G000131303

Restoring Order

The Ecole des Chartes and the Organization of Archives and Libraries in France, 1820–1870

Restoring Order

The Ecole des Chartes and the Organization of Archives and Libraries in France, 1820–1870

By Lara Jennifer Moore

Litwin Books, LLC
Duluth, Minnesota

Copyright Lara Jennifer Moore, 2001

Published in 2008

Litwin Books
PO Box 3320
Duluth, MN 55803
http://litwinbooks.com/

This book is printed on acid-free paper that meets all present ANSI standards
for archival preservation.

Cover design by Topher McCulloch

The cover image is an engraving of the Salle de Lecture of the French National
Library, by Victor-Adolphe Malte-Brun (1816–1889).

Library of Congress Cataloging-in-Publication Data

Moore, Lara Jennifer.
  Restoring order : the Ecole des chartes and the organization of archives and
libraries in France, 1820-1870 / by Lara Jennifer Moore.
     p. cm.
  Includes bibliographical references and index.
  ISBN 978-0-9778617-9-8 (acid-free paper)
  1. Ecole nationale des chartes (France)--History. 2. Archives--France--History--
19th century. 3. Libraries--France--History--19th century. 4. France--Charters,
grants, privileges--History--19th century. I. Title.
  CD1191.M66 2008
  027.744--dc22
                              2007047772

Table of Contents

Preface

Anyone who witnessed the acrid, prolonged debates in the 1990s concerning the new French national library, La Bibliothèque Nationale de France, knows that libraries are not spared politics, at least in France. Geographical location, architectural design as well as the electronic cataloguing of the collection—all these issues sparked such controversy among French government officials, librarians, archivists and scholars that the construction of the library itself was prolonged, if not entirely threatened. While everyone in France could agree that a more spacious, modern, and efficient library was needed, few concurred on how these goals could be achieved. At stake was the nation's *patrimoine* or heritage—the pamphlets, books, documents and manuscripts which represented France's history and inherited wisdom over the past centuries.

Such disputes would not have come as a surprise to the reader of Lara Moore's provocative history of the "national" library in the nineteenth century, *Restoring Order: The Ecole des Chartes and the Organization of Archives and Libraries in France, 1820-1870*. Since the time of the French Revolution in 1789, Moore argues, the library and the archive have often been at the center of political controversy. When the Jacobins did their best to destroy the French monarchy and bring down the aristocratic elite, they also had to deal with a "pell-mell" system of private and royal libraries in which the French national heritage had been preserved. The millions of books and documents the Jacobins had seized awaited a new system of order and classification. How would they be organized and made accessible to the public? How, indeed, would the *patrimoine* of the *ancient régime* become a part of the modern nation? Moore sets out to answer this question for the crucial middle years of the nineteenth century, beginning in 1820, in the Restoration period, and ending in 1870, just before the establishment of the Third Republic. To tell her story, she draws on an impressive range of sources, including documents from obscure archives throughout France, as well as rich collections housed in the Archives Nationales, the Bibliothèque nationale de France, l'Institut de France, and the Ecole Nationale des Chartes. To focus her topic, Moore follows the history of the Ecole des Chartes, the state school for librarians and archivists in France. She asks: what clues can their professional training provide about the ways in which the archival system was being re-imagined, and documents re-organized? How, in short, was "order" being restored?

Despite her focus on the Ecole des Chartes, Moore's study is no institutional history. Rather, she uses ongoing changes in the training of the *chartistes* as a mere starting point. Her analysis extends outward to much wider questions concerning revolutionary process and the evolution of the French state during the years 1820 to 1870.

In the separate periods of the Restoration, the July Monarchy, the Second Republic and the Second Empire, she asks the same questions: How did each successive regime seek to classify and make accessible the components of a public library and archival system? How did such conceptions of "restoring order" to the nation's patrimony reflect political ambitions and notions of the state at the time? How did libraries and archives themselves act as political forces? In short, what role did they play in the transition from monarchy to Republic during this turbulent period? By asking these questions, Moore helps us to comprehend the revolutionary process which so shaped the political turmoil of the nineteenth century.

Besides expanding our knowledge of the French state in this way, *Restoring Order: The Ecole des Chartes and the Organization of Archives and Libraries in France, 1820-1870* makes a significant contribution to the scholarship on the cultural production of knowledge. Such historians as Roger Chartier and Pierre Nora have shown how seemingly "neutral" cultural artifacts, such as books, monuments, and museums, have a deeply-textured politics of their own. They have shown how monuments, for example, "forget" certain elements of an event as much as they "remember" others. These boundaries of memory and forgetting are political in both cause and effect. Those who construct monuments shape and even distort the knowledge produced through their design; in wishing to forget something, they force others to forget it as well. In the same way, Moore reveals how libraries and archives, largely ignored by cultural historians, have been shaped by political concerns and ambitions; as a result, the way they classify, organize and make accessible the documents of the past make the production of some historical narratives possible, while excluding others. Moore's aim, as she writes at the end of her introduction, is to alert historians to "consider the archival and bibliographical practices that have shaped the collections on which they rely." In other words, rather than view archival collections as neutral repositories of documents, we must better appreciate the politics which shape them, and take this into consideration when producing our own narratives of the French past.

Lara Moore wrote *Restoring Order: The Ecole des Chartes and the Organization of Archives and Libraries in France, 1820-1870* as a dissertation at Stanford University. For her research in Paris, she won a prestigious Fulbright fellowship during the academic year 1998-1999. She completed her work in March of 2001, producing a dissertation that was broad in scope, meticulous in research, and clear and original in analysis. In short, it was a *tour de force*. She graduated from Stanford University, and soon after, took a job as the History Librarian in the Collection Development Department at Princeton University in Princeton, New Jersey. In July 2003, Lara Moore passed away after a spirited and courageous battle against cancer. Because of her untimely death, she was unable to revise this work in the way she would have wanted. However, it is a measure of her talents as a scholar that her unrevised dissertation is so eminently worthy of publication. Those who knew Lara well, including her immediate family, colleagues and friends, felt strongly that *Restoring Order* should be made accessible to the large readership it deserves and will no doubt enjoy. Lara was a consummate professional, and would want to be remembered for her intellectual life rather than her tragic death.

Still readers of *Restoring Order* will now discover what all of us who had the honor of working with Lara already know: her death was an incomparable loss.

Mary Louise Roberts
Madison, Wisconsin, 2007

Acknowledgments

It gives me great pleasure to acknowledge the people and institutions that allowed me to complete this project.

An invaluable pre-dissertation trip to Paris was funded by the University of California's Center for German and European Studies. Funding from Stanford University and the Mellon Foundation supported me as I completed my secondary research in the United States. A Fulbright grant from the Franco-American Commission for Educational Exchange and a fellowship from the Bibliographical Society of America supported a year of more intensive research in France, while a Mabelle McLeod Lewis Memorial Fund award allowed me to complete the writing phase in a timely fashion.

The faculty, students, and staff of the Ecole Nationale des Chartes have been tremendously generous with their time and resources. I am particularly grateful to Yves-Marie Bercé, director of the school, for sponsoring my visit to Paris in 1998-99 and for granting me access to the school's archives. I would also like to express my gratitude to professors Olivier Guyotjeannin, Marc Smith, Annie Charon, Elisabeth Parinet, and Bruno Delmas, and to students Marc Verdure and Agathe San Juan for sharing their thoughtful comments as well as examples of their own research. Two of the school's alumni, Jean Le Pottier and Vincent Mollet, kindly allowed me to consult their Ecole des Chartes theses, both rich mines of information and insight. I would also like to acknowledge the invaluable assistance of the Ecole's librarian, Isabelle Diu, who very graciously granted me access to the library's wonderful collections. Finally, I must thank the members of the school's alumni organization, the Société de l'Ecole des Chartes, who allowed me to consult their archives.

French scholars outside the Ecole des Chartes also did a great deal to support the project. I am forever indebted to historian Jean Hébrard, who was the first to suggest that I focus on the Ecole des Chartes and who has continued to provide both warm encouragement and perceptive advice. Dominique Varry of the Ecole nationale supérieure des science de l'information et des bibliothèques welcomed me to the school during a brief visit and shared his tremendous expertise in French library history. Historian and librarian Laure Lévillé took the time to meet with me in Paris and allowed me to consult her excellent thesis on public libraries.

As a historian of French archives and libraries, I owe a double debt of gratitude to French archivists and librarians (many of them *chartistes*), who not only helped me find the materials I needed but offered great insight into their own professions. In Paris, Françoise Hildesheimer and Odile Krakovitch of the Archives nationales very generously shared their own work in archival history. Pierre Portet and Emmanuel Rousseau helped me locate materials in the "archives of the Archives," while Patricia Gillet went far beyond the call of duty in granting me access to the unprocessed archives of the Ecole des Chartes. At the Bibliothèque nationale, Emmanuel Le Roy Ladurie and Kinga Maria Kantorska offered useful advice in the early stages of the project. Later, Pierre Janin, Raymond-Josué Seckel, Jean-François Foucaud, and Eve Netchine also provided important research leads. I would also like to thank Yann Sodet of the Bibliothèque Sainte-Geneviève, Mme Mezerolles of the Bibliothèque de l'Arsenal, and Fabienne Queyroux and Mireille Lamarque of the Institut de France for their able assistance.

Archivists in France's departmental depositories proved exceptionally helpful and kind. I am especially grateful to Xavier de la Selle of the Archives départmentales de l'Aube, Martine Salmon-Dalas of the Archives départmentales de Lot-et-Garonne, Elisabeth Verry of the Archives départmentales Maine-et-Loire, Arnaud Ramière de Fortanier of the Archives départmentales des yvelines, Yves Soulinges of the Archives départmentales de l'Isère, and the staffs of the departmental archives of the Allier, Indre-et-Loire, Nièvre, and Rhône. J.-Y-. Mariotte of the Archives municipales de Strasbourg and Marie Michaut of the Bibliothèque municipale d'Auxerre also provided welcome assistance.

Professors and colleagues in the United States offered unfailing encouragement, even when I could only see gaps and obstacles. At the University of California, Los Angeles, historians Edward Berenson, Kathryn Norberg, David Sabean, and David Myers helped me refine my ideas and my writing. In the library science program, John Richardson and Elaine Svenonius pushed me to think more theoretically about how information is organized. At Stanford University, I felt myself fortunate to work with Keith Baker, whose challenging questions and perceptive comments helped make this a better dissertation. I am also enormously indebted to Mary Louise Roberts for her energetic encouragement, insightful editing, and professional perspicacity. It is rare to find a thesis advisor so giving of her time and attention. My third reader, Paula Findlen, offered wonderfully helpful comments on my work, often encapsulating my arguments in a way that allowed me to see their strengths and limitations more clearly. A fourth

Stanford professor, James Sheehan, also deserves my thanks; it was in his excellent research seminar in Modern European History that I developed my early interest in nineteenth-century France into a more coherent research proposal. Finally, I would be greatly remiss if I did not recognize Mary Jane Parrine, Curator of Romance Language Collections for the Stanford Libraries, and Sonia Moss, former head of Interlibrary Services, for their expert assistance.

Scholars at a number of other institutions helped me think through certain sections of my dissertation. I am particularly grateful to Dena Goodman, Colin Jones, Sheryl Kroen, Nancy Bartlett, Joan Schwartz, Lauren Clay, Richard Keller, J. P. Daughton, and the late Laura Kinsey for their comments. Yet I am most grateful to my fellow Stanford graduate students for their patient readings (and often rereadings) of my work. Gillian Weiss, Sarah Sussman, Shana Bernstein, Jana Bruns, Tim Brown, Malick Ghachem, Ben Kafka, Charly Coleman, and Claire Salinas offered frank comments and friendly encouragement in equal doses. I must give special thanks to Sara Pritchard and Tara Nummedal, fellow dissertators, who read the various drafts of this dissertation more carefully than anyone else and whose comments not only profoundly shaped the pages that follow but also helped me to understand the way I think and the way I write.

In closing, I would like to offer my deepest thanks to my undergraduate adviser and now good friend, Gary Kates, whose course on the French Revolution first fired my interest in history more than a decade ago and whose energy and conviction continue to inspire me. I must also thank my dearest friends Tal Gozani and Didier Reiss, who, with Sasha Reiss, helped sustain me (culinarily and otherwise) through the final grueling months of writing. Finally, I give my neverending thanks to my family: my brother, Clark Moore, and my parents, Ellen and Tony Moore. This dissertation is dedicated to them.

List of Abbreviations

AD	Archives départementales (Departmental Archives)
AEC	Archives de l'Ecole des Chartes (Archives of the Ecole des Chartes, housed at the Ecole Nationale des Chartes, Paris)
AEC-SC	Archives of the Ecole des Chartes (materials in-process, housed at the Archives Nationales, Section Contemporaine)
AN	Archives nationales (National Archives, Paris)
BEC	*Bibliothèque de l'Ecole des chartes* (1839-)
BN mss.	Bibliothèque Nationale, Département des Manuscrits (Manuscripts Department of the National Library, Paris)

Introduction

The crowd of revolutionaries that pushed its way across the drawbridge of the Bastille on July 14, 1789 found more than just a rag-tag group of royal prisoners. As they made their way through the fortress's subterranean labyrinth, they came upon the Archives of the Bastille. Here, like a secret within a secret, were the records of one of the most despised practices of the Bourbon regime: arbitrary imprisonment. Here were the notorious *lettres de cachet*, royal letters used to detain French subjects without trial. Here, too, were files on some four thousand former prisoners, from the so-called "Man in the Iron Mask" to the *philosophe* Voltaire. Fully aware of the symbolic (and commercial) value of this collection, the conquerors of the Bastille began grabbing documents by the armful. Some, like the playwright Beaumarchais, quickly fled the prison grounds, hoarding their treasures until calmer times, while others stayed to celebrate their victory by torching police files, shredding old logbooks, and flinging prison records from the fortress towers.

The dispersal of the archives was not to last for long, however. By the end of the day on the 15th, the municipal government had sent guards to protect the conquered prison from the hordes of excited Parisians, and on the 16th, it dispatched a special commission to help preserve the prison archives, which it described as "authentic evidence of all the excesses of arbitrary power." The commissioners, at first overwhelmed by the "complete disorder" of the collection, soon began gathering up the remaining documents and trying to persuade their fellow citizens that the prison's records constituted "national" property. As one poster proclaimed: "The Public is requested not to enter the Bastille until the papers of interest to the Nation have been gathered and put in a safe place." Meanwhile, the government also tried to recover some of the documents taken beyond the fortress walls, reminding its citizens that surrendering the stolen archives was "the only way of guaranteeing this precious knowledge to the present generation, and to future generations, and of forming a national collection that will provide History with authentic materials." Though some of the Bastille's records were never returned (only to resurface in collections as far away as Saint Petersburg), the rest were eventually assembled in a former convent. The succeeding revolutionary governments all promised to ensure public access to the collection by publishing excerpts from it, but progress

was slow, and in 1798 the French state abandoned the project, transferring
the Archives of the Bastille to the Arsenal Library of Paris, where they
remain today.[1]

If the storming of the Bastille has come to symbolize France's passage
from absolute monarchy to revolutionary republic, the storming of the
Bastille Archives might be said to represent the parallel transformation of
the Old Regime's network of private (and sometimes secret) archives and
libraries into a set of "national" and "public" collections. Between 1789 and
1793, the revolutionary French state nationalized thousands of libraries and
archival depositories, thus becoming the proprietor of many millions of
books and documents, ranging from Montesquieu's *Persian Letters* to
proclamations signed by Charlemagne. Unsure whether to condemn these
materials as vestiges of feudalism and tyranny or to preserve them as the
core of the nation's historical patrimony, the revolutionaries initiated a
series of overlapping and contradictory plans to remake French archives and
libraries. Few of these plans were carried out, however, and by the close of
the eighteenth century, most of the collections nationalized during the
revolution sat abandoned and deteriorating in provincial warehouses.

This book is about how the French governments of the nineteenth
century dealt with the collections left behind by the revolution. What did
they choose to preserve, or ignore? How did they distinguish between the
authentic sources of national history and the irrelevant debris of a bygone
age? How did they organize the materials they did deem relevant into a
national network of libraries and archives? And who did they imagine would
use these new collections? Who was included in the post-revolutionary
"public"? According to most histories of French archives and libraries, the
nineteenth century was a period of slow but steady recovery from the
trauma of the revolutionary era. Confronted with the "chaos" of the
nationalized collections, it is said, a few forward-thinking archivists and
librarians gradually restored bibliographic and documentary order,

---

[1] This account of the Bastille archives is based on the introduction to Frantz Funck-
Brentano, *Catalogue général des manuscrits des bibliothèques publiques de France. Paris.
Bibliothèque de l'Arsenal. Tome Neuvième: Archives de la Bastille* (Paris: Librairie Plon,
1892), and, to a lesser extent, on François Ravaisson and Louis Ravaisson-Mollien,
Archives de la Bastille, d'après des documents inédits (Paris: A. Durand et Pedonne-Lauriel,
1866-1904). The quotations are from Funck-Brentano, pp. xxxvi, xxxvii, xxxix, and
xliii, respectively. See also Arlette Farge and Michel Foucault, *Le désordre des familles:
lettres de cachet des Archives de la Bastille* ([Paris], Gallimard, 1982). All translations are
mine unless otherwise noted.

sheltering the state's collections from destruction and decay, preparing suitable catalogues, and improving public access. In contrast, I argue here that the organization of archives and libraries in nineteenth-century France was neither steady nor progressive. By following the development of the Ecole des Chartes, the state school for archivists and librarians, I show that conceptions of "order" changed dramatically from one decade to the next. More important, I argue that these changing notions of "order" were directly connected to contemporary shifts in state politics. Since each new political regime had its own conceptions of both national history and public knowledge, each one worked to "restore order" in a different way.

On the eve of the French Revolution, French archives and libraries were neither "national" nor "public." A visitor to France in 1788 would have discovered a dizzying array of privately-owned collections reflecting the social and political complexity of the Old Regime. According to the few recent studies of eighteenth-century archives, most administrative entities, ecclesiastical institutions, and noble families had archival collections of some kind, whether locked in armoires, piled into sacks, or laid out on depository shelves, as at the Bastille.[2] Perhaps the most famous of these collections was the royal *Trésor des Chartes* (Treasury of Charters), created in 1194 to hold monarchical treaties and decrees.[3] Many cities and towns had their own "treasuries," containing charters, edicts, and other testaments to local privileges.[4] Meanwhile, particularly during the "seigneurial reactions" of the late 1700s, individual *seigneurs*, or noble landowners, worked hard to

---

[2] See Paul Delsalle, "L'archivistique sous l'ancien régime, le trésor, l'arsenal, et l'histoire," *Histoire, Economie, et Société* 12, no. 4 (1993): 447-472; and Françoise Hildesheimer, *Les Archives de France: Mémoire de l'Histoire* (Paris: Honoré Champion, 1997).

[3] On the development of the Trésor des Chartes, see footnote 2 as well as L[éon] Dessalles, *Le Trésor des chartes, sa création, ses gardes et leurs travaux, depuis l'origine jusqu'en 1582...*(Paris: Imprimerie royale, 1844); H[enri]-François de Laborde, *Etude sur la constitution du Trésor des chartes et sur les origines de la série des sacs dite aujourd'hui Supplément du Trésor des chartes* (Paris: Plon-Nourrit, 1909); and Krzysztof Pomian, "Les archives, du Trésor des chartes au CARAN," in *Les lieux de mémoire*, ed. Pierre Nora (Paris: Gallimard, 1992), vol. 3, pt. 3, pp. 162-233. As Pomian and Hildesheimer explain, relatively few documents were added to the Trésor after the late sixteenth century, when royal offices began maintaining their own records, yet the core collection remained under careful guard through the end of the Old Regime.

[4] Marcel Baudot, "Les archives municipales dans la France de l'ancien régime," *Archivum* 13 (1963): 23-30.

construct and maintain their estate archives, often with the help of a specialized lawyer, or *feudiste*.[5] Yet some of the richest archival collections belonged to the various institutions of the Catholic Church, from the modest holdings of country parishes to the massive collections of the great Paris abbeys. Pre-revolutionary libraries, more carefully studied by historians, were equally diverse. None could compete in size or renown with the Royal Library, which since its foundation in the fourteenth century had become, at more than 300,000 volumes, the largest in Europe. Yet France could also boast of thousands of ecclesiastical libraries, including the vast collection of the Benedictine Abbey of Saint-Germain-des-Près, in Paris, as well as convent and church libraries scattered throughout the countryside. As we know from auction records and booksellers' catalogs, the great figures of the literary world also maintained enormous libraries, often intermingled with collections of scientific instruments and works of art.[6] A small but increasing number of these pre-revolutionary archives and libraries (such as the Bibliothèque Mazarine in Paris) declared themselves open to the local or general public in the late eighteenth century. Nevertheless, even these publicly accessible collections remained privately owned. It was left to the revolutionary governments of the 1790s to establish—at least in principle—national collections that were both publicly owned and publicly accessible.[7]

Though the Archives of the Bastille became "national" property in July 1789, it was several years before the rest of the Old Regime's archives and libraries followed suit. Between 1789 and 1793, the revolutionary government gradually acquired the major book and document collections of the Old Regime through two basic approaches: confiscation and absorption.

---

[5] See especially Albert Soboul, "De la pratique des terriers à la veille de la Révolution," *Annales, Economies, Sociétés, Civilisations* 19, no. 16 (1964): 1049-1065; and Hilton Lewis Root, "Challenging the Seigneurie: Community and Contention on the Eve of the French Revolution," *Journal of Modern History* 57, no. 4 (1985): 652-681.

[6] The definitive source on pre-revolutionary libraries is Claude Jolly, ed., *Les bibliothèques sous l'Ancien Régime, 1530-1789*, vol. 2 of *Histoire des bibliothèques françaises* (Paris: Promodis, 1988). The volume also contains an excellent bibliography of local studies.

[7] On the rise of publicly-accessible libraries in the late eighteenth century, see Louis Desgraves, "Vers la bibliothèque publique," in *Histoire des bibliothèques françaises*, 2: 391-413. On the "publicity" of certain archival collections, see Robert-Henri Bautier, "La phase cruciale de l'histoire des archives: la constitution des dépôts d'archives et la naissance de l'archivistique (XVIe-début du XIXe siècle)," *Archivum* 18 (1968): 139-149.

The confiscations began in November 1789, when the new National
Assembly, desperate to solve the ongoing economic crisis, declared all
ecclesiastical property—including thousands of archives and libraries—"at
the disposal of the nation." Two more waves of confiscations followed in
February 1792 and July 1793, as the government seized first the property of
the *émigrés* (exiled nobles) and *condamnés* (convicted counter-revolutionaries,
soon to include King Louis XVI) and then that of the Old Regime
academies and scholarly societies.[8] The revolutionary state expanded its
holdings still further by absorbing the collections belonging to the various
components of the now-dismantled Bourbon administration. Hence in April
1790 the records of the provincial governors, or *intendants*, along with those
of the various pre-revolutionary "estates" fell to the newly created
administrative districts, while in August of that same year the papers of the
Royal Council and Paris magistracy were taken over by the National
Assembly.[9]

Like the Archives of the Bastille, many of the Old Regime archives and
libraries nationalized between 1789 and 1793 were at first assembled in
what were meant to be temporary warehouses. Most of the former
ecclesiastical, noble, and royal libraries, for example, were concentrated into
a network of "literary depositories" housed in abandoned monasteries,
church attics, and unused granaries throughout Paris and the countryside.[10]
Meanwhile, the revolutionaries gathered most provincial archives into
district and departmental depositories, often in the local administrative

---

[8] On the revolutionary confiscations, see especially Dominique Varry, "Les
confiscations révolutionnaires," in *Histoire des bibliothèques françaises* (Paris: Promodis,
1991), 3: 2-27; his "Les saisies révolutionnaires: une source inexploitée," in
Transactions of the Eighth International Congress on the Enlightenment, Studies on Voltaire
and the Eighteenth Century, nos. 303-305 (Oxford: Voltaire Foundation, 1992), pp.
1011-1015; and Luc Passion, "Les confiscations: contribution à l'étude des mesures
législatives (1789-1793)," in *Patrimoine parisien, 1789-1799: destructions, créations,
mutations*, ed. Alfred Fierro (Paris: Délégation à l'action artistique de la ville de Paris;
Bibliothèque historique de la ville de Paris, 1989), pp. 32-46.
[9] See Ministère de l'instruction publique et des beaux-arts, *Lois, instructions et
règlements relatifs aux Archives départementales, communales et hospitalières* (Paris: H.
Champion, 1884); Gabriel Richou, *Traité théorique et pratique des archives publiques*
(Paris: Paul Dupont 1883); and Hildesheimer, *Les Archives de France*.
[10] See especially J[ean]-B[aptiste] Labiche, *Notice sur les dépôts littéraires et la révolution
bibliographique de la fin du dernier siècle, d'après les manuscrits de la Bibliothèque de l'Arsenal*
(Paris: Typographie de A. Parent, 1880); and Maryse Goldemberg, "Les
bibliothèques parisiennes et les dépôts littéraires," in *Patrimoine parisien*, pp. 64-81.

offices, and divided Parisian archives into neighborhood collections.[11] By all accounts, the creation of these depositories was messy and uneven. As soon as the confiscations began, abbots and bishops spirited their most valuable collections out of the country, while booksellers and collectors, eyeing an unprecedented opportunity, bought precious volumes from departing noblemen. Local guardians, if they existed, had great difficulty simply assembling and transporting the nationalized collections, let alone protecting them against destruction and theft. And throughout, the central government issued enough competing instructions as to confuse even the most determined of provincial agents.[12]

What did the revolutionaries plan to do with all of these materials? If the vast bibliographic and documentary collections of the Old Regime were now "at the disposal of the nation," how would the "nation" proceed? The years 1789-95 generated intense debates about the fate of these collections, debates which I will only outline here. Whatever their differences, the participants in these debates could all agree that first and foremost, the amassed papers and volumes had to be inventoried. If the government did not know what it owned, it could not properly "dispose" of its new property. Hence from the start the revolutionary leaders called repeatedly for the creation of "catalogs," "lists," "summaries," and "accounts." Though this effort clearly extended to the new archival warehouses, the most ambitious attempts to inventory the nation's collections focused on the "literary depositories." In late 1790, the National Assembly began laying plans for a *Bibliographie universelle de la France* (Universal Bibliography of France) intended to include every book in every depository in the country. In a steady stream of instructions and decrees, the central government ordered local officials to record the contents of their depositories not in the usual bound registers, but on the backs of playing cards, an innovation which, it was thought, would

---

[11]   In 1790, the revolutionary Constituent Assembly divided France into departments [*départements*], each of which was further subdivided into districts, cantons, and communes. In 1800, Napoléon changed some of the smaller subdivisions but retained the basic system of departments, which persists in France to this day.

[12] See chap. 1 of Graham Keith Barnett, *Histoire des bibliothèques publiques en France de la Révolution à 1939*, trans. Thierry Lefèvre and Yves Sardat (Paris: Promodis; Editions du Cercle de la librairie, 1987), originally presented as "The History of Public Libraries in France from the Revolution to 1939," (thesis, Library Association [Great Britain], 1973); and Varry, "Les confiscations."

ensure the rapid assembly of a unified catalog.[13] Once armed with a comprehensive listing of its books and documents, the government would be ready to use these collections in the best interests of the revolutionary public.

What constituted the public interest, however, was a matter of serious dispute. Throughout the 1790s, revolutionary leaders argued about whether to preserve or eliminate the vast legacy of the Old Regime. We can see the essence of this debate in the speeches made by two successive heads of the Universal Bibliography project, Urbain Domergue and Henri Grégoire, at the height of the Terror. In November 1793, Domergue delivered a report to the National Convention that quickly moved from a measured discussion of cataloging techniques to an impassioned diatribe on the dangers lurking in Old Regime books. He declared: "We rightly send to the scaffold all authors or accomplices of counter-revolution. Our libraries also have their counter-revolutionaries; I vote for their deportation." Domergue called for the creation of a "bibliographic jury," that, much like the recently established Revolutionary Tribunal, would eliminate all works of "despotism," "superstition," and "trickery" so as to avoid "poisoning" the French citizenry.[14] Six months later, his successor, the Abbé Grégoire, tried to counter Domergue's anti-preservationist rhetoric in his own report on the national bibliography. In a speech that anticipated many of his later arguments against the "vandalism" of national property, Grégoire argued that pre-revolutionary books and manuscripts, however "scandalous to

---

[13] The definitive study of the bibliography project is Pierre Riberette, *Les bibliothèques françaises pendant la Révolution (1789-1795): recherches sur un essai de catalogue collectif* (Paris: Bibliothèque nationale, 1970). See also Judith Hopkins, "The 1791 French Cataloging Code and the Origins of the Card Catalog," *Libraries and Culture* 27, no. 4 (1992): 378-404; Jack A. Clarke, "French Libraries in Transition, 1789-95," *Library Quarterly* 37, no. 4 (1967): 366-372; and Hélène Richard, "Catalogue collectif et échange de documents: un utopie révolutionnaire," *Bulletin des bibliothèques de France* 34, nos. 2-3 (1989): 166-173. On earlier visions of the "universal" library, see chap. 3 of Roger Chartier, *The Order of Books: Readers, Authors, and Libraries in Europe between the Fourteenth and Eighteenth Centuries*, trans. Lydia G. Cochrane (Stanford: Stanford University Press, 1994); originally published as *L'ordre des livres: lecteurs, auteurs, bibliothèques en Europe entre le XIVe et le XVIIIe siècle* (Aix-en-Provence: Alinea, 1992). On efforts to compile inventories of archival depositories, see *Lois, instructions et règlements.*

[14] Urbain Domergue, "Rapport fait au Comité d'Instruction Publique sur la Bibliographie Générale" 21 Brumaire Year II (11 Nov. 1793), in *Procès-verbaux du Comité d'Instruction publique de la Convention nationale*, ed. J[ames] Guillaume (Paris: Imprimerie nationale, 1891-1907), 2: 795-799.

reason," had much to teach the present: "false ideas [and] absurd systems at least have the advantage of functioning as beacons…; they point out the pitfalls." More important, Grégoire maintained, French libraries were part of the "common heritage" and thus worthy of careful preservation. If only the citizens of the Republic could have access to the "immense riches" of the national depositories, they would be able to prepare themselves to serve the *patrie*.[15]

The revolutionary government's inability to decide between Domergue's program of cultural purification and Grégoire's conception of national heritage produced a series of rather contradictory policies regarding the new literary and archival depositories. While holding local officials responsible for preserving the vast archival holdings of the Church and the nobility, the central government also periodically instructed them to destroy certain categories of documents. In June 1792, for example, the Legislative Assembly told the departments to burn all "genealogical titles" housed in public depositories, and according to local archival histories, many provincial officials readily obliged, burning heaps of noble records in their town squares.[16] Similarly, in early October 1793, the Convention ordered

---

[15] [Henri] Grégoire, "Rapport sur la bibliographie…séance du 22 germinal, l'an 2 de la République [11 Apr. 1794]," in *Procès-verbaux du Comité d'instruction publique*, 4: 120-129. See J. Tourneur-Aumont, "Idées bibliographiques en l'an II: Les rapports d'Urbain Domergue et Henri Grégoire," *Revue des bibliothèques* 37 (1927): 362-391; and Michel Delon, "La bibliothèque est en feu: rêveries révolutionnaires autour du livre," *Bulletin des bibliothèques de France* 34, nos. 2-3 (1989): 120-121. In a set of three reports to the Convention, Grégoire coined the term "vandalism" to describe the destruction of national monuments, including books and documents. See Joseph L. Sax, "Heritage Preservation as a Public Duty: The Abbé Grégoire and the Origins of an Idea," *Michigan Law Review* 88, no. 5 (1990): 1142-1169; Catherine Volpilhac, Dany Hadjadj, and Jean-Louis Jam, "Des Vandales au vandalisme," in *Révolution française et 'vandalisme révolutionnaire': Actes du colloque international de Clermont-Ferrand, 15-17 décembre 1988*, ed. Simone Bernard-Griffiths, Marie-Claude Chemin, and Jean Ehrard (Paris: Universitas, 1992), pp. 15-27; Alfred Fierro, "L'Abbé Grégoire et la sauvegarde des monuments du passé," in *Patrimoine parisien*, pp. 132-137; and the work of Dominique Poulot, including *Musée, nation, patrimoine, 1789-1815* (Paris: Gallimard, 1997) and *'Surveiller et s'instruire': la Révolution française et l'intelligence de l'héritage historique*, Studies on Voltaire and the Eighteenth Century, no. 344 (Oxford: Voltaire Foundation, 1996).

[16] See for example Jacques Charpy, "Les archives en révolution: les premières années des Archives départementales d'Ille-et-Vilaine, 1789-1802," *Bulletin et mémoires de la Société archéologique du département d'Ille-et-Vilaine* 93 (1991): 33-60; A[imé] Champollion-Figeac, "Notice sur les Archives départementales de France," *Bulletin*

the removal of all signs of feudalism and royalty from public property, including books, yet just two weeks later reversed itself, making it illegal to apply the earlier ruling to the nation's books and chastising those who had cut *fleurs-de-lis* from fine leather bindings.[17]

From a certain perspective, of course, such policies were not contradictory at all, for both the preservation of French heritage and the destruction of feudal monuments were part of the revolutionary effort to "regenerate" the French nation by offering it powerful lessons in civic virtue.[18] And indeed both preservation and destruction were included in what might be seen as the most typical of revolutionary policies toward archives and libraries: triage. While the term was most often applied to archival depositories, the revolutionary regimes were constantly trying to separate both archival and library collections into items to keep, items to sell, and items to eliminate. The key piece of legislation on this point is the Law of 7 Messidor Year II (25 June 1794), which, in addition to identifying the attributions of the new National Archives, announced a nationwide campaign to "triage" all existing Old Regime titles. All documents that were no longer useful or were "purely feudal" were to be destroyed immediately. Those related to "history, the sciences, and the arts" or that might be "useful for instruction" would go to the National Library or to one of the new provincial public libraries, while the remaining documents would either be sold or divided among a set of publicly-accessible archival depositories.[19]

---

de l'*Académie delphinale* 21 (1886): 179-209; and Vincent Mollet, "Les archives départementales du Tarn de 1790 à 1946: constitution et mise en valeur d'un patrimoine écrit," (Thesis, Ecole nationale des chartes, 1992). One can find similar examples in the Archives nationales (hereafter AN) series F2 I (particularly the responses to the surveys of 1807 and 1812), and in the *Guides* published by individual departmental archives.

[17] See Varry, "Les confiscations," p. 14; and Anne Kupiec, "Le livre sauveur," *Bulletin des bibliothèques de France* 34, nos. 2-3 (1989): 129. For the text of the second law, see Ulysse Robert, ed., *Recueil de lois, décrets, ordonnances, arrêtés, circulaires, etc. concernant les bibliothèques publiques, communales, universitaires, scolaires et populaires* (Paris: H. Champion, 1883), pp. 21-22.

[18] On the revolutionary notion of "regeneration," see especially Mona Ozouf, "Regeneration," in *Critical Dictionary of the French Revolution*, ed. François Furet and Mona Ozouf, trans. Arthur Goldhammer (Cambridge: Harvard University Press, Belknap Press, 1989), pp. 781-790; originally published as *Dictionnaire critique de la Révolution française* (Paris: Flammarion, 1988).

[19] For the text of the law, see Henri Bordier, *Les Archives de la France, ou l'histoire des Archives de l'Empire, des Archives des Ministères, des départements, des communes, des hôpitaux,*

The revolutionary nation would glean all that was useful and instructive from the Old Regime collections and eliminate the rest.

In some respects, the revolutionary effort to nationalize French archives and libraries, inventory them, and then redistribute their most useful components through a network of public collections was a dismal failure. After six years, the great "Universal Bibliography" project ground to a halt, with only a handful of catalog cards to show for its efforts. The triage campaign, never seriously underway in most provincial depositories, eventually folded in Paris on the eve of the Napoleonic Empire.[20] And despite numerous proposals for the development of public libraries and archives, many of the nationalized collections of books and manuscripts remained in their "temporary" warehouses well into the nineteenth century, where they were often subject to theft, destruction, and neglect.[21] Nevertheless, the revolutionaries did lay the institutional groundwork for France's current system of archives and libraries. In 1790, the revolutionary assembly established the National Archives, comprised of the new government's papers as well as the collections of Old Regime administrative, judicial, and historical papers (including the *Trésor des Chartes*) generated by the program of triage.[22] In the provinces, the Law of 5 Brumaire Year V (26 October 1796) instituted a national network of departmental archives, again meant to include both the nationalized collections of the former provinces as well as the administrative records of

---

des greffes, des notaires, etc., contenant l'inventaire d'une partie de ces dépôts (Paris: Dumoulin, 1855), pp. 384-389.

[20] See Gustave Desjardins, *Le service des archives départementales: conférences faites aux élèves de l'Ecole des chartes les 10, 18, 25 et 30 juin 1890* (Paris: E. Bourloton, 1890); and Olivier Guyotjeannin, "Les premières années des archives départementales françaises (1796-1815)," in *Les archives en Europe vers 1800: les communications présentées dans le cadre de la journée d'études du même nom aux Archives générales du Royaume à Bruxelles le 24 octobre 1996*, Miscellanea Archivistica Studia, no. 103 (Brussels: Archives générales du royaume et archives de l'état dans les provinces, 1998), pp. 7-36.

[21] Varry, "Vicissitudes et aléas des livres placés 'sous la main de la Nation'," in *Révolution française et 'vandalisme révolutionnaire'*, pp. 277-284; his "'Il faut que les lumières arrivent par torrents': La Révolution française et la création des bibliothèques publiques: projets et réalités," *Bulletin des bibliothèques de France* 34, nos. 2-3 (1989): 160-165; and Hélène Richard, "Des bibliothèques des districts aux bibliothèques municipales," in *Histoire des bibliothèques françaises*, 3: 43-59.

[22] See the work of Françoise Hildesheimer, especially *Les Archives de France*; and "Les Archives nationales," in *Patrimoine parisien*, pp. 84-95.

the departments themselves.[23] As for French libraries, the Revolution substantially enriched the major Parisian collections (the National Library, the Mazarine, the Arsenal, and the Sainte-Geneviève), all of which became "public" in the 1790s and had their pick of books and manuscripts from the literary depositories.[24] The revolutionaries also created a system of provincial public libraries, albeit in embryonic form. After attempting to link public libraries with provincial schools in the mid-1790s, the central government eventually entrusted both the school libraries and the remaining literary depositories to local officials, thus preparing the way for the emergence of what are today known as municipal public libraries.[25]

Beyond these institutional innovations, however, the revolutionary period generated new ways of thinking about archives and libraries. First, the legislative debates of the years 1789-95 produced the idea of "national" archives and libraries. Whether revolutionary legislators sided more closely with the cathartic impulses of Urbain Domergue or the preservationist views of Henri Grégoire, they all seemed to agree that the libraries and archives of the Old Regime were not simply useless refuse but national property whose management (whether destructive or conservationist) would reflect upon the nation itself. They all agreed, in other words, that the bibliographic and documentary legacy of the Old Regime was strongly connected to French national identity. The second key concept produced by the revolutionary experiments with archives and libraries was the idea that national

---

[23] See Guyotjeannin, "Les premières années," and Mollet, "Les archives départementales."

[24] On the National Library, see Simone Balayé, *La Bibliothèque nationale: des origines à 1800* (Geneva: Droz, 1988) and her "La Bibliothèque nationale pendant la Révolution," in *Histoire des bibliothèques françaises*, 3: 71-83. On the Arsenal, Mazarine, and Sainte-Geneviève, see Thérèse Charmasson and Catherine Gaziello, "Les grandes bibliothèques parisiennes," also in *Histoire des bibliothèques françaises*, 3: 61-69.

[25] The first provincial public libraries created out of the literary depositories were the district libraries, instituted on 8 Pluviôse Year II (27 Jan. 1794); however, it seems that none of the new libraries ever actually opened. Then in October 1795, the Convention called for a network of *écoles centrales* (central schools), each of which was to include a public library. Again, this program was largely unsuccessful; less than thirty-two of the projected 108 school libraries were established. Provincial public libraries and literary depositories became the responsibility (though not the property) of the municipalities in 1803. See especially Barnett, *Histoire des bibliothèques*, pp. 33-64; Richard, "Des bibliothèques"; and Henri Comte, *Les bibliothèques publiques en France* (Lyon: Imprimerie BOSC Frères, 1977).

collections ought to be publicly accessible. The surfeit of laws and proposals
on libraries and archives in this period all emphasized that the books and
documents of the Old Regime were no longer secret; under the New
Regime, it was believed, these collections would help educate and inform
the entire citizenry.[26] Though the revolutionaries did not take many
practical steps to ensure public access to the new depositories, nor did they
attempt to limit the library and archival "public" in any explicit way. It was
thus left to the New Regimes of the nineteenth century to grapple with the
notions of "public access" and "national property" articulated by the
revolutionaries.

   Just as studies of the 1789 revolution dominate the historiography on
France in general, so do studies of revolutionary book and manuscript
collections loom large in the historiography on French archives and
libraries. In the decade following the 1989 bicentennial, historians produced
an unprecedented number of articles and essays on revolutionary
collections.[27] Yet the focus on the revolutionary period is certainly nothing
new; nearly all of the historical notices on French collections written in the
early nineteenth century placed overwhelming emphasis on the
revolutionary decade, whether to condemn it as a time of brutal
"vandalism" or (less often) to praise it as an era of unparalleled progress.[28]
The debate between the champions and the denouncers of the Revolution
came to a head during the Second Empire (1852-70), when Imperial
Archives Director Léon de Laborde challenged archivist Henri Bordier's *Les
Archives de la France* (1855) with his own work of the same title (1867). Bordier
had made every effort to absolve the revolutionaries of charges of
"vandalism," arguing that the feverish tales of archival bonfires had been

---

[26] While I cannot offer a full discussion of these proposals here, interested readers
can consult Barnett, *Histoire des bibliothèques*; and Riberette, *Les bibliothèques françaises*,
both of which cite the relevant primary texts.

[27] See *Patrimoine parisien*; *Révolution française et 'vandalisme révolutionnaire'*; "Archives et
Révolution: création ou destruction? Actes du colloque organisé par l'Association
des archivistes français (groupe régional Provence-Alpes-Côte-d'Azur),
Châteauvallon, 10-11 mars 1988," published in *Gazette des Archives* nos. 146-147
(1989); and the 1989 issues of *Bulletin des bibliothèques de France* devoted to
revolutionary libraries (vol. 34, nos. 2-3).

[28] For early histories of French libraries, see the bibliography in vol. 3 of *Histoire des
bibliothèques françaises*. For historical accounts of archives, see especially the
Bibliothèque de l'Ecole des Chartes [hereafter *BEC*], the early volumes of the Ministry of
Public Instruction's *Collection de documents inédits sur l'histoire de France*, as well as my
bibliography.

seriously exaggerated, and that while the revolutionaries did destroy some papers, these were "almost entirely devoid of historical or literary value."[29] Laborde, meanwhile, countered that the revolutionaries' "ignorance" and "incompetence" had led them to "dishonor" French archives by destroying some two-thirds of them in a burst of "barbarism" and "brutality."[30] Since the Bordier-Laborde debate, historians of French archives and libraries have taken somewhat less extreme positions on the policies of the revolution; nevertheless, many of them continue to focus on the issue of revolutionary "vandalism" and "disorder" to the exclusion of other aspects of library and archival history.[31] Historians of archives, for example, often characterize the triage campaign of the 1790s as a violent "dismemberment" of the Old Regime's supposedly orderly and coherent collections.[32] Historians of libraries, for their part, still point to the bibliographic destruction and dispersal of the revolutionary period as the primary cause of the "backwardness" of modern French libraries.[33]

Perhaps because scholars tend to see the French Revolution as the defining moment in the history of archives and libraries, they have as yet given relatively little attention to nineteenth-century developments. In the past forty years, there have been only a few general, book-length studies of

---

[29] Bordier, *Les Archives de la France*, p. 329.

[30] Léon de Laborde, *Les Archives de la France: leurs vicissitudes pendant la Révolution, leur régénération sous l'Empire* (Paris: Vve. Renouard, 1867), pp. 90-91 and 125-127.

[31] See for example Xavier Charmes, *Le Comité des travaux historiques et scientifiques (histoire et documents)* (Paris: Imprimerie nationale, 1886), which states: "All things considered, the point is neither to condemn nor to glorify the Revolution in any absolute fashion but to note the advantages of its work without covering up the disadvantages" (pp. lxxxv-lxxxvi). The emergence of more measured accounts of revolutionary policies in the 1870s can probably be connected to the contemporary interest in the archives produced by the Revolution itself, and, perhaps, to the growing emphasis on historical "impartiality" in the early Third Republic. For a brief discussion of these developments, see the epilogue.

[32] See for example Pierre Santoni, "Archives et violence. A propos de la loi du 7 messidor an II," in *Gazette des Archives* nos. 146-147 (1989): 199-214; Charpy, "Les archives en révolution"; and Françoise Hildesheimer, "Des triages au respect des fonds: les archives en France sous la monarchie de Juillet," *Revue historique* 286, no. 2 (1991): 295-312.

[33] See especially Comte, *Les bibliothèques publiques*; and Jean Hassenforder, *Développement comparé des bibliothèques publiques en France, en Grande-Bretagne, et aux Etats-Unis dans la seconde moitié du XIXe siècle (1850-1914)* (Paris: Cercle de la Librairie, 1967).

nineteenth-century French libraries, notably Jean Hassenforder's *Développement comparé des bibliothèques publiques en France, en Grande-Bretagne, et aux Etats-Unis dans la seconde moitié du XIXe siècle (1850-1914)* (1967), Henri Comte's *Les Bibliothèques publiques en France* (1977), and Graham Keith Barnett's *Histoire des bibliothèques publiques en France de la Révolution à 1939* (a 1987 French translation of his 1973 English thesis). Most of the remaining accounts of this period focus on a single library (such as Jean-François Foucaud's *La Bibliothèque Royale sous la monarchie de juillet (1830-1848)* (1978)) or set of libraries (like Noë Richter's *Les bibliothèques populaires* (also 1978)). Some of the most useful article-length studies of this type can be found in *Les bibliothèques de la Révolution et du XIXe siècle, 1789-1914* (1991), volume three of the four-volume compendium, *Histoire des bibliothèques françaises*. Meanwhile, the published literature on nineteenth-century French archives includes neither monographic studies nor major compendia.[34] Perhaps the most prolific scholar in this field is Françoise Hildesheimer, who has produced numerous articles on the development of the National Archives as well as a useful survey of French archival history.[35] Yet despite what appears to be a growing academic interest in archives more generally, aside from Hildesheimer and a handful of French and North American scholars, historians have yet to demonstrate a sustained interest in nineteenth-century French archives.[36]

---

[34] Unfortunately, two of the most important recent studies of post-revolutionary French archives, Jean Le Pottier's "Histoire et érudition: recherches et documents sur l'histoire et le rôle de l'érudition médiévale dans l'historiographie française du XIXè siècle" (1979) and Vincent Mollet's "Les archives départementales du Tarn de 1790 à 1946: constitution et mise en valeur d'un patrimoine écrit" (1992), both theses completed at the Ecole nationale des chartes, have not been published. I am grateful to both Jean Le Pottier and Vincent Mollet for allowing me to consult their theses at the Archives nationales.

[35] For Hildesheimer's articles, see the bibliography. The survey is entitled *Les Archives de France* (1997).

[36] Recent articles on this period include Guyotjeannin, "Les premières années"; Pomian, "Les archives"; Michel Duchein, "La clef du trésor. L'évolution des instruments de recherche d'archives du Moyen Age à nos jours d'après des exemples français," *Archives et bibliothèques de Belgique (Miscellanea Carlos Wyffels)* 57, nos. 1-2 (1986): 109-126; Odile Krakovitch, "La découverte des sources révolutionnaires il y a cent ans: les inventaires et collections de documents sur la Révolution publiés à l'occasion du Centenaire," *Gazette des archives* 148 (1990): 157-179; Nancy Bartlett, "*Respect des Fonds*: The Origins of the Modern Archival Principle of Provenance," in *Bibliographical Foundations of French Historical Studies*, ed.

Much of what has been published on post-revolutionary archives and libraries offers either implicitly or explicitly what is in essence the flip side of the argument made about revolutionary collections. While historians associate the revolution with the destruction and disruption of Old Regime archives and libraries, they tend to present the nineteenth century as a time of restoration and recovery for these collections. Where the revolutionary period had created disorder, the post-revolutionary era created (or recreated) order. According to this argument, though the beginning of the nineteenth century found state-owned book and document collections in a dreadful state, impossibly disorganized and often abandoned to the elements, a small cadre of French archivists and librarians gradually repaired these collections by preserving them from dilapidation and theft, providing them with increasingly accurate inventories and catalogues, and opening them to an ever-expanding reading public. Archivists undid the effects of revolutionary triage by reconstituting Old Regime collections, while librarians transformed deteriorating literary depositories into properly functioning public libraries. Nevertheless, these histories often add, French libraries and archives never fully overcame the trauma of the 1789 upheaval. Even though France's librarians and archivists often led the world in developing new bibliographic and documentary principles, because of the difficult legacy of the revolution, France's libraries and archives often lagged behind those of other Western states.[37]

Interestingly, while historians are quick to point to the political context for revolutionary policies on libraries and archives, this context seems to drop out of discussions of the nineteenth century. Though many of these

---

Lawrence McCrank (New York: Haworth Press, 1991), pp. 107-115; and V. Duclert, "Archives politiques et politiques d'archives sous la IIIe République," *Jean Jaurès: Cahiers trimestriels* no. 135 (Jan. 1995): 11-19. The interdisciplinary seminar on "Archives, Documentation, and the Institutions of Social Memory" currently in progress at the University of Michigan's Advanced Study Center and the recent publication of works like Jacques Derrida's *Archive Fever: A Freudian Impression* (1995, in French 1994) and Shawn Michelle Smith's *American Archives: Gender, Race, and Class in Visual Culture* (Princeton: Princeton University Press, 1999) suggest that the "archive" is becoming an increasingly important academic trope.

[37] For arguments about French "backwardness," see especially Hassenforder, *Développement comparé*, and Comte, *Les bibliothèques publiques*. For a thoughtful analysis of these arguments, see the introduction to Laure Léveillé, "Les petites bibliothèques de la République: aux origines de la lecture publique parisienne, des années 1870 aux années 1930," (doctoral thesis, Université de Paris X-Nanterre, Jan. 1998). I am grateful to Laure Léveillé for sharing her work with me.

accounts are organized according to traditional political markers (1814, 1830, 1848, etc.), these dates seem to be merely convenient stopping points rather than key argumentative shifts. In most cases, libraries and archives are described as developing according to their own internal logic: when collections are disorganized, classification schemes are developed; when classification is complete, catalogues are prepared; and when catalogues attract the attention of researchers, new public access policies are created.[38] This internalist view of French collections is undoubtedly at least partly attributable to the fact that most historians of archives and libraries are professional archivists and librarians, many of them writing about their own institutions. Like their nineteenth-century predecessors, these professionals often appear reluctant to identify connections between archival and library policies and national politics, perhaps fearing that perceptions of the former will be tainted by the conflicts of the latter. They are thus more likely to place nineteenth-century French collections against the backdrop of other libraries and archives than against that of nineteenth-century France.

My investigation of post-revolutionary archival and library policies, however, shows that the story of nineteenth-century French archives and libraries cannot be separated from the story of nineteenth-century French politics. After many centuries of Bourbon rule, France entered an extremely volatile political phase. Between 1800 and 1870, the French went through five different political regimes (the Napoleonic Empire of 1804, the Bourbon Restoration of 1814, the July Monarchy of 1830, the Second Republic of 1848, and the Second Empire of 1852) before instituting the relatively durable Third Republic, which would last until France's defeat in 1940. One might expect that in a time of such political turmoil, the organization of libraries and archives would have been a relatively low government priority, but each of these short-lived regimes showed a strong interest in the collections constituted by the revolutionary state. Moreover, rather than simply continuing the policies established by their predecessors, each of these governments developed its own approach (or approaches) to libraries and archives, reconceptualizing them in ways best suited to its particular political predicament. The Bourbon Restoration, for example, explored the great Parisian collections for Old Regime precedents for the 1814 Charter, while the late July Monarchy organized provincial archives so as to divert

---

[38] Exceptions to this general rule include Le Pottier, "Histoire et érudition"; Pierre Casselle, "Les pouvoirs publics et les bibliothèques," in *Histoire des bibliothèques françaises*, 3: 109-117; and the work of Noë Richter, including *Les bibliothèques populaires* (Paris: Cercle de la librairie, 1978).

scholarly attention from the revolutionary records. Decisions about preservation, classification, inventory, and access were therefore the result not just of practical considerations or the opinions of individual archivists and librarians but also of key shifts in national politics.

Of course, in order for each new post-revolutionary regime to justify its own reconfiguration of archives and libraries, it had to dismiss existing configurations as unsatisfactory. From the end of the eighteenth century to the final quarter of the nineteenth, government officials constantly described French archives and libraries as "chaotic," "disorderly," and, perhaps most memorably, "pell-mell." Interestingly, while these officials sometimes explicitly blamed their immediate predecessors for wreaking such havoc, they were more likely to blame the revolutionaries of the 1790s. For each New Regime, then, the revolutionary upheaval (both political and bibliographical-documentary) had to be invoked anew in order to attempt, once again, to end it.[39] Seen in this light, the development of state-owned archives and libraries in post-revolutionary France appears less as gradual progression from disorder to order than as a series of very different attempts to recreate both "disorder" and "order."

My analysis of changing state conceptions of archives and libraries in this period takes as its point of departure the Ecole des Chartes (School of Charters), the state school for archivists, librarians, and historians established in Paris in 1821.[40] I have chosen to focus on the Ecole des Chartes for a number of reasons. First and foremost, because the school was not the product of the Church or of a private association but of the French state, it offers a useful way of tracking government perceptions of the "national" and "public" collections created in the 1790s. Even though the

---

[39] Readers familiar with the work of François Furet will recognize how much my argument here and throughout owes to his *Interpreting the French Revolution*, trans. Elborg Forster (Cambridge: Cambridge University Press, 1981), first published as *Penser la Révolution française* (Paris: Editions Gallimard, 1978); and especially to his *Revolutionary France, 1770-1880*, trans. Antonia Nevill (Cambridge: Blackwell, 1992), originally published as *La Révolution: de Turgot à Jules Ferry, 1770-1880* (Paris: Hachette, 1988). In a sense, this dissertation might be considered a case study of Furet's assessment of post-revolutionary France, investigating how each successive government contended with the dual legacies of monarchy and revolution.

[40] While some scholars will undoubtedly disagree with my characterization of the Ecole des Chartes as the "school for archivists, librarians, and historians," here I have chosen to use the most expansive definition of the school's mission; the chapters that follow will explore the key shifts in this definition over the period 1821 to 1870. For the historical literature on the Ecole des Chartes, see the bibliography.

Ecole was first founded under the much-belittled Bourbon Restoration, subsequent governments maintained and even expanded the school, each according to its own vision of archives, libraries, and the French past. Second, from its inception, the Ecole des Chartes was meant to contend especially with the library and archival collections nationalized during the French Revolution. Since the religious orders (the term is particularly appropriate here) once responsible for maintaining many of these collections had been largely dispersed in the 1790s, it was hoped that the Ecole des Chartes would provide "new Benedictines" capable of reviving the precious vestiges of the Old Regime. And while the school's graduates, or *chartistes*, did work with post-revolutionary books and documents, through most of the nineteenth century, Old Regime (and especially medieval) collections remained their primary focus. Their work therefore teaches us a great deal about state views of both the Old Regime and the revolution that ended it.

Another reason for concentrating on the Ecole des Chartes is that it affords a look at both archives and libraries. With rare exceptions, historical studies of French collections treat archives and libraries as entirely distinct.[41] Libraries are described as encyclopedic collections—primarily consisting of books—of use to the general public. Archives, meanwhile, are characterized as coherent bodies of records—usually documents—naturally produced by institutions and individuals in the regular course of their activities, and of special interest to the historians and administrators of those institutions and individual estates. Thus historians of archives do not mention libraries, and vice versa. Yet before the 1860s, these modern distinctions between archives and libraries were still being drawn. The revolutionary program of triage, as we have seen, made only a rather vague distinction between confiscated titles destined for archives and those destined for libraries.[42] The Bourbon Restoration and July Monarchy, for their part, often emphasized the similarities between archives and libraries as much as they did their differences. In this same period, moreover, it still seemed possible that the Ecole des Chartes would train both state archivists and public librarians (even if in practice few of its graduates became library administrators). It

---

[41] The exceptions consist primarily of studies of the struggle between the Imperial Archives and the Imperial Library in the early 1860s. For more on this struggle, see chap. 5.

[42] While a thorough investigation of the revolutionary understandings of the terms "libraries" and "archives" is beyond the scope of this study, it would be intriguing to study revolutionary reports and correspondence, particularly those produced as part of the triage campaign, to see how they deploy these two terms.

was not until the latter half of the Second Empire that the French began to clearly differentiate between archives and libraries and to definitively associate the Ecole des Chartes with the archival world. Hence by exploring the changing conceptions of the Ecole in this period, we can learn more about how modern notions of the state archive and the public library emerged.

The fourth and final reason why I have focused on the Ecole is that doing so allows me to explore the development of the archival profession in nineteenth-century France. While I did not set out to tell this story, it became clear in the course of my research that the corps of *chartistes* produced by the school (most of whom were archivists) came to exert a major influence on state archival policies.[43] At the same time, the French government came to view the politically neutral "expert" archivist as crucial to maintaining the status and authority of state archives. Thus it became just as important for me to investigate archivists' perceptions of themselves and their work as it was to explore ministerial officials' perceptions of them. By studying the Ecole des Chartes as well as its very active alumni organization, the Société de l'Ecole des Chartes, I was able to outline the complex relationships among archives, archivists, and the French state.[44]

It should be emphasized, however, that while my study concentrates on the Ecole des Chartes, it makes no attempt to provide a comprehensive history of the school and its students.[45] I have not tried, for example, to give detailed accounts of the careers of individual professors and alumni, except

---

[43] I do not mention libraries here because unlike the archival profession, which can be said to have its roots in the mid-nineteenth century, the library profession took much longer to coalesce, emerging only in the early decades of the twentieth century. For more on these developments, see chap. 5 and the epilogue.

[44] My study thus provides a complement to recent studies of the growth of "neutral" medical and scientific professions in this period. See especially Jan Goldstein, *Console and Classify: The French Psychiatric Profession in the Nineteenth Century* (Cambridge: Cambridge University Press, 1987); and Gerald L. Geison, ed., *Professions and the French State, 1700-1900* (Philadelphia: University of Pennsylvania Press, 1984).

[45] As a number of scholars have pointed out (see for example Anne-Marie Chartier and Jean Hébrard, *Discours sur la lecture (1880-1980)* (Paris: Bibliothèque publique d'information, Centre Georges-Pompidou, 1989), p. 86; and Bertrand Joly, "L'Ecole des Chartes et l'Affaire Dreyfus," *BEC* 147 (1989): 612), there is as yet no comprehensive, critical history of the Ecole des Chartes. However, the recent anthology edited by Yves-Marie Bercé, Olivier Guyotjeannin, and Marc Smith, *L'Ecole nationale des chartes: histoire de l'école depuis 1821* (Thionville, France: Gérard Klopp, 1997), points out some interesting paths for future research.

as these bear on the development of official policies or programs. My aim throughout has been to use the school as a way of understanding the French state's shifting approach to archives and libraries. Thus in Chapter 1, I show how the creation of the school figured in a moderate royalist campaign to preserve the Charter of 1814 by identifying its legal precursors among the collections of the Royal Library and Royal Archives. In Chapter 2, I argue that with the rise of the Liberals in 1828-29, the state reconfigured the Ecole des Chartes so that its graduates might help mine provincial archives and libraries for evidence of the Third Estate's glorious past. Chapter 3 shows that the next major turning point in state policy came not with the fall of the Liberal July Monarchy, but with the regime's shift to the right in 1840. As the constitutional monarchy of Louis-Philippe became increasingly rigid and conservative, it became particularly interested in archival classification, establishing a new classification scheme for departmental archives that reflected its strong misgivings about the revolutionary past. Chapter 4 takes on two major shifts in state policies, the first coinciding with the rise of the Second Republic in 1848 and the second with the start of the "authoritarian" Second Empire in 1852. Here I explore how, after a series of brief yet crucial experiments with public libraries under the Second Republic, the early Empire began dispatching "expert" *chartistes* to provincial archives in an attempt to both counteract the effects of 1848 and promote a new kind of allegiance to the central government. Finally, in Chapter 5, I investigate the decisive period of the late Empire, situating two major debates about the role of public libraries in France—the debate on "popular" libraries and the fierce struggle between the Imperial Library and the Imperial Archives—in the context of the Empire's halting efforts to come to terms with the political implications of the "public." I argue that in the course of these debates, not only did libraries and archives begin to take on their modern connotations, but the Ecole des Chartes, once linked with a variety of scholarly practices, became more firmly associated with archival work, an association that only intensified with the rise of the French historical profession after 1866. Meanwhile, as the Second Empire became the Third Republic, the French state spent less time grappling with the Old Regime collections confiscated during the 1789 revolution and more time working with the collections generated by the revolution itself. Though national archives and libraries and national politics would remain intertwined, the era of constant reconceptualizations of the pre-revolutionary collections had come to a close.

My decision to explore French library and archival policies from the perspective of the Ecole des Chartes meant, of course, forgoing certain

intriguing aspects of the general topic. Perhaps the most obvious of these is
the First Napoleonic Empire (1804-14), which I discuss only briefly in my
opening chapter. Aside from the fact that the Ecole des Chartes was not
founded until 1821, my preliminary investigations of the sources for this
period suggested that the Napoleonic state was less preoccupied than
subsequent regimes with the collections nationalized during the 1790s.
Nevertheless, Napoleon's seizure of collections from conquered European
countries and his (unfulfilled) plans for an archival "palace" are interesting
developments that have only begun to be explored by historians.[46] Another
topic that is largely absent from my study is private or individual initiatives
on behalf of libraries and archives. Though I discuss some of these ideas as
roads not taken by the various post-revolutionary regimes, it was not
possible to include nearly all of them here. Nor am I able to discuss the
fascinating issue of how nineteenth-century readers made use of state
collections. Though the records on this topic are relatively sparse, it would
be intriguing to pair my discussions of the state's imagined "public" with an
analysis of French readers' understandings of their own library and archival
practices.[47] Finally, I recognize that my analysis of state policies carries its
own internalism; while I situate libraries, archives, and the Ecole des
Chartes in the context of national politics, I do not place them in other
potentially illuminating contexts (the rise of scientific disciplines, for
example). In future work on this subject, I hope to explore whether or not
the shifts I identify here might be traced in other contexts.

For the moment, however, this study aims to provide a worthwhile
contribution to a number of historical fields. First, it offers an intriguing
retelling of the familiar story of post-revolutionary politics, showing how
changing conceptions of both the Old Regime and the French Revolution
played themselves out in the organization of archives and libraries. I also
hope to contribute to the growing literature on the history of collecting and
classification, a literature that has thus far concentrated primarily on

---

[46] See Raymond J. Maras, "Napoleon's Quest for a Super-Archival Center in
Paris," *Consortium on Revolutionary Europe, 1750-1850: Selected Papers* (1994): 567-578;
and, to a lesser extent, Frances E. Montgomery, "Tribunes, Napoleon and the
Archives Nationales," *Consortium on Revolutionary Europe, 1750-1850: Selected Papers* 19,
no. 1 (1989): 437-459.

[47] Though the literature on the history of reading in France is quite large, it does
not as yet include many studies of state-owned collections. Readers interested in this
topic might begin with James Smith Allen's *In the Public Eye: A History of Reading in
Modern France, 1800-1940* (Princeton, NJ: Princeton University Press, 1991).

collections of artistic and scientific objects.[48] Third, my analysis of libraries and archives is meant to serve as a complement to recent studies of French monuments and national memory.[49] Readers familiar with the large and growing literature on the construction of national memory will find strong parallels in my discussions of the making of national history. Finally, I hope this book will serve as a contribution to the study of French historians and historical practices. Scholars have paid particular attention in recent years to the connection between the rise of "positivist" history and the fetishization of archives as bearers of historical truth in the late nineteenth century; my work offers a kind of pre-history of this conception of historical practice, exploring the relationship between French historians and historical collections in the era before professional, "scientific" history.[50] For if my study is in part an attempt to encourage archivists and librarians to consider their collections in historical and political terms, it is also an effort to encourage historians—and particularly historians of France—to consider the archival and bibliographical practices that have shaped the collections on which they rely.

---

[48] While this literature is vast, some particularly thoughtful recent works include Krzysztof Pomian, *Collectors and Curiosities: Paris and Venice, 1500-1800* (Cambridge, England: Polity Press, 1990), originally published as *Collectionneurs, amateurs et curieux: Paris, Venise, XVIe-XVIIIe siècle* (Paris: Gallimard, 1987); Paula Findlen, *Possessing Nature: Museums, Collecting, and Scientific Culture in Early Modern Italy* (Berkeley: University of California Press, 1994); Andrew McClellan, *Inventing the Louvre: Art, Politics, and the Origins of the Modern Museum in Eighteenth-Century Paris* (Cambridge: Cambridge University Press, 1994); and Harriet Ritvo, *The Platypus and the Mermaid and Other Figments of the Classifying Imagination* (Cambridge: Harvard University Press, 1997).

[49] See especially the essays in Pierre Nora's compendium, *Les lieux de mémoire* (Paris: Gallimard, 1984-1992) as well as Daniel Sherman, *Worthy Monuments: Art Museums and the Politics of Culture in Nineteenth-Century France* (Cambridge: Harvard University Press, 1989); and Stephane Gerson, "Pays and nation: the uneasy formation of an historical patrimony in France, 1830-1870," (Ph.D. diss., University of Chicago, 1997).

[50] See in particular Bonnie G. Smith, The Gender of History: Men, Women, and Historical Practice (Cambridge: Harvard University Press, 1998); and William Keylor, Academy and Community: The Foundation of the French Historical Profession (Cambridge: Harvard University Press, 1975).

Chapter One

Of Kings and Charters: Restoration Politics and the Creation of the Ecole des Chartes

To listen to the reports of provincial administrators in the early Restoration, one would think that an enormous tornado had just blown through the archives and libraries of France. Surveying the collections now under their control, these officials saw before them only "chaos," "disorder," and "destruction." In the spring of 1816, for example, the newly appointed Prefect of the Indre-et-Loire described his department's archives to the Minister of the Interior:

> Everywhere...we were surprised by the disorder, by the dirtiness that prevailed. Dust, in prodigious quantities, hardened by the water that has run in from all sides due to the humidity, covers the surfaces of all the masses of papers...All research seems impossible until a certain order has been established....[1]

Officials in other provincial capitals filed similar reports. In 1817, the Secretary-General of the Nièvre wrote that his department's archives were "in a painful <u>disorder</u>, which ordinary means will not be sufficient to remedy," while his counterpart in the Allier noted that documents had been thrown "pell-mell" into the local depository, creating total "disorder and confusion."[2]

Despite such reports, throughout most of the Restoration, the central government paid little attention to the preservation and classification of the book and manuscript collections confiscated in the 1790s. As we will see, the monarchy did show considerable concern for the two largest state-run collections, the Royal Library and the Royal Archives, but left local and

---

[1] Bacot (prefet d'Indre et Loire), "Préfecture d'Indre et Loire [report on state of departmental archives]," 1 Jun. 1816, AN, box F2 I 371⁵.

[2] Secrétaire-général [de la Nièvre] to Son Excellence le Ministre Secrétaire d'Etat de l'Intérieur, Nevers, 12 Dec. 1817, AN, box F2 I 374⁴, p. [2], emphasis in original; Duchezot (Secrétaire-général), "Etat Statistique des Archives du département de l'Allier," 1 Aug. 1817, AN, box F2 I 367⁴, p. [3].

regional collections almost entirely at the disposition of provincial officials. In April 1817, for example, the Minister of the Interior issued a circular ordering all prefects to ensure that their archives were safe from both fire and humidity and instructed them to hire a clerk to classify and maintain their collections. However, aside from sending a brief reminder to the prefects in late 1820, the Ministry made no effort to enforce this circular.[3] Provincial libraries received even less attention from the central government. The only ministerial decision related to libraries before 1828 was the creation of an "Inspector-General of Libraries and Literary Depositories" in 1822, yet the first and only appointee, Charles-Hyacinthe His, conducted few inspections and produced no reports.[4] The restoration of the Old Regime, then, did not necessarily involve the physical restoration of its provincial collections.

In fact, far from attempting to preserve these collections, the Restoration government often seemed to do just the opposite. In 1817, for instance, the head of the Royal Archives, De Larue, outlined a plan for France's departmental archives in which he proposed four key tasks: first, to get rid of "useless" documents; second, "to return to private individuals the titles that belong to them"; third, to maintain in departmental archives only documents relevant to local administration; and fourth, to transfer all documents "related to constitutions, [laws], properties, and the institution of the state" to the Royal Archives in Paris.[5] Though De Larue's plan was

---

[3] Lainé (Le Ministre Secrétaire d'état de l'intérieur), "Circulaire No. 38" [with marginal heading "Instructions, 1. sur l'ordonnance du 9 avril 1817, qui supprime les Secrétaires généraux de préfecture; 2. sur les archives des départemens [sic]."], 28 Apr. 1817, and Mounier (Directeur général de l'administration départementale et de la police), "Circulaire," 11 Dec. 1820, both in AN, box AB XXXI 41. A lengthy excerpt from the 1817 circular can be found in [Tanneguy Duchâtel], *Rapport au Roi sur les archives départementales et communales* (Paris: Imprimerie royale, May 1841), which can in turn be most easily located in the appendix to [Maximilien] Quantin, *Dictionnaire Raisonné de Diplomatique Chrétienne…* (Paris: Chez l'Editeur [the Abbé Migne], 1846), cols. 841-968.

[4] Corbière (Le Ministre Secrétaire d'Etat au Dept. de l'Intérieur) and Bon. Capelle (Le Conseiller d'Etat Secrétaire général), Rapport au Roi, 1 Jun. 1822, AN, box AB II 11, folder "Correspondance 1822." On His's appointment, see Maurice Caillet, "L'inspection générale des bibliothèques," *Bulletin des Bibliothèques de France* 15, no. 12 (1970): 597-608; and his "Les inspecteurs généraux des bibliothèques," in *Histoire des bibliothèques françaises* (Paris: Promodis, 1991), 3: 131.

[5] [Isidore Etienne De Larue], "Observations," [1817], AN, box AB VI 1, folder "Rapport et observations de Mr. de La Rue…," p. [1].

never articulated as an official policy, correspondence between provincial officials and the Ministry of the Interior in this period shows that the Ministry generally followed his recommendations, never preventing local administrators from removing documents from their archives, and often giving its explicit approval for them to do so. For example, in 1821, the Prefect of the Aube confidently claimed, "The real way to put [the archives] in order and to be able to find useful papers easily would be to eliminate the mass of papers that can never be used for anything and which in thirty years have not been interrogated a single time either in the public interest or in the private interest." The ministerial reply of May 1821 made no mention of this suggestion, simply encouraging the Prefect to "accelerate" his efforts.[6]

However, the Restoration government's lack of interest in preserving and classifying provincial collections does not mean that it did not care about the bibliographic and documentary legacy of the Old Regime. It simply did not deal with this legacy as one might expect. Rather than undertaking a national campaign to rescue dilapidated archives and libraries, the government of Louis XVIII chose to establish the Ecole des Chartes, or "School of Charters." Readers familiar with the modern incarnation of the school, now housed at the Sorbonne, might not find this choice so surprising; after all, these days most of the school's graduates, known as *chartistes*, spend their entire careers in provincial archives and libraries, working on just those problems of preservation and classification that so troubled local officials in the early Restoration. Yet as first instituted in February 1821, the school was not supposed to train archivists and librarians. According to the royal ordinance establishing the school, its sole mission was to teach its students "to read the various manuscripts and to explicate the French dialects of the Middle Ages."[7] Why did such a mission suddenly become important in 1821? Why did accomplishing this mission entail creating a "School of Charters"? And most important, what does the

---

[6] Préfet du Département de l'Aube to Monsieur le Baron Mounier, Pair de France, Directeur général de l'Administration Départementale et de la Police, Troyes, 12 Apr. 1821, AN, box F2 I 367[12], pp. [1-2]; Mounier to Mr. le Préfet de l'Aube, Paris, 7 May 1821, Archives départementales [hereafter AD] de l'Aube, box 3T 32, folder labelled [incorrectly] "1840," p. [1].

[7] Louis [XVIII], Siméon, and Bon. Capelle, "Ordonnance du Roi," Paris, 22 Feb. 1821, Archives of the Ecole nationale des chartes [hereafter AEC], folder "Ecole des Chartes. établie....," p. [2]; also published in *Le Moniteur Universel*, 2 Mar. 1821. I am very grateful to Yves-Marie Bercé, Director of the Ecole nationale des chartes, for granting me access to the school's archives.

creation of such a school tell us about how the Restoration thought about the legacy of the Old Regime?

While there is as yet no in-depth history of the Ecole des Chartes, most discussions of the school's founding—nearly all of them by *chartistes*—do little to help answer these questions. These accounts usually take one of two tacks. The first takes great pains to portray the 1821 Ecole des Chartes as a failure, a kind of false start before the school really got underway in the 1830s and 1840s. According to this version of the story, because the 1821 ordinance did not reserve any government posts for the school's graduates, the school could not attract enough students and was forced to fold at the end of 1823. It was not until the reorganization of November 1829, or, according to some accounts, that of December 1846, that the school could be described as "truly constituted."[8] The second approach to the history of the school emphasizes that its true origins are to be found not in the royal ordinance of 1821 but in the proposals presented to Napoleon Bonaparte by the Ideologue philosopher and philanthropist Joseph-Marie Degérando in 1806-7. Degérando's idea was to set up a "new Port-Royal," a calm provincial retreat where an "erudite senate" of revered elder scholars would help a young "noviciate" perfect his literary skills. As the story goes, although Napoleon tabled the proposal, saying it needed "development," Degérando renewed his request in 1819 or 1820 and this time found official support for what became the Ecole des Chartes.[9] A few accounts push the origins of the school even farther back, to late 1793, when legal scholar

---

[8] See for example [Henri Bordier], *Programme de l'Ecole Nationale des Chartes. Historique de l'Ecole des Chartes...*(Paris: Chez Dumoulin et Chez Auguste Durand, 1848), Paul Frédéricq, "L'enseignement supérieur de l'histoire à Paris, notes et impressions de voyage," *Revue internationale de l'enseignement* (1883): 742, and Henri-Jean Martin, "Les chartistes et les bibliothèques," *Bulletin des bibliothèques de France* 17 (1972): 529-537. The quotation is from Charles Samaran, "L'école des Chartes et les Chartistes," *La Revue de la Semaine* 8 (25 Feb. 1921): 445-446.

[9] See for example, A[uguste] Vallet de Viriville, "Notes et documents pour servir à l'histoire de l'Ecole royale des chartes," *BEC* 9 (1848): 153-176, and [Jean-Marie Pardessus], "Note sur l'ecole des chartes," [1845?], AN, Box F17-4024. Although Degérando's original proposal, probably drafted in 1806, has been lost, the communications between Champagny, then Minister of the Interior, and the Emperor on this subject can be found in AN, box AF IV 1289, folders 74, 75, and 77.

Antoine Maugard proposed—also unsuccessfully—that the Bibliothèque Nationale offer courses in paleography to future archivists and librarians.[10]

While neither of these two versions of the school's history is inaccurate— the school really was closed two years after it opened, and the 1821 ordinance does indeed have affiliations with earlier projects—neither story helps us situate the foundation of the school in the context of Louis XVIII's France. Neither tells us why it was in 1821, not in 1793, 1807, 1829, or 1846, that the government created an "Ecole des Chartes." As an 1839 letter from the *chartiste* Vallet de Viriville to his colleague Le Roux de Lincy suggests, this effort to locate the origins of the school outside the Restoration may reflect an effort to distance the school from a discredited Bourbon legitimism. Upon hearing of the unearthing of Degérando's proposals to Napoleon, Vallet de Viriville remarked, "We now date to 1806. Certainly I sincerely congratulate this new discovery. I like much better for my part to descend from Napoleon than from [Restoration minister] Monsieur the Abbé de Montesquiou."[11] Subsequent historians of the school seem to have followed suit, preferring to link the school to a revolutionary, Bonapartist, or Orleanist tradition rather than to a Bourbon one.

There are two important exceptions to this general tendency. The first is Albert Mathiez's 1921 article, "Le centenaire de l'Ecole des chartes," which while championing the *chartistes'* "scientific rigor," characterizes the school in just the way Vallet de Viriville had hoped to avoid:

> It is under the reign of the Bloc National that is celebrated the centenary
> of the Ecole des Chartes, founded by Louis XVIII to rekindle in [his

---

[10] See especially "Projet d'un enseignement historique et diplomatique à la Bibliothèque nationale sous la Convention," *BEC* 52 (1891): 353-355; and Henri Omont, "Rapport sur la Bibliothèque Nationale fait à la Commission d'Instruction Publique de la Convention Nationale," *Revue des Bibliothèques* (1905): 98, footnote 1. The "projet de rapport" cited by Omont can be found in AN, box D XXXVIII 2, folder 20 (labelled "Bibliothèques, XX").

[11] Aug[uste] Vallet [de Viriville] to Mons[ieur] Le Roux de Lincy (secrétaire de la Société de l'Ecole des chartes), Troyes, 16 Nov. 1839, AN, Archives of the Société de l'Ecole des Chartes, box 11 AS 11. I am very grateful to the Société de l'Ecole des chartes for allowing me to use these materials. Vallet de Viriville probably mentions the Abbé de Montesquiou in particular because two years earlier, Achille Jubinal had published an article claiming it was the Abbé, at the prodding of the Academician Raynouard, who first proposed an Ecole des Chartes to Louis XVIII. Jubinal does not cite any sources, and I have not found any evidence to corroborate his story. See his "Ecole des Chartes," in *Paris pittoresque*, ed. G. Sarrut and B. Saint-Edme (Paris: D'Urtubie, Worms et Cie., 1837), 2:54-68.

subjects'] minds the cult of divine-right monarchy. To what extent have Louis XVIII's hopes been fulfilled? To what extent has the Ecole des Chartes rehabilitated feudalism, the monarchy, and the Church? It would take too long to find out. But, what is sure is that the great majority of *chartistes* have remained attached, by their preferences and by their sympathies, to the parties of social conservatism.[12]

For Mathiez, the Ecole was not a creation of the French Revolution, the First Empire, or the July Monarchy, but clearly owed its scholarly mission and political leanings to the ultraroyalism of the Bourbon Restoration.

The second exception that bears mentioning is Yves-Marie Bercé's contribution to the recent anthology on the history of the Ecole des Chartes. Bercé, currently the school's director, argues that the 1821 ordinance is best understood in the context of Degérando's intellectual and political career. Though his scholarly interests ranged widely, from Kantian philosophy to elementary education, Degérando was particularly fascinated by the study of language. As a founding member of the *Société des observateurs de l'homme*, he produced a number of studies of "savage peoples" and deaf-mutes in an attempt to work out the connections between mental mechanisms and the production of language. Yet unlike many of his contemporaries, Degérando believed that the study of ancient manuscripts could be just as useful in this effort as the observation of living subjects, for both revealed language in its most "primitive" state. Bercé suggests, however, that Degérando would likely never have been able to transform this idea into the Ecole des Chartes if not for his political connections. A Councilor of State and Secretary-General to the Minister of the Interior under the Empire, Degérando was so little scathed by the upheavals of 1814-15 that in 1820 he was able to call upon his friend at the Ministry of the Interior, the Comte Siméon, for help in establishing the Ecole des Chartes.[13]

Thus Mathiez and Bercé, while both diverging from the general tendency to locate the founding of the school outside the Restoration, offer remarkably different explanations for why the school was created under

---

[12] Albert Mathiez, "Le centenaire de l'Ecole des chartes," *Annales révolutionnaires* 13 (1921): 174.

[13] Yves-Marie Bercé, "Aux origines de l'Ecole des chartes: le baron de Gérando," in *L'Ecole nationale des chartes: histoire de l'école depuis 1821*, ed. Yves-Marie Bercé, Olivier Guyotjeannin, and Marc Smith (Thionville, France: Gérard Klopp, 1997), pp. 20-25. On Degérando's career, see J.-B. Bayle-Mouillard, *Eloge de Joseph-Marie Baron de Gérando* (Paris: Jules Renouard, 1846); and Georges Berlia, *Gérando: Sa vie -- son oeuvre* (Paris: R. Pichon et R. Durand-Auzias, 1942).

Louis XVIII. If we believe Mathiez, the school was the natural product of a government obsessed with reviving the Old Regime. For Bercé, on the other hand, the school was largely the work of a single man who in the 1820s saw his political opportunities and intellectual interests converge. I would like to offer an explanation that lies somewhere between these two. Mathiez's conclusion is provocative, but imprecise. If the school was simply a legitimist strategy, then why was the school closed at the end of 1823, just as the Ultraroyalists were consolidating their power? What *kind* of legitimism was the school meant to promote? What particular aspects of the Old Regime was it intended to revive, and why? This chapter will attempt to answer these questions. Yet in doing so, it will look beyond the life and work of Degérando to examine the complex of political and historiographical currents that combined to establish—and then quickly disestablish—the Ecole des Chartes. As we will see, although Degérando proposed an Ecole des Chartes in 1806 and again in 1820, the institution that opened in 1821 differed significantly from his proposals. In order to explain how his bucolic "Port-Royal" became the Ecole des Chartes, we need to understand the political and intellectual struggles of the early Restoration.

This is no small task, given the state of scholarly work on the period. Sandwiched between two seemingly more politically exciting and culturally productive eras, the Restoration attracts relatively few historians. Surveys of French history generally dash through the Hundred Days, the Carbonarist revolts, and Byron's death at Missolonghi before skipping on to the barricades of July 1830, while the small number of monographs on the Restoration tend to emphasize a single political camp, focusing either on the Bourbon kings and their circle of advisors or on the Liberal opposition. This pattern has begun to shift, as historians like François Furet, Pierre Rosanvallon, and Sheryl Kroen have begun investigating the "political culture" of Restoration France; nevertheless, constructing a convincing picture of Restoration politics still requires a good measure of ingenuity and speculation.[14]

Part of what makes this task so difficult is that it is not clear—nor was it so at the time—what the Restoration was supposed to restore. International

---

[14] François Furet, *Revolutionary France, 1770-1880*, trans. Antonia Nevill (Cambridge: Blackwell, 1992); originally published as *La Révolution: de Turgot à Jules Ferry, 1770-1880* (Paris: Hachette, 1988); Pierre Rosanvallon, *La monarchie impossible: les Chartes de 1814 et de 1830* (Paris: Fayard, 1994); Sheryl Kroen, *Politics and Theater: The Crisis of Legitimacy in Restoration France, 1815-1830* (Berkeley: University of California Press, 2000).

peace? The rule of law? The Old Regime? The House of Bourbon? If the last of these seems the most obvious answer, this was not the case in early 1814. Even as the royal family began making its way from England to France, the provisional government vacillated between recalling the aging brother of Louis XVI and supporting a Bonapartist regency under Empress Marie Louise.[15] And though the provisional government and the victorious European monarchs soon came to advocate Louis XVIII's return, the relationship between the Restoration regime and the Old Regime remained hazy. After all, this Bourbon monarchy was neither the absolutist one of 1715 nor the constitutional one of 1791, but one whose principles and practices had yet to be tested out: it was a monarchy by Charter.

The *Charte constitutionnelle* promulgated by Louis XVIII in June 1814 is a tremendously ambiguous document. Some of this ambiguity might be attributed to the fact that the king and his advisors produced it in enormous haste, drafting seventy-six articles and a preamble in less than two weeks.[16] However, as a number of historians have pointed out, its fundamental contradictions stem primarily from its attempt to strike a kind of "compromise" between the Old Regime and the Revolution.[17] While the proclamation—commonly known simply as *la Charte*—affirms the absolute power of the king, it also establishes a bicameral parliament and guarantees equality before the law, freedom of religion, and freedom from arbitrary arrest. Though claiming to "efface" the Revolution from memory, it nevertheless maintains all extant legislation, including the Napoleonic Code.

The tensions in the Charter are apparent even in its title. In early 1814, there appear to have been three definitions of the word *charte* available in French. As described in the *Encyclopédie* of 1751, the first and most general use of the term was a modification of the Latin *charta*, meaning "paper or parchment." In this usage, *chartes*, sometimes spelled *chartres*, referred simply to "letters, or old titles and instructions." Yet according to the *Encyclopédie*, by the eighteenth century, the term was used primarily to describe a

---

[15] Paul Bastid, *Les Institutions politiques de la monarchie parlementaire française (1814-1848)* (Paris: Recueil Sirey, 1954), pp. 43-45.

[16] The text of the Charter can be found in Charles Debbasch and Jean-Marie Pontier, eds., *Les Constitutions de la France*, 3rd ed. (Paris: Dalloz, 1996), pp. 116-122.

[17] See especially Furet, *Revolutionary France*, pp. 271-275; Guillaume Bertier de Sauvigny, *The Bourbon Restoration*, trans. Lynn M. Case (Philadelphia: University of Pennsylvania Press, 1966), pp. 65-72; originally published as *La Restauration* (Paris: Flammarion, [1955]); and Gordon Wright, *France in Modern Times: From the Enlightenment to the Present*, 5th ed. (New York: W. W. Norton, 1995), p. 92.

particular set of titles: that is, the "customs, privileges, and concessions" granted under the Merovingian, Carolingian, and early Capetian kings, or until the mid-fourteenth century.[18] Thus in its second and more common usage, a "charter" meant a written concession made by a medieval French king, or more rarely, it seems, by a feudal lord. But a concession to whom? Both the *Encyclopédie* and Dom de Vaines' classic *Dictionnaire Raisonné de diplomatique* of 1774 give multiple examples of medieval charters: *chartes de commune, de fidelité, d'obéissance, d'hommage, d'abjuration, de mundeburde,* etc.[19] Yet none of these many kinds of charters was granted to the entire mass of the king's subjects; a "charter," in this sense, gave privileges to a particular individual (such as a nobleman) or corporation (such as a town) and to that person or group alone.

We cannot forget, however, that there was a third definition of the term floating about in early nineteenth-century France, a definition that raised a whole different set of political possibilities. This version was not just *une charte* but *la Grande Charte,* better known in English as the Magna Carta of 1215. As the *Encyclopédie* explains, "the reason why one calls it *magna,* great, is because it contains freedoms and prerogatives [that are] precious to the nation...." Unlike the charters granted by French kings, which were never national in scope, the Magna Carta extended rights to "all the free men of our realm."[20] Yet there was another difference between "*la Grande Charte*" and medieval French charters, one not mentioned by the *Encyclopédie* but undoubtedly clear to most post-revolutionary politicians and jurists.[21] Whereas French charters were simply royal "concessions," the Magna Carta was a pact between King John and a group of powerful barons who had demanded guarantees of their liberties before they would continue to fund his military engagements. If the king did not hold up his end of the bargain, the Magna Carta declared, the barons were free to "distrain and distress" him "in every way they can, namely by seizing castles, lands and

---

[18] *Encyclopédie, ou dictionnaire raisonné des sciences, des arts et des métiers, par une société de gens de lettres* (Paris: Briasson [etc.], 1751-80), 3: 218-223, s.v. "charte" and "chartre."
[19] De Vaines, Dom J., *Dictionnaire Raisonné de diplomatique* (Paris: Chez Lacombe, 1774), pp. 242-243.
[20] An English translation of the Magna Carta can be found in J. C. Holt, *Magna Carta,* 2d ed. (Cambridge: Cambridge University Press, 1992), Appendix 6. The phrase quoted here is from Holt's p. 451.
[21] According to Bastid, *Institutions politiques,* p. 33, "In 1814 England was in fashion. At no other moment in our history did British institutions enjoy as much prestige."

possessions."[22] Thus while in the first kind of charter the prerogative clearly rested with the king, in the English version it could be seen as belonging to the barons, and by extension, to the nation as a whole. Following this line of reasoning, the Magna Carta could be interpreted less as a royal concession than as a kind of proto-constitution.

Of course, in 1814, Louis XVIII and his advisors had no intention of agreeing to a written national constitution, with all the revolutionary connotations that would have entailed. In fact, when in April 1814 the provisional government sent the king a proposal for a new "constitution," requesting that he sign it before taking the throne, the king rejected it, choosing instead to prepare what became the Charter of June 1814.[23] So perhaps this Charter was meant to refer only to the French tradition of concessionary charters and not to the Magna Carta? The commentary offered by Beugnot, the royal advisor responsible for the selection of the term "Charter" in 1814, tries to skirt the issue:

> [I]n general, and especially in France, according to the opinions that have prevailed there in the last twenty-five years, the word constitution supposes a gathering to establish a new order of things between the king and the representatives...and it is quite evident that no such thing is occurring here...Since it is about a concession freely made by a king to his subjects, the name once in common use, the one consecrated by the history of several peoples and by our own is [the name] Charter: we will call it...the Charter of rights, the Great Charter, as in England, or else the Constitutional Charter.[24]

While explicitly rejecting the term "constitution," Beugnot both acknowledges the Magna Carta and suggests the name "Constitutional Charter."[25] Thus his commentary on this point, like the Charter he helped to compose, keeps in play the tension between concession and constitution, between *charte* and *Charte*.

Thus despite Beugnot's assertion that the Restoration did not "establish a new order of things," monarchy by Charter *was* new in France. The Charter of 1814 attempted to fuse two traditions—one French and one

---

[22] Holt, *Magna Carta*, p. 471. See also A. E. Dick Howard, *Magna Carta: Text and Commentary*, rev. ed. (Charlottesville: University Press of Virginia, 1998).

[23] Rosanvallon, *Monarchie*, Part I, Chap. 1.

[24] Beugnot, *Mémoires* (Paris: E. Dentu, 1868) 2:250-251, quoted in Maurice Barbé, *Etude historique des idées sur la souveraineté en France de 1815 à 1848* (Paris: F. Pichon, 1904), p. 52.

[25] Bastid, *Institutions*.

English—into a monarchical system that both refused and acknowledged the constitutional experiments of the revolutionary era. Consequently, like any compromise, it was vulnerable. Supporters of the Bourbons could not simply rely on Louis XVIII's birthright to legitimate and stabilize his regime; rather, they would have to repeatedly interpret and defend its founding document if the newly-invented system of monarchy by Charter was to hold.

What then did the Charter created in 1814 have to do with the School of Charters founded in 1821? None of the surviving documents related to the establishment of the school shows an explicit connection; none of the reports, letters, and royal decrees outlining the school's curriculum makes any reference to the Charter of 1814, even in passing. While a few secondary sources on the school mention the Charter, only Bercé's essay on Degérando hints that there was an ideological connection between it and the Ecole des Chartes.[26] Nevertheless, the timing of the school's establishment and subsequent disestablishment, as well as the claims made in the early 1820s about the school's potential usefulness to the State, make it difficult not to see the Ecole des Chartes as a response to a particularly difficult moment in the short life of the 1814 Charter.

It took nearly two years for the first experiment in monarchy by Charter to get underway. Just nine months after the Charter's promulgation, Napoleon made his last sally against the French monarchy, returning to power for the Hundred Days. After Napoleon's final defeat, the most conservative among his royalist enemies struck back against his supporters, launching the counter-revolutionary "White Terror" in the provinces and securing an Ultraroyalist triumph in the parliamentary elections of late 1815. Though in practice the new Ultra majority used the institutions established by the Charter to its own political advantage, in principle it objected to what it perceived as the Charter's constraints on royal authority.[27] Fearful that this drastic swing to the right was endangering his fragile regime, Louis XVIII dissolved the Ultra-dominated Chambers in

---

[26] Bercé, "Aux origines," p. 25. Bercé develops this idea a bit more in an unpublished essay on the history of the school that he was kind enough to share with me on one of my visits to the school. See also Olivier Guyotjeannin, "Aperçus sur l'Ecole des Chartes au XIXe siècle," in *Erudicion y discurso historico, las instituciones europeas, s. XVIII-XIX*, ed. Gimeno Blay (Valencia: Universitat de Valencia, 1993), p. 287; and Auguste Vallet de Viriville, *L'Ecole des Chartes. Son passé, son état présent, -- son avenir* (Paris: Ch. Schiller, 1867), p. 12.

[27] Rosanvallon, *Monarchie*, pp. 75-81.

September 1816, opening the way for a moderate royalist majority. And for
the next three and a half years, the compromise established by the Charter
seemed—if only barely—to hold. Because the Charter itself was so
ambiguous, a wide spectrum of French subjects, from Liberals (supporters of
the 1789 revolution) to Conservatives (moderate royalists, advocates of
limited monarchy) to Ultras (extreme royalists, wary of any limits on royal
power) could champion it for their own ends. Even as boundaries among
these political factions became sharper, the new monarchy seemed to have
achieved some measure of balance.[28]

In early 1820, however, an unexpected crisis jolted the regime off
balance and unleashed the political tensions that had been developing since
1816. On February thirteenth, the Bonapartist Pierre Louvel surprised the
king's nephew, the Duke de Berri, outside the Paris Opera and stabbed him
to death. If the bloody demise of the popular Duke was not horrifying
enough to Bourbon supporters, his death was even more appalling because
it seemed to jeopardize the entire future of the French monarchy. Since
Louis XVIII, in an ironic twist of fate, was impotent, and the Duke had
been the only Bourbon still young enough to produce a male heir, how
would the Bourbon regime survive? Seven months later, the anxiety about a
royal heir evaporated as the Duke's widow gave birth to a son; nevertheless,
the political conflicts ignited by the assassination kept the regime in a state
of crisis for nearly four more years.[29]

As early as the morning after the assassination, the Ultras seized the
opportunity to blame the ruling Conservatives for the murder. The
parliamentary session had hardly begun on February fourteenth when the
Ultra Clausel de Coussergues accused the Conservative chief minister,
Decazes, of being an "accomplice" to the assassination:

> In view of such a deplorable attack, the first thought of a political body
> must therefore be to destroy the seeds of a fanaticism that leads to such a
> deadly result, because it is only in chaining anew the revolutionary spirit
> that an iron arm had long restrained, [and] because it is only in dealing
> ruthlessly with the reckless writers emboldened for impunity, that you will
> stop these scandalous and reprehensible productions that overheat all
> heads, foment new revolutions, and excite the most odious crimes.[30]

---

[28] Bastid, *Institutions*, p. 100; Wright, *France in Modern Times*, pp. 94-95.
[29] See David Skuy, "The Politics of Assassination: The Death of the Duke of Berry,
February 14, 1820 and its Aftermath" (Ph.D. diss., University of Toronto, 1997).
[30] *Le Moniteur Universel*, 15 Feb. 1820.

In Clausel's analysis, it was not Pierre Louvel but the "revolutionary spirit" that had killed the Duke, and it was the pro-Charter politics of Decazes and his supporters that had allowed this spirit to reappear. This chain of reasoning proved quite persuasive in early 1820; under pressure from the Ultras, Decazes resigned as minister, to be replaced by the somewhat more conservative Richelieu. The Ultra reaction then extended beyond the ministry with the June 1820 "Law of the Double Vote," which gave the wealthiest (and presumably most fiercely royalist) quarter of Frenchmen double representation in parliament. When such drastic changes provoked student protests and Carbonarist insurrections, the regime used the "iron arm" so admired by Clausel to quash revolts, close left-leaning schools, and arrest students who shouted not *"Vive le Roi!"* but *"Vive la Charte!"*[31] By the time of Louis XVIII's death in 1824, the Ultras had gained political control, taking the lead both in parliament and in the royal ministries.

The Duke's assassination, then, marked a key shift in Restoration politics, from a Conservative, pro-Charter regime to an Ultra, anti-Charter one. However, this shift did not take place instantaneously; between 1820 and 1824, and especially between February 1820 and December 1821, when the Ultra Villèle became chief minister, Conservatives and Ultras were still wrangling for control of the government, as is clear from the constant clashes over the Charter in the parliamentary discussions of the time.[32] It was in this period of crisis that the Ecole des Chartes was established. In late 1820, Degérando asked the Minister of the Interior, his friend and fellow moderate royalist the Comte Siméon, to help him create the school. On 22 February 1821, Siméon presented the idea in a report to Louis XVIII, who then signed the ordinance founding the Ecole des Chartes. If none of these early documents mentions the Charter of 1814 by name, it was perhaps because they did not need to. As monarchy by Charter faced its fiercest challenge ever, a state institution devoted explicitly

---

[31] M. D. R. Leys, *Between Two Empires: A History of French Politicians and People between 1814 and 1848* (London: Longmans, Green, and Co., 1955), p. 108; on student revolts and Carbonarism, see Alan B. Spitzer, *The French Generation of 1820* (Princeton: Princeton University Press, 1987) and his *Old Hatreds and Young Hopes: The French Carbonari Against the Bourbon Restoration* (Cambridge: Harvard University Press, 1971).

[32] See for example the minutes of parliamentary debates published in *Le Moniteur Universel*, ca. 1820-1821, and the description of these debates as "wrangles" in Leys, *Between Two Empires*, pp. 112-113.

to the study of *chartes* could hardly have been seen as anything less than a
Conservative effort to defend *la Charte*.

But how would offering courses in medieval French and Latin
paleography contribute to this effort? Consider the dilemma facing the
moderate royalists. In order to defend monarchy by Charter, they had to
make their case not to the Liberals, who already supported the Charter (if
not exactly as the Conservatives would have wished), but to the Ultras, who
seemed ready to jettison it completely. Therefore, they could hardly claim
that the Charter ought to be maintained because it was innovative and
forward-thinking, let alone revolutionary. To convince an audience
committed to the full restoration of the absolutist Old Regime, they had to
show that the Charter—which, as we have seen, was an invention, a fusion
of legal practices—had deep roots in pre-revolutionary France. It was the
job of the Ecole des Chartes to find these Old Regime precedents.

This search for precedents for the Charter can be seen as a return to a
strategy first elaborated in the preamble to the Charter itself. Here Louis
XVIII and the royal advisors who helped prepare the Charter do a
complicated rhetorical dance as they try to present the proclamation as
business-as-usual without acknowledging its revolutionary precursors. In this
version of the French past, the revolution simply does not exist. Indeed, the
preamble explicitly excludes the revolutionary era from its discussion of
French history, describing it only as a set of "fatal gaps" and stating that "we
have effaced from our memory, as we would like to be able to efface from
history, all the troubles that afflicted the country during our absence."
Leaping over the revolutionary "gap," the preamble attempts to cast the
Charter as a return to practices of governance employed by generation after
generation of French kings:

> We have considered that, although all authority in France resided in the
> person of the King, our predecessors did not hesitate at all to modify the
> exercise [of this authority], according to the different times; it is thus that
> the communes owed their emancipation to Louis le Gros, the
> confirmation and extension of their rights to Saint Louis and to Philippe le
> Bel; that the judiciary order was established and developed by the laws of
> Louis XI, Henri II, and Charles IX; finally, that Louis XIV regulated
> almost all aspects of public administration....

According to this view, although French kings have traditionally been all-
powerful, they have also traditionally chosen to limit their power ("modify"
its "exercise") by passing laws that respond to the needs of their subjects. As

the inheritor of this tradition, Louis XVIII could only follow suit. The preamble continues:

> We have had, following the example of our predecessors the Kings, to appreciate the effects of the ever-increasing progress of knowledge [*lumières*], the new relationships that this progress has introduced to society, the direction imprinted on minds in the last half-century, and the serious alterations that have resulted....

Yet, the preamble implies, new problems do not necessarily require entirely new legislation. The Charter's authors emphasized that they had

> looked for the principles of the constitutional charter in the French character, and in the venerable monuments of past centuries. Thus, we have seen in the renewal of the peerage a truly national institution, and which must link all memories to all hopes, in reuniting ancient times and modern times.[33]

Thus according to the preamble, the Charter of 1814 was both inspired by and contributed to the ancient collection of laws promulgated by beneficent French kings.

During the political crisis that followed the Duke de Berri's assassination, this point had to be made much more forcefully. In order to muster Ultra support for monarchy by Charter, the Conservatives had to actually produce the "venerable monuments of past centuries" to which the Charter's preamble had only alluded. The Ecole des Chartes, I would like to suggest, offered a means to this end. Unfortunately, and rather ironically, there are very few archival sources related to the creation of the school.[34] Even if we pool the resources of the National Archives, the Archives of the Institut, and those remaining at the school itself, we have only a handful of letters, speeches, and reports. Nevertheless, a careful analysis of these texts suggests important links between the goals of the Ecole des Chartes and those of the moderate royalist faction in the early 1820s.

The earliest available Restoration text related to the Ecole des Chartes is Degérando's proposal of late 1820.[35] This plan contains in draft form many

---

[33] Debbasch and Pontier, eds., *Les Constitutions*, pp. 117-118.

[34] As a number of archivists and *chartistes* repeated to me during my research, "The shoemaker's son is always the most poorly shod."

[35] Although histories of the school usually locate this undated manuscript at the end of 1820, it is possible that it was written as early as 1819 (that is, before the assassination), which might help explain the differences between it and the final ordinance of February 1821. See Emmanuel Poulle, "Historiens ou fonctionnaires de la conservation?" in *L'Ecole nationale des chartes: histoire de l'école depuis 1821*, p. 26.

of the elements that would later be incorporated into the official ordinance of February 1821. Abandoning his earlier idea of a provincial "Port-Royal," here Degérando prescribes a series of "free courses in all branches of the study of Diplomatics," or the study of official documents, to be held jointly at the Royal Archives and the Royal Library. In order to secure one of the twelve seats in these courses, prospective students would have to pass an examination "on our antiquities and on the literary history of France and on [the history] of our public law up until the fifteenth century." The successful students would then study diplomatics for two years in order to prepare for work on one of the many historical projects overseen by the Ministry of the Interior.[36]

While historians of the Ecole des Chartes have been quick to emphasize the similarities between these prescriptions and the 1821 ordinance, the differences between the two texts are just as telling. Degérando's plan imagines that graduates of the school will do extensive work in archives and libraries both in France and around Europe. According to article ten of his proposal,

> a certain number of them [i.e., graduates of the school] will be sent by turns to visit the archives in the departments. [T]hey will also be able to be sent to England, Germany, [and] Italy to look in various depositories for unpublished documents that might be related to our history.

And in article fourteen, Degérando states that these students were also given "priority" in appointments to "posts in public libraries, archives, museums, and the various public collections in Paris and the departments."[37] However, neither of these articles appears in the final ordinance; in fact, the ordinance does not mention libraries and archives at all, except to say that the school will be under the joint authority of the head of the department of manuscripts at the Royal Library and the Guardian-General of the Royal Archives.[38] In the *Rapport au Roi* that accompanied the published ordinance, this rejection of non-Parisian archives and libraries is made more explicit:

> the depositories...of old titles that have escaped the ravages of the revolution exist in very small numbers in the interior of France; most have been transported to Paris. Thus it is now only in Paris that the science of charters can be reborn, either by the torch of enlightenment that the

---

[36] Degérando, [untitled manuscript], [late 1820?], AN, Archives de la Société de l'Ecole des Chartes, box 11 AS 1, folder "8. Archives de la Société, 1821-1984," p. [1].

[37] Ibid., pp. [3-4].

[38] Louis [XVIII], Siméon, and Capelle, "Ordonnance du Roi," p. [2].

> Academies have not allowed to extinguish, or with the help of the
> immense depositories that this capital possesses.[39]

Thus as the Minister of the Interior (perhaps with the assistance of
Degérando himself) shaped Degérando's 1820 proposal into the 1821
ordinance, the school's focus shifted, from the provinces and even beyond to
Paris alone, and from a whole range of "public collections" to a single type
of document, "charters."

Descriptions of the school from the period 1821-1824 suggest that this
focus persisted throughout the school's early years. On 4 March 1822, the
head of the Royal Archives, De Larue, welcomed his new students with a
lesson on the importance of *chartes*:

> Charters, which will become the subject of your studies, are quite rightly
> regarded as the torches [*flambeaux*] of chronology and history. They make
> up for what is lacking in coins, inscriptions, and other monuments of that
> type. Without them, all is obscure, all is uncertain in the Middle Ages;
> without them genealogies only offer problems or fables; without them the
> origin of our principal institutions would remain enveloped in shadows; in
> a word every historian, every chronologist who does not take Charters as
> guides into the labyrinth of former times, risks becoming lost.[40]

Although De Larue does not define "charters" in any careful way, it seems
clear his students were not meant to explore, as Degérando had once
envisioned, all of the historical materials available in public collections, but
rather a particular subset, one more reliable and authentic than all the rest.
In 1824, a report to the Academy of Inscriptions defined the school's focus
even more narrowly, arguing that the school had been created specifically to
help continue the work begun by the Academy in the eighteenth century on

---

[39] Siméon (ministre secrétaire-d'état au département de l'intérieur), "Rapport au
Roi," 22 Feb. 1821, *Moniteur Universel*, 2 Mar. 1821. By the 1830s, as we will see in
the next chapter, the central government's perception of provincial collections had
changed dramatically.

[40] [De Larue]. [speech on the opening day of the Ecole des Chartes], [4 Mar.
1822], AEC, folder "Ecole des Chartes. établie...," p. [1]. Author, title, and date
taken from note added by Pavillet, then one of the school's professors. The Ecole
des Chartes was divided into two sections; for reasons that remain unclear, the first
section, housed at the Royal Library, began its classes in July 1821, while the
second, at the Royal Archives, did not begin until the following March.

the famous *Trésor des Chartes*, or "Treasury of Charters."[41] This once "secret" collection of official royal deeds from the twelfth through seventeenth centuries had been transferred to the National Archives after being appropriated by the revolutionary government.[42] Here again, medieval charters housed in Parisian collections lay at the center of the Ecole's investigations.

What was the point of studying this particular set of documents? We find a concise answer to this question in the 1821 ordinance, which begins:

> Louis, by the grace of God, King of France and of Navarre...Wishing to revive a type of studies indispensable to the glory of France, and to provide our Academy of Inscriptions and Belles-Lettres with all the means necessary for the advancement of the projects entrusted to its care, We have ordained and we ordain that which follows....[43]

According to this decree, in addition to the intellectual goal of learning about medieval charters, the school had a more practical aim: to provide what the accompanying report called "auxiliaries" for the Academy of Inscriptions. First developed by Colbert as an offshoot of the Académie Française, the Academy of Inscriptions evolved under the Old Regime from a commission concerned quite literally with crafting inscriptions for royal coins, statues, and other monuments to a full-fledged royal academy charged with a wide range of historical projects. Like the other academies, it was closed in 1793 only to be revived in 1795 as part of the new Institut; it regained its old title, "Academy of Inscriptions and Belles-Lettres," in 1816.[44]

---

[41] Degérando et al., on behalf of the "Commission chargé de proposer un nouveau règlement pour l'Ecole des chartes," to the Académie des Inscriptions, Paris, 23 Jan. 1824, AN, box F17-4024, p. [2].

[42] H[enri]-François de Laborde, *Etude sur la constitution du Trésor des chartes...*(Paris: Plon-Nourrit, 1909). See also Krzysztof Pomian, "Les archives, du Trésor des chartes au CARAN," in *Les lieux de mémoire*, ed. Pierre Nora (Paris: Gallimard, 1992), vol. 3, part 3, pp. 162-233. If I understand Pomian's argument correctly, he tries to distinguish between the Trésor des Chartes, which was about the creation of memory, and the Ecole des Chartes, which was about the creation of history. However, for my purposes, the similarities between the two are more important, for in its earliest incarnation, at least, the school adopted the central goal of the Trésor des Chartes: to establish a complete chronological record of royal charters.

[43] Louis [XVIII], Siméon, and Capelle, "Ordonnance du Roi," p. [1].

[44] See L[ouis]-F[erdinand] Maury, *L'ancienne Académie des Inscriptions et Belles-Lettres*, 2d ed. (Paris: Didier et Cie, 1864), and Institut de France, *L'Académie des Inscriptions et Belles-Lettres* (Paris: Auguste Picard, 1924).

In the post-revolutionary era, the Academy's members, who ranged from linguists to archeologists to literary scholars, took on a wide variety of individual projects, not all of which focused on France.[45] Yet the Academy as a body also undertook a series of large-scale French history projects that had been initiated under the Old Regime but set aside during the Revolution. It was this set of massive scholarly enterprises, notably the *Recueil des historiens de la France*, the *Histoire littéraire de la France*, the *Ordonnances des rois de France de la troisième race*, and the *Table chronologique des diplômes, titres et chartes concernant l'histoire de France*, to which the Ecole des Chartes was expected to contribute.[46] As these titles suggest, although the projects emphasize distinct themes and sources, they have important features in common. First, they are all, to one degree or another, collections of primary sources. While they include extensive scholarly commentary, they also contain numerous transcriptions or translations of historical documents, and most often, of official royal documents. Second, they are all organized chronologically, usually by king or line of kings. Rather than dealing with cross-cutting themes in French history (war, religion, etc.), they map the entire history of France onto a kind of genealogy of monarchs. What emerges, then, is an account of French history that highlights both the continuity of kings and the continuity of royal law. Given the historical conceptions outlined in the preamble to the 1814 Charter, it is hardly surprising that defenders of the Charter would find these projects particularly appealing.

If continuing these historical collections was the goal, it may seem odd that the moderate royalists did not simply push for the expansion of the Academy of Inscriptions in the wake of the Ultra resurgence of 1820. However, in the eyes of the school's creators, scholars capable of the kind of specialized paleographic work required by these collections were a dying

---

[45] Between 1804 and 1819, of 405 communications by Academy members, only 52 dealt specifically with France. See Pierre Marot, *L'essor de l'étude des antiquités nationales à l'Institut, du Directoire à la monarchie de juillet... Lecture faite dans la séance publique annuelle du 22 novembre 1963* (Paris: n.p., 1963), p. 6.

[46] On the development of individual projects, see Adrien Blanchet, et al., *Les Travaux de l'Académie des Inscriptions et Belles-Lettres: histoire et inventaire des publications* (Paris: C. Klincksieck, 1947). Note that although the Academy did not begin work in earnest on the continuation of the *Table chronologique des diplômes* until 1832, the Academy made a brief effort to further the project in 1820-1822. See Charles-Olivier Carbonell, *L'autre Champollion: Jacques-Joseph Champollion-Figéac (1778-1867)* (Toulouse: Presses de l'Institut d'études politiques de Toulouse et l'Asiathèque, 1970), pp. 164-165.

breed. As early as 1810, the head of the Academy had warned the Emperor, in language remarkably similar to that of the 1821 ordinance, that diplomatics would die out "unless one of your powerful gazes [*regards*] revives this type of studies in which France has distinguished itself for more than two centuries."[47] In 1821, Siméon's *Rapport au Roi* echoed this fear:

> Sire, a branch of French literature in which your majesty takes a particular interest (that relative to the history of the *patrie*) will, if a remedy is not soon brought about, be deprived of a class of collaborators that are indispensable to it; I wish to speak, Sire, of those men who, by long efforts of application and patience, have acquired the knowledge of our manuscripts; have made themselves familiar with the writings of our archives, of our charters, of the documents of all kinds that our ancestors have left to us; and know how to translate all the dialects of the Middle Ages.[48]

In Siméon's view, in addition to dismantling the great archives and libraries of the Old Regime, the Revolution had dispersed the corps of *érudits* who alone could understand their contents. Thirty years later, most of these scholars were dead, and the few that remained would not live long. If France did not train a new generation of paleographic specialists, Siméon feared, whole categories of books and manuscripts would be completely illegible and therefore lost to history.

Interestingly, although paleographic experts appeared in a variety of contexts in the final decades of the Old Regime, Siméon's report, along with nearly every description of the Ecole des Chartes written since, draws attention to the loss of a single group: the Benedictines of Saint-Maur. Completely overlooked are the Old Regime *feudistes*, legal experts charged with maintaining noble *terriers*, or archives of written claims to property and taxes. Absent, too, are the other ecclesiastical orders, such as the Benedictines of Saint-Vannes, who were known for their skill in deciphering historical documents.[49] In the case of the *feudistes*, the omission is perhaps not so surprising, as they had come to symbolize all that was deceptive and

---

[47] [Bon-Joseph] Dacier, introduction to *Rapport historique sur les progrès de l'histoire et de la littérature ancienne depuis 1789, et sur leur état actuel...*(Paris: Imprimerie Impériale, 1810), pp. 16-17.

[48] Siméon, "Rapport."

[49] See David Knowles, *Great Historical Enterprises* (London: Thomas Nelson and Sons, 1963).

oppressive in the application of feudal law.[50] But why the focus on the Maurists? By examining the reverential and often sentimental references to the order in accounts of the Ecole des Chartes, we can better understand the school's early goals.

As a rule, descriptions of the Ecole des Chartes generally emphasize two moments in the history of the Order of Saint-Maur. The first is the publication of *De re diplomatica* ("On Diplomatics") by the Maurist monk Jean Mabillon in 1681. In an effort to defend the order against charges that its collections of medieval charters contained forgeries, Mabillon sketched out a method for the authentication of archival documents, one based on careful comparisons of writing styles, material supports, official seals, etc. Yet at the same time, he warned that such comparisons alone could not determine whether a document was genuine; in the end, only the long experience of studying medieval sources and the frequent consultation of colleagues would allow a scholar to authenticate a source.[51] It is not hard to see why *chartistes* and their supporters have always focused on Mabillon's work; his famous treatise not only offered a method for doing diplomatics but also provided a justification for reviving a community of "experts" capable of applying this method successfully.

The other key moment in *chartiste* accounts of the Benedictines of Saint-Maur is the period roughly from 1762 to 1789, when the order placed its scholarly labor and paleographic expertise at the disposal of the French monarchy. As Keith Baker has shown, in the early 1760s, both the Maurist order and the Bourbon regime were in crisis. Confronted on the one hand by debates over Jansenism and on the other by the influence of Enlightenment philosophy, the Order of Saint-Maur seemed to have lost its

---

[50] The practices of the *feudistes*, some of whom produced lengthy treatises on archival management, are largely unexplored. For general background information, see P. de Saint-Jacob, *Les Paysans de la Bourgogne du Nord au premier siècle de l'ancien régime* (Paris: Société Les Belles Lettres, 1960), pp. 432-434; Albert Soboul, "De la pratique des terriers à la veille de la Révolution," *Annales: Economies, sociétés, civilisations* 19, no. 6 (1964): 1049-1065; J. Q. C. Mackrell, *The Attack on 'Feudalism' in Eighteenth-Century France* (London: Routledge and Kegan Paul, 1973), pp. 56-65; and Jean Bastier, *La féodalité au siècle des lumières dans la région de Toulouse* (1730-1790) (Paris: Bibliothèque nationale, 1975), pp. 63-67.

[51] *De Re Diplomatica* has never been translated into English in its entirety. However, for Mabillon's views on the importance of experience, see Richard Wertis' translation of the "supplement" to *De Re Diplomatica* in Peter Gay and Victor Wexler, eds., *Historians at Work* (New York: Harper and Row, 1972), 2: 161-198.

ability to maintain discipline among its members.[52] Meanwhile, these same influences had helped fuel a fierce struggle between King Louis XV and members of the *parlements*, or high courts, that registered and enforced royal edicts. In an effort to buttress their claims against the king, the *parlements* had begun amassing enormous collections of legal and historical documents that seemed to support parliamentary authority. Faced with these "ideological arsenals," the monarchy soon concluded that it would have to create documentary arsenals of its own if it was to counter the parliamentary attack. Therefore, in the late 1750s, the royal historiographer, Jacob-Nicolas Moreau, launched a hugely ambitious campaign to locate, copy, verify, organize, and preserve all documents related to French history and public law. In Moreau's view, the Benedictines of Saint-Maur would provide the ideal footsoldiers for this campaign. They were not only experts in diplomatics and veteran compilers of historical sources but would also be less likely to incite proprietary hostilities when foraging in provincial archives. For the Maurists, too, Moreau's project seemed fortuitous, offering the struggling order both a scholarly purpose and a claim to public utility. Beginning in September 1762, then, Maurist monks began working for Moreau, gathering archival documents and participating in his increasingly elaborate attempts to organize and evaluate the assembled materials, known collectively as the *Cabinet des Chartes*. Moreau even initiated efforts to revamp the order's internal rules and procedures to help it meet his own research goals more efficiently.[53]

Nevertheless, by 1789, Moreau's great campaign had disintegrated in the face of increasingly radical (and anti-historical) political struggles, and in 1790, the Order of Saint-Maur itself was dissolved by the Constituent

---

[52] On the double threat of Jansenism and Enlightenment philosophy, see Philibert Schmitz, *Histoire de l'ordre de Saint-Benoît* ([Paris]: Maredsous, 1956), 4: 43-69.

[53] Keith Michael Baker, "Controlling French history: the ideological arsenal of Jacob-Nicolas Moreau," Chap. 3 in *Inventing the French Revolution: Essays on French Political Culture in the Eighteenth Century* (Cambridge: Cambridge University Press, 1990). Moreau's plans for reforming the order in 1766 even included a new course of study for young monks, prompting one Interior Ministry official in the late 1820s to claim that the Ecole des Chartes really dated to 1766. See [Rives?] (Directeur des belles lettres, sciences, et beaux arts), *Rapport présenté à Son Excellence le Ministre Secretaire d'Etat au Departement de l'Interieur*, [1828?], AN, box F17-4024. For the text of the reform, see the "Plan d'études pour la congrégation de Saint-Maur...," in [Louis Georges Oudart Feudrix de] Bréquigny and J[acques]-J[oseph] Champollion-Figeac, *Lettres de rois, reines et autres personnages...tirées des archives de Londres par Bréquigny* (Paris: Imprimerie Royale, 1839), 1: xliv-lxxix.

Assembly, despite the Maurists' insistence on the benefits their work brought to the French nation.[54] Though most of Moreau's *Cabinet des Chartes*, quickly incorporated into the Manuscripts Department of the National Library, survived the revolutionary era, the Benedictines of Saint-Maur did not. After an effort to reestablish the order failed in 1815 for lack of adherents, it seemed that the Maurist tradition would have no successors.[55] In 1821, presumably just before the announcement of the Ecole des Chartes, the British bibliophile and traveler Thomas Fragnall Dibdin solemnly recounted his visit with the elderly Dom Brial, one of the last remaining Maurist scholars:

> 'When he is dead, he will not have any students at all'—says his old and intimate friend the Abbé Betencourt; an observation which, when I heard it, filled me with mingled regret and surprise—for why is this valuable, and most *patriotic* of all departments of literature, neglected abroad as well as *at home?*...[A]nd France...was once rich in historical literati.[56]

According to the heroic legend of the Ecole des Chartes, a legend created along with the school itself, the Ecole des Chartes rescued the "patriotic" study of diplomatics and created a cadre of young, vigorous, "new Benedictines."[57] Inspired by the methodological prescriptions of Mabillon and the scholarly investigations of the Maurists who worked for Moreau, this legend claims, the early *chartistes* not only helped tie the Restoration to the great scholarly traditions of the Old Regime but also began undoing the destructive and disorienting effects of the Revolution. So was the Ecole des Chartes really just the Order of Saint-Maur under a new name? The similarities between the Maurists and the *chartistes* are indeed striking. Both

---

[54] Pierre Gasnault, "Motivations, conditions de travail et héritage des Bénédictins de Saint-Maur," *Revue d'histoire de l'église de France* 71 (Jan. 1985): 13-23.

[55] Schmitz, *Histoire de l'ordre*, p. 176.

[56] Tho[mas] Fragnall Dibdin, *A bibliographical, antiquarian and picturesque tour in France and Germany*...(London: W. Bulmer and W. Nicol, Shakespeare Press, and sold by Payne and Foss [etc.], 1821), 2: 424-425. Dibdin's emphasis.

[57] Descriptions of the Ecole des Chartes as the successor to the Order of Saint-Maur are too numerous to list, but see for example Dorothy Mackay Quynn, "The Ecole des Chartes," *American Archivist* 13, no. 3 (1950): 271-283, and Leon de Laborde, as quoted in Françoise Hildesheimer, "Les Archives nationales au XIXe siècle: établissement administratif ou scientifique?" *Histoire et Archives* 1 (1997): 120. *Chartistes'* vision of themselves as the successors to the Maurists is especially striking to visitors to the school, who find a portrait of Mabillon hanging in the director's office and an enormous painting of the Maurists' headquarters, the Abbey of Saint-Germain des Près, in the main lecture hall.

institutions channeled their collective efforts into the exploration of manuscript collections, and, more specifically, medieval French manuscript collections. In fact, they often worked with the very same documents, since several of the large historical projects shouldered by the Academy of Inscriptions in the early nineteenth century (e.g., the *Recueil des historiens de la France* and the *Histoire littéraire de la France*) were actually continuations of Maurist collections begun in the early eighteenth century.[58]

More important, however, both the late eighteenth-century Maurists and the early nineteenth-century *chartistes* conducted their documentary investigations in the service of a particular vision of French monarchy. Though they encountered very different opponents (magistrates arguing for representative institutions in the case of the Maurists, politicians advocating divine-right absolutism in the case of the *chartistes*), they deployed similar strategies.[59] These strategies can perhaps be best understood in the context of what Baker has described as the "discourse of justice." In Baker's analysis, the traditional conception of royal authority had attempted to fuse three "strands of discourse": justice, will, and reason. The king exercised justice, "by which each receives his due in a hierarchical society of orders and estates." Justice was then "given effect by the royal will," which was in turn "preserved from arbitrariness by reason and counsel." However, mid-eighteenth-century political conflicts produced a "disaggregation of the attributes traditionally bound together in the concept of monarchical authority...and their reconceptualization as the basis of competing definitions (or attempted redefinitions) of the body politic." In a particularly potent redefinition of monarchical justice, parliamentary magistrates argued that the king had to maintain "a traditional constitution," or "a historically constituted order of things which both defines and limits royal power." Royal power, they claimed, should not be arbitrary but rather should operate "according to constitutionally prescribed legal forms," forms they attempted to make manifest in their enormous collections of legal and historical documents.[60] Thus in order to regain control of the "discourse of justice," and with it a key element of royal authority, the monarchy had to show that it was *not* arbitrary, that it *did* adhere to legal forms. As

---

[58] See Blanchet, et al., *Les Travaux*.

[59] I do not wish to imply that every Maurist was anti-parliamentary (indeed, the prevalence of Jansenism in the order would suggest otherwise), nor that every *chartiste* was anti-Ultra, rather that their work as members of a group had these political valences.

[60] Baker, *Inventing*, p. 25.

understood by Moreau, "the crown had to recover the mantle of law" by creating its own "arsenal" of legal and historical sources with the help of the scholarly Maurists.[61] More than a half-century later, the moderate royalists of the Restoration revived this discursive strategy, establishing the Ecole des Chartes in an equally desperate effort to locate the current king in a tradition of just and lawful monarchs.

Despite these remarkable similarities, the Ecole des Chartes was not simply a reincarnation of the Order of Saint-Maur. Perhaps the most obvious difference between the two institutions is that whereas the Maurist order was an ecclesiastical body subject to the rulings of the Catholic Church, the Ecole des Chartes was founded as a secular agency of the French State. While working on the *Cabinet des Chartes* allowed the Maurists to demonstrate that they could contribute to the French State, the Ecole des Chartes' very purpose was to be useful to the State. According to the passage from the 1821 ordinance cited earlier, the school was to "revive a type of studies indispensable to the glory of France." Thus while the Maurists carried out a whole variety of functions (indeed, it has been estimated that at any one time, only two percent of the order's members were working on scholarly projects), *chartistes* were expected to devote all their energies to diplomatics.[62] And whereas the Benedictine order proved difficult for Moreau to reshape for his own purposes, the Ecole des Chartes came under the direct authority of the Ministry of the Interior, and could be—and indeed often was—swiftly reformed or restructured. If the early *chartistes* were in some respects "new Benedictines," they were so in a thoroughly nineteenth-century way, one more suited to the political imperatives of a modern bureaucratic state.

The Ecole des Chartes of 1821 was also different from the Order of Saint-Maur of the late 1700s in that the school was intended to work primarily on reading or "deciphering" medieval manuscripts rather than collecting them. In the 1760s, the scholarly team assembled by Moreau and the powerful magistrates of the *parlements* had been engaged in what might be seen as a kind of elaborate scavenger hunt. Each side believed that accumulating a bigger pile of legal and historical documents than the other would allow it to win the struggle to define French monarchical authority. Thus Moreau's instructions to the Benedictines of Saint-Maur exhorted them to find every available document in every available depository, carefully transcribing those that seemed especially important and

---

[61] Ibid., p. 64.
[62] Gasnault, "Motivations," p. 14.

summarizing all the rest.[63] Their goal was less to interpret individual documents than simply to capture them and bring them back to Paris. In the early 1820s, however, the creators of the Ecole des Chartes faced a different kind of challenge. At that time, there was no shortage of medieval French charters in Paris. Moreau's work on the *Cabinet des Chartes* and the revolutionary confiscations of the 1790s had concentrated substantial collections at the Royal Archives and the Royal Library. Yet after thirty years of war and revolution, these charters had become illegible, both literally and metaphorically. Hardly anybody alive could decipher the medieval scripts in which they were written, nor could they understand the legal traditions that the texts represented. If the Restoration's Conservatives wanted to transform the great Parisian collections of charters into a comprehensible legal "pedigree" for the Charter of 1814, they would have to begin by making them legible.

In this context, the Ecole des Chartes' initial mission—to teach students "to read the various manuscripts and to explicate the French dialects of the Middle Ages"—does not seem quite so narrowly academic.[64] Though there seems to have been widespread concern among Restoration *érudits* that the paleographic expertise of the Maurists was in danger of disappearing, this fear alone cannot explain why the Restoration monarchy chose to establish an Ecole des Chartes in February 1821. Only by mapping scholarly concerns onto political ones can we begin to understand the emergence of the school at this particular historical moment. One might object, however, that identifying the Ecole des Chartes with a Conservative effort to defend the Charter is intriguing, but potentially anachronistic. How do we know that French politicians and intellectuals at the time saw any connection between the two? As mentioned earlier, at a moment when simply shouting "*Vive la Charte!*" might get one arrested, it seems highly unlikely that an Ecole des Chartes could have been seen as politically neutral. Yet we find even more compelling linkages between the Charter of 1814 and the Ecole des Chartes in what remains one of the most widely-read publications of the Restoration period, Isambert's *Recueil général des anciennes lois françaises*, which first appeared in 1822.[65]

---

[63] See the instructions issued by Moreau and his chief assistant, Bréquigny, in the early 1760s, reproduced in Bréquigny and Champollion-Figeac, eds., *Lettres de rois*, 1: v-xiii.

[64] See above, note 7.

[65] [Athanase Jean Leger] Jourdan, Decrusy, and [François-André] Isambert, eds., *Recueil général des anciennes lois françaises, depuis l'an 420 jusqu'à la révolution de 1789,*

   The bulk of this twenty-nine-volume collection consists of transcriptions
of laws issued by French kings from the Merovingians of the early fifth
century to the Bourbons of the late eighteenth. In the lengthy preface to the
first volume, dated 1 August 1822, the lawyer and future politician François-
André Isambert attempts to justify his enterprise by linking it to
contemporary political and legislative concerns. His first section, "On the
Importance of Studying Ancient French Laws," begins: "The study of the
legislative monuments of the former French monarchy is not only a subject
of great curiosity for men who are eager to learn. It is an everyday necessity
for publicists, magistrates, administrative officials, and legal experts" (i).
Despite the great changes wrought by the revolution, the laws of the Old
Regime have not become at all outdated:

> If all is not good, all is not bad in the old laws; and that legislative
> disposition that has not produced the good that one expected of it, only
> needs to be modified, or better applied, in order to be useful. This way of
> proceeding is often preferable to innovations (vii).

Indeed, Isambert argues, it was the French predilection for innovation that
had fueled the destruction of the revolutionary era:

> Among us,...the spirit of innovation has been permanent.—It was
> encouraged by our Kings, first to shake off the feudal yoke, and then to
> diminish the prerogatives of a nobility and clergy [that had become] too
> powerful. We proceeded in this direction until the moment when the
> government became so to speak absolute in their hands; then we wanted
> to stop; but the impulse had been given...the revolution broke out; a
> constitution was so to speak improvised on the dispersed debris of the
> former monarchy; [and] the hatred for former institutions showed
> itself...we very nearly repealed all former legislation in a single move. This
> senseless project would have been fulfilled, if it had been possible to
> replace with improvisations civil and administrative laws, the fruit of so
> many meditations and so many years of experience (ix).

According to Isambert, his contemporaries could only reverse the negative
effects of so much innovation by exploring "the monuments the monarchy

---

*contenant: la notice des principaux monuments des Mérovingiens, des Carlovingiens et des
Capétiens, et le texte des ordonnances, édits, déclarations, lettres patentes, règlements, arrêts du
Conseil, etc., de la troisième race, Qui ne sont pas abrogés, ou qui peuvent servir, Soit à
l'interprétation, soit à l'histoire du droit public et privé, avec notes de concordance, table
chronologique et table générale analytique et alphabétique des matières...*(Paris: Berlin le Prieur,
[1822-33]) [hereafter page numbers are cited parenthetically]. This collection is still
a key source of Old Regime legislative texts.

has left behind" and then "combining [them] with our political condition" (viii).

The echoes of the Charter of 1814 in these passages are no accident. Isambert's preface is filled with references to the Charter, and particularly to the preamble, which he quotes extensively as justification for his own work:

> The author of the CHARTER, in appreciating the ever-increasing progress of knowledge, informs us that he has *drawn from the venerable monuments of past centuries*.... Those whom he has called to share the legislative power, will not scorn more than he the careful study of ancient laws (i, emphasis in original).

Like the authors of the preamble, Isambert maintains that the Charter is fully compatible with the legislative tradition of the Old Regime, stating that "there is nothing about this study [of old laws] that does not reconcile itself perfectly with the principles of the Charter" (xvii). He even goes beyond the claims made in the preamble to identify specific Old Regime laws as "*chartes*," claiming, for example, that while the Magna Carta dates to the thirteenth century, "we obtained from the second of the Valois [kings]...the Ordinance of 1356, which an illustrious Peer calls the great Charter of the French" (xi)

As his choice of the phrase "we obtained" suggests, although he lavishes praise on the "author" of the Charter, Isambert was no Beugnot. He saw the Charter less as a royal concession than as an agreement between the king and his subjects. This view of the Charter becomes particularly clear toward the end of his preface:

> In itself, *Charte* indicates a feudal concession; it is in this sense that it was used by the first Kings of the third race [i.e., royal line], and by all the great barons of France. But ever since the English turned King John's *Charter* to such good account, and took it as the basis of their constitution, bigger ideas [*idées de supériorité*] have naturally attached themselves to this word. It is thus not surprising that Louis XVIII adopted it, at the time of his restoration, in preference to [the term] *constitution*. He wanted to attach to it a character of stability and perpetuity, that the preceding constitutions had not at all yet obtained (lxxx, emphasis in original).

As in the passage from Beugnot's memoirs cited earlier, here Isambert attempts to root the Charter in history, linking it both to the French feudal tradition and to the English Magna Carta. However, while Beugnot claims that he chose the term Charter in order to counter the possibility that the proclamation might be seen as a "constitution" (which would have established a "new order of things between the king and the representatives"), Isambert turns this argument on its head. In Isambert's formulation, the Charter *is* a kind of constitution, one so momentous and so enduring that it could only take its name from the greatest of all constitutional documents, the Magna Carta. Whereas Beugnot's conception of the Charter had emphasized the continuity of the rule of kings, Isambert's version plays up the continuity of the rule of law.

Though Isambert makes no direct references to the political crisis set off by the assassination, he does make it clear that he believes the rule of law may be in danger. He notes that even while politicians all over Europe have praised the Charter, some French subjects continue to oppose it: "How is it then that what in the eyes of foreigners is France's claim to fame could be the object of contempt or indifference among the French?" (xiii). He therefore offers his countrymen his vast *Recueil* of French laws in the hopes that it will help them appreciate and defend monarchy by Charter:

> The study [of French legal history]...is not only necessary for legal experts, not only for lawyers,...it is necessary for all men whose situation involves the practice of law. They will find there the origin and the successive attributions of the various ministerial offices, and the public functions that derive from them, *and consequently the means of defending them, if they come to be attacked or misunderstood.* To understand what one is, one must know what one has been (xx, my emphasis).

The study of history, in this conception, is not a purely intellectual enterprise but rather a legal and political one central to assuring the stability of the Restoration government.

Not surprisingly, Isambert does his best to play up the contribution of his own *Recueil* to this larger political project; nevertheless, his preface also includes lengthy descriptions of earlier efforts to accomplish similar goals and pays particular attention to the Ecole des Chartes. According to his account, despite formidable accomplishments in the late seventeenth and early eighteenth centuries, French legal historiography in his own time is in a frightful state. The great documentary collections begun by scholars like Baluze, Bouquet, and Bréquigny remain unfinished, and the archival sources necessary to complete them "are so poorly maintained, and are in such disorder, that one finds it very hard to locate the documents one needs" (xlviii). Yet amid this tale of frustration, Isambert offers special praise for the Ecole des Chartes, touting it as a solution to the crisis in the study of legal history. He argues that the school will help "fill the gap" left by the interruption of Old Regime collections by deciphering the charters in the

Trésor des Chartes (at the Royal Archives) and in the *Cabinet des Chartes* (at the Royal Library):

> If one gives the young men who make up this school proper supervision, there is no doubt that they will be able to render very great services, and that in a small number of years, they will be able to recover monuments that one perhaps did not suspect existed (xxvi, xlix).

For Isambert, in an era neglectful of the crucial links between legal history and contemporary politics, the Ecole des Chartes is a bright spot, offering the possibility of finally producing a complete chronological record of French monarchical laws.

Few other legal historians of this period make direct references to the Ecole des Chartes; however, it seems unlikely that Isambert's conception of the school was unusual. After all, as Donald Kelley has pointed out, the notion that legal history should form the basis for modern jurisprudence

> was in effect the axiom of legal studies in the Restoration, and the consequences were momentous for the legacy of the Enlightenment and of the Revolution. What this principle signified, not to put too fine a point on it, was simply a return to many of the assumptions, attitudes, methods, and materials of the Old Regime, even for lawyers who were busy summoning up a bourgeois future.[66]

Often heavily influenced by German legal theorists like Friedrich Karl von Savigny and Karl Friedrich Eichhorn, these French lawyers and jurists pushed legal history to the center of their field. In 1819, for example, a committee that included Victor Cousin, André Dupin, and Isambert founded the first French legal history journal, the enormously successful *La Thémis*. The following year, the Paris Faculty of Law began offering a course in "the philosophical history of Roman and French law" taught by jurist F. F. Poncelet.[67] Thus just at the time that the Ecole des Chartes was being established, French legal scholarship was beginning to emphasize the connections between legal history and contemporary jurisprudence.

Interestingly, placing the Ecole des Chartes in the context of legal scholarship brings us full circle back to Joseph-Marie Degérando. Historians of the school focus exclusively on Degérando's roles as philosopher,

---

[66] Donald R. Kelley, *Historians and the Law in Post-Revolutionary France* (Princeton: Princeton University Press, 1984), p. 56.

[67] Ibid., Chap. 7; see also Madeleine Ventre-Denis, *Les sciences sociales et la faculté de droit de Paris sous la Restauration. Un texte précurseur: l'ordonnance du 24 mars 1819* (Paris: Aux amateurs de livres, 1985), pp. 21 and 57.

philanthropist, and government official, but Degérando was also widely known as a legal theorist. A longtime admirer of German scholarship, he helped import the ideas of what Kelley calls the "historical school of law" from Germany to France.[68] In 1819, the same ordinance that created Poncelet's course in legal history led to Degérando's appointment as professor of "positive public law and administrative law" at the Paris Faculty. In his opening lecture, he emphasized his support for the Charter:

> Our positive public law…is entirely in that solemn and imperishable act, [that has] become the patrimony of every Frenchman, in that Charter, august promulgation of a venerable monarch, restorer of France, and restorer of public liberties; in that Charter which is the expression and the accomplishment of the wishes of France as a whole.[69]

Here Degérando, like Isambert, presents legal scholarship as the articulation of the principles of the Charter, a document at once historical (the "patrimony" of every Frenchman, "restoring" public liberties) and perpetual (an "imperishable act").

But what do Degérando's interest in law and support for the Charter have to do with his involvement in the Ecole des Chartes? The connection would seem only coincidental if not for two letters by Degérando that have so far been ignored by historians of the school. On 1 March and again on 5 March 1821, Degérando wrote to Bon-Joseph Dacier, then head of the Academy of Inscriptions and thus responsible for selecting students for the Ecole des Chartes, to ask that three of his law students be included in the first class. Expressing the hope that Dacier would not think his recommendations "too indiscreet," Degérando wrote: "You will have the goodness to forgive me for them in thinking that this establishment was formed essentially for the students in my course, at my request, and in considering all the care I have taken to secure its creation."[70] If we put this

---

[68] Kelley, *Historians and the Law*, pp. 72-73.

[69] Joseph-Marie Degérando, *Thémis* 1 (1819): 76, quoted in Ventre-Denis, *Les sciences sociales*, pp. 82-83.

[70] Degérando to Monsieur le Chr. Dacier Secretaire Perpetuel de l'Acade. Rale. des inscriptions & Belles Lettres &c., 1 Mar. and 5 Mar. 1821, Archives de l'Académie des Inscriptions (housed at the Archives de l'Institut), folder E 6. The quotation is from the letter of 1 March, pp. [1-2]. Both Marot, *L'essor*, and the very useful dissertation by Jean Le Pottier, "Histoire et érudition: recherches et documents sur l'histoire et le rôle de l'érudition médiévale dans l'historiographie française du XIXè siècle" (Thesis, Ecole nationale des chartes, 1979), cite this letter, but neither includes this particular passage.

claim together with the law school lecture quoted above, it seems that
Degérando proposed the Ecole des Chartes in order to promote the study of
public law in general and the study of the Charter in particular. In this light,
Degérando's idea for the school appears to have emerged less directly out of
his interests in philosophy and language than out of a conception of the
connections between law and history that had become common among
supporters of the 1814 Charter.

Therefore, the creation of the Ecole des Chartes can be seen as a
response to three demands expressed by politicians and intellectuals in the
early 1820s: to continue the historical projects of the Academy of
Inscriptions, to revive the Maurist practice of diplomatics, and to promote
the study of public law and its history. As I have tried to demonstrate, all of
these demands were part of a larger goal: to stabilize monarchy by Charter
by rooting it in the Old Regime. In this context, the study of medieval
documents was not at all an esoteric enterprise but rather a key strategy in
the Conservatives' effort to find a middle ground between absolutism and
revolution.

Between 1821 and 1823, the goals of the Ecole des Chartes seem to have
held considerable appeal. In March 1821, so many students applied for
admission to the school that the Academy of Inscriptions asked to subject
them all to a year of study and testing before selecting those who would
receive government stipends.[71] Soon after, though, the Academy settled on
an entering class of twelve students—including the three law students
recommended by Degérando—to undergo a two-year program of study.[72]

---

[71] Draft of letter from [Jacques-Joseph Champollion-Figeac, probably in his
capacity as secretary to Dacier, head of the Academy] to M. le Cte. [probably
Siméon, then Minister of the Interior], 29 Mar. 1821, AD Isère, Fonds
Champollion, microfilm reel 30. See also minutes of the Academy's meeting of 30
Mar. 1821, AI, Procès-verbaux, volume for 1818-1823. It does not appear that this
request was granted; students began receiving government stipends as early as July
1821.

[72] Biographical information on the school's first students (Ernest Augustin Xavier
Clerc de Landresse, Léon Lacabane, Alexandre Lenoble, Gustave Marin d'Arbel,
Honoré Capefigue, Pierre Augustin Faudet, Jules Pétigny, Alexandre Barbier [or
Barbié] du Bocage, Eugène Burnouf, Benjamin Guérard, Levaillant de Florival,
and Hippolyte Rolle) can be found in *Ecole Impériale des Chartes. Liste des élèves
pensionnaires et des archivistes-paléographes depuis la fondation de l'Ecole en 1821 jusqu'au 1er
mai 1870* (Nogent-le-Rotrou: Impr. de A. Gouverneur, [1870?]), AN, box F17-
4024; in the *Livret de l'Ecole des Chartes, 1821-1966* (Paris: Ecole nationale des chartes,
1967), which updates the 1852 and 1879 editions.

By mid-1821, the section of the school housed at the Royal Library had begun classes under the direction of Pierre de Lespine, a genealogist and archivist specializing in the history of the Périgord, and by early 1822, Joseph-Nicolas Pavillet, the former head of the archives of Notre-Dame de Paris, had started conducting courses for the section housed at the Royal Archives.[73] Although no examinations or student notebooks from these early courses have survived, it is clear from passing references that they focused mainly on the "decipherment" (*déchiffrage*) of medieval manuscripts and that they drew heavily on the methods of the Benedictines of Saint-Maur. A list of "books necessary to the Ecole des Chartes" dated 11 March 1822 consists primarily of Maurist publications, such as the "Diplomatics of D. Mabillon" and the "Dictionary of Diplomatics by Dom de Vaines."[74]

However, at the end of December 1823, classes at the Ecole des Chartes ground to a halt. Though the Ministry of the Interior made no official move to close the school, it refused to fund a new class of students (scheduled to begin in early 1824), and thus effectively consigned the school to a state of dormancy from which it would not emerge until the late 1820s.[75] As I mentioned earlier, most histories of the Ecole des Chartes see the withdrawal of government funding as a logical response to a basic flaw in the 1821 ordinance. Because the ordinance did not set aside any government posts for the school's graduates, the first *chartistes* were left without any career prospects, and thus the school could not attract enough new students to continue its classes. Interestingly, this account seems to

---

[73] AEC, folder "Ecole des Chartes. établie...." On Lespine, see especially L. de Lanzac de Laborie, "La Révolution en Périgord et l'émigration périgourdine d'après les notes et correspondances inédites de l'abbé Lespine," *Revue des questions historiques* (1 Jul. 1895): 96-148; on Pavillet, see Samaran, "L'Ecole des Chartes," and Paul Delsalle, "L'archivistique sous l'Ancien Régime, le trésor, l'arsenal, et l'histoire," *Histoire, Economie, Société* 12, no. 4 (1993): 454.

[74] See for example descriptions of Pavillet's course in "Etat des Travaux des Employés aux Archives du Royaume," AN, box AB VIII 1, folder "Travail du Secretariat general...1816-1829"; see also "Livres nécessaires à l'Ecole des chartes," 11 Mar. 1822, AEC, folder "Ecole des Chartes. établie...."

[75] The exception here is Amable Floquet, who did not begin classes until late 1822 (replacing Marin d'Arbel) and thus continued to study under Lespine and receive a stipend until the end of his two-year program, in late 1824 ; for reasons I do not understand, the school's professors (including Ponsar, hired after Pavillet's death in August 1823) continued to receive salaries from the Ministry of the Interior until the school reopened in 1829. See AN, box F17-4026 and F17-4027 [both *cotes* in same box], folder "Ecole des Chartes. Dépenses 1821-1840."

reproduce the explanation provided at the time by the Ministry of the Interior. In November 1824, the head of the ministerial division responsible for the Ecole des Chartes wrote to the Minister of the Interior, Corbière, to report that because local governments had refused to hire members of the first graduating class as archivists, he was not able to fill the next class of students.[76] That same month, Corbière gave official word that the Ministry would no longer provide stipends for the school's students.[77]

This explanation for the closure of the school has its merits, but it is ultimately unsatisfactory. The National Archives' files on the school do contain a draft of an Interior Ministry circular dated March 1824 that asks French prefects to determine if their local councils would be willing to pay for a departmental archivist.[78] Yet despite careful searches of seven departmental archives, I have not found any evidence that this circular was actually sent, nor that departmental councils made any explicit decisions against hiring archivists. Moreover, even if these councils did refuse to hire the school's graduates, this clearly did not prevent the school from attracting new students. According to the Academy of Inscriptions' own records, it did indeed have trouble finding as many interested applicants as in 1821; nevertheless, on 19 December 1823, it proposed a list of seventeen candidates to the Minister of the Interior, asking him to select twelve.[79] Despite several pointed reminders, the Minister made no selection, in effect

---

[76] Lourdoueix (Le Chef de la 2e division), "Rapport présenté à Son Excellence le Ministre Secrétaire d'Etat au Département de l'Intérieur," Nov. 1824, AN, box F17-4024.

[77] [Corbière] (Le Ministre de l'Intérieur) to Ponsard [sic] and Lespine, Paris, Nov. 1824, AN, box F17-4046, F17-4047 and F17-4048 [all *cotes* in same box], folder "Ecole des Chartes. 1. Nominations 1821-46 (demandes de places d'élèves), 2. Arrêtés de nomination, 1833-43."

[78] [Corbière] (Le Ministre secrétaire d'Etat de l'Intérieur) to Monsieur le Préfet, Paris, Mar. 1824, AN, box F17-4024. Historian Vincent Mollet comes to the same conclusion about this circular in "Les chartistes dans les Archives départementales avant le décret de 1850," *BEC* 151 (1993): 124.

[79] Dacier, "Extrait du procès-verbal de la Séance du vendredi 19 Décembre 1823 [of the Académie Royale des Inscriptions et Belles-Lettres]," AN, box F17-4046, F17-4047, and F17-4048, folder "Ecole des Chartes. 1. Nominations 1821-46 (demandes de places d'élèves), 2. Arrêtés de nomination, 1833-43"; see also descriptions of each candidate (including the now-famous Emile Littré) in AN, box M 257 B; on the Academy's attempts to attract more candidates, see Degérando et al., to the Académie des Inscriptions, p. [3].

placing the school on hold until his decision to eliminate student funding in November 1824.[80]

If the Minister of the Interior had a sufficient number of candidates, why did he first ignore the Academy's submissions and then refuse to support a new class at all? I would like to suggest that the answer has less to do with the lack of suitable jobs for *chartistes* than with a contemporary shift in Restoration politics. As I have noted, although the 1820 assassination of the Duke de Berri prompted the resurgence of the Ultraroyalist faction, the Ultras did not consolidate their ministerial and parliamentary power until late 1824. Already in 1822, the Ultra presence had begun changing the face of public instruction in France. That year, Villèle and Corbière, the chief spokesmen of the Ultras, began using their new authority as ministerial leaders to silence Liberal university professors (including François Guizot and Victor Cousin) and eliminate potentially left-leaning law courses (including those taught by Degérando and Poncelet).[81] But the real Ultra triumph came in 1824. In March, parliamentary elections returned a solidly Ultra majority. Then in mid-September, Louis XVIII, who had generally proven sympathetic to Conservative policies, died, ushering in the longtime Ultra favorite, Charles X.

As a number of historians have pointed out, Charles X barely concealed his hostility to the 1814 Charter. Soon after its proclamation, he told the moderate royalist Pasquier, "we will have to try it, but the experiment will be over soon, and if at the end of a year or two we see that it is not working promptly, we will go back to the natural order of things."[82] For Charles X and his Ultra supporters, the "natural order of things" was quite different from that outlined in Isambert's *Recueil des lois* or in the founding documents

---

[80] See for example Lourdoueix (Le Chef de la 2e division), "Rapport présenté à Son Excellence le Ministre Secrétaire d'Etat au Département de l'Intérieur," 29 Sept. 1824, AN, box F17-4026 and F17-4027, which states that "although the Royal academy of inscriptions and belles-lettres has presented candidates, Your Excellency has not yet made any determination."

[81] Stanley Mellon, *The Political Uses of History: A Study of Historians in the French Restoration* (Stanford: Stanford University Press, 1958), p. 14; Ventre-Denis, *Les sciences sociales*.

[82] Pasquier added, "I note these words because Monsieur, without any doubt, mentioned similar ones to many others besides me, and from there the opinion that did not take long to establish itself, that he did not want the Charter and that he was very determined to destroy it as soon as he found the opportunity." [Etienne-Denis] Pasquier, *Mémoires* (Paris: Plon, 1894), 3: 40-41, quoted in Rosanvallon, *Monarchie*, p. 89, footnote 4.

of the Ecole des Chartes. These texts had envisioned the French monarchy—both past and present—as steadfastly committed to the rule of law. The normal state of affairs, in this conception, meant that the king upheld existing laws and issued new ones appropriate to the needs of his subjects. But for Charles X, to "go back to the natural order of things" meant to revoke existing laws—in this case, the Charter—and return to rule by divine right alone, or by what Baker has called the "discourse of will," rather than the "discourse of justice."[83]

Of course, Charles X did not revoke the Charter upon his ascension in 1824. Undoubtedly afraid that an all-out assault on the Charter would provoke an unmanageable reaction from the growing Liberal opposition movement, the king left the 1814 proclamation in place. Instead, he and his Ultra advisors tried to recast the relationship between the Charter and the monarchy. While the supporters of the Charter—including, as I have argued, supporters of the Ecole des Chartes—had emphasized the enduring nature of the proclamation, Charles X tried to present it as a temporary measure, inessential to the success of his regime. In other words, he tried to push the term "Charter" away from its English definition and back toward its medieval French definition. His Charter would not be a constitution, but rather a simple concession, subject to revocation at any moment.

However, in order to redefine the Charter, Charles also had to redefine the Old Regime. Since his opponents had argued for the power and stability of the Charter by connecting it to an enduring body of pre-revolutionary law, Charles and his supporters had to provide their own conception of the Old Regime, one that emphasized divine absolutism and minimized the role of law. Perhaps the most striking example of their efforts to create such a conception is Charles X's coronation in May 1825. While Louis XVIII had never managed to organize a coronation, Charles X spent many months and many thousands of francs preparing an elaborate ceremony at Reims Cathedral. In spite of these detailed preparations, it was not clear until the ceremony began whether or not the king would deign to mention the Charter. In the event, the Charter made a passing appearance during the coronation oath, as "the Most Christian King and the Eldest Son of the Church" swore to uphold both the "laws of the kingdom" and the "Constitutional Charter." Yet this was the only mention of French law in a three-day celebration of royal power and divinity. The rest of the coronation festivities played up not the continuity of law, but rather the continuity of the line of kings selected by God to govern France. The rituals

---

[83] Baker, *Inventing*, pp. 25-26.

included in the ceremony, from the touching of scrofula patients to the shouting of "*Vivat rex in aeternum*" ("May the king live forever"), invoked royal traditions dating to the Middle Ages. The archbishop of Reims even anointed Charles X with holy oil from the same ampulla—"miraculously" rescued after being smashed by revolutionaries—used to anoint every French king since Clovis.[84]

Given this reconceptualization of the Charter and of the Old Regime, it is not surprising that the decision to withdraw support for the Ecole des Chartes occurred less than two months after Charles became king. Under the new Ultraroyalist monarchy, a School of Charters was no longer useful, for an absolute king did not need to invoke a legal tradition to justify his method of rule. Indeed, it seems the new monarchy required no documentary justification at all. By the mid-1820s, even the two collections that had begun to be explored under Louis XVIII, the Royal Library and the Royal Archives, seemed to hold little appeal for Charles' regime. In early 1827, for example, Corbière rejected a proposal to reorganize and consolidate the Royal Library's *Cabinet des Chartes*.[85] Though by this time scholars like Guizot, Thierry, and Mignet had begun to turn to archival and manuscript sources in their investigations of French history, they had to do so without government support.[86] For Charles X, it seems, the maintenance of royal power required not historical documents, but medieval rites; not legal texts, but holy images.

Therefore, the establishment and disestablishment of the Ecole des Chartes reflect key shifts in Restoration politics. When the school was created in February 1821, moderate royalists were in the midst of a fierce struggle to defend monarchy by Charter. The school's emphasis on reading

---

[84] Richard A. Jackson, *Vive le Roi! A History of the French Coronation from Charles V to Charles X* (Chapel Hill: University of North Carolina Press, 1984), pp. 191-197.

[85] In his *Notice sur le cabinet des chartes et diplômes de l'histoire de France* (Paris: Firmin Didot, 1827 [dated at end, 20 Apr. 1827]), Jacques-Joseph Champollion-Figeac asks Corbière to support a reorganization of the Cabinet. On the rejection of this plan, see Jean-Marie Pardessus, *Institut royal de France. Rapport fait à l'Académie royale des inscriptions et belles-lettres, au nom de la commission des travaux littéraires, sur la continuation des tables des chartes imprimées, et la publication des textes des chartes concernant l'histoire de la France...*(Paris: Firmin-Didot, [1835]), pp. 27-28.

[86] See for example Jean Walch, *Les Maîtres de l'histoire, 1815-1850: Augustin Thierry, Mignet, Guizot, Thiers, Michelet, Edgard Quinet* (Geneva and Paris: Editions Slatkine, 1986); and Anne Denieul Cormier, *Augustin Thierry: l'histoire autrement* ([Paris]: Publisud, 1996).

medieval legal manuscripts and, in particular, royal charters, fit neatly with
the Conservative effort to identify Old Regime precedents for the 1814
proclamation and thereby stabilize Louis XVIII's regime. However, by the
time of Charles X's ascension in 1824, such precedents were no longer seen
as necessary to royal legitimacy. As the last of the Bourbon monarchs took
on the mantle of divine-right absolutism, the Ecole des Chartes lost its
official support. Thus the school was not simply, as Mathiez claims, a
product of Bourbon legitimism but rather of a certain kind of Bourbon
legitimism, one tied to a particular vision both of the Charter and of the Old
Regime.

By late 1827, however, neither the Conservative nor the Ultraroyalist
brand of legitimism seemed capable of stabilizing the Bourbon regime.
Nearly three years before Charles X's ordinances of July 1830 dealt a final
blow to the 1814 Charter and set off a new revolution, the Liberal
opposition had already gained a parliamentary majority and begun pressing
its claims on the Ultraroyalist administration. Like the Conservatives of the
early 1820s, the Liberals of the late 1820s looked to the archival vestiges of
the Old Regime in their efforts to defend monarchy by Charter. Yet while
the Conservative supporters of the Ecole des Chartes had concentrated their
efforts on the royal charters housed in Parisian collections, the Liberals of
the late Restoration began turning to the myriad provincial collections
created by the Revolution as a way of promoting a new kind of
constitutional monarchy. As we will see in Chapter Two, it was this
reconceptualization of the French state and of its archives and libraries that
gave rise to a new and dramatically different Ecole des Chartes.

Chapter Two

Constructing an Authentic National History: Archives and Libraries Under Liberal Rule

In the summer of 1830, the French overthrew the Bourbon monarchy for the second and final time. On July 25, after parliamentary elections again returned a vigorously anti-Ultra majority, Charles X made a desperate play for control of the government. Invoking the emergency powers supposedly granted him by the Charter of 1814, he ordered the dissolution of the new parliament, the severe reduction of the electorate, and the elimination of freedom of the press.[1] Within days, widespread revulsion at these drastic measures, known as the July Ordinances, mingled with frustration at the ongoing economic crisis to fuel a nationwide reaction. Angry artisans and journalists revolted against royal troops in the streets of Paris, while demonstrators in the provinces chanted "*A bas les rats! A bas les royalistes!*" ("Down with the rats! Down with the royalists!"). Fearful of the escalating violence, Liberal opposition leaders acted quickly to form a new government, and by the beginning of August, they had engineered the abdication of Charles X and the ascension of the Duke d'Orléans, now called Louis-Philippe, King of the French.[2]

Unlike the revolution of July 1789, that of July 1830 did not cause any major upheaval in the world of libraries and archives. No crowds stormed through provincial depositories; no politicians urged the destruction of "counter-revolutionary" manuscripts. In fact, most accounts of libraries and

---

[1] Charles relied on article fourteen of the Charter, which states: "The king is the supreme head of the State; he commands the land and sea forces, declares war, makes treaties of peace, alliance, and commerce, appoints all public officials, *and makes the rules and ordinances necessary for the execution of the laws and the security of the State* [my emphasis]." His opponents claimed that this article was not intended to give the king full emergency powers. For the text of the Charter, see chap. 1, footnote 16.

[2] The classic account of July 1830 is David H. Pinkney, *The French Revolution of 1830* (Princeton: Princeton University Press, 1972). Pamela Pilbeam's *The 1830 Revolution in France* (New York: St. Martin's, 1991) offers a useful reassessment of the event in light of recent "revisionist" scholarship.

archives from this period fail to mention the revolution at all, except perhaps to note the arrival of a new administrator. At the National Archives, the fall of Charles X apparently prompted the suicide of the head archivist, the royalist Etienne De Larue, on August 13.[3] Yet the events of July seemed to have no impact on the collections for which De Larue was responsible. The week before his death, De Larue reported to the Minister of the Interior that despite the intense streetfighting in the vicinity of the Archives, "proper order has not ceased to reign even for an instant."[4]

The lack of revolutionary drama in such reports would seem to imply that the advent of the so-called July Monarchy in 1830 brought no significant change in attitudes toward libraries and archives. However, the state's approach to these collections in the early 1830s was quite different from what it had been ten years earlier. As we saw in Chapter One, the early Restoration vacillated between two views of libraries and archives. On the one hand, supporters of the Ecole des Chartes, most of them moderate royalists, saw the Royal Archives and Royal Library as precious sources of legal precedents for the 1814 Charter. Ultraroyalist opponents of the school, on the other hand, suggested that historical documents, as well as the collections from which they came, were unimportant to the French monarchy. Yet by the 1830s, this split no longer existed; intellectuals and government officials now agreed that the preservation and exploration of French libraries and archives were national priorities. At their instigation, the state not only laid claim to the thousands of provincial collections it had abandoned after the first French Revolution but began mining these depositories for new kinds of documents, such as municipal records, tax registers, government correspondence, and even poetry. French libraries and archives no longer just offered legal buttressing for current political practices; they now held out the possibility of producing an authentic national history capable of rallying the French people around the new Liberal regime.

If descriptions of July 1830 do not announce this sea change in perceptions of archives and libraries, it is perhaps because the change had begun more than two years earlier. In January 1828, the Restoration government decided to revive the Ecole des Chartes, inactive since

---

[3] [Jacques-Pierre] Coru Sarthe to Monsieur [Daunou], Paris, 13 Aug. 1830, AN box AB IVc 3, folder on De Larue; and Ch. Choisnard to Monsieur, Paris, 13 Aug. 1830, AN box BB 17a 75, folder 19 bis.

[4] De Larue to S. Exce. le Mtre. de l'Intr., 7 Aug. 1830, AN box AB II 12, folder "Correspondance 1830."

Corbière's decision to withdraw student funding in November 1824.[5] The Minister of the Interior began soliciting advice from prominent scholars, and, after nearly two years of discussion and experimentation, signed the new school into law on November 11, 1829. However, the Ecole des Chartes that finally opened its doors in January 1830 bore only minimal resemblance to that of February 1821. As we will see, although the school still offered courses in medieval paleography, both its mission and its curriculum had changed considerably, reflecting an important shift in government conceptions of archives and libraries. This shift, already underway in January 1828, became even more noticeable after July 1830, as the new government rearticulated the ideas expressed in the 1829 reorganization of the Ecole des Chartes and placed archives and libraries at the center of national politics.

If the turning point for French library and archival policies came in 1828, not 1830, then it may be worth re-evaluating the significance of the July Revolution for the history of French cultural policies more generally. Until about twenty years ago, the cultural policies of the early nineteenth-century French governments hardly seemed worth writing about. Most historians described the political leaders of the Restoration and July Monarchy as decadent, self-serving elites, hopelessly out of touch with the rest of French society. More recently, however, historians have begun to isolate the July Monarchy as a time of particularly productive cultural cooperation between Liberal politicians on the one hand and historians, archeologists, and literati on the other. For example, a series of articles in Pierre Nora's enormously successful compendium, *Les lieux de mémoire* ("The Sites of Memory"), published in the mid-1980s, argues that the Liberal triumph in July 1830 prompted a nationwide surge of interest in the vestiges of the French past, from medieval statues to crumbling manuscripts to provincial chateaux.[6] Similarly, the spate of recent work on François Guizot, the July Monarchy's most powerful politician, attempts to

---

[5] See chap. 1, footnote 77.

[6] See especially the articles by Laurent Theis, François Bercé, Dominique Poulot, Edouard Pommier, and André Chastel in vol. 2, pt. 2 of Pierre Nora, ed., *Les lieux de mémoire* (Paris: Gallimard, 1986). Another recent example of this historiographical trend is Stephane Gerson, "Pays and nation: the uneasy formation of an historical patrimony in France, 1830-1870" (Ph.D. diss., University of Chicago, 1997).

recuperate Guizot in large part by crediting him with promoting a national historical revival in the wake of 1830.[7]

Although this chapter draws heavily on this new work, it also argues for a reconsideration of its chronological parameters. Discussions of libraries and archives in the late Restoration suggest that government support for the collection, preservation, and publication of French historical sources emerged well in advance of the 1830 Revolution. Furthermore, a careful study of libraries and archives in the 1830s and 1840s suggests that the state's approach to such sources shifted yet again in 1840. As I will show in Chapter Three, by 1840, the state began concentrating less on locating and publishing key historical documents than on classifying and cataloguing entire collections. Some of the historical projects initiated by Guizot and other Liberal intellectuals in the early 1830s began to lose steam, while new projects took their place. Although there are clear affiliations between these two sets of initiatives, 1840 did mark a substantial shift in library and archival policy. Therefore, seen from the perspective of libraries and archives, the July Revolution neither inaugurated an entirely new set of cultural policies nor signaled the rise of a distinctly "Orleanist" approach.

Since the major turning points in library and archival policies (1828 and 1840) do not seem to fit with the usual political markers (1830 and 1848), one might conclude that libraries and archives had little to do with major political changes in this period. But 1828 and 1840 were years of major political change. 1828 saw the revival of the moderate and Liberal opposition movement that would remove Charles X from the throne in July 1830, while 1840 marked the emergence of a much more conservative and inflexible regime than had existed in the 1830s. Though neither year witnessed the kind of public drama found in July 1830 or February 1848, both saw significant shifts in political power. The task of this chapter (on the period 1828-1840) and the next (on the period 1840-1849) is to show how these political shifts are connected to changes affecting libraries and archives. In the process, I hope to suggest new ways of understanding the July Monarchy and its relationship to the French past.

For nearly four years, from early 1824 to late 1827, Charles X and his Ultraroyalist ministers managed to maintain control of the government. But

---

[7] See for example Marina Valensise, ed., *François Guizot et la culture politique de son temps: Colloque de la Fondation Guizot-Val Richer* (Paris: Gallimard, 1991); and Pierre Rosanvallon, *Le Moment Guizot* (Paris: Gallimard, 1985).

at the end of 1827, the tide turned.[8] In November, chief minister Villèle called for new parliamentary elections, hoping to further solidify Ultra control. However, Villèle greatly underestimated the vigor of the Liberal opposition. The same historians, philosophers, and other intellectuals who had been pushed out of state posts in the early 1820s and who would soon comprise the leadership of the July Monarchy had organized themselves into a formidable campaigning alliance. Guizot, the Liberal historian and politician who had lost his university chair in 1822, helped create the network of campaign committees known as *Aide-toi, le ciel t'aidera* (Heaven helps those who help themselves). In cooperation with opposition newspapers, these committees helped return a Liberal majority in late November 1827.[9] And while Charles X made a series of attempts to control this new parliamentary force—culminating in the "royal coup d'état" of July 25, 1830—his efforts served only to strengthen the opposition. The Liberal victory of 1830 thus had its roots in that of 1827-1828.

New state policies on libraries and archives followed closely on the heels of the Liberal conquest of parliament. On January 3, 1828, hoping to appease the Liberal majority, Charles X fired Villèle and replaced him with the moderate royalist Joseph de Martignac. Less than three weeks later, on January 22, Martignac wrote to Dacier, head of the Academy of Inscriptions, announcing his plans to reopen the Ecole des Chartes and asking the Academy to select a new list of twenty-four candidates.[10] Martignac evidently did not intend simply to reactivate the old Ecole des Chartes, because he began gathering proposals about how to revamp the school's curriculum. At the same time (perhaps while waiting for the Academy of Inscriptions and other scholars to advise him on this new curriculum), he drew on Ecole des Chartes funds to hire the historian Alexandre Buchon as "Inspector-General of the Archives of the Kingdom" and created a new section at the National Archives charged solely with the

---

[8] I am certainly not the first to see 1827-1828 as a key political turning point. See for example Pinkney, *French Revolution,* p. 3, and Jean-Claude Caron, *Générations romantiques: les étudiants de Paris & le quartier latin* (1814-1851) (Paris: Armand Colin, 1991) p. 281.

[9] See Pilbeam, *1830 Revolution*, pp. 27-36.

[10] Ministre Secrétaire d'Etat de l'Intérieur [Martignac] to M. Dacier, Secrétaire perpétuel de l'Académie des Inscriptions et B.B. L.L. [Belles-Lettres], Paris, 22 Jan. 1828, AN, box F17-4024.

organization of departmental archives.[11] Interestingly, this renewed concern for state-owned collections did not cease when, on August 8, 1829, Charles X made the far more conservative Jules de Polignac chief minister and named his fellow Ultra, François-Régis de la Bourdonnaye, Minister of the Interior.[12] Although La Bourdonnaye soon revoked the appointment of Buchon, a well-known Liberal, as archives inspector, he continued with plans to reopen the Ecole des Chartes and formally reestablished the school on November 11, 1829. Thus despite the series of standoffs between Liberals and Ultras in this period, the new attitude toward libraries and archives seemed to hold.[13]

The Ecole des Chartes that emerged out of the reorganization of 1828-1829 was to persist virtually unchanged until the late 1830s. It differed in important ways from the Ecole of 1821. With its expanded curriculum, commitment to historical publication, and attention to provincial depositories, the new school took a much broader view of state-owned

---

[11] Martignac, "Arrêté," 31 Jul. 1829, AN, box F17-4052 and F17-4053 (in same box), folder "Archives départementales...Projet d'ordonnance...."

[12] Following the shifts in ministerial positions in early nineteenth-century France can be a challenge. From January 1828 to August 1829, Martignac was both Minister of the Interior and chief minister of the cabinet. In August 1829, even though La Bourdonnaye became Minister of the Interior, Polignac (the Minister of Foreign Affairs) became chief minister. See Pinkney, *French Revolution*, p. 6, and, for a broader chronological view, Association du corps préfectoral et des hauts fonctionnaires du ministère de l'Intérieur, *Histoire du Ministère de l'Intérieur, de 1790 à nos jours* (Paris: La Documentation française, 1993).

[13] It is difficult to explain why La Bourdonnaye, renowned as the most rabid of Ultra politicians, signed the ordinance reorganizing the Ecole. One possibility is that La Bourdonnaye only supported the school as a way of diverting funds away from Buchon, who was being paid out of the Ecole's budget. Another possibility is that La Bourdonnaye -- who, like the rest of the Ultras, supported the Charter in its most narrow interpretation as a royal "grant" -- hoped to reappropriate the school for his own ends. In any case, the final ordinance, as we will see, was not the work of La Bourdonnaye himself but primarily that of Rives, an Interior Ministry official, and Jacques-Joseph Champollion-Figeac, a young *érudit*. On the Buchon affair, see Rives, "Rapport au Ministre [de l'Intérieur]," 22 Sept. 1829, AN, box F17-4024, and La Bourdonnaye, "Arrêté," 22 Sept. 1829, AN, box F17-4052 and F17-4053, folder "Archives départementales...Projet d'ordonnance...," as well as discussions in P. Piétresson de Saint-Aubin, "Un projet de réforme des archives départementales en 1829," *Gazette des Archives* (1970): 46-48; and in Jean Longnon, introduction to *Voyage dans l'Eubée, les Iles ioniennes et les Cyclades en 1841*, by Alexandre Buchon (Paris: Emile-Paul, 1911), pp. xxv-xxvii.

collections than its early Restoration predecessor. Although these innovations had little direct impact on French libraries and archives until after the July Revolution, it is significant that the conceptual shift underlying these changes came earlier, with the Liberal triumph of 1828.

Let us take a closer look at the changes wrought by the 1829 reorganization. Perhaps the most obvious change was the expansion of the curriculum. The school's first courses had emphasized the painstaking "decipherment" of royal charters. Yet by the late 1820s, both the methods and the materials used in these early courses began to seem unnecessarily restricted. In 1829, a member of the school's first graduating class, Alexandre Lenoble, urged the Minister of the Interior to reinvigorate the curriculum, claiming that in 1821,

> Students were taught to read and nothing more. The respectable men charged with teaching the courses, poorly versed in the art of speaking and too old to start practicing a kind of teaching that was completely foreign to their habits of retirement and tranquillity, never went beyond this first step.[14]

Jacques-Joseph Champollion-Figeac, elder brother of Jean-François Champollion and an accomplished *érudit* in his own right, echoed Lenoble's complaint in a set of notes sent to the Interior Ministry in late September 1829:

> The two professors designated [to teach the original courses] limited their instruction to the simple reading of charters from various periods. They gave the student a charter to copy; the student conveyed his copy to the master, who corrected it, and that was all.[15]

Not everyone agreed with this critique of the first Ecole des Chartes. In fact, in an April 1828 letter to Martignac, the ill-fated Etienne De Larue argued that the 1821 institution's main defect was that it placed too little emphasis on reading and transcription. Because students had only had three hours of paleographic instruction per week, they lacked the intimate familiarity with medieval documents that came from "permanent study":

---

[14] Alexandre Lenoble, "Note sur la nécessité de créer une chaire de Diplomatique et de Paléographie étrangère près le collège royal de France," Paris, 1829, AN, box F17-4052 and F17-4053, p. [1].

[15] [Jacques-Joseph Champollion-Figeac], notes on the reorganization of the Ecole des chartes, sent to [Rives (Directeur des belles-lettres, sciences, & beaux-arts at the Ministry of the Interior)], 28 Sept. 1829, AD Isère, Fonds Champollion, microfilm reel 30.

The decipherment of old manuscripts is composed of two parts, one of which undoubtedly depends on the intellect, but the other of which is acquired by what might be called mechanical habit. The eye, glued to the manuscripts, has to accustom itself by inspection alone to grasp with sureness and without confusion the traits, abbreviations, etc., that from country to country and from century to century offer such a great variety and infinitely nuance the physiognomy of these documents.[16]

The solution, De Larue claimed, was to incorporate the Ecole des Chartes into the Royal Archives, where students could work as full-time apprentices and then become archivists themselves as positions became available.

While De Larue's proposal might have attracted supporters in the early 1820s, by the late 1820s, "decipherment" was not enough. According to La Bourdonnaye's "Report to the King" that accompanied the 1829 ordinance,

> the lessons [of 1821-1824], limited to just the reading and correct copying of Charters from various periods, did not cover *Diplomatics* and *Paleography*. It is nevertheless this science that aims to establish the authenticity of documents...to determine incontestably the dates of deeds...to specify, always in the interest of historical certitude, the formulas and protocols proper to each period...and to expose the characteristics that differentiate *Charters, Diplomas, Letters, Epistles, Indicules, Rescripts, Edicts, Capitularies,* etc.[17]

Consequently, the 1829 ordinance combined the two original courses (one at the Royal Library and one at the Royal Archives) into a single "elementary course," and then added a two-year advanced course in diplomatics and paleography, designed to "explain the various dialects of the Middle Ages to the students and guide them in the critical understanding [*science critique*] of the written monuments of the period, as well as in the means of determining authenticity and verifying dates."[18]

---

[16] Le Garde General des archives du Royaume [De Larue] to Son Excellence le Ministre Secrétaire d'Etat de l'Intérieur [Martignac], Paris, 3 Apr. 1828, AEC, folder "Ecole des Chartes. établie...," p. [4].

[17] La Bourdonnaye, "Rapport au Roi," Paris, 11 Nov. 1829, AN, box F17-4024. Also in *BEC* 1 (1840): 30-31. His emphasis.

[18] Charles X and La Bourdonnaye, "Ordonnance du Roi concernant la remise en activité de l'Ecole royale des chartes" [ms. copy of original?], 11 Nov. 1829, AN, box F17-4024. Also in *BEC* 1 (1840): 32-33. Despite the official merger of the two original courses at the Royal Archives, because the new advanced course could not start until the first group of students had passed the elementary course (i.e., in January 1831), for a time Lespine, who had been assigned to teach the advanced

Of course, the school's first professors, Lespine and Pavillet, had believed that their courses in reading and transcription *were* courses in diplomatics and paleography; but by 1829, conceptions of these fields had changed. This shift is particularly apparent in records from the new elementary course, taught by a member of the class of 1823, Benjamin Guérard. While in 1822, De Larue had welcomed students to the Ecole des Chartes by telling them that charters alone would occupy their attention, in 1831, Guérard opened his course with the following admonition:

> Gentlemen, the goal of our studies is not only to read and critique Charters, as the title of our Ecole would seem to indicate; our studies are much broader and must include histories, chronicles, biographies, notes, poems, sermons, breviaries, deeds, letters, in short, all kinds of written or figured monuments from the Middle Ages....[19]

Moreover, whereas De Larue's speech never mentioned the issue of authenticity (charters, which he described as "torches" that would guide students through the "shadows" of the Middle Ages, were assumed to be authentic), Guérard made authentication a central task of his new course. According to a student notebook from the 1830s, though Guérard did cover "some exercises in paleography," or ancient writing, the focus of the class was Diplomatics, "defined as the art of recognizing authentic deeds and charters."[20] Thus instead of simply reading and transcribing charters, *chartistes* were now dating and authenticating a whole range of historical documents.

The second innovation introduced by the 1829 Ecole des Chartes was a new commitment to publishing these documents. The authors of the 1821

---

course, offered a second elementary course at the Royal Library. See [Guillaume Isidore], comte de Montbel, and Baron de Balzac, "Ministre de l'Intérieur. Règlement provisoire de l'Ecole des Chartes. Conformément à l'article 11 de l'ordonnance royale du 11 novembre 1829," 29 Dec. 1829, AEC, folder "Ecole des Chartes. établie...."

[19] Benjamin Guérard, "Ecole des chartes. Discours d'ouverture du cours de première année," *La France littéraire* 1 (1832): 268. On De Larue's 1822 speech, see chap. 1, footnote 40. The unprecedented number of paleography and diplomatics manuals and treatises that appeared in the 1830s (notably Natalis de Wailly's *Eléments de paléographie* of 1838) also reflect the expanding conceptions of these fields.

[20] H[ercule] Géraud, "Résumé du Cours de Diplomatique de Mr. Guérard. Notes diverses," Jan. 1836 - [1841 or 1842?], AN Section Contemporaine, Archives of the Ecole des Chartes (materials in-process) [hereafter AEC-SC], series B, item 2, fol. 3r.

ordinance had certainly intended that the school would help publish medieval manuscripts; after all, the first *chartistes* were supposed to serve as "auxiliaries" to the members of the Academy of Inscriptions, which had been charged with the continuation of the great Old Regime compendia.[21] Nevertheless, the earliest students had not been responsible for any government-funded publications of their own. The 1829 ordinance, by contrast, made no mention of the Academy's projects, ordering the school's students to produce two completely new publications: the *Bibliothèque de l'Ecole royale des Chartes*, and the *Bibliothèque de l'histoire de France*. The first of these would be composed of student translations of historical documents, while the second was to include "national charters, in chronological order and with critical commentary."[22] Now, rather than simply providing the readers and copyists necessary for the completion of the Academy's collections, *chartistes* would serve as editors and compilers of their own publications.

Perhaps the most far-reaching of the changes included in the 1829 ordinance, however, was a new concern for provincial depositories. Even though the nationalizations of the revolutionary era had wrought an enormous transformation in provincial archives and libraries, replacing ecclesiastical, administrative, and family collections with a network of literary depositories, municipal libraries, and departmental archives, the First Empire and early Restoration had largely ignored provincial collections in favor of the great Parisian depositories. With the reorganization of the Ecole des Chartes at the end of the Restoration, this pattern began to shift. The 1829 ordinance stipulated that after working at the Royal Library and Archives during their student years, the school's graduates would be eligible "in preference to all other candidates," for "half of the positions vacant in public libraries (with the exception of our library on the Rue de Richelieu [i.e., the Royal Library]), at the Royal Archives,

---

[21] See chap. 1.

[22] Charles X and La Bourdonnaye, "Ordonnance." For reasons I will explain shortly, both of these publications were cancelled in early 1832. Thus the 1829 *Bibliothèque de l'Ecole royale des chartes* is not to be confused with the journal of the same name (now called simply *Bibliothèque de l'Ecole des Chartes*) that began publication in 1839-40 under the direction of the school's alumni organization, the *Société de l'Ecole des chartes*.

and in the various literary depositories."[23] Once limited to the capital, *chartistes* would now begin to look beyond it.

This new concern for provincial collections is even more striking when we set the 1829 ordinance in the context of several contemporary initiatives related to departmental archives. In early 1828, Joseph Boudot, head of the departmental archives in the Côte-d'Or, offered to establish a new Ecole des Chartes at the departmental headquarters in Dijon. He argued that while the Paris school of 1821 had been "so useful for the royal *Trésor des Chartes*, Royal Archives, and Royal manuscript library," it had "left no hope for the departmental archives," which, though in a "sort of chaos," contained "riches that would both illustrate the works of the Academy of Inscriptions and interest religion, customs, and jurisprudence."[24] While the previous minister, Corbière, might have dismissed such a project, Martignac supported it, and Boudot began offering courses in diplomatics and paleography at the Dijon archives in November 1829.[25]

At the same time that Boudot was lobbying for a provincial Ecole des Chartes, scholars and archivists in the capital were also putting forth proposals aimed at the revitalization of departmental archives. One of the many proposals Alexandre Lenoble presented to the Minister of the Interior

---

[23] Charles X and La Bourdonnaye, "Ordonnance." The explicit exception of the Royal Library was apparently made at the request of Dacier (a manuscripts curator at the Royal Library, as well as Permanent Secretary of the Academy of Inscriptions), who argued that the Library's ruling *conservatoire* had long established its right to appoint all Library employees. See Dacier's letter to Rives, reproduced in *BEC* 1 (1840): 29-30.

[24] Joseph Boudot (Le conservateur des archives de la préfecture du dept. de la côte d'or), "Projet d'une Ecole gratuite des Chartes près les archives du département de la Côte d'or," [1827 or 1828], AEC, folder "Ecole des Chartes. établie...."

[25] On the Dijon school, which lasted until Boudot's resignation as archivist in 1836, see for example [Maximilien Quantin], "L'Ecole des chartes de Dijon," *Bulletin historique et philologique du Comité des travaux historiques* 1-2 (1887): 305-311; J[oseph] G[arnier], "Souvenirs Bourguignons: la mésaventure d'un Conseiller au Parlement," *Le Bien Public*, 30 Apr. 1893, p. 1; and "L'Ecole des Chartes de Dijon," *BEC* 83 (1922): 271. It is even possible that it was Boudot's proposal that sparked Martignac's interest in reviving the Paris Ecole des Chartes. The draft of a February 1, 1828 letter from Dacier to Martignac, for example, suggests that the two schools were discussed simultaneously (see AEC, folder "Ecole des Chartes. établie...."). See also Pierre Marot, *L'essor de l'étude des antiquités nationales à l'Institut, du Directoire à la monarchie de juillet... Lecture faite dans la séance publique annuelle du 22 novembre 1963* (Paris: n.p., 1963), p. 13.

in these years argued that only the creation of an Inspector-General of Departmental Archives (a position for which he thought himself remarkably well suited) would relieve "the state of abandon and deterioration afflicting the majority of our departmental archives."[26] Alexandre Buchon apparently had a similar idea, for in 1828, he began conducting inspections of provincial archives and libraries and sending his findings back to Martignac. In Buchon's eyes, France's departmental archives demanded immediate government action:

> The archives are in a still greater disorder [than neighboring libraries], even in places that have the appearance of order... I know a town where the person charged with guarding the archives put them all in barrels and sent them far away, in order to ensure that they would be sold...[In such places,] if we are to save what remains, reform is urgently necessary.[27]

In July 1829, Martignac responded to these pleas, naming Buchon as the first Inspector-General of Archives and creating a special section at the Royal Archives to deal with departmental collections.[28] The Minister also sent off a new circular to his prefects requesting information about departmental archives and asked his "Bureau of Sciences" for ideas about how to get the Ecole des Chartes involved in inspection work. Thus at the very moment that the central government was working to reorganize the Ecole des Chartes, it also embarked on a whole series of efforts to bring provincial archives back into its administrative purview.[29]

---

[26] Alexandre Le Noble [more often printed Lenoble], "Rapport à Son Excellence le Ministre Secrétaire d'Etat au département de l'Intérieur, sur la nécessité de nommer un Inspecteur des Archives des Départemens [sic]," 1 Jul. 1829, AN, box F17-4052 and F17-4053, folder "Archives départementales...Projet d'ordonnance...," p. [1].

[27] J. A. C. Buchon, *Quelques souvenirs de courses en Suisse et dans le pays de Bade, avec des notices sur plusieurs anciens manuscrits des bibliothèques publiques ou particulières relatifs à l'histoire littéraire ou politique de la France* (Paris: Librairie de Gide, 1836), pp. 49-52, quoted in Piétresson de Saint-Aubin, "Un projet," pp. 47-48. See also J. A. C. Buchon, "Rapport à Son Exc. le Vicomte de Martignac, sur la situation des bibliothèques publiques en France," *Revue de Paris* 5 (1829): 24-38; 8 (also 1829): 30-45 and 262-278.

[28] See above, footnote 11. Buchon's appointment was, not surprisingly, extremely galling to Lenoble (see his letter of 5 Aug. 1829 in AN, box F17-4052 and F17-4053, folder "Archives départementales...Projet d'ordonnance....").

[29] Martignac, "Circulaire [addressed to "Monsieur le Préfet"]," 17 Jul. 1829, AN, box AB Vf 1, folder "Archives départementales (1820-1857)..."; [official at the "Bureau des sciences"], "Note sur l'établissement d'une section départementale aux

Given these archival initiatives, it is tempting to identify the reorganized Ecole with yet another innovation: the creation of the profession of "archivist." After all, unlike the texts associated with the 1821 version of the school, those connected with the 1829 ordinance repeatedly refer to the school's graduates as "archivists." This shift is especially clear in a report presented to La Bourdonnaye, the Minister of the Interior, by Rives, his agent responsible for the Ecole des Chartes, in September 1829. Much of Rives's report is a verbatim transcription of the report on the Ecole submitted by the Comte Siméon to King Louis XVIII in February 1821. Repeating Siméon's dramatic phrasings, Rives argues that "if a remedy is not soon brought about," diplomatics will soon "be deprived of a class of collaborators that are indispensable to it." However, Rives also alters Siméon's text in important ways. Whereas Siméon had no precise term for the practitioners of diplomatics, referring to them sometimes as "those instructed in the science of our charters and our manuscripts," and elsewhere as the "guardians" of provincial depositories, Rives replaces all of these phrases with the word "archivist." Similarly, while Siméon often referred to diplomatics simply as "these studies," Rives calls it "the archivists' science."[30]

The November 1829 ordinance, based largely on Rives's own work, solidifies this connection between the Ecole des Chartes and the role of "archivist." The ordinance states that at the end of their three years of coursework, students will take an exit examination, and that those who pass this examination will be awarded the new title of *archiviste-paléographe*, or "Archivist-Paleographer," a title which, however cumbersome, persists to this day.[31]

This change in terminology is certainly significant. While the term "archivist" had long been used to describe keepers of archival depositories (whether ecclesiastical, familial, or administrative), and while the eighteenth

---

archives du Royaume et sur la création d'une place d'Inspecteur des archives," [between 31 Jul. and 22 Sept. 1829], AN, box F17-4052 and F17-4053, folder "Archives départementales...Projet d'ordonnance...." Interestingly, although Buchon, Lenoble, and Champollion-Figeac all called upon the Minister to begin the classification of departmental archives, the government initiatives of the period 1828 to 1838 focused far less on classification than on preservation and publication. However, as I will discuss in the following chapter, in 1838-1840, classification quite suddenly became the Ministry's chief priority.

[30] Rives, "Rapport." On Siméon's report, see chap. 1, footnote 39.

[31] Charles X and La Bourdonnaye, "Ordonnance."

century had seen the publication of several archival manuals and treatises, never before in France had there been any standard conception of the "archivists' science," or any formal way of training its practitioners.[32] Furthermore, if we look ahead to the remainder of the nineteenth century, we can see that after 1829, both the graduates of the Ecole des Chartes and the ministerial officials responsible for the school increasingly came to view it as a training ground for professional archivists. Nevertheless, it would be quite misleading to characterize the graduates of the revamped Ecole as "professional archivists." Two of the three job categories the new ordinance reserved for Archivist-Paleographers were not in archives but in libraries and literary depositories (most of which would later become libraries). And indeed in the early years of the July Monarchy very few of the school's graduates were actually appointed as archivists (two at the Royal Archives, four in various positions in provincial archives).[33] Instead, most of the school's graduates in this period were hired to work on historical projects that took them to both archives and libraries. In these situations, they served more as experts in historical documents than as administrators of particular collections. It was not until the 1840s and 1850s, then, that *chartistes* would begin to be perceived as professional archivists.

To sum up, then, the reorganization of the Ecole des Chartes that began in early 1828 and was completed in late 1829 signaled a major turning point in the French government's approach to archives and libraries. On the eve of the July Revolution, the state demonstrated a broader conception of historical methods and materials, a new commitment to the publication of historical documents, and a growing preoccupation with provincial collections. What was the connection between these developments and the Liberal parliamentary triumph of 1827-1828? If one looks only at sources from the late Restoration, it is very difficult to tell. Liberal politicians of the period did not offer great pronouncements about archives and libraries, nor

---

[32] On pre-revolutionary archival manuals, see chap. 1, footnote 50, and Paul Delsalle, "L'archivistique sous l'Ancien Régime, le trésor, l'arsenal, et l'histoire," *Histoire, Economie, Société* 12, no. 4 (1993): 447-472.

[33] Alexandre Teulet was hired at the Royal Archives in 1834, followed by Eugène de Stadler in 1836. As we will see shortly, Louis Redet (in the Vienne) and Claude Chelle (in the Rhône) became the first *chartistes* to head departmental archives in 1834. Meanwhile, Louis Hugot became the archivist of the city of Colmar in 1837, and Edouard [or Edward] Leglay became the assistant archivist of the Nord in 1838.

did the new archival and library policies make obvious reference to Liberal campaigns. Yet if one looks at the sources for the early 1830s, the connections between archival and library policies, on the one hand, and Liberal (now "Orleanist") politics, on the other, are both strong and explicit. While the early Orleanist approach to state collections was largely an extension of the approach initiated in the late Restoration, the new government articulated the political motives for this new approach in ways the Bourbon regime never had.

For the victors of July 1830, the connection between national politics and national history—including not only historical books and manuscripts but also coins, tombstones, cathedrals, and all other sorts of "monuments"—was axiomatic. While each of the post-revolutionary governments tried to craft a national history consonant with its own political principles, the leaders of the July Monarchy moved history-making to the very center of national political life. Indeed, many of the most prominent politicians and government officials of the era, including Guizot, Adolphe Thiers, Jules Michelet, Auguste Mignet, and Ludovic Vitet, were well-known historians.[34] After being ejected from their university posts in 1820-1822, they had spent the years of Ultraroyalist domination poring over historical sources in French libraries and archives, only to return to the political stage with the Liberal triumph of 1827-1828.[35] By 1840, this coalition of Liberal historians was beginning to fall apart, but for most of the 1830s, it helped foster a remarkably coherent program of state-sponsored historical research.[36]

However, the presence of such men in the early Orleanist administration cannot by itself explain the intensity with which the regime promoted the study of national history. The rest of the explanation lies in the peculiar dilemma facing the French state in the wake of July 1830. In less than a week, the Liberals had fomented a popular revolt against Charles X, convinced the Duke d'Orléans to take the throne, and compelled him to

---

[34] See Ceri Crossley, *French Historians and Romanticism: Thierry, Guizot, the Saint-Simonians, Quinet, Michelet* (London: Routledge, 1993); Jean Walch, *Les Maîtres de l'histoire, 1815-1850: Augustin Thierry, Mignet, Guizot, Thiers, Michelet, Edgard Quinet* (Paris: Editions Slatkine, 1986); and Yvonne Knibiehler, *Naissance des sciences humaines: Mignet et l'histoire philosophique aux XIXe siècle* (Paris: Flammarion, 1973).

[35] Anne Denieul Cormier, *Augustin Thierry: l'histoire autrement* ([Paris]: Publisud, 1996), pp. 189 and 247-248.

[36] On the breakdown of the consensus among Liberal historians, see my chap. 3 as well as Laurent Theis, "Guizot et les institutions de mémoire," in *Les lieux de mémoire,* vol. 2, pt. 2, p. 577.

uphold a new constitution, the Charter of 1830. The result was a
government that, as François Furet explains, had no clear source of political
legitimacy.[37] Unlike Louis XVIII and Charles X before him, Louis-Philippe
could not claim hereditary or "divine" right to the French throne; in fact,
Louis-Philippe's father, known in the 1790s as Philippe-Egalité, had voted
for the execution of Louis XVI.[38] Nor could the new king look to the force
of the popular revolution to justify his rule. Even though the new Charter
emphasized the contractual nature of the relationship between the king and
the people, dubbing him "King of the French" rather than "King of
France," there could be no ignoring that Louis-Philippe had been the choice
of a few Liberal politicians rather than the popular favorite. Well into the
1830s, worker revolts in Paris and Lyon reminded Liberal leaders that not
all French subjects had wanted to see the July Revolution end so quickly;
many artisans, especially, hoped for a more radical and egalitarian
transformation of the government. In this context, to cast Louis-Philippe as
the "revolutionary" king would be to risk encouraging a potentially volatile
popular movement.[39]

   Thus the second experiment in monarchy by charter was in certain
respects even more precarious than the first.[40] In their efforts to stabilize the
fragile regime, the Orleanist leaders were certainly not afraid to use force, as
evidenced by the swift repression of the worker revolts of 1831 and 1834.
But they placed considerably greater faith in the power of national historical
consciousness to ease political tensions and ensure future stability. Perhaps
the most cogent statement of this belief is the speech Guizot delivered to the
Société des Antiquaires de Normandie (Antiquarian Society of Normandy) in
August 1837. Here Guizot argues that "nothing...can contribute more
certainly and more honorably" to the "moral, public, and lasting
reconciliation" of the country than "national historical studies":

> It is the misfortune, and I must say the vice of times of great political
> upheavals, that men arrange themselves in very separate camps, each one
> under its own flag, pledged to the service of a single idea, a single interest.

---

[37] François Furet, *Revolutionary France, 1770-1880*, trans. Antonia Nevill (Cambridge:
Blackwell, 1992); originally published as *La Révolution: de Turgot à Jules Ferry, 1770-
1880* (Paris: Hachette, 1988), p. 351.
[38] H. A. C. Collingham, *The July Monarchy: A Political History of France, 1830-1848*
(London: Longman, 1988), p. 3.
[39] Ibid., chaps. 5 and 12; Furet, *Revolutionary France*, p. 340.
[40] The best discussion of the two Charters is Pierre Rosanvallon, *La monarchie
impossible: les Chartes de 1814 et de 1830* (Paris: Fayard, 1994).

> Out of which comes a passionate, narrow, exclusive spirit; one sees, hears, and understands only one's own party; one is blind and unjust toward all others. The study of national history fights forcefully against this disastrous situation.[41]

Urging his listeners to redouble their scholarly efforts, Guizot assured them that an ever more zealous program of historical research would ensure that "impartiality, tolerance, and peace" returned to the nation.

In Guizot's view, historical study would act on the national consciousness in two ways. First, by learning the history of the various regions of France, French subjects everywhere would become more respectful, more understanding of each other. "We are quite rightly advised," Guizot maintained, "not to limit ourselves to local or parochial patriotism, [but] to rise up to the idea of national unity, to include all of France in our thoughts, in our affections, [and] in our work." Historical study would make this happen, for "one easily acquires some benevolence for that which one studies with care; one easily becomes equitable toward that which one has fully understood."[42] But beyond gaining sympathy for people from other regions, the French would also gain new respect for people from other periods in French history, and, by extension, Guizot claimed, for different political views. For according to Guizot, each of the political camps found in his own time was in a sense a vestige of a past regime:

> What separates us, what divides us, is that morally speaking, we all belong in part, in ideas, feelings, tastes, [and] interests, to the various national historical periods. All these periods have left traces and still survive on our soil. Every past France, the France of the Old Regime, the France of the Revolution, the France of the Empire, the France of the Restoration, has its representatives in the France of today.[43]

If only the royalists, the republicans, and the Bonapartists would study French history, they would identify an underlying Frenchness that would make political divisions irrelevant: "[F]or us, all these various periods that we are learning to understand, to appreciate equitably, they are all our *patrie*; it is France, France, at the various stages of life, in the various phases of civilization."[44] For Guizot, then, as for many of his Liberal contemporaries, the study of the French past across both time and space was

---

[41] [François] Guizot, "Allocution de M. Guizot [at the meeting held 2 Aug. 1837]," *Mémoires de la Société des Antiquaires de Normandie* 11 (1840): xlii.

[42] Ibid.

[43] Ibid., pp. xliii-xliv.

[44] Ibid., p. xliii.

an extraordinarily powerful catalyst that would in turn produce French identity, national unity, and political stability.

This approach to the French past at first appears as a radical departure from that of the Bourbon Restoration. While Louis XVIII's Charter chopped the story of France into knowable and unknowable segments, claiming to "efface" the French Revolution (and undoubtedly the Empire, as well) from the national memory, Guizot seems to offer a much wider vision, embracing the great sweep of national development from Clovis to Louis-Philippe.[45] But in fact the Liberal historians of the 1830s had their own blind spots, which are central to our understanding of how they shaped the library and archival collections around them. Despite Guizot's rhetoric of sympathy and inclusion, the state-sponsored historical projects of this period focused almost exclusively on one geographical setting—towns—and on one chronological period—the high Middle Ages. The theory behind such projects was that the urban centers of the twelfth and thirteenth centuries had formed the cradle of modern French civilization. While early medieval France had been dominated by struggles between the clergy and the nobility, by the end of the eleventh century, a growing bourgeoisie (here used in its literal sense, as "town dwellers") had started to make its presence felt. Towns throughout France began revolting against feudal authority, and, in many cases, obtaining royal charters guaranteeing their political rights. Soon the bourgeoisie was speaking for the "Third Estate" at the Estates-General, or meetings of the three orders that made up France. For a time, this bourgeois "revolution" also produced a tremendous cultural transformation, including a great literary and artistic revival, but the rise of absolute monarchy in the sixteenth century squelched the urban renaissance, condemning the bourgeoisie to nearly three centuries of royal oppression. Yet in 1789, Liberal historians argued, the bourgeoisie once again surfaced as the rightful leaders of the Third Estate, and, after a series of temporary derailments by enemy forces (notably Jacobins, Bonapartists, and Ultraroyalists), succeeded in July 1830 in establishing a new compact with the king in the form of a constitutional monarchy.[46]

See Gooch p. 197 →

---

[45] See chap. 1, footnote 33.

[46] For a concise discussion of Liberal historiography, see Christopher M. Greene, "Romanticism, Cultural Nationalism, and Politics in the July Monarchy: The Contribution of Ludovic Vitet," *French History* 4, no. 4 (1990): 487-509. See also Paul Viallaneix, "Guizot historien de la France," in Valensise, ed., *François Guizot*, pp. 235-246.

Even if the Liberal historians devoted most of their scholarly attention to the medieval bourgeoisie, it would still be unwise to dismiss Guizot's language of unity and understanding as hypocritical posturing. For Guizot, Michelet, Thierry, and many other historians of the 1830s, the medieval bourgeoisie was not simply the most important or worthy segment of the French nation but rather stood for it in synecdochal fashion. While the Restoration regimes had tried to bolster their own authority by promoting the history of kings to the exclusion of all other groups, the July Monarchy, at least in its early years, tried to argue that all Frenchmen could find themselves in the history of the medieval bourgeoisie. Because the bourgeoisie had given birth to the French nation in the twelfth and thirteenth centuries, it was around the bourgeoisie that the French should rally in the 1830s. The emphasis on national unity and the focus on medieval townspeople thus went hand in hand.

In the early 1830s, the political and historiographical imperatives articulated by Orleanist leaders and the methodological and administrative innovations outlined in the 1829 Ecole des Chartes ordinance came together, with powerful consequences for the relationship between the French state and its Old Regime collections. As the new government looked for ways to engage the French nation in the study of its past, it took up the new approaches to archives and libraries that were first expressed in the late Restoration. Just as the organizers of the new Ecole had begun to look beyond charters to a variety of historical sources and beyond Paris to a range of provincial collections, the Liberal leaders of the 1830s worked to comb depositories throughout the country for authentic vestiges of the national past. Like the authors of the 1829 ordinance, they created new series of historical publications to accommodate all their findings. And finally, they gave the school's graduates new and more prestigious roles to play in the production of national history.

The new regime began by working to eliminate the Ecole des Chartes' subservience to the Academy of Inscriptions. While the 1829 ordinance had only hinted at a diminished role for the Academy by ignoring its ongoing publications, the new Minister of the Interior (the ubiquitous Guizot) began undermining the Academy's authority almost as soon as he arrived in office. In one particularly telling exchange, Guizot rejected the Academy's appointment of Joseph Naudet to the school's governing Commission, claiming that only the Minister could make such appointments, and that he was therefore selecting Naudet himself.[47] Undaunted, the Academy continued to assert its authority. The head of the Commission, the Academician Jean-Marie Pardessus, opened the December 1830 examination session by stating that the Ecole des Chartes, which he claimed was intended specifically to help the Academy complete the *Table chronologique des diplômes*, was subject to the sage counsel of the Academy's members.[48] And in March 1832, with Guizot no longer Minister, the Academy forced the cancellation of the two publications that the 1829 ordinance had prescribed for the Ecole, demanding that the school's students instead devote their time to helping with the *Table chronologique*.[49] Seven months later, however, Guizot returned to the royal cabinet, and calling himself the "protector of the students of the Ecole des Chartes" against the Academy, acted quickly to bring the school under his new Ministry (Public Instruction) and begin developing plans for its students.[50]

The culmination of this administrative arm-wrestling came in 1834, when Guizot drew the Ecole des Chartes into the vast network of historians, antiquarians, and literati known as the *Comité des travaux historiques* (Historical Works Committee). Based in Paris as of July 1834, the Committee quickly established connections to scholarly societies and individual *érudits* from Marseille to Metz in an enormously ambitious effort to develop the kind of

---

[47] Guizot to Mr. le Secrétaire Perpétuel de l'académie des Inscriptions et belles lettres, 27 Oct. 1830, ms. copy in AEC, volume labeled, "Ecole royale des Chartes. Section de la Bibliothèque du Roi. Registre contenant les ordonnances et règlemens [sic] relatifs à l'Ecole; et servant à l'Inscription des Elèves," p. [13].

[48] Pardessus, "Discours Prononcé à l'ouverture du concours par M. Pardessus Président de la Commission," [13 Dec. 1830], ms. copy in AEC, volume "Ecole royale des Chartes. Section...," pp. [35-38]. On Pardessus' scholarly career, see G[abriel] Demante, "M. Pardessus, sa vie et ses ouvrages," *BEC* 15 (1854): 453-467.

[49] Louis-Philippe and Cte. d'Argout (Le Pair de France Ministre Secrétaire d'Etat au département du Commerce et des Travaux Publics), "Ordonnance," 1 Mar. 1832, AN, box F17-3602, folder "Académie des Inscriptions. Publications. Tables des chartes...."

[50] Passage quoted is from [Guizot], note written across first page of 27 Nov. 1832 letter he received from Ecole des Chartes students Chelle, Hugot, and Le Roux de Lincy, complaining that the Academy had picked a non-*chartiste* to help with the *Table chronologique*, AN, box F17-3602, folder "Académie des Inscriptions. Publications. Tables des chartes...." See also Guizot to Monsieur Champollion-Figeac, Paris, 23 Oct. 1832, AD Isère, Fonds Champollion, microfilm reel 30; and Guizot to Daunou (Garde Général des Archives du Royaume), 24 Jul. 1833, AN, box F17-4024.

national history the Liberal historians thought so crucial to French unity. As Guizot explained to the king in November 1834, the Committee was intended to explore

> all the sources in the archives and libraries of Paris and the departments, in the public and private collections; to collect, examine, and if necessary, publish all the important original documents of a historical nature, such as manuscripts, charters, diplomas, chronicles, memoirs, correspondence, even works of philosophy, literature, or art, provided that they reveal some hidden side of the customs and social condition of a period of our history.[51]

Although the Ecole des Chartes never became a formal subsidiary of this new organization, the Committee's goals soon far overshadowed those of the Academy in determining the school's direction. Both of the school's professors served on the original executive board, and by the late 1830s, most of the school's students were engaged in one or more Committee projects.[52]

How are we to interpret Guizot's appropriation of the Ecole des Chartes? Guizot's efforts to bring as many cultural and educational programs as possible under the control of his Ministry of Public Instruction are well known. As he noted in his memoirs, he endeavored to "reclaim for this ministry its natural limits and possessions" by moving institutions like the Collège de France and the Museum of Natural History from other

---

[51] Guizot, "Rapport au roi sur les mesures prescrites pour la recherche et la publication de documents inédits relatifs à l'histoire de France," 27 Nov. 1834, in *Rapports au Roi et pièces. Collection de documents inédits sur l'histoire de France, publiés par ordre du Roi et par le soins du Ministre de l'Instruction publique* (Paris: Imprimerie royale, 1835), pp. 12-13. Xavier Charmes, *Le Comité des travaux historiques et scientifiques (histoire et documents)* (Paris: Imprimerie nationale, 1886), published under the auspices of the Committee itself, is the key reference work for any study of the Committee's development, notwithstanding Charmes's fawning descriptions of Guizot. For more recent evaluations of the Committee's work, see Gerson, "*Pays* and *nation*," and Charles-Olivier Carbonell, "Guizot, homme d'Etat, et le mouvement historiographique français du XIXe siècle," in Société de l'Histoire du Protestantisme Français, *Actes du Colloque François Guizot (Paris, 22-25 octobre 1974)* (Paris: Au siège de la société, 1976), pp. 219-237.

[52] On the professors, see Guizot, "Arrêté [creating the Historical Works Committee]," 18 Jul. 1834, in *Rapports au Roi*, pp. 41-42. On the students, see, for example, Guizot, "Rapport au Roi sur l'etat des travaux relatifs à la recherche et à la publication des documents inédits relatifs à l'histoire de France," 2 Dec. 1835, also in *Rapports au Roi*, pp. 25-40.

ministries over to his own.[53] Similarly, while he at first considered charging the *Société de l'histoire de France* (the French History Society, which he had helped to found in 1833) with the task of reviving national historical research, he quickly decided that a private organization was not up to the job:

> It is to the government alone, in my opinion, that belongs the power to accomplish the great project of a general publication of all the important and still-unpublished materials on the history of our *patrie*. The government alone possesses the resources of all kinds that this vast enterprise requires.[54]

But if it was a central government agency that was required, then why not assign this duty to the Academy of Inscriptions, which, after all, had long been responsible for official historical publications and had developed extensive connections with provincial scholars? Guizot argued in late 1833 that "the extreme meagerness of the resources available to the Academy for the publication of its collections, and...the slowness that is the result," disqualified it from consideration, even though as Minister he was in an ideal position to remedy this problem.[55] That Guizot chose to create the Historical Works Committee rather than trying to reinvigorate the Academy of Inscriptions suggests that he was after more than just increasing the central government's control of historical research; he wanted to refuse the kind of French history that the Academy had come to represent. As we saw in Chapter One, the Academy, itself a product of absolute monarchy, had largely devoted itself to completing the great compendia of royal deeds and charters. Guizot's decision to recenter historical study—including the Ecole des Chartes—around the Historical Works Committee signaled a desire for a more Liberal sort of history, one less about monarchical edicts than municipal protestations, less about kingly glory than "national" triumph.

Since Guizot's plans for the Historical Works Committee were nothing if not ambitious, it is perhaps not surprising that most historians of the Committee have offered rather hyperbolic accounts of its accomplishments, crediting it with the large-scale classification, preservation, and

---

[53] Guizot, *Mémoires pour servir à l'histoire de mon temps*, 2d ed. (Paris: Michel Lévy frères, 1860), 3: 34. On Guizot as centralizer, see Theis, "Guizot et les institutions."

[54] Guizot, *Mémoires pour servir*, p. 5.

[55] [Guizot], "Extrait du Rapport au Roi sur le budget du Ministère de l'instruction publique pour l'exercice 1835," 31 Dec. 1833, in *Rapports au Roi*, p. 4.

interpretation of French historical monuments.[56] Yet if we look closely at the way the Committee deployed its key group of experts—the students and professors of the Ecole des Chartes—we can see that in the 1830s, at least, the Committee funneled its energies into two main tasks: first, identifying a national "patrimony" in the form of documents, books, and other historical objects; and second, extracting from this patrimonial material a kind of Liberal "archive," containing only the most authentic testaments to the evolution of the French nation. In addition, we can see that key elements of both of these projects are to be found in the Ecole des Chartes reorganization of 1828-1829.

If the 1829 ordinance had begun to lay claim to the thousands of provincial depositories produced by the confiscations of the 1790s, the mid-1830s Historical Works Committee renewed this claim with near-obsessive urgency. Guizot, Thierry, Michelet, and other Committee leaders broadcast their horror not only at the "chaos" caused by the revolutionary governments but also at the failure of subsequent regimes to acknowledge and protect French historical sources. For example, Guizot's "Rapport au Roi" of November 1834 stated:

> In Paris, and in a small number of towns, there are archives that are methodically classified and for which an exact inventory...has been prepared; but everywhere else, disorder and confusion reign. At the time of the revolutionary troubles, masses of documents, until then kept in former monasteries, in castles, or in communal archives, were suddenly given up to pillage and devastation. Heaps of papers and parchments, transported to neighboring municipalities, were thrown pell-mell into warehouses or abandoned rooms....[57]

Nevertheless, Guizot explained, many of these depositories still contained precious historical sources, sources that could only be saved by a massive and ongoing government campaign to locate and preserve them.

Provincial scholars soon took up the Committee's call to preserve local collections. In 1837, an official in the Indre-et-Loire told his departmental council:

> Everything that escaped the spoliations of public monuments, the ruin of monasteries, the sale of property, [and] all the vicissitudes of our long revolutions; everything that we were able to save from...all these vast establishments that once covered our soil, has been collected [in our

---

[56] See above, footnote 6.
[57] Guizot, "Rapport au Roi," 27 Nov. 1834, pp. 13-14.

departmental depository]…; it is this precious debris, these priceless fragments…that I ask you to preserve religiously.[58]

The following year, Jules Ollivier made an even more dramatic plea in an article in the *Revue du Dauphiné*, claiming that while the Old Regime corporations had ensured the "continual transmission" of historical sources, all this had ended with the Reign of Terror:

'93 broke out: archivists, monks, municipal magistrates disappeared, and the work of so many centuries was swept away in an instant; so many historical treasures…dispersed, condemned, tossed to the flames and to the worms: brutally inept proscriptions that, trying to kill an undying past, deprived a great nation of the glory of its ancestors, to throw it naked and desolate into a future bereft of the prestige of its memories!

Like Guizot, Ollivier blamed the "administrative negligence" of succeeding governments for the persistence of this problem; he argued that those provincial collections not mutilated by worms and rodents in the post-revolutionary period were further harmed by "the prefects of the Empire and Restoration" who "took care not to preserve from a slow but infallible ruin the sad debris, that, according to their reasoning, was fit only to shut up in a cabinet."[59]

Such tales of destruction and dilapidation were not new; provincial officials of the early 1820s had also expressed their alarm at the "chaos" caused by the revolutionary seizure of books and manuscripts.[60] Why was the central government suddenly so eager to encourage these kinds of reports? The answer becomes clear when we consider the kinds of documents that could be found in France's provincial depositories. Most departmental archives in this period contained, among other materials, tax records, parish registers, municipal rulings, feudal documents—in short, the very sorts of materials appropriate to a history of the medieval bourgeoisie. Municipal libraries and literary depositories, too, though less well-documented for this period, undoubtedly contained personal and familial records as well as local literary and artistic treasures. As the Liberal regime looked for its own origins in the urban renaissance of the high Middle Ages,

---

[58] Vte. Bretign[ières?] de Courteille[s?], "Archives de la Préfecture," 1837, AD Indre-et-Loire, T 1627, folder "Rapports des commissions. 1837 et 1839," pp. [1]-2.

[59] Jules Ollivier, "De l'importance des recherches à faire sur l'histoire générale de la France et en particulier sur l'histoire du Dauphiné," *Revue du Dauphiné* 4 (1838): 70-73.

[60] See chap. 1.

it began to reclaim the dust-filled granaries and warehouses of the French countryside as "national property" requiring immediate attention.

This process of reclamation involved repeated public condemnations of revolutionary destruction and negligence; at the same time, however, it involved constant evocation of the revolutionary conception of national "patrimony." Under the Old Regime, "patrimony" had referred to the goods one inherited from one's father (*pater*). Yet as we saw earlier, the French Revolution transformed this idea in what can be seen as a series of three conceptual moves. First, the revolution redefined the "nation" as the ultimate sovereign body. Next, it declared ecclesiastical, royal, and noble possessions "national property." And finally, it argued that the nation had a collective responsibility to protect its new property, or "patrimony." This last claim, significantly, was not fully articulated until the radical phase of the revolution, when Grégoire developed the notion of a "common heritage" in conjunction with the concept of revolutionary "vandalism."[61] Much like Grégoire, Guizot and the other Liberal historians celebrated the early revolution's nationalization of corporate property while roundly condemning the radical revolution's disregard for this property. As Guizot explained to the king in 1833, the national government was the "guardian and trustee of this precious legacy of past centuries," and therefore had an obligation to recognize and protect it.[62]

Seen from the perspective of archives and libraries, however, the early July Monarchy's treatment of its patrimony involved far more recognition than it did protection. Recent histories of this period have undoubtedly been correct in crediting Guizot and friends with returning the subject of the nation's "heritage," including state-owned books and manuscripts, to the center of public discussion. The Historical Works Committee and the Ministry of Public Instruction sent out dozens of circulars reminding provincial officials and scholars of the national import of their local

---

[61] See the introduction. On the evolution of the term "patrimony," see André Chastel, "La notion de patrimoine," in *Les lieux de mémoire*, vol. 2, pt. 2, pp. 405-450; Dominique Poulot, "The birth of heritage: 'le moment Guizot'," *Oxford Art Journal* 11, no. 2 (1988): 40-56; as well as the introduction to Gerson, "Pays and nation."

[62] See above, footnote 55. Unlike the Liberal historians of the 1830s, however, Grégoire did not attack the radical revolution (of which he was a part) directly, choosing instead to associate the destruction of national property with enemies of France. An extended comparison of Grégoire's and Guizot's discussions of patrimony lies beyond the scope of this chapter, but certainly would merit scholarly attention.

collections.[63] The central government also incorporated libraries and archives into its new program of official inspections of historical monuments. In October 1830, despite the fact that the Restoration appointee Charles-Hyacinthe His was still technically the Inspector-General of Libraries and Literary Depositories, Guizot made Ludovic Vitet (and later Prosper Mérimée) Inspector-General of Historical Monuments, responsible for surveying not only buildings and sculptures but also libraries and archives.[64] By propagating the idea that so many piles of musty books and manuscripts were actually national "monuments" (from the Latin for "memorials"), the regime surely helped transform French conceptions of archives and libraries.

Yet even as the rearticulation of a national patrimony conferred a privileged status on these collections, the Orleanist leaders of the 1830s actually made little effort to preserve archival and library materials. We can see this in the way the regime made use of its new cadre of Archivist-Paleographers. Both Vitet and Michelet (who conducted several official inspections for the Ministry of Public Instruction even though he did not have the title of Inspector-General), recommended sending available *chartistes* to protect and maintain neglected provincial collections. For example, reporting on southwestern France, Michelet argued that while collections everywhere needed protection from fire, rain, and theft, the magnificent depositories in Bordeaux and Toulouse, at least, had "the right to get a student from the Ecole des Chartes."[65] Nevertheless, between 1829 and 1838, only two *chartistes* were assigned to head departmental depositories: Louis Redet, to the archives of the Vienne, and Claude Chelle,

[63] Some of these are reprinted in Charmes, *Le Comité*.

[64] Guizot, "Rapport présenté au Roi le 21 octobre 1830, par M. Guizot, ministre de l'intérieur, pour faire instituer un inspecteur général des monuments historiques en France," in Guizot, *Mémoires pour servir*, 2: 385-389. Some of the most useful recent works among the many on French monuments are: Dominique Poulot, "Alexandre Lenoir et les musées des Monuments français," and André Fermigier, "Mérimée et l'Inspection des monuments historiques," both in *Les lieux de mémoire*, vol. 2, pt. 2; the prefatory material accompanying the reedition of Prosper Mérimée and Ludovic Vitet, *La naissance des monuments historiques: la correspondance de Prosper Mérimée avec Ludovic Vitet (1840-1848)* (Paris: Comité des travaux historiques et scientifiques, 1998); and Daniel Sherman, *Worthy Monuments: Art Museums and the Politics of Culture in Nineteenth-Century France* (Cambridge: Harvard University Press, 1989).

[65] [Jules] Michelet, *Rapport au Ministre de l'Instruction Publique sur les bibliothèques et archives des départements du sud-ouest de la France (août-septembre 1835)* (Paris: Imprimerie de Ducessois, 1836), p. 18.

to the archives of the Rhône.[66] What is more, the government's official instructions to these two archivists make no mention of preservation.[67]

So what was the point of training Archivist-Paleographers, if not to preserve France's deteriorating collections from further ruin? The instructions given to Redet and Chelle in 1834 show that after making a preliminary assessment of their depositories, they were expected to accomplish two basic tasks. First, they were to create an inventory of the collection, noting each document on a separate card [*bulletin*] and making a copy of each card to send to the Minister in Paris. The instructions do not say how these cards should be prepared or organized, only that they ought "to include an indication of documents of interest for the history of the province or the kingdom." The second task was to send the Minister a "special catalogue of the manuscript works in all subjects, especially cartularies, feudal registers, cadastral surveys, old inventories of titles or libraries, [and] church and monastery treasures that can be found in the archives...."[68] While it is possible that such reports were intended to prepare the way for later preservation efforts, no inkling of that intention is provided here. Nor do the instructions make any mention of classification, which by the 1840s would be the primary focus for nearly all *chartistes*. Instead, the instructions show that Redet and Chelle's mission was to carefully examine their collections in order to inform the central government about the historical sources, and especially manuscript sources, that they contained.

This mission brings us to the heart of the Liberal historical project of the 1830s. Far more than classifying or preserving French archives and libraries,

---

[66] On Redet's appointment, see AN, box F2 I 378², folder "Archivistes départementaux. Tableaux du personnel"; on Chelle's, see AN, box F17-4052 and F17-4053, folder "Demandes de chartistes pour travaux d'inventaires et classements [dans?] les depts." Maximilien Quantin, a graduate of the Dijon Ecole des Chartes, became departmental archivist of the Yonne in April 1833; however, because he was neither an "Archivist-Paleographer" nor a central government appointee, I do not count him here. For a useful survey of the first *chartistes* in the departments, see Vincent Mollet, "Les chartistes dans les Archives départementales avant le décret de 1850," *BEC* 151 (1993): 123-154.

[67] "Copie des instructions données par M. le Ministre de l'instruction publique à l'élève de l'Ecole des Chartes nommé archiviste à Poitiers [i.e., Redet]," [1834], AD Isère, Fonds Champollion, microfilm reel 30. A note on this same reel says the same instructions were given to Chelle. Since Redet was appointed before the end of Guizot's term as Minister of Public Instruction in November 1834, these instructions probably came from Guizot himself.

[68] Ibid.

the early July Monarchy planned on mining them for historically useful documents. After reasserting its "patrimonial" claim to the materials confiscated during the Revolution, the national government hoped to cull from these materials a collection—a kind of "archive" in itself—of the most important and authentic documents in French history. We see this goal reflected in the Historical Works Committee project that occupied the majority of *chartistes* in the 1830s: the *Collection de documents inédits sur l'histoire de France* (Collection of original documents on the history of France). Now a fixture in most modern research libraries, this enormous compendium (some 200 volumes) went through its period of greatest growth under the July Monarchy, when Ecole des Chartes students and professors alike served as some of its most active contributors.[69]

We can best understand the scope and purpose of this massive publication by looking at some of the series that it contains. Perhaps the most wide-ranging of those produced during the July Monarchy was the *Documents historiques inédits tirés des collections manuscrites de la Bibliothèque Royale et des archives ou des bibliothèques des départements* (Original historical documents drawn from the manuscript collections of the Royal Library and the archives or libraries in the departments), begun in late 1834. As the Minister of Public Instruction, Salvandy, explained in 1837, each volume in this series contains two parts: first, "Rapports et notices," containing reports and inventories sent in by provincial correspondents or by *chartistes* on "mission" to particular depositories; and second, "Texte de documents," including "in chronological order, all the documents of a truly historical interest [*d'un intérêt réellement historique*] that come from [Committee] correspondence, work carried out at the Royal Library, or any other authentic source."[70]

The task of coordinating the elaborate process of gathering reports and selecting and copying "authentic" documents for this series fell to Ecole des Chartes professor and Royal Library manuscripts curator Jacques-Joseph Champollion-Figeac. Under his direction, the Manuscripts Department at the Royal Library became a beehive of paleographic activity, as a dozen young assistants, most of them *chartistes*, began reading and creating

---

[69] In *History as a Profession: The Study of History in France, 1818-1914*, p. 68, Pim den Boer calculates that between 1835 and 1852, "103 volumes had been published. After that the enthusiasm subsided: 37 volumes appeared in 1853-70; 44 in 1870-85, and 22 in 1886-1900."

[70] [Narcisse de] Salvandy, "Arrêté," 22 Jul. 1837, AN, box F17-3283, folder "Champollion-Figeac. 1ere série des Mélanges. Direction du dépouillement de manuscrits à la bibliothèque Royale, de 1835 à 1846," p. [2].

catalogue cards for the masses of manuscripts in the Library's collections. Progress was exceedingly slow; according to Champollion-Figeac, the Library contained roughly one million manuscripts, which he estimated it would take his team seventy years just to inventory.[71] With this daunting task in mind, he soon switched gears, assigning half of his workers to select documents for publication.[72] Unfortunately, the team left behind no formal rules for choosing publishable manuscripts, but if we look at the four volumes they eventually produced, we can see that they included a wide range of documents, from royal correspondence to the "Association between the commune of Agen and several other places in the county of Agenais." They also covered a remarkably broad chronological span, with the greatest number of documents coming from the thirteenth century.[73] Thus the work of the *chartiste* was no longer to decode royal charters but to read and evaluate a broad range of French historical sources.

At first glance, the *Documents inédits* series produced by the other Ecole des Chartes professor, Benjamin Guérard, seems far less in keeping with a Liberal vision of French historical development. In 1836, Guérard began editing a set of cartularies (registers containing copies of charters) and by his death in 1854 had prepared for publication the cartularies of four major ecclesiastical institutions, including Notre-Dame de Paris.[74] The idea of publishing yet another collection of charters, and particularly a collection of ecclesiastical charters, seems more in line with the work of the Maurists than with that of the early Orleanists. However, the proposal Guérard sent to the Minister of Public Instruction in December 1836 reveals that he saw these sources through distinctly Liberal lenses. Here Guérard argues that a cartulary begun in the early Middle Ages would offer "a faithful image of the institutions, customs, and practices of the French nation in all periods."

---

[71] Jacques-Joseph Champollion-Figeac, preface to *Documents historiques inédits tirés des collections manuscrites de la Bibliothèque Royale et des archives ou des bibliothèques des départements* (Paris: Firmin Didot, 1841), 1: iv. See also Charles-Olivier Carbonell, *L'autre Champollion: Jacques-Joseph Champollion-Figeac (1778-1867)* (Toulouse: Presses de l'Institut d'études politiques de Toulouse et l'Asiathèque, 1970), pp. 225-236.

[72] Champollion-Figeac to Monsieur le Ministre, Paris, 15 Oct. 1835, in his *Documents historiques*, 1: x.

[73] Champollion-Figeac, *Documents historiques*.

[74] The *Cartulaire de l'abbaye de Saint-Père de Chartres* (2 vols., 1840), the *Cartulaire de l'abbaye de Saint-Bertin* (1 vol., 1840), the *Cartulaire de l'église Notre Dame de Paris* (4 vols., 1850), and the *Cartulaire de l'abbaye de Saint-Victor de Marseille* (2 vols., published posthumously in 1857).

Thus by studying the contents of such a cartulary, one could trace the development of the nation from "servitude" to "sovereignty":

> In [a cartulary] one follows step by step the progress of modern civilization:...First man is a slave and possesses only his life, then he passes to the state of colonist or farmer; then he is a property owner, and having become his master he rises to the government of the commune and of the province, and does not stop until he gets to the government of the State: beginning in servitude he ends with sovereignty.[75]

Cartularies, then, were crucial sources not for the history of French monarchs but for the history of the French "nation," now at the height of its sovereign powers.

How did the cartularies of churches and abbeys fit into this conception of French history? If one looks beyond the title pages of Guérard's cartularies to the documents and commentary he includes, it becomes clear that he was not only or even especially interested in the inner workings of Church institutions. For example, the 277-page preface to the *Cartulaire de l'abbaye de Saint-Père de Chartres* allots only thirty pages to the abbey itself, devoting the remaining 247 to such topics as "Property," "Coins," "Measures," "Arts and Crafts," and "Feudal Laws." Guérard uses the documents contained in the abbey's cartulary to produce a kind of social history of medieval Chartres, ranging from the development of surnames to the impact of wars.[76] Moreover, Guérard's proposal suggests that he never meant to limit his "Cartularies of France" series to ecclesiastical collections alone. His plan gives as much attention to civil cartularies (i.e., those maintained by "general, provincial, or communal institutions") as to ecclesiastical ones and implies that both are useful for "geography, chronology, and general history" as well as for "the history of localities."[77]

Guérard acknowledged that his approach to French charters set his project apart from the Old Regime collections maintained by the Academy of Inscriptions. He pointed out that while Academy publications like the *Table chronologique* and the *Recueil des historiens de la France* printed charters in chronological order, it was much more useful and efficient to publish entire cartularies. Instead of having to "see everything, collect everything, and classify everything" from a particular period before producing a new volume

---

[75] [Benjamin Guérard], "Note relative à la publication des Cartulaires de France," [15 Dec. 1836], AN, box F17-3263, folder "Cartulaires de France...," p. [5].
[76] [Benjamin Guérard], "Prolégomènes," *Cartulaire de l'abbaye de Saint-Père de Chartres* (Paris: Imprimerie de Crapelet, 1840), 1: v-cclxxxii.
[77] Ibid., pp. [3-4].

of charters, one could simply copy all the documents from a single cartulary and print them as they appeared. This approach would also allow historians to study the evolution of institutions and practices in particular locations rather than by period alone.[78] Interestingly, Guérard did not point out another potential advantage of his approach. Since cartularies only contain copies of charters received by a particular individual or institution rather than issued by them, Guérard's "Cartularies of France" project meant organizing French charters according to their recipients rather than their authors.[79] A charter granted by the king to a town would thus appear in the volume containing that town's cartulary, not among the charters issued by the same king in the same period. This organizational approach seems remarkably consonant with the aims of the Charter of 1830, which reversed the emphasis of the Charter of 1814 by shifting attention away from the king as grantor of legal concessions and toward the French people as the recipients of political rights. Whereas chronological series of royal charters had been well-suited to the defense of the first monarchy by charter, the publication of entire cartularies was more appropriate to the defense of its successor.[80]

If Guérard limited discussion of the contemporary political implications of his *Documents inédits* work to rather general remarks about the transition from servitude to sovereignty, his more famous colleague, Augustin Thierry, made the connection between medieval manuscripts and Orleanist politics much more explicit. In 1836, Thierry began work on his own contribution to the *Documents inédits* series, the *Recueil des monuments inédits de l'histoire du tiers état* (Collection of original monuments on the history of the third estate). He believed that this new collection would do for the Third Estate what the great Old Regime compendia had done for the first two.[81] Instead of

---

[78] Ibid., pp. [5-6].

[79] On the distinction between a cartulary, which contains charters received by a particular body, and a register, which contains charters issued by that body, see James J. John, "Cartulary," in *Dictionary of the Middle Ages*, ed. Joseph R. Strayer (New York: Charles Scribner's Sons, 1983), 3: 120.

[80] Guérard's approach to the publication of cartularies can also be read as an early articulation of the late Orleanist principle of *respect des fonds* (respect for the collections), according to which all archival documents were to be arranged in their "original" order. For a fuller discussion of this principle, see chap. 3.

[81] Augustin Thierry, "Avant-propos," *Recueil des monuments inédits de l'histoire du tiers état* (Paris: Firmin Didot, 1850), 1: [v]. The best overview of this project is Robert-Henri Bautier, "Le recueil des monuments de l'histoire du tiers état et l'utilisation

collecting documents that emphasized the power of the nobility and clergy, his project would assemble four new sets of sources: first, documents on the "condition of towns, boroughs, and parishes in the former French kingdom," such as communal charters and municipal laws; second, sources on the "condition of the bourgeoisie in its various corporations," such as guild statutes; third, materials related to the "convocation and proceedings of the provincial estates and estates general"; and finally, sources revealing "the condition of the common people [personnes roturières]."[82] Thierry soon set these last two sets of sources aside, however, opting to focus on what he saw as the central theme in French history: the "bourgeois struggle," first against feudalism and then against absolutism. In his view, the story of the bourgeois "revolutions" of the twelfth and thirteenth centuries was the story of modern France. As he explained in his introduction to the Recueil: "Here we are at the origins of the social world of modern times; it is in the liberated, or rather, regenerated towns that appears, in a great variety of forms, more or less free, more or less perfect, the first manifestations of its character."[83] More to the point, the story of the bourgeoisie was the story of the Orleanist regime. In Thierry's view, his task was "to collect and assemble in a single corpus all the authentic documents on the history of these families [who were] without names, but not without glory, from which have come the men who made the revolution of 1789 and that of 1830."[84]

It is difficult to imagine how Thierry was able to develop such a corpus when one considers that by the mid-1830s, he was completely blind. He managed to overcome this physical failing by hiring a team of assistants, mostly students or recent graduates of the Ecole des Chartes. Under the strict supervision of Martial Delpit (class of 1837), these young men became, as Thierry put it, his "eyes," inventorying, deciphering, and transcribing documents and then reading them aloud for his approval.[85] They began their work in Paris, toiling alongside Champollion-Figeac's assistants on the

---

des matériaux réunis par Augustin Thierry," *Annuaire-bulletin de la Société de l'histoire de France* (1944): 89-118.

[82] Augustin Thierry, "Rapport," 10 Mar. 1837, in *Rapports au Ministre. Collection de documents inédits sur l'histoire de France publiés par l'ordre du Roi et par les soins du Ministre de l'instruction publique* (Paris: Imprimerie royale, 1839), pp. 2-3.

[83] Thierry, "Introduction," *Recueil des monuments*, 1: XXIV.

[84] Thierry, "Rapport," 10 Mar. 1837, p. 13. See also A. Augustin-Thierry, *Augustin Thierry (1795-1856) d'après sa correspondance et ses papiers de famille* (Paris: Plon, 1922), p. 149.

[85] Thierry, "Rapport," 6 May 1838, in *Rapports au Ministre*, p. 24.

Royal Library's *Cabinet des Chartes* and in the company of still more *chartistes* on the Royal Archives' *Trésor des Chartes*. Yet while Thierry admired these Parisian collections for their "incontestable authenticity," he nevertheless maintained that "the largest portion of the documents that must be included in the great *recueil*…are still buried in provincial archives."[86] His *chartistes* therefore soon embarked on a series of "missions" to departmental collections, where they "unearthed" such sources as the municipal statutes of Périgueux and minutes of the meetings of the Estates of Languedoc.[87] At the same time, they maintained a huge network of provincial correspondents eager to contribute their local treasures. While this enormous expenditure of scholarly labor generated tens of thousands of *bulletins*, translations, and transcriptions of documents, only a fraction of these (mostly on the town of Amiens) were actually published. The rest, largely abandoned by Thierry after the Liberal defeat of 1848, have sat ever since in the Manuscripts Department of the Bibliothèque Nationale, dusty testament to the archiving impulses of the July Monarchy.[88]

A number of scholars have seen the work of Liberal historians like Thierry and Guizot during the early July Monarchy as evidence of a long-anticipated merger between "erudition" and "philosophy." According to

---

[86] Ibid., p. 23, and his 10 Mar. 1837 "Rapport," p. 6.

[87] Martial Delpit, "Département de la Dordogne. Premier rapport de M. Martial Delpit à M. le Ministre de l'Instruction publique. Novembre 1838," in Champollion-Figeac, *Documents historiques*, p. 98; and Louis de Mas Latrie to Monsieur le Ministre [de l'Instruction publique], Paris, 10 Feb. 1839, AN, box F17-3283, folder on Mas Latrie, pp. [2-4].

[88] Though I cannot discuss them all here, other *Documents inédits* projects from this period to which the school's students contributed include Claude Fauriel's *Histoire de la croisade contre les hérétiques Albigeois*; Arthur Auguste Beugnot's *Olim, ou registres des arrêts rendus par la Cour du roi sous les règnes de saint Louis - Philippe le Long*; Berger de Xivrey's *Recueil des lettres missives de Henri IV*; and Jules Michelet's *Procès des Templiers*. Besides serving as assistants on such projects, *chartistes* also made individual contributions to the series. For instance, before dying of consumption at the age of thirty-two, Hercule Géraud (class of 1839) worked on three different *Documents inédits* projects and published a volume of his own, *Paris sous Philippe-le-Bel* (Paris: Imprimerie de Crapelet, 1837). Though far more modest in scale than many of the publications in the series, the volume nevertheless expresses the same enthusiasm for the urban culture of the High Middle Ages, providing a transcription of the Royal Library's copy of the Paris tax roll of 1292 along with an extended discussion of the manuscript's usefulness for the study of geography, architecture, population, commerce, and industry in this period of "greatness" in the city's development.

this argument, between roughly the late seventeenth century and the early nineteenth, historical work was either "erudite" (based on "original" documents, often with little accompanying description or commentary) or "philosophical" (based on secondary texts, with an emphasis on narrative or theoretical structure). In the period 1820-1830, however, the Liberal historians forced the "marriage" of these two historiographical approaches, creating the kind of document-based narrative history that would reach its apogee under the Third Republic.[89] While this argument may apply to the commercially-published work of individual historians (Thierry, Mignet, etc.), it is perhaps less appropriate to the state-published histories like the *Documents inédits* series we just examined. Unlike the historical monographs published in the early 1830s, which often wove documentary references into a running narrative, the historical series produced by the French government in this same period kept documents and commentary physically separate, leaving primary source transcriptions intact inside a kind of envelope of introductory matter, tables, and appendices. In the pages of these volumes, then, "erudite" sources and "philosophical" description were not so much merged as simply juxtaposed.[90]

Why was this the case? Why did Champollion-Figeac, Guérard, Thierry, and the other leaders of the *Documents inédits* project not try to incorporate the sources they found in French libraries and archives into a more readable narrative? One answer to this question is that to have done so would have been to rob these sources of their political potency. As we have seen, the Orleanist regime—neither sanctified by divine authority nor supported by popular mandate—was desperately in need of a convincing source of legitimacy. "Original documents" culled from the supposedly untouched depositories of the French provinces appeared to provide this legitimating power; duly authenticated by the new corps of *chartistes*, they gave seemingly infallible proof of the political destiny of the French bourgeoisie. To have

---

[89] See especially Chantal Grell, *L'histoire entre érudition et philosophie: étude sur la connaissance historique à l'age des lumières* (Paris: Presses universitaires de France, 1993) and, on the earlier period, Blandine Barret-Kriegel, *La défaite de l'érudition* (Paris: Presses universitaires de France, 1988). The term "marriage" comes from Marcel Gauchet, "Les Lettres sur l'histoire de France d'Augustin Thierry," in *Les lieux de mémoire*, vol. 2, pt. 1, p. 280. For a countervailing view of eighteenth-century historical practices, see Lionel Gossman, *Medievalism and the Ideologies of the Enlightenment: The World and Work of La Curne de Sainte-Palaye* (Baltimore: The Johns Hopkins Press, 1968).

[90] See also Gerson, "Pays and nation," pp. 269-272.

divided these testaments to Liberal authority into a multitude of quotations and footnotes would therefore have been to diminish their legitimating force.

Yet there is also another answer to the question. If the editors of the *Documents inédits* did not weave these sources into a readable narrative, it was undoubtedly in part because the series was not really meant to be "readable." Rare is the volume that does not require either a strong background in medieval history or a firm grasp of Latin, or both. Guérard's *Cartulaires*, for example, provide transcriptions but not translations of his Latin sources, while Champollion-Figeac's *Documents historiques* intersperse municipal rulings, tax laws, and royal correspondence without providing any unifying commentary. Thus although Guizot believed that historical understanding would unify the nation, causing French people everywhere to respect and embrace the views of their countrymen, the form and content of his great historical publications suggest that he intended for the transmission of this understanding to be largely indirect. In Guizot's system, politicians and historians (or, in many cases, politician-historians), the elite cadre of the new regime, would be able to refer to the *Documents inédits* as to a sacred text as they told and retold the history of France. Promoting the publication of historical documents, it seems, was not necessarily about making these documents directly accessible to the French public.

Descriptions of state-owned archives and libraries from the early 1830s tend to confirm this conclusion. Reports filed by section heads at the Royal Archives show that the largest of French archival collections received only a trickle of visitors, most of them prominent Parisian scholars. For example, Michelet's monthly reports as head of the Archives' Historical Section rarely mention more than three or four visitors, usually members of the Academy or the Historical Works Committee. Since the Archives had no public reading room, these researchers had to consult their materials in his office or in neighboring workrooms.[91] The records of provincial archives, for their part, mention no visitors at all. Though it seems likely that members of the scholarly societies so favored by Guizot made occasional visits to their local depositories, the extant reports do not discuss research requests, reading

---

[91] Michelet's reports are in AN, box AB IX 1. On his work as head of the Historical Section, see Bernard Mahieu, "Michelet aux Archives nationales," *Annuaire-Bulletin de la Société de l'histoire de France* (1946-47): 71-86; his "Les inventaires d'archives selon Michelet," *Gazette des archives* 16 (1954): 16-22; and Félix Rocquain, "Les travaux de Michelet aux Archives nationales," *Notes et fragments d'histoire* (Paris: Plon, 1906), pp. 61-92. The first public reading room at the Royal Archives opened in 1842.

rooms, or public hours.[92] More important, the numerous circulars, decrees, and instructions emitted by the central government in this period make no provisions whatsoever for direct public access to provincial archives. They repeatedly urge provincial scholars to send copies of municipal "treasures," but never recommend that such treasures be shared with local residents.

The Liberal government's shyness about opening its collections to the reading public becomes even more apparent when we look at public libraries. Most historians of French libraries present the early years of the July Monarchy as a kind of heroic age, when forward-thinking Paris politicians began awakening provincial officials to the moral and intellectual benefits of public libraries. For example, Graham Keith Barnett, author of a lengthy study of public libraries in modern France, argues that Guizot and his ministerial successors worked hard to promote "new ideas" about public libraries but had to struggle "against a strong conservative tradition, going back to the monastic libraries with their chained books."[93] In this account, though Orleanist leaders tried to open France's long-abandoned libraries to the general public, protective local officials refused to cooperate with their efforts. In fact, the new government's attitude toward its library-going public was rather more complex.

It is certainly true that the 1830s witnessed a surge of interest in public libraries. Perhaps in part due to the expansion of both the publishing industry and the demand for books (consider, for example, the rise of *cabinets de lecture,* or commercial lending libraries, in this period), public libraries suddenly became the focus of a number of treatises and reports.[94] Scholars,

---

[92] Based on an examination of records of seven departmental archives (Allier, Aube, Indre-et-Loire, Lot-et-Garonne, Maine-et-Loire, Nièvre, and Seine-et-Oise), both in the National Archives and in the departments themselves.

[93] Graham Keith Barnett, *Histoire des bibliothèques publiques en France de la Révolution à 1939* (Paris: Promodis, 1987), p. 125. For a similar account, see Pierre Casselle, "Les pouvoirs publics et les bibliothèques," in *Histoire des bibliothèques françaises* (Paris: Promodis, 1991), 3: 109-117.

[94] The rapid expansion of the publishing industry and of the reading public certainly predated the 1830 revolution, but with the exception of the articles produced by Buchon in 1829 (see above, footnote 36), discussions of public libraries seem not to have emerged in force until the 1830s. On the complex relationship between literacy and reading, see James Smith Allen, *In the Public Eye: A History of Reading in Modern France, 1800-1940* (Princeton, NJ: Princeton University Press, 1991). On *cabinets de lecture,* see his article, "The Cabinets de Lecture in Paris, 1800-1850," *Journal of Library History* 16, no. 1 (1981): 199-209; and François Parent-

librarians, politicians, and even publishers all began touting the glories of public reading and calling for the reform of state-owned collections. In particular, they called for public libraries to adapt themselves to the needs of modern readers. For example, after an 1831 inspection tour of public libraries in five northern departments, Ludovic Vitet declared:

> [I]n [the government's] hands, libraries can become a powerful means of instruction ...Until now, they have been abandoned and have gradually become like warehouses of unfashionable merchandise,without consumers. We must bring them back to life by connecting them with the present.[95]

Connecting libraries to the present, for Vitet, meant both promoting the contemporary relevance of existing collections and expanding the collections to include books in new fields:

> [We must] establish...a relationship between the old library books that no one thinks about and the current things that everyone is eager for. Too often theology alone is appropriately represented in these heaps of books, gathered from the monasteries and clerical institutions, while the exact sciences, history, geography, statistics, etc., barely appear in the catalogues.[96]

In 1837, Henri Ternaux-Compans made a similar case in a report on the public libraries of Paris. He argued that although the "utility of public libraries" was "generally recognized," the main Parisian collections were in need not of "a reform, but a complete reorganization."[97] The Bibliothèque Mazarine, renowned as the oldest public library in France, was so outdated that it was "becoming useless to the majority of its readers," while the Bibliothèque de l'Arsenal, despite its many rich collections, offered little to instruct the "youth of the Marais."[98] Public libraries, in short, had to become more public.

However, catering to the greater reading public also had its dangers. Many of the new treatises on public libraries vacillated between calling for greater publicity and cautioning against its pernicious effects. François-

---

Lardeur, *Les cabinets de lecture: la lecture publique à Paris sous la Restauration* (Paris: Payot, 1982).

[95] L[udovic] Vitet, *Rapport à M. le ministre de l'intérieur sur les monumens, les bibliothèques, les archives, et les musées des départemens* [sic] *de l'Oise, de l'Aisne, de la Marne, du Nord et du Pas-de-Calais* (Paris: Imprimerie royale, 1831), p. 71.

[96] Ibid., p. 73.

[97] H[enri] Ternaux-Compans, *Lettre à M. le Ministre de l'Instruction publique, sur l'état actuel des bibliothèques publiques de Paris...*(Paris: Delaunay, 1837), pp. 5-6.

[98] Ibid., pp. 8-9 and 14-15.

Marie Foisy's manual on public library management, for instance, advised library employees to "provide the public with the most complete enjoyment of the library by anticipating its desires" for new and interesting books, yet devoted nearly half its space to instructions on how to discipline this same public.[99] Foisy claimed that most public libraries faced the same set of problems:

1) The librarian's office invaded on crowded days by a tumultuous public....
2) Disorder in catalogue searches.
3) Expectant readers rummaging unnoticed among the returned books.
4) The catalogue at first up for pillage, then more or less thrown aside.
5) Pell-mell comings and goings, hence an increase in noisy tremors.
6) Books not returned properly.
7) Possibility of robbing the library, without being seen by anyone.

In order to prevent such ills, Foisy argued, "the public must take care of the books, [and] one must keep an eye on the public."[100]

In "Paris Public Libraries in 1831," published in 1836, the outspoken bibliophile Paul Lacroix made a similar claim. While maintaining that no library should require an "attestation of capacity" from its readers ("genius," he said, had always appeared among those with holes in their sleeves), he expressed his horror at the "swarm of readers" in Parisian collections.[101] "It seems certain," he wrote, "that the reading multitude that flocks to the Rue de Richelieu [home of the Royal Library] is lacking in studious types: laziness and insouciance bring in these homeless loafers and *flaneurs* who delight in the Pirates' Adventures and the Causes Célèbres." Even worse, the flood of the "curious" was fast depleting the Library's once-rich collections: "Unique editions have disappeared, pages have been cut, engravings stolen, autographs torn out; people have dared to mutilate priceless manuscripts in order to remove the miniatures!"[102] Interestingly, Lacroix blamed these losses on the collection's status as national "patrimony." Since "this great, free lending library is considered patrimonial property," "it is enough to be an academician or the cousin of a

---

[99] F[rançois]-M[arie] Foisy, *Sommaire d'un opuscule intitulé: Essai théorique et pratique sur la conservation des bibliothèques publiques* (Paris: Typographie de Lachevardière, [1833]), p. [30].
[100] Ibid., pp. [12-14].
[101] Paul Lacroix Jacob, "Les bibliothèques publiques de Paris en 1831," in *Mon Grand Fauteuil* (Paris: E. Renduel, 1836), 2: 195-196.
[102] Ibid., p. 199.

cousin of an academy doorman" to obtain borrowing privileges and thus make off—perhaps forever—with the library's treasures.[103]

By far the most striking argument for the supervision of the library-going public, however, appeared in philanthropist Benjamin Delessert's *Mémoire sur la Bibliothèque Royale* of 1835. Drawing implicitly on the work of the English philosopher Jeremy Bentham, Delessert called for the construction of a new "panoptic" reading room for the Royal Library. As he explained in the text and in an accompanying floor plan, Delessert envisioned a large, circular room in which aisles of bookshelves would converge, much like the spokes of a wheel, on a central librarians' station. Though Delessert believed that this layout would make the provision of library "service" "easy and convenient," he placed particular emphasis on how it would facilitate "surveillance." From the center of the room, library personnel would be able keep watch on all of the books—and all of the readers—at the same time:

> One can easily see...that this surveillance will be complete, since the library head or librarian in charge, installed in the middle of the rotunda, will see at a glance the far ends of the all the galleries, and all the people that are circulating through them.[104]

According to Delessert's vision, then, the French public would be welcome to explore the library's collections for themselves, but only under the constant supervision of library officials.

State policies on public libraries in this period reflect the same kind of ambivalence toward the reading public, though this ambivalence is rarely so explicit. Like Vitet and Ternaux-Compans, Guizot and his fellow ministers proclaimed their support for public library reform. In an oft-cited November 1833 circular to departmental prefects, Guizot explained:

---

[103] Ibid., pp. 185-187.

[104] B[enjamin] Delessert, *Mémoire sur la Bibliothèque royale, ou l'on indique les mesures à prendre pour la transférer dans un bâtiment circulaire d'une forme nouvelle, qui serait construit au centre de la place du Carrousel* (Paris: Imprimerie de Henri Dupuy, 1835). The passage quoted is from p. 4. Though Delessert's plan was not adopted by the Royal Library, we can see echoes of his work in the circular reading rooms of the British Library (completed 1857) and the Library of Congress (completed 1897). See also Jean-François Foucaud, "Extensions et travaux de la Bibliothèque nationale," in *Histoire des bibliothèques françaises*, 3: 340-341. On the panopticon as a means of extending the state's disciplinary control over its citizens, see Michel Foucault, *Discipline and Punish: The Birth of the Prison*, trans. Alan Sheridan (New York: Vintage, 1979), pp. 200-228; originally published as *Surveiller et punir: naissance de la prison* (Paris: Gallimard, 1975).

> The public libraries in the departments have been for forty years in a situation that one might call provisional: created, in general, by accident, ...[these] precious but still incoherent collections of works of all kinds, once piled up in monasteries and transported pell-mell to every district in the department, these are quite often depositories of books rather than libraries.

> This state of affairs must end. I intend to take or to provoke measures that will allow me to revive [*vivifier*] these establishments and to make them into a powerful means of instruction, not only by coordinating their riches, but by increasing them, and especially by adapting them to the special needs of the populations.[105]

A series of government decisions gave substance to Guizot's plan. The early 1830s saw the appointment of a commission on Paris public libraries as well as the opening of a new Royal Library reading room, whose unrestricted access policy was soon attracting more than 500 readers a day.[106] Then in late 1830s, Guizot's successor at the Ministry of Public Instruction issued a number of new programs, including general inspections of public libraries, a public library office, and a system of book exchanges among libraries. The culmination of all of these measures was the royal ordinance of February 1839, the first major French law on public libraries since the turn of the century.[107]

However, with the exception of the new Royal Library reading room, these measures did not work to connect the French public with its "patrimonial" collections. As the Minister of Public Instruction himself acknowledged, the Paris libraries commission proved unable to carry out its recommendations.[108] The new Inspector-General of Public Libraries, historian Félix Ravaisson, concentrated on locating and preserving

---

[105] [François] Guizot, "Circulaire," Nov. 1833, in *Rapports au Roi*, p. 45.

[106] Cte d'Argout (Ministre Secrétaire d'Etat au Département du Commerce & des Travaux publics), "Arrêté," 15 Aug. 1831; and Jean-François Foucaud, *La Bibliothèque Royale sous la monarchie de juillet (1830-1848)* (Paris: Bibliothèque Nationale, 1978), p. 123.

[107] See Casselle, "Les pouvoirs publics," pp. 110-111, as well as Barnett, *Histoire des bibliothèques*, chap. 3.

[108] [Narcisse de] Salvandy, "Rapport au Roi concernant l'organisation des bibliothèques publiques," in Ulysse Robert, *Recueil de lois, décrets, ordonnances, arrêtés, circulaires, etc. concernant les bibliothèques publiques, communales, universitaires, scolaires et populaires...*(Paris: H. Champion, 1883), p. 50.

"original" documents, not on opening libraries to the public.[109] And finally, the famous 1839 law, in which one might expect to find idealistic evocations of the French public, never discussed how public libraries ought to be used, only how they ought to be managed. The bulk of the ordinance's provisions had to do with changes in the personnel structure of the Royal Library, long resistant to ministerial control, and in that of the large Paris libraries. The few articles related to provincial libraries made no mention of library readers, noting only that town mayors should send in catalogues of their local collections and set up municipal "inspection" committees as soon as possible.[110]

It will come as no surprise, then, that although the 1829 ordinance giving half of all public library positions to Archivist-Paleographers remained on the books throughout the July Monarchy, not a single graduate of the new Ecole des Chartes was appointed as a public librarian in the 1830s. At least a dozen *chartistes* worked at the Royal Library (and occasionally also in provincial libraries), but as employees and emissaries of the Historical Works Committee, not as librarians. In fact, the only graduate of the school hired as a regular library employee in this period worked for the Institut Library, which was open only to Academy members.[111]

Thus contrary to many histories of French libraries, the 1830 revolution did not mark the beginnings of a great government campaign to open the nation's libraries to the reading public. The new rulings on public libraries made few overtures to provincial collections, leaving them largely to local control. What is more, provincial officials were not necessarily the stubbornly "conservative" administrators Barnett and others make them out to be; indeed, these local officials were sometimes among the most radical of library reformers. For example, in his rather innocuously titled *Notice sur la bibliothèque publique de Chalon-sur-Saône* (Note on the public library of Chalon-sur-Saône), published in 1834, Aimé Baune berates Guizot for his lack of

---

[109] See for example Ravaisson, *Rapports au Ministre de l'Instruction Publique sur les bibliothèques des départements de l'ouest, suivis de pièces inédites* (Paris: Joubert, 1841).

[110] Louis-Philippe and [Narcisse de] Salvandy, "Ordonnance du Roi concernant l'organisation des bibliothèques publiques," in Robert, *Recueil de lois*, pp. 57-66. On the long battle between the Ministry and the Royal Library's ruling conservatoire, see Foucaud, *La Bibliothèque*, chap. 1.

[111] See Henri-Jean Martin, "Les chartistes et les bibliothèques," *Bulletin des bibliothèques de France* (1972): 529-537. On individual *chartistes*, see my chap. 1, footnote 72.

attention to public libraries. While Guizot had once planned to open these libraries to everyone,

> Today, M. Guizot is a minister, occupied with the improvisation of his speeches to future parliaments, the transformation of conscientious jurors into obliging judges, the task of washing our cities of the blood with which the government has stained them, the creation of new political prisons…How would he allot a single minute to our libraries?[112]

In Baune's view, public libraries needed to serve not only "professional scholars" but the "people," especially workers [*la classe ouvrière*] and women (library access, he claimed, would promote "women's liberty"). Yet instead of forcing libraries to address these groups, Guizot had simply sent out more and more circulars, for Baune proof that "the library question has never been a serious one for our political leaders" and that the government had only wanted to "make a display of its solicitude for the world of letters," in order to "distract its opponents [*amuser le tapis*]."[113] The new government's public libraries, in other words, were never intended to be "popular."[114]

Why was the early July Monarchy so ambivalent about public access to libraries and archives yet so enthusiastic about making the contents of these collections the very basis of French national identity? The new regime's treatment of libraries and archives—prefigured, as we have seen, by the policies of the late Restoration—suggests that it had not yet worked out the relationship between the "nation" and the "public." The first French Revolution had attempted to fuse these two concepts, expanding the limits of the "nation" and borrowing the authority of the "public" in order that the government might speak for both. While the Bourbon Restoration avoided these two terms (preferring instead the *patrie* or the "state"), the 1830 regime, eager to continue what it saw as the unfinished work of the 1790s, revived the language of the "nation" and the "public." Promoting the first of these terms in the 1830s proved relatively easy. The great campaign to rescue the nation's "patrimony" met with tremendous support, never encountering charges that it was insufficiently "national." Indeed, the concept of the "nation" in this period seemed to have a kind of centripetal force, pulling the French in toward a common core. All the government had to do was define this core by creating a pure, authentic source of national

---

[112] Aimé Baune, *Notice sur la bibliothèque publique de Chalon-sur Saône* (Chalon-sur-Saône: J. Ducresne, June 1834), p. 10.

[113] Ibid., p. 9.

[114] On later discussions of "popular libraries," see chap. 5.

history: the "archive" of *Documents inédits*. However, invoking the "public" proved far more difficult. If the "nation" was centripetal, the "public" was centrifugal, capable of infinite expansion. By opening up archives and libraries to the "public," the regime would be opening up the possibility of multiple uses and, perhaps more important, multiple interpretations of historical materials. The "people," so quickly rejected in the wake of the July revolution, might extract its own archive from these collections and thus rob the Liberal regime of its monopoly on national history. The "public," in other words, was potentially damaging to the "nation."

During the second half of the July Monarchy (ca.1838-1848), the government's mistrust of library and archival "public" remained largely unchanged. Yet as the Orleanist regime entered its second decade, it began to develop new ways of approaching the "nation" and national history. No longer content simply to study and organize selections from French libraries and archives as representative of the nation's history, the central government began to study and organize the libraries and archives themselves with an eye to how they might serve the production of national history. That is, instead of working to publish individual historical documents, the late Orleanist regime—with its expanding corps of *chartists*—began to classify entire collections. It is to these projects that we now turn.

Chapter Three

Putting the Past in Order: Archival Classification and the Ecole des Chartes in the late July Monarchy

In 1838, François Morand, archivist for the town of Boulogne-sur-Mer and official correspondent of the Historical Works Committee, fired off a series of letters to Augustin Thierry, editor of the Committee's much-anticipated *Recueil des monuments inédits de l'histoire du Tiers Etat*. Morand warned Thierry that his great *Recueil*, intended as the definitive collection of French municipal documents, already contained serious gaps. Though Thierry and his team of *chartistes* had spent years exploring France's historical collections, they had overlooked enormous caches of medieval sources. The problem was not that Thierry and his assistants were incompetent researchers, Morand explained, but rather that provincial archives—by far the richest depositories of municipal records—were so "chaotic" as to be practically impenetrable. Foolishly defying the "logical order" of operations, the Guizot government had begun dispatching researchers to these collections without making any effort to organize them first. Therefore, Morand argued, if Thierry wanted his *Recueil* to be complete, he would convince his powerful Parisian friends to impose a single standard of organization on all provincial archives. In Morand's view, this program would be two-fold: first, each depository would be assigned its own permanent archivist. Second, each archivist would classify his entire collection, taking care to separate the "public" archives (which Morand described as documents produced before 1789) from the "secret" archives (produced after 1789). By rigorously applying such a standard, he claimed, the government would not only greatly facilitate the work of historians of the Old Regime, like Thierry, but also protect the populace against the "revolutionary passions" of the post-1789 era.[1]

---

[1] François Morand, *Lettres à Augustin Thierry et autres documents relatifs à un projet de Constitution des Archives communales, proposée en 1838 et années suivantes...*(Paris: J.-B. Dumoulin, 1877), pp. 2, 12, and 6. The letters are dated 24 Jul. 1838, Nov. 1838, and Mar. 1839. On Thierry's *Recueil*, see chap. 2.

Preparing to publish his letters to Thierry in 1877, Morand maintained that they had had no impact whatsoever on official policy. Thierry, seemingly "annoyed" by Morand's requests, had referred him to the Historical Works Committee, which in turn had passed him along to the Chamber of Deputies and later the Minister of the Interior, all to no avail.[2] Nevertheless (as Morand himself was doubtlessly aware, or he would not have published his letters), his plan for the reorganization of provincial archives proved remarkably prescient. Between 1839 and 1841, the French state began shifting its attention away from locating and publishing key historical sources to cataloguing and classifying entire collections. While the Historical Works Committee continued to produce new compilations of medieval documents, it did so with considerably less fervor and efficiency than in the mid-1830s.[3] Now instead of employing *archivistes-paléographes* as Committee researchers, the government began appointing them as departmental archivists, charged with the classification and inventory of local collections. At the same time, it developed an elaborate new classification scheme for departmental archives, a scheme which, like that envisioned by Morand, made special provisions for revolutionary materials. Thus as the July Monarchy entered its second decade, it became less preoccupied with extracting its own "archive" from state-owned depositories than with forming these seemingly inchoate masses of documents into "orderly" collections.

The new preoccupation with cataloguing and classification seems to have affected a whole range of public collections, including libraries. In March 1839, for example, the Royal Library received an infusion of government money to complete its public catalogues, long a source of frustration and complaint.[4] The Library's first catalogue of printed books, developed by Nicolas Clément in the 1680s, had already become seriously outdated by the 1790s, when the influx of revolutionary confiscations brought cataloguing efforts nearly to a standstill. Instead of creating new catalogues, overwhelmed librarians had simply combined the confiscated

---

[2] Morand, *Lettres*, p. vii.

[3] The first issue of the *Bibliothèque de l'Ecole des Chartes* (1839-40), for example, warned against suspending Claude Fauriel's *Histoire des Albigeois*, a key Committee project, saying that such a move would only further the widespread perception that the *Documents inédits* series was "unraveling" (in the anonymous "Chronique" section, p. 216).

[4] Paulin Paris, *De la Bibliothèque Royale et de la nécessité de commencer, achever et publier le catalogue général des livres imprimés...*(Paris: Techener, 1847), pp. 32-34.

books with the existing backlog to form an enormous *fonds non-porté* (uncatalogued collection), estimated in 1842 to include some 300,000 volumes, or roughly half of the Library's printed books.[5] For decades, the only guide to this *fonds* was librarian Joseph Van Praët, known as the Library's "living catalogue." But after Van Praët's death in 1837, state officials and Library patrons alike began clamoring for a public catalogue, and in the 1840s, the Library finally began work on its Old Regime collections.[6] Similarly, in 1841, the Ministry of Public Instruction enlisted a team of librarians and *érudits* (including two *chartistes*) in the production of a union catalogue of manuscripts housed in provincial public libraries, eventually published as the *Catalogue général des manuscrits des bibliothèques publiques des départements.*[7]

However, the late July Monarchy's attempts to catalogue and classify public library collections pale in comparison with its forceful and sustained efforts to reorganize departmental archives. Despite a growing literature on library classification (including L.-A. Constantin's *Bibliothéconomie*, probably the first use of the French term for "library science," in 1839), most public libraries continued to organize their collections according to the five "great divisions" developed in the seventeenth century: theology, jurisprudence,

---

[5] Ch. Magnin et al., "Rapport des conservateurs du dept. des imprimés sur les travaux du catalogue," Sept. 1842, AN, box 3473, folder "Catalogues. Affaires générales. 1837-1852 (Ancien dossier)," p. [5]. See also E[ugène]-G[abriel] Ledos, *Histoire des catalogues des livres imprimés de la Bibliothèque nationale* (Paris: Editions des Bibliothèques nationales, 1936); Jean-François Foucaud, *La Bibliothèque Royale sous la monarchie de juillet (1830-1848)* (Paris: Bibliothèque nationale, 1978), pp. 115-128; and Simone Breton-Gravereau and François Dupuigrenet Desroussilles, "'Lever la carte': la politique des catalogues de livres imprimés à la fin du XIXe siècle," *Revue de la Bibliothèque Nationale* 49 (1993): 4-7.

[6] On Van Praët, see Ledos, chap. 11, as well as Dominique Varry, "Joseph Van Praët," in *Histoire des bibliothèques françaises* (Paris: Promodis, 1991), 3: 302-303. On Clément's scheme, see especially Laurent Portes, "L'ordre des livres selon Nicolas Clément," in *Mélanges autour de l'histoire des livres imprimés et périodiques*, ed. Bruno Blasselle and Laurent Portes (Paris: Bibliothèque nationale de France, 1998), pp. 64-92. And on the cataloging efforts of the 1840s, see AN, box 3473, folder "Catalogues...."

[7] The catalog, launched by Villemain in August 1841, has been published in two series, the first in-quarto (Paris: Imprimerie nationale, 1849-1885) and the second in-octavo (Paris: Plon, 1886-). See Marcel Thomas, "Les manuscrits," in *Histoire des bibliothèques françaises*, 3: 172-175. On the two *chartistes* involved (Jules Quicherat and Raymond Thomassy), see AN, box F17-3340, and AEC-SC, series B, item 103.

sciences and arts, *belles-lettres*, and history.[8] For instance, though the Royal
Library began reworking Clément's catalogue, it left his classification
scheme (also based on these five divisions) basically untouched. In contrast,
departmental archives in this period underwent a complete reclassification.
Abandoning the classification schemes of the Old Regime, Revolution, and
Restoration, the central government of the 1840s energetically reconstituted
provincial archives to suit its own scholarly and ideological goals. Since it
was on departmental archives, rather than libraries, that the organizing
impulses of the late July Monarchy left their clearest stamp, these archives
form the primary focus of this chapter.

Archivists the world over have heard about the classification of French
departmental archives in the 1840s. For not only is the classification scheme
of 1839-41 still used in departmental archives today, but the archival
principles associated with that scheme (namely the idea of *respect des fonds*, or
the "principle of provenance") are seen as the founding tenets of modern
archival practice. Indeed, many archivists argue that the principle of *respect
des fonds* is what distinguishes their work from that of librarians, museum
curators, and other record-keepers.[9] Perhaps because this and related

---

[8] Although we find traces of these five divisions in classification schemes from as
early as the mid-seventeenth century, they are usually attributed to the Parisian
bookseller Gabriel Martin (1679-1761). The divisions were slightly revised and
greatly popularized by Martin's nineteenth-century counterpart, Jacques-Charles
Brunet, author of the enormously successful *Manuel du libraire et de l'amateur de livres*
(first ed., Paris, 1810). On the development of these divisions, see especially Claude
Jolly, "Naissance de la «science» des bibliothèques," in *Histoire des bibliothèques
françaises*, 2: 381-385. On library classification in the July Monarchy, see especially
Constantin [pseud. for Léopold-Auguste Hesse] (Paris: Techener, 1839); and J. F.
M. Albert, *Recherches sur les principes fondamentaux de la classification bibliographique* (Paris:
Chez l'auteur, 1847).

[9] See for example, Michel Duchein, "Le respect des fonds en archivistique:
principes théoriques et problèmes pratiques," *Gazette des archives* 97 (1977): 71-96;
Hilary Jenkinson, "Reflections of an Archivist," *Contemporary Review* 165 (Jun. 1944):
355-361; and T.R. Schellenberg, "Archival Principles of Arrangement," *American
Archivist* 24 (Jan. 1961): 11-24. The latter two articles can be found in *A Modern
Archives Reader: Basic Readings on Archival Theory and Practice*, ed. Maygene F. Daniels
and Timothy Walch (Washington, D.C.: National Archives and Records Service
and the U.S. General Services Administration, 1984), pp. 15-21 and 149-161,
respectively. Though in recent years, some archivists, particularly in the United
States and Canada (see for instance the running discussions in the Canadian journal

principles have attained a kind of sacred status in the archival community, archivists have so far refrained from exploring the political context in which they first emerged. Two recent articles describe the archival debates surrounding the publication of the new scheme but never mention the political struggles that framed these internal discussions.[10] Thus the first task of this chapter is to investigate the political motives for—and implications of—the new archival order.

The second task of this chapter is to show how it was that the archival principles of 1839-41 first came to be seen as central to the archival profession. If today's archivists define themselves as enforcers of *respect des fonds*, this was not necessarily the case in the early 1840s. The French state did not simply imprint its new methods of classification and description on the latest generation of Archivist-Paleographers. Rather, at the very moment that the central government was developing these methods, the graduates of the Ecole des Chartes were organizing themselves into a new quasi-professional association, the Société de l'Ecole des Chartes, which had its own ideas about the proper functions of an Archivist-Paleographer. As this chapter will show, while the state increasingly characterized *chartistes* as expert classifiers, the members of the new Society worked to represent themselves primarily as medieval historians. It was not until the second reorganization of the Ecole des Chartes in the late 1840s that these two conceptions came together in the curriculum that would guide the school—and state archival practice—for the next twenty years.

To understand how the state reclassification campaigns of the 1840s transformed departmental archives, it would be useful to know how these collections were organized before the campaigns began. Yet assessing these early collections can be extraordinarily difficult. As we have seen, scholars and administrators in the period 1800-1840 routinely described provincial archives as "disorderly" and "pell-mell," making it impossible to determine what earlier organizational schemes might have escaped their attention. To compound the problem, the reclassification projects of the 1840s tended to

---

Archivaria), have begun to re-evaluate the principle of provenance, few have suggested it be abandoned.

[10] See Nancy Bartlett, "*Respect des Fonds*: The Origins of the Modern Archival Principle of Provenance," in *Bibliographical Foundations of French Historical Studies*, ed. Lawrence McCrank (New York: Haworth Press, 1991), pp. 107-115; and Françoise Hildesheimer, "Des triages au respect des fonds: les archives en France sous la monarchie de Juillet," *Revue historique* 286, no. 2 (1991): 295-312.

efface existing organizational schemes, both physically (by rearranging documents in depositories) and intellectually (by dismissing previous collections as "chaotic"). Recent historians and archivists have generally followed suit, lauding the archivists of the 1840s for finally bringing order to the chaos of departmental archives.

However hopelessly chaotic departmental archives may have seemed in 1839-41, most of these depositories probably carried traces of earlier attempts at classification. A summary of responses to a September 1812 ministerial questionnaire, for example, suggests that at the end of the First Empire, many departmental archival inventories (and perhaps the documents themselves?) were organized by "subject" [matière] rather than by title, format, or administrative division.[11] In April 1817, under the Bourbon Restoration, the Minister of the Interior issued a circular asking that all departmental prefects organize their archives according to the "four principal periods of public administration in France." Thus each set of archives would include: "1) those spoken of in the royal proclamation of April 20, 1790 [transferring provincial archives to the departments]; 2) those of the departmental administrations, up until the establishment of the prefects [February 1800]; 3) those of the prefects, up until the Restoration of 1814; and 4) finally, those of the prefects since the government of the king" [see Figure 1].[12] Unfortunately, we know next to nothing about the origins of this intriguing scheme, which seems to treat the archives confiscated during the Revolution like any other government records: that is, as simple products of an administration, devoid of historical value.[13] What we do know is that the Ministry made little effort to enforce or elaborate on this

---

[11] For the circular, issued by Interior Minister Montalivet, see AN, box AB Vf 1, folder "Archives départementales...1812." For the summary, which includes responses from forty of the eighty-seven departments, see "Tableau de situation des Dépôts d'archives des Départements de l'ancienne France, au 1er novembre 1812. contenant les réponses aux 16 questions adressées aux préfets par la circulaire ministérielle du 22 septembre," [Nov. 1812?], AN, box AB Vf 1* (bound volume). See also Olivier Guyotjeannin, "Les premières années des archives départementales françaises (1796-1815)," in Les archives en Europe vers 1800: les communications présentées dans le cadre de la journée d'études du même nom aux Archives générales du Royaume à Bruxelles le 24 octobre 1996, Miscellanea Archivistica Studia, no. 103 (Brussels: Archives générales du royaume et archives de l'état dans les provinces, 1998), pp. 7-36.
[12] See chap. 1, footnote 3.
[13] And indeed this fits with the Restoration policies discussed in chapter 1, which generally ignored departmental archives, looking instead to the Royal Library and Royal Archives for historically useful documents.

scheme, leaving its implementation entirely to local officials. Remarkably, despite the Restoration government's general lack of interest in archival classification, a number of departmental administrators began applying the 1817 categories, and well into the 1840s, many prefects were still describing the organization of their collections in terms of "the four periods."[14]

Some early nineteenth-century prefects claimed adherence to the 1817 scheme but then modified it for their own purposes. For example, as early as July 1817, the Secretary-General of the Department of the Maine-et-Loire had altered the official scheme—without explanation, unfortunately—to include just three divisions: before 1790, 1790 to 1800, and after 1800.[15] Other departmental administrators, perhaps sensing there would be no repercussions from Paris, made up their own classification schemes. Sometime in 1833, for instance, the prefect of the Seine-et-Oise (now the Yvelines) determined that the local archives ought to be organized by *décennales* (decades), starting with the most recent documents and working backward.[16] Six years later, just before the emergence of the new classification standard, another Seine-et-Oise official discarded the prefect's *décennales* system and instead split the collection into "current" archives (those still in use by departmental officials) and "old" archives (those no longer necessary to departmental administration).[17]

Yet the most intriguing (and best-documented) attempts at archival classification before 1839 are those undertaken by students from the Ecole des Chartes. Between 1838 and early 1839, the Minister of Public Instruction sent four of the school's students on "missions" to catalogue and classify departmental archives. As we saw in Chapter 3, *chartistes* had often served as missionaries of the Historical Works Committee, scouring regional collections for ecclesiastical cartularies or municipal charters. While such missions continued (and were sometimes even combined with classifying

---

[14] See the reports by departmental prefects and archivists in AN series F2 I.

[15] [Massin?] (Secrétaire-général), "Rapport sur la situation du dépôt des Archives de la Préfecture du Département de Maine et Loire, En conformité de la circulaire de son Excellence le Ministre Secrétaire d'Etat de l'intérieur du 28 avril 1817," 10 Jul. 1817, AN, box F2 I 373[1].

[16] Crosnier, "Rapport à Monsieur le Secrétaire général sur les travaux faits aux Archives pendant le mois d'avril 1833," 2 May 1833, AD Yvelines, box 3T/AD 1.

[17] Breval, "Rapport à Monsieur le Préfet sur la situation du classement des Archives du département de Seine-et-Oise, au 1er Août 1839…," 26 Aug. 1839, AN, box F2 I 376[11].

missions), a new group of missionary *chartistes* was expected to make organization and cataloguing its primary goals. Interestingly, the Paris Ministry did not give these new missionaries any clear guidelines, leaving each one to construct his own classification scheme. By taking a closer look at these schemes, we can better understand not only what was new about the 1839-41 organization, but also what it might have borrowed from earlier sources.[18]

The first *chartiste* assigned to classify a departmental depository was Charles Louandre, sent to the Sarthe in April 1838. Though Louandre had not done well enough on his first-year examinations to continue on at the Ecole des Chartes, his work on behalf of Thierry's *Tiers Etat* project apparently earned him the chance to test his mettle in a provincial depository. And by all accounts, Louandre set at the dusty documents in the Sarthe with a furious energy, classifying the entire collection in only four months. Perhaps drawing in part on the classification scheme of 1817, Louandre divided his archives into three chronological groupings: *archives anciennes* (old archives), *archives révolutionnaires* (revolutionary archives), and *archives postérieures à 1800* (post-1800 archives) [see Figure 1]. As one might expect from a scholar trained under Thierry, Louandre paid special attention to the *archives anciennes*, creating a separate table of their contents; yet he also explored the *archives révolutionnaires*, among which he identified twenty boxes of "'major interest'."[19]

For the next two *chartistes* dispatched to classify departmental archives, revolutionary documents held no such interest. Marius Clairefond, sent to the Allier in late April 1838, separated the depository into just two categories: documents produced before the creation of the departments in April 1790, and those produced afterward [Figure 1]. As the Prefect of the Allier explained to the Minister of the Interior in 1839:

> [Clairefond] thought that the division of the archives into four great periods prescribed by the ministerial circular of 28 April 1817 had the disadvantage of separating items and processes that often are related to the same subject, splitting the documents, and inverting the chronological order. It seemed preferable to him to divide [the archives] into just two

---

[18] Unfortunately, it seems that no evidence remains of the classification work done by one of these missionaries, Eugène de Certain, who spent 1839 in the Mayenne. This discussion therefore focuses on the remaining three.

[19] Louandre quoted in Vincent Mollet, "Les chartistes dans les Archives départementales avant le décret de 1850," *BEC* 151 (1993): 132-134.

periods, and…it is according to this system that work was begun and is continuing.[20]

For Clairefond, then, documents from the 1790s through the 1830s constituted a single set of "items and processes," completely distinct from documents from the 1780s and before. Thus whereas Louandre had identified "revolutionary" documents as a special category, Clairefond subsumed these archives under the larger category of post-1790 collections. And as if to confirm the insignificance of "revolutionary" archives, Clairefond, unlike Louandre, never spent any time cataloguing materials from the 1790s, devoting all his energies to the *vieilles archives*, or "old archives."

Clairefond's classmate, Auguste Vallet de Viriville, developed a similar approach to departmental archives upon arriving in the Aube in November 1838. Like Clairefond, Vallet separated his collection into two main categories, before and after the creation of the departments. Yet if Clairefond was simply more interested in the pre-departmental *vieilles archives*, Vallet made them his obsession. During his three years in the Aube, he sent off eight highly detailed reports to Paris, later published as the core of his *Archives historiques du département de l'Aube et de l'ancien diocèse de Troyes* (1841).[21] As the title of this book suggests, though Vallet's original mission was to classify the department's collections, he quickly refashioned himself as the region's chief historian, responsible for the rescue and rehabilitation of its Old Regime treasures. Thus his first report opens with a long lamentation for ecclesiastical archives of Troyes, noting that after fifty years, most of them "can be found thrown in no order whatsoever in old crates, stuffed into sacks, or even…gathered pell-mell into shapeless piles on the dusty floor." He adds, "in short, Monsieur the Minister, my pen refuses to describe in any more detail this inexpressible disorder."[22] His other reports continue in the same vein, often careening off into erudite meditations on the region's most precious collections.

---

[20] Ed[mond] Méchin, (Préfet de l'Allier) to Monsieur le Ministre Secrétaire d'état au département de l'Intérieur, Moulins, 7 Sept. 1839, AN, box F2 I 367[4], p. [2].

[21] Auguste Vallet de Viriville, *Les archives historiques du département de l'Aube et de l'ancien diocèse de Troyes, capitale de la Champagne…*(Troyes: Bouquot, 1841).

[22] Auguste Vallet de Viriville, "Premier rapport adressé à Monsieur le Ministre de l'Instruction publique sur les archives du département de l'Aube," Troyes, 15 Feb. 1839, AN, box F2 I 367[13], p. 3.

Figure 1

	Lainé (1817)	Louandre (1838)	Clairefond (1838)	Vallet (1838)	Seytre (1839)	De Wailly (1841)
1788	epoque #1	archives	epoque #1	archives		archives
1789		historiques	(vieilles archives)	historiques contentieuses		historiques
1790	-------	-----------	-------------	-------------	----------	----------
	epoque #2	archives revolutionnaires	epoque #2	archives administratives	archives historiques	periode intermediaire
1800						
	epoque #3	archives administratives				archives administratives
1814						
1815	epoque #4				archives administratives	
1830						
1848						

Vallet's passion for historical sources may help explain why he chose to overlay his basic chronological classification with a more elaborate topical one. He argued in his first report that the archives of the Aube would "naturally divide themselves" into three "sections," two pre-1790 and one post-1790:

Historical section, including all documents interesting to some branch of history.

Legal section [*section contentieuse*], composed of documents that serve to establish rights of servitude, prescription, or property for individuals or towns.

Departmental administration section, containing all acts that have emanated from the local authority since the organization of France into departments.[23]

---

[23] Ibid., p. 11-12.

As Vallet explained, this scheme represented a simplified version of the one used by the Royal Archives. Under the Empire, Head Archivist P.-C.-F. Daunou had divided the Royal Archives into six sections: legislative, administrative, historical, topographical, judicial, and *domaniale* [property-related]. While this classification was somewhat modified in subsequent decades, the Archives of Vallet's time still had functional "sections" rather than chronological groupings.[24] By imitating Daunou's scheme, Vallet implied that it was less important to know when a document had been produced than how it was going to be used (by lawyers, departmental administrators, or, more significantly for Vallet, historians).

Yet if Vallet, Clairefond, and Louandre at least began with a chronological division circa 1790,[25] a fourth *chartiste*, Jean-Claude-Marius Seytre, chose a different moment of rupture. After beginning coursework at the Ecole des Chartes in the mid-1830s, Seytre left Paris for the provinces, eventually landing a post as departmental archivist of the Indre-et-Loire in March 1839.[26] There he divided the depository into two main categories: "historical" (before 1815) and "administrative" (after 1815). In the earlier group, Seytre explained,

> I include not only the documents related to the great political events of France or of the province; not only the old charters and chronicles that introduce us to the inner life of…the Middle Ages,…But I consider as precious monuments all those [documents] that relate to the history of the Third Estate before its emancipation in '89; and, since then, all the documents that allow us to understand the men and events of the revolution and of the bloody period of the terror.[27]

---

[24] See Françoise Hildesheimer, "Les Archives nationales au XIXe siècle: établissement administratif ou scientifique?" *Histoire et Archives* 1 (1997): 105-135. As Hildesheimer points out, the division of the Archives into "sections" actually dates to 1793, but the elaboration of this idea is particularly associated with the era of Daunou (head of the Archives 1804-1815 and again 1830-1840).

[25] It is not clear exactly what year (1789? 1790?) separated "old" from "revolutionary" archives in Louandre's scheme.

[26] Thus unlike Louandre, Clairefond, and Vallet, Seytre was not a missionary but a permanent employee of the archives. See Mollet, "Les chartistes," pp. 142-144.

[27] Seytre, "Rapport de l'Archiviste à Mr. le Préfet d'Indre et Loire," Aug. 1840, AN, box F2 I 371[5], pp. [4-5]. Though it is possible that Seytre's scheme was a response to the new classification guidelines of August 1839, documents in the Indre-et-Loire (see especially box T 1627, folder "Rapports des commissions. 1837 and 1839") suggest that he began developing this scheme upon his arrival in early 1839.

Seytre allowed that placing Old Regime and revolutionary documents in the same category had its risks; as he told the Prefect in 1840, "I understand that it is disagreeable to certain families to count Jacobins among their close associates, but what can one do, it is part of history [*qu'y faire, c'est de l'histoire*]."[28] For Seytre, then, the archives of the revolutionary period did not represent the beginnings of modern "administration," but rather the end of France's long and tumultuous "history." However controversial, these archives needed to be studied and understood.

These four classification schemes—especially when combined with François Morand's hypothetical scheme, devised at the same time—suggest that the years 1838-1839 witnessed increasing concern about how to categorize and interpret the documentary vestiges of the French past. Until 1838, archival classification had generated little interest, especially among Parisian scholars and *chartistes*; but suddenly government missionaries and provincial archivists began questioning the categories prescribed in 1817 and developing their own groupings of archival sources. Interestingly, despite the potentially infinite number of axes along which such sources might be divided (author, subject, location, size, shape, value, color . . .), all of these archivists and missionaries chose to emphasize chronological divisions. Yet they did not agree on where these divisions ought to occur: 1790? 1800? 1815? Nor did they agree on how to describe the categories generated by these divisions. Were documents from before 1790 "historical," "legal," or just "old"? Were the archival remnants of the 1790s "revolutionary," "historical," or "administrative"?

Beginning in 1839, the central government tried to put an end to this classificatory confusion. In August, the new Minister of the Interior, the Guizot supporter Tanneguy Duchâtel, issued a circular to his prefects that announced a new approach to departmental archives. He claimed that while previous ministerial instructions had encountered "various obstacles," he planned to make departmental collections "truly useful to the administration, to families, and to scholarship." The key to this plan was the creation of a "vast inventory of all the sources" in departmental archives; and the key to this inventory, in turn, was the development of "certain rules of classification that can be more or less generally followed." In 1839, Duchâtel could only promise to deliver these rules in "subsequent instructions," but in April 1841, he issued a second circular that not only

---

[28] Seytre, "Rapport," pp. [7-8].

laid out new rules of classification but offered an entirely new classification scheme to be applied to all departmental archives.[29]

Unfortunately, the discussions and negotiations that transpired between the circular of 1839 and that of 1841 are lost to us, but the 1841 instructions (in many sources listed simply as "Circular no. 14") are usually attributed to Natalis de Wailly, head of the administrative section at the Royal Archives, active member of the Historical Works Committee (for whom he had prepared a widely-used manual on paleography), and future head of the advisory council for the Ecole des Chartes. And indeed it was most often De Wailly who articulated and defended the circular's precepts in the early 1840s.[30] Nevertheless, the famous circular was most likely a collaborative effort involving De Wailly, Léon Gadebled (bureau chief at the Minister of the Interior), the Comte de Portalis (member of the Chamber of Peers), and Auguste Leprevost (Liberal legislator and co-founder of the Antiquarian Society of Normandy).[31] For Duchâtel, it seems, the reclassification of departmental archives was too important a task to be left to *érudits* alone.

Though the authors of the circular claimed to have drawn on the work of both departmental and royal archivists, its most celebrated principle—the idea of *respect des fonds*—seems to run counter to these earlier approaches. According to the circular, the basic unit of archival classification is the *fonds*, or "collection of all the titles that derive from a body, an establishment, a

---

[29] T[anneguy] Duchâtel (Ministre Secrétaire d'Etat de l'Intérieur), "Circulaire [with marginal heading: "Archives départementales. Instructions pour la garde et la conservation de ces archives"]," Paris, 8 Aug. 1839, AN, box AB XXXI 41, and in the appendix to [Maximilien] Quantin, *Dictionnaire Raisonné de Diplomatique Chrétienne...*(Paris: Chez l'Editeur [the Abbé Migne], 1846), cols. 841-968.

[30] See H. Wallon, "Notice sur la vie et les travaux de M. Joseph-Natalis de Wailly...," *BEC* 49 (1888): 581-598. I am grateful to Ecole des Chartes student Marc Verdure for sharing with me his unpublished essay on De Wailly.

[31] Both Hildesheimer (in "Des triages," p. 306) and Christine Nougaret (in "De Nathalis de Wailly à MIRA: 150 ans de normalisation des instruments de recherche aux Archives nationales," in *Histoires d'archives: recueil d'articles offert à Lucie Favier par ses collègues et amis* (Paris: Société des amis des Archives de France, 1997), p. 87) suggest that Daunou also participated in the preparation of the circular, but if so, he was only involved in the early stages, as he died in June 1840. In any event, the final circular clearly challenged the classification methods Daunou had developed at the Royal Archives. On the involvement of Gadebled and Portalis, see Bibliothèque nationale, Département des manuscrits [hereafter BN mss.], n.a.f. 21578.

family, or an individual."[32] What did this mean, exactly? The authors of the
circular were quick to explain how classification by *fonds* differed from other
classification methods. For instance, they immediately pointed out that
classification by *fonds* was not the same as classification by author; to "derive
from" a person or group was not the same as to have been "produced by"
that person or group. As the circular explains:

> In regard to *fonds*, it is important to understand clearly that this method of
> classification consists in uniting all the titles that were the property of the
> same establishment, the same body, [or] the same family. Thus the official
> copy of a parliamentary decision issued to a private individual will not be
> classified in the *fonds* of the *parlement*, but in that of the person that had the
> copy made; an original request addressed to the *parlement* by a town or a
> family will not be classified among the papers of the town or the family,
> but among those of the *parlement* to which the request was addressed. Thus
> again a draft of a letter cannot be part of the same *fonds* as the letter itself,
> because the   draft letter belongs to the person that wrote it; the letter, on
> the contrary, is the property of the person to whom it was addressed.[33]

Nor was classification by *fonds* to be confused with classification by
subject. Shortly after the publication of the circular, De Wailly explained
that classification methods based on "systems," (i.e., predetermined subject
lists or trees) actually created more confusion than order in archival
collections. No archivist could possibly have the breadth of knowledge
required to choose the correct subject category for each of the many
documents he might confront; and if he chose inappropriately, the archives
would "fall into a disorder that it would be difficult to remedy."[34] In all
likelihood, De Wailly's apprehensions about classificatory "systems" were
the product of his own experience at the Royal Archives. Since the early
1830s, he had been struggling to organize the vast and unwieldy Series F
("General French Administration") within the constraints of Daunou's

---

[32] T[anneguy] Duchâtel (Ministre Secrétaire d'Etat au département de l'Intérieur),
"Circulaire [with marginal heading, "Instructions pour la mise en ordre et le
classement des archives départementales et communales"]," Paris, 24 Apr. 1841,
AN, box AB Vf 1, folder "Archives départementales (1820-1857)," p. 2. In French,
the verb I have translated as "derive" is *proviennent*, hence the usual English
translation of *respect des fonds* as the "principle of provenance."
[33] Ibid., p. 3.
[34] Commission des archives départementales et communales, "Procès-verbaux," 8
Jun. 1841, AN, AB XXVI 1*, 2*, and 3* (three bound volumes covering May 1841
to January 1854), 1: 20-21.

system of "sections."[35] While to Daunou, born in the age of the *Encyclopédie*, it seemed possible to classify documents according to a fixed hierarchy of sections and series, to De Wailly, nearly a half-century Daunou's junior, such "theoretical" classifications made little sense; archival arrangements had to arise out of the documents themselves, or, as he put it, out of the "nature of things."[36]

De Wailly and the other authors of the circular used a similar argument to attack a third method of classification: classification by time period. Though the circular made no mention of the chronological categories developed by Louandre, Clairefond, Vallet de Viriville, and Seytre in the late 1830s, it explicitly rejected the ministerial classification scheme of 1817, which, as we know, had divided departmental archives into four periods (before 1790, 1790 to 1800, 1800 to 1814, and 1814 on):

> [E]xperience has shown that classification must not be subordinated principally, as the circular of 28 April 1817 prescribes, to divisions based on political periods, and that one must above all seek to arrange them in an order drawn not from the times [*temps*] but from the very nature of the documents and the actual sequence of affairs [*enchaînement réel des affaires*].[37]

In this view, archival collections are not the product of a particular period, much less a particular political regime, but the product of people and institutions; and like those people and institutions, they develop organically and continuously. The only "natural" organizational scheme, then, is one reflective of the continuity of people and institutions: classification by *fonds*.

But what hope was there of assembling these *fonds*? If, as so many government officials maintained, provincial collections had been tossed "pell-mell" into dilapidated granaries, how were departmental archivists ever supposed to form neat collections of "all the titles that derive from a body, an establishment, a family, or an individual"? In June 1841, De Wailly had no doubts about the feasibility of his method. "Above all else," he declared, "it is easier than any other to put into practice: for in the first place it consists only of a simple bringing together [*rapprochement*] of documents, and [for this] it is only a question of discerning their origin." Yet

---

[35] Gustave Desjardins, *Le service des archives départementales: conférences faites aux élèves de l'Ecole des chartes les 10, 18, 25 et 30 juin 1890* (Paris: E. Bourloton, 1890), pp. 35-36. A careful study of De Wailly's work on series F has yet to be undertaken.

[36] Commission des archives, "Procès-verbaux," 8 Jun. 1841, 1: 21. Daunou's dates are 1761-1840.

[37] Duchâtel, "Circulaire," 24 Apr. 1841, p. 2.

aside from recommending that archivists consult "old inventories" (which not all departmental archives possessed), De Wailly made no suggestions about how to determine what he later called the "primitive order" of departmental documents.[38] His assumption, apparently, was not only that there was an original, "natural" order to these collections, but that this order was discernible, even through the "disorder" of departmental depositories.

De Wailly's notion of an organic, perdurable archival order has had generations of adherents. For example, in an 1890 lecture to the students of the Ecole des Chartes, archivist Gustave Desjardins proclaimed:

> Monsieur de Wailly was right to say that the principle of classification by *fonds* was in the natural order of things. There were not just dates, facts, [and] individuals in the past: one also found there institutions, bodies, families—moral and collective beings that had a life of their own...Classification by *fonds* has the effect of preserving [and] perpetuating the memory of these moral beings who played such a large role; all other [methods], in dissecting them, would leave in place of these bodies only isolated fragments ready to crumble into dust. In the *fonds*, we rediscover the physiognomy of the vanished establishment, its members, its organs, the products of its activity, and, as the established term expresses so well, *its acts*.[39]

More than a century later, professional archivists still rely heavily on this kind of imagery. Like Desjardins and De Wailly, they describe archival development as "organic and automatic" and thus condemn all classifications not based on *fonds* as violent "dissections."[40] A recent article on *respect des fonds*, for example, describes the revolutionary program of triage as "the dismemberment of *fonds*," while the 1993 edition of the standard manual for French archivists calls the first post-revolutionary efforts at classification a "veritable massacre of *fonds*."[41]

---

[38] Commission des archives, "Procès-verbaux," 8 Jun. 1841, 1: 20.

[39] Desjardins, *Le service*, pp. 31-32. In French, as in English, the term "acts" means both "actions" and "official records."

[40] See for example Michel Maréchal, *Guide des Archives de l'Allier* (Yzeure: Département de l'Allier, Direction des services d'archives, 1991), p. 15; and Jacques Charpy, *Guide des Archives du Finistère* (Quimper: Archives départementales du Finistère, 1973), p. 17.

[41] Hildesheimer, "Des triages," p. 300; Michel Duchein, "Archives, archivistes, archivistique: définitions et problématique," in *La pratique archivistique française*, ed. Jean Favier (Paris: Archives nationales, 1993), p. 34. In "Archives et violence. A propos de la loi du 7 messidor an II," (*Gazette des archives* n.s., nos. 146-147 (1989):

Not surprisingly, then, historical accounts of the 1841 circular, all of them written by professional archivists, see its emphasis on classification by *fonds* as eminently practical, a logical response to the dismemberment of *fonds* in the previous half-century. In this view, when confronted with the broken and battered remains of once-orderly collections, the archivists of the 1840s had little choice but to "re-member" them, thus restoring them to life.[42] But if one does not assume that archives (in France or anyplace else) possess a natural and enduring order, then the 1841 circular appears less about restoring order than about creating it. Faced with the supposed "chaos" of provincial archives, the government of the 1840s might have chosen any number of classification methods, but it chose instead to elaborate a new approach, one based on *respect des fonds*. Why did it make this choice?

Perhaps the most general answer to this question is that organicist ideas were simply "in the air" in the early nineteenth century. In *The Order of Things*, Michel Foucault argues that at any given historical moment, there are unconscious rules, or "epistemes," that determine how knowledge can be produced. Thus ideas generated in seemingly disparate fields (biology and economics, for example) in fact share certain crucial assumptions. And according to Foucault, the episteme in place in the early nineteenth century, or what he calls the "modern" episteme, was characterized by just those notions of organic development that we find in discussions of *respect des fonds*. While the natural history enthusiasts of the eighteenth century had categorized living things based solely on their visible characteristics, the biologists of the nineteenth century made their categorizations based on how these beings developed over time. Similarly, while linguists had once perceived language as largely static, the linguists of the "modern" era saw words as constantly evolving through "systems of kinship." Indeed, scholars from a whole range of fields began to describe their world as fundamentally historical, the product of a long and steady evolution.[43] In this context, the

---

210), Pierre Santoni makes the interesting if undeveloped claim that this organic language may reflect the "sacred" role of archives in modern French culture.

[42] Hildesheimer, "Des triages."

[43] Michel Foucault, *The Order of Things: An Archaeology of the Human Sciences* (New York: Vintage, 1970); originally published as *Les mots et les choses: une archéologie des sciences humaines* (Paris: Gallimard, 1966). It should be noted that while Foucault particularly associates classification as a mode of knowledge with the "Classical" episteme (roughly 1660-1800), he argues that "modern" thinkers still created classification schemes, just now based on more organic conceptions of knowledge (emphasizing

idea that archives are composed of naturally-developing *fonds* looks less like the product of Louis-Philippe's France than like the product of the "modern" shift in Western thought.

Nevertheless, it might be said that the July Monarchy was particularly committed to an organicist conception of history. As we saw in the previous chapter, the Orleanist regime, neither fully Bourbon nor fully revolutionary, lacked a clear source of political legitimacy. Its leaders therefore tried to justify the regime's authority by describing it as the triumphant product of the centuries-long evolution of the French "nation." Of course, Restoration officials had also tried to locate their regime in the great sweep of French history, but without relying on an evolutionary model; they emphasized the continuity and stability of monarchical rule, not its progress over time.[44] Orleanist politicians, on the other hand, repeatedly likened the nation (held as the basis of Orleanist rule) to a living being that had slowly grown into full maturity. In this model, the various epochs of French history were not radically distinct but rather represented, as Guizot put it, "France, at the various stages of life, in the various phases of civilization."[45] Given this conception of French history, it is hardly surprising to find the nation's archives described in organic terms.[46]

Thus far, the 1841 circular would seem to represent less a radical shift from the archival policies of the early July Monarchy than an extension of its historical vision into the realm of classification. The newly "restored" archival *fonds* would offer documentary proof of the slow and inexorable progress of the French "nation" from the struggles of the medieval period to the triumph of the July regime. And to read most accounts of the famous circular, one would think it was entirely devoted to the notion of *respect des*

"successive" or diachronic similarities and differences rather than synchronic ones). However, as we will see in a moment, the 1841 circular also included some synchronic divisions, resulting in a scheme that does not fit quite so neatly into Foucault's framework.

[44] See chapter 1.

[45] See chapter 2, footnote 44.

[46] Yet interestingly, the *fonds* of the 1841 circular are not the *products* of historical bodies, but their *property*. The French "nation" would therefore appear in archival form in terms of property-owners rather than in terms of actors and producers, a scheme quite appropriate to a regime associated especially with property-owning "notables." See André Jardin and André-Jean Tudesq, *Restoration and Reaction, 1815-1848*, trans. Elborg Forster (Cambridge: Cambridge University Press, 1983), originally published as *La France des notables* (Paris: Seuil, 1973).

fonds. However, one has only to look at the actual classification "framework" published at the back of the circular (and still found in slightly modified form in today's archival guides) to see that this was not the case. The *fonds* was only one of several cross-cutting categories prescribed by the Minister of the Interior [Figure 2]. Nor could *fonds* properly be described as the basic building block of the new classification scheme, since other categorizations both precede and follow it in the order of operations. Extrapolating from the instructions accompanying the new scheme, this order of operations would involve a series of categorizations:

1. By period (before or after 1790)
2. By lettered series (representing various subjects, or types of *fonds*)
3. By *fonds*
4. By matières(topics) organized chronologically, alphabetically, or geographically[47]

Thus despite De Wailly's criticism of classification schemes based on subjects and periods, the circular he helped prepare actually incorporates elements of these earlier approaches, resulting in a complex framework not easily reducible to a single principle of classification.

Figure 2
1841 Classification Scheme: Departmental Archives

(or "Framework for the classification of the various archival *fonds* kept in prefectoral depositories)

First part of the framework, containing archives prior to 1790

    Civil archives
    A. Acts of the sovereign power and public domain
    B. Courts and jurisdictions
    C. Provincial administrations
    D. Public instruction, sciences and arts
    E. Feudalism, communes, bourgeoisie and families
    F. Miscellaneous civil *fonds*

---

[47] The 1841 circular does not list these operations in such a concise fashion, but we find a similar summary of the 1841 instructions in Commission des archives, "Procès-verbaux," 26 Jan. 1843, 1: 103.

Ecclesiastical archives
G. Secular clergy
H. Regular clergy
I. Miscellaneous ecclesiastical *fonds*

Second part of the framework, containing archives after 1790, or departmental archives, properly speaking

K. Laws, ordinances, and decrees
L. Documents especially related to departmental, district, and canton administrations, from the division of France into departments [in 1790] until the creation of prefectures in the Year VIII [i.e., 1800]
M. Personnel and general administration
N. Departmental administration and accounting
O. Communal administration and accounting
P. Finances
Q. Domains
R. War and military affairs
S. Public works
T. Public instruction, sciences and arts
U. Justice
V. Cults
X. Charitable institutions
Y. Repressive institutions
Z. Miscellaneous

From T[anneguy] Duchâtel, (Minister of the Interior), "Circulaire," Paris, 24 Apr. 1841, AN, box AB Vf 1, pp. 17-19.

The basic division in this framework is between archives from before 1790 (part one) and archives from after 1790 (part two). As the accompanying instructions explain:

> The distinction to be made in the prefectoral archives between the documents prior to the division of France into departments and the documents after this period is fundamental and of universal application because of the essential difference in nature and object between these two classes of documents.[48]

This distinction, as we know, was not new; the ministerial circular of 1817 as well as the schemes developed by students of the Ecole des Chartes (with the exception of Seytre) in 1838-39 had all included a major division in

---

[48] Duchâtel, "Circulaire," 24 Apr. 1841, p. 2.

1789 or 1790. We also find hints of this division in Duchâtel's preliminary circular of August 1839, which claimed that departmental archives were comprised of "historical" documents (before 1789) and "administrative" ones (after 1789).[49] The 1841 circular was nevertheless the first to declare this distinction "fundamental" and "essential"; now all eighty-six departmental collections would be permanently split at 1790. It was also the first text to articulate this division in the language of *fonds*. The circular insists that while the first part of the framework (series A-I) contains many different *fonds*, the second part (series K-Z) technically contains only one enormous *fonds*, since all the post-1790 documents in a given collection would have come from a single institution, the department itself. Thus the various sub-divisions within series K-Z are not properly *fonds*, but only "analogous" to *fonds*.[50]

This distinction between pre- and post-1790 *fonds* has several intriguing implications. First, it suggests that for the authors of the 1841 circular, the year 1790 did not just mark a change in administration (as the 1817 instructions had emphasized) but a kind of social and institutional death. In 1790, the circular seems to imply, the various individual, familial, and corporate *fonds* that had been organically growing and evolving in pre-revolutionary France suddenly and collectively expired. Now administratively "dead," they passed all at once into the realm of the "historical." While French governments had long looked to pre-1790 collections for "historical" documents, that of 1841 was the first to describe these collections as *uniquely* historical rather than legal or administrative. The Old Regime was now definitively "old."

The corollary to the "death" of pre-1790 *fonds*, of course, was the "birth" of a single post-1790 *fonds*. Though the April 1841 circular gives only the briefest of explanations for the decision to create only one post-1790 *fonds*, a May 1841 report by Duchâtel to Louis-Philippe offers a somewhat more elaborate justification. Duchâtel argues that the archives from before 1790 "present...the varied image of a society formed by successive agglomerations of diverse nationalities, whose individual eccentricities were only fully eliminated by the revolution." The post-1790 archives, by

---

[49] Duchâtel, "Circulaire," 8 Aug. 1839, col. 878. The Royal Library's manuscripts department seems to have experimented with a similar distinction; see Bibliothèque Royale, Département des manuscrits, "Renseignements sur l'état des Catalogues et sur le projet de Catalogues raisonnés," 28 Nov. 1838, AN, box 3473, folder "Catalogues...."

[50] Duchâtel, "Circulaire," 24 Apr. 1841, p. 6.

contrast, "are everywhere the same, being the product of a uniform administrative regime."[51] In this vision of the French past, although the various organic components of the "nation" were combining and evolving over the course of the Old Regime, it was not until the moment of the Revolution that these various entities could be reborn as a fully unified nation-state.

But what about the revolution of 1830? Considering that it was the revolution of July 1830, not that of July 1789, that brought Duchâtel and his fellow Orleanists into power, one would think that 1830 would have been the more appropriate moment of rupture between the era of heterogeneity and the era of uniformity. Yet neither the circular nor its accompanying classification scheme makes any mention of the July revolution, subsuming it completely under the "administrative" section of the framework. Like the 1789 revolutionaries themselves, then, the authors of the 1841 circular define the first revolution as the end of history, the ultimate passage from the conflicts and struggles of the Old Regime to the *tabula rasa* of the new. Even the language of *fonds* recalls the revolutionary discourse of "regeneration," in which the nation appeared as an organic unity whose purity and health required constant vigilance. In this respect, the 1841 circular seems to bear out François Furet's contention that in the eyes of the Orleanist leaders, 1830 was merely an "epilogue" to 1789 rather than a second revolution. By emphasizing 1789 over 1830, the July regime hoped not only to associate itself with the unity and optimism of 1789, but also to discourage the notion that France might need still more revolutions to reach its ideal state.[52] In the vision promoted by the new archival classification scheme, France after 1790 was not "revolutionary" but stable, uniform, and homogeneous.

---

[51] T[anneguy] Duchâtel (Ministre Secrétaire d'Etat au département de l'intérieur), *Rapport au Roi sur les archives départementales et communales* (Paris: Imprimerie royale, May 1841), pp. 2-5. See also chap. 1, footnote 3.

[52] François Furet, *Revolutionary France, 1770-1880*, trans. Antonia Nevill (Cambridge: Blackwell, 1992); originally published as *La Révolution: de Turgot à Jules Ferry, 1770-1880* (Paris: Hachette, 1988), chap. 7. On regeneration, see especially Mona Ozouf, "Regeneration," in *A Critical Dictionary of the French Revolution*, ed. François Furet and Mona Ozouf, trans. Arthur Goldhammer (Cambridge, MA: Harvard/Belknap, 1989), pp. 781-791; originally published as *Dictionnaire critique de la révolution française* (Paris: Flammarion, 1988).

Yet the post-1790 *fonds* is less homogeneous than it first appears. If we look even more closely at the 1841 classification scheme, we can see that it contains not one chronological rupture, but two. Under "Archives after 1790," Series L, we find: "Documents especially related to departmental, district, and cantonal administrations, from the division of France into departments [in 1790] until the creation of prefectures in the Year VIII [1800]." In other words, all departmental archives from the period 1790 to 1800 were to be placed in a special category, Series L.[53] As we have seen, several earlier classification schemes had also included such a category, yet they had all made it a first-order division, on par with "archives before 1790" and "archives after 1800." Louandre, one of the missionary *chartistes*, had even given the category its own name: "revolutionary archives." The 1841 circular, however, makes every effort to downplay the category's importance, not only by burying it amid the other post-1790 series but also by replacing the term "revolutionary" with the administrative language of "departments" and "prefectures."

The term "revolutionary" is also absent from the instructions accompanying the 1841 framework. Here under the heading "Exception," the authors of the circular work to justify the inclusion of Series L:

> The special series that relates to the interval of time between 1790 and the Year VIII must be the subject of an observation. Although it may hardly seem in keeping with the general method of this second part of the framework, it has been indispensable to include [this series] due to the special character of the events, the political or administrative measures that relate to the period at hand, [and] of the format and even the material assembly of the documents…[54]

In this intriguing passage, the circular's authors both assert the absolute uniqueness of the documents from this period (their "special character") and at the same time sidestep the question of what makes them so unique. They claim that the archives of Series L are politically, administratively, and even materially different, but say nothing about the nature of these differences. Unlike the other series in the scheme, then, Series L has no obvious content; it is defined not by its subject, but by its "specialness."

---

[53] The exceptions to this rule were documents that fell under the heading of *domaines* (state properties). *Domaines* documents from all periods were to be placed in Series Q. I hope in later work to offer a more extended analysis of the relationship between Series L and Q.

[54] Duchâtel, "Circulaire," 24 Apr. 1841, p. 7.

The very avoidance of the term "revolutionary," however, suggests that the Interior Ministry's decision to create a special series for the archives of the 1790s was an attempt to isolate and control the political energies of the French Revolution. As we have seen, the July Monarchy had never been particularly eager to promote "revolutionary" activity; as soon as Louis-Philippe had been installed on the throne of France, Orleanist leaders had begun working to control the revolutionary fervor unleashed in 1830 in order to create a stable, "orderly" regime. Yet for most of the 1830s, the historian-politicians at the head of the July regime had generally supported a holistic vision of the French past that included (even if it did not emphasize) the 1789 revolution. If Orleanist leaders like Guizot, Thiers, Michelet, Mignet, Quinet, and Thierry had their points of disagreement, these were still in the 1830s less marked than their points of consensus. In their published histories, university lectures, and, especially, in their work on the *Documents inédits*, they described the continuous and progressive development of the French nation, from its origins in the bourgeois renaissance of the high Middle Ages through the dark days of absolutism, and from the hard-won triumph of the Revolution to the final victory of the Orleanist constitutional monarchy.[55]

By the early 1840s, however, this scholarly and political consensus had begun to fall apart. Michelet and Quinet began to shift to the left, using their positions as university lecturers to attack ministerial policies and to rally the youth of the Latin Quarter behind a vision of the revolutionary destiny of the French people.[56] By 1843, Michelet had put aside the Old Regime volumes of his *History of France*, skipping ahead three centuries to begin work on the period of the French Revolution. At the same time, Guizot and his circle began shifting to the right. While Guizot had moved in and out of ministerial office in the 1830s, in 1840 he emerged from the country's latest diplomatic and economic crisis as the *de facto* prime minister of France. With the cooperation of King Louis-Philippe and a core group of loyal ministers (Duchâtel among them), Guizot embarked on an extended campaign to stabilize French institutions and squelch all efforts at radical reform. As Furet explains:

> The obsession with public order, which was the dominant political feature
> of [Guizot's] ministry, tended to bring the country back to a situation
> comparable with the one which had preceded 1830…there was the same

---

[55] See chap. 2.

[56] Eric Fauquet, *Michelet, ou la gloire du professeur d'histoire* (Paris: Editions du cerf, 1990), chap. 7.

inability to accept the expression of citizens' hostile opinions or political activity, the same will to govern through the police and the administration.[57]

While the Guizot of the 1830s had emphasized national unity and reconciliation, then, the Guizot of the 1840s was increasingly given to the harsh repression of opposing views.

In this political and intellectual context, it is hardly surprising that the Interior Ministry would institute an archival classification scheme that bracketed and subordinated the documents of the 1790s. Indeed, the very notion that French archives ought to be classified, rather than simply copied and explored, can be interpreted as a conservative maneuver.[58] For classification is ultimately about establishing control; faced with an unruly mass of objects or ideas, the classifier names them, separates them, and fixes them into place.[59] Yet it is the inclusion of the "special" Series L that marks the scheme with conservatism particularly characteristic of the late July Monarchy. Just as the political and intellectual unity of the July regime was beginning to dissolve and a new wave of scholarly interest in the 1790s was starting to emerge, the government defined the archives of the revolutionary period as outside the nation's "historical archives," and, by extension, outside of national history. While the state acknowledged the first revolution as the key transformation in France's history (hence the division at 1790), it worked to discourage the study of the presumably "disorderly" workings of

---

[57] Furet, *Revolutionary France*, p. 364. For similar interpretations of the late July Monarchy, see H.A.C. Collingham, *The July Monarchy: A Political History of France, 1830-1848* (New York: Longman, 1988), chap. 21; and Gordon Wright, *France in Modern Times: From the Enlightenment to the Present*, 5th ed. (New York: W.W. Norton, 1995), chap. 10.

[58] In *Painting Politics for Louis-Philippe: Art and Ideology in Orléanist France, 1830-1848* (New Haven: Yale University Press, 1988), Michael Marrinan links the "glacially immobile narrative" of Louis-Philippe's art-historical "galleries" of the 1840s with the "ossification" of the late July regime. Marrinan's intriguing analysis suggests the need for further investigation of the connections between the classification of archival documents and the classification of other kinds of objects (paintings, buildings, sculpture, etc.) in this period.

[59] Of course, as the Enlightenment *Encyclopédie* demonstrates, classification need not uphold the political status quo; nevertheless, any classification scheme inevitably creates its own stasis, preventing alternate conceptions of the same objects and ideas.

the transformation itself.[60] In this respect, it is intriguing to note that Series L begins in 1790, not 1789; the new classification scheme thus retained the most optimistic and "liberal" phase of the revolution for "history" but left the more radical and violent phase in the supposedly "administrative" Series L.

Of course, this attempt to isolate and control the departmental records of the 1790s had what was surely an unintended consequence: the constitution of France's "revolutionary archives." Before 1841, the archives from 1790 to 1800 were not necessarily grouped together, particularly in those departments that had ignored the 1817 circular; after 1841, however, these archives were permanently united in a single category that could then be used for a variety of purposes, both counter-revolutionary and pro-revolutionary. As we will see in later chapters, as the republican historians of the 1870s began to study the first revolution, they turned immediately to Series L, which they called the *archives révolutionnaires*. The divisions created in 1841 not only greatly facilitated their work but helped define it; for generations of future historians, the period covered by Series L became their "Revolution."[61]

But why did the classification scheme of 1841 prove so durable? After all, implementing a new scheme, especially one as complicated as that contained in the 1841 circular, is tremendously labor-intensive. One might expect, then, that departmental prefects and archivists of the 1840s would

---

[60] After all, not only was this series not "historical," but unlike the other two chronological categories (before 1790 and after 1800), it contained no internal divisions, ensuring that in most departmental depositories it would remain one large, undifferentiated mass -- hardly easily accessible to scholars -- until the 1870s. On this point see for example Ch[arles]-V[ictor] Langlois and H[enri] Stein, *Les archives de l'histoire de France* (Paris: Alphonse Picard, 1891), who maintain that the July Monarchy "intentionally mixed" the papers of the revolutionary era with "modern papers so it would be more difficult to consult them and awaken irritating memories" (p. 71). Interestingly, none of Langlois and Stein's successors have pursued this important observation. For an uneven but provocative discussion of a more recent case of archival "repression" -- the "silencing" of World War II-era documents in French archival collections -- see Sonia Combe, *Archives interdites: les peurs françaises face à l'histoire contemporaine* (Paris: Albin Michel, 1994).
[61] On Series L's influence on French historiography, see Françoise Hildesheimer, "Périodisation et archives," in *Périodes. La construction du temps historique. Actes du Ve colloque d'histoire au présent* (Paris: Editions de l'Ecole des Hautes Etudes en Sciences Sociales et Histoire au Présent, 1991), pp. 39-46.

have resisted the Minister's instructions, preferring to maintain their own systems of classification. And in fact, in the first months after the circular's publication, many local officials did exactly that, though some with more strategic finesse than others. In the Aube, the *chartiste* "missionary" Vallet de Viriville was just completing his final report on the department's archives when the 1841 circular arrived. Within weeks, Vallet had dashed off a letter to the Minister, claiming that although he would not be able to implement the new scheme himself, "I hasten to inform you that the analytical procedure that I have followed is exactly that prescribed in the 'first part of the framework.'"[62] By August, he was even more confident, publishing his own listing of what he now termed "*fonds*" in the archives of the Aube alongside a "concordance" between this listing and the 1841 framework.[63] Even a quick glance at this concordance reveals major disparities between the two structures: next to three of the nine pre-1790 series in the 1841 scheme, Vallet marked "nil," and next to two others he added "will eventually be part of the Legal Section [*section contentieuse*]." Yet by describing his framework in the language of the 1841 circular, he undoubtedly hoped to stave off what threatened to become a major overhaul of the organizational scheme it had taken him nearly three years to create.

Other archivists took a more confrontational approach. In June 1841, the archivist of the Seine-et-Oise, Breval, submitted a lengthy critique of the ministerial circular. While he agreed that a "uniform method of classification" for departmental archives was highly desirable, he feared that the method required by the Minister would prove impractical. Already burdened by the tasks of "locating and communicating documents to offices and administrative units, as well as supervising the return and preservation of these documents," he had no time to reclassify his collection. More important, he worried that instituting so many chronological divisions would serve to hinder research. Breval was particularly troubled by Series L:

> [T]he method proposed by Monsieur the Minister, which divides administrative affairs since the revolution into two series, that is, into one series from 1790 to the Year VIII, and into a second from the Year VIII to the present day and hereafter, could have serious drawbacks...because of the numerous changes that have taken place, both in the names of the

---

[62] A[uguste] Vallet de Viriville ("arch. paléographe") to Monsieur le Ministre [de l'Intérieur], Troyes, 12 May 1841, AN, box F2 I 367[13], folder "Ensemble du service. Personnel," pp. [1-2]. Vallet's emphasis.

[63] Vallet de Viriville, *Les archives historiques*, pp. 75-80.

various administrations that have followed one another and in the
different modifications in the local administrative districts that have been
made and may be made again.[64]

In Breval's view, the decade 1790-1800 was no different from the period
after 1800 since both had been marked by constant changes in local
administrations. He therefore argued against the special series and in favor
of organizing all post-1790 archives by a single set of subjects.

In August 1841, an Interior Ministry official responded to Breval's
criticisms, saying that while he thought the changes in administration were
not really so hard to follow, Breval was free to omit the special series if he
wished. "You must have noticed," wrote the Paris official, "that as far as
concerns the formation of this special series, my circular does not carry any
strict obligation."[65] However, the Ministry soon changed its tune, making a
steadily greater effort to enforce Circular No. 14 over the course of the
1840s. The ministerial agency responsible for mounting this effort was the
Commission des archives départementales et communales (Departmental and
communal archives commission, hereafter simply the Archives
Commission), appointed by Duchâtel in May 1841. The new commissioners
were a powerful group, including among them the authors of the 1841
circular (De Wailly, Portalis, Gadebled, and Leprevost), as well as four
legislators (including Ludovic Vitet) and several prominent scholars
(including writer Prosper Mérimée and Ecole des Chartes professor
Benjamin Guérard).[66] In their monthly meetings, regular correspondence,
and frequent inspection trips to provincial depositories, they not only
enforced and interpreted the new classification scheme but also began
associating this scheme with the work of the Ecole des Chartes. Thus by
looking at the Archives Commission's records, we can see how the central

---

[64] Breval, "Rapport du Conservateur des Archives de la Préfecture de Seine et Oise
à Monsieur le Préfet, en réponse aux instructions ministérielles du 24 avril 1841,
circulaire No. 14, sur la mise en ordre et le classement des Archives," 21 Jun. 1841,
AD Yvelines, box 3T/AD1, p. 3.
[65] [signature illegible] (Pour le Ministre [de l'Intérieur] et par autorisation, Le Sous
Secrétaire d'Etat) to Monsieur le Préfet de Seine-&-Oise, Paris, 7 Aug. 1841, AD
Yvelines, Box 3T/AD1, pp. [3-4].
[66] T[anneguy] Duchâtel, "Arrêté portant création, près le Ministère de l'intérieur,
d'une Commission des archives," Paris, 6 May 1841, ms. copy in AN, box AB
XXVI 1*, pp. 3-4 . The commission met more or less monthly from 25 May 1841
to 18 Jan. 1854.

government of the 1840s began to refashion both state archives and state archivists.

The commission's primary function, according to these records, was to review the archival inventories that the 1841 circular had required prefects to submit to the Ministry of the Interior. Like the Historical Works Committee established by Guizot in 1834, Duchâtel's Archives Commission paid special attention to the historical "treasures" mentioned in these listings, often requesting that prefects embellish their inventories with "historical notes." The Commission's requests could be remarkably demanding. For example, in May 1844, Commissioner De Wailly said of an inventory submitted by the Haute-Saône:

> It would be good, for the documents susceptible to an historical interest, to provide dates in detail and verbatim, [to give] an analysis of each document from before the fourteenth century, to say if the acts are on parchment or paper, originals or copies, in Latin or French, with or without their seals, [and] to make known, along with the exact location of each place, its Latin name with [its] modern equivalent.[67]

Far more often, however, the Commission expressed less interest in historical detail than in classificatory precision. The Commission refused to accept any inventories that did not adhere to the 1841 circular, often returning submissions again and again for departmental revision. The commissioners expressed particular frustration with archivists who seemed not to have understood the concept of a *fonds*, thus "mixing" documents that ought to have remained distinct. In November 1843, for example, they explained to the officials of the Ille-et-Vilaine:

> The words *fonds* and *article* have been poorly used. Indeed, one reads at the bottom of the first page of the inventory, '*Fonds* 1H, male religious orders,' which indicates that in the archivists' thinking, the '*Fonds* 1H' includes all male religious orders, while the circular of 24 April 1841 calls *fonds* the collection of titles that were the property of a single establishment...Messieurs the archivists have also made poor use of the word *article*...By reading the circular of 24 April 1841 with more attention, Messieurs the archivists would easily avoid errors of this kind.[68]

They also chastised archivists for ignoring the circular's chronological divisions, reiterating the circular's claim that such divisions were "fundamental" to provincial collections. Yet while the circular had only

---

[67] Commission des archives, "Procès-verbaux," 23 May 1844, 2: 20-21.
[68] Ibid., 16 Nov. 1843, 1: 154-155.

described Series L as the "period between 1790 and the Year VIII," the Commission started calling it the "intermediary" period, thus further emphasizing its marginal status within the framework. For example, in response to an inventory from the Ain whose main categories were "1st Room" and "2nd Room," the Commission noted that the archivist "has confused that which relates to state property, to secular and regular clergy, to corporations, to establishments, to families, to times before 1790, to the intermediary times from 1790 to the Year VIII, etc. . . . ." Soon archivists across France had adopted this language, and even today many Series L *dossiers* still bear the heading "Intermediary Period."[69]

The Archives Commission also went beyond the 1841 instructions by explicitly linking classification with preservation. Duchâtel's circulars of 1839 and 1841 had both claimed that the reclassification of departmental archives would make the collections more "useful" to local administrators, to families, and especially to historians. Although the Commission certainly never abandoned this claim, it appeared increasingly interested in how classification might improve the material preservation of archival documents. As early as its second meeting, the Commission concluded that while sturdy walls and clean floors might help protect provincial archives, classification was the best guard against theft and disorder; when every document had a number marking its proper place in the collection, nothing would be lost or neglected. This argument soon became a central component of state archival policy, as is clear from Duchâtel's circular of June 1844, apparently based on an Archives Commission proposal.[70] Rather misleadingly titled "Instructions concerning the elimination and sale of useless papers," this new circular ordered prefects not to destroy any archival documents before the classification by series and *fonds* was complete, since there were certain series—including all of those prior to 1790—that could never be eliminated for any reason.[71]

---

[69] Ibid., 26 Jan. 1843, 1: 102-103. The phrase "intermediary period" undoubtedly has its origins in the field of law; under the Empire, legal experts had referred disparagingly to the period between the start of the Revolution and the elaboration of the Napoleonic Code as the time of *droit intermédiaire*, or "intermediary law." I am grateful to Malick Ghachem and Peter Sahlins for alerting me to this connection.

[70] Commission des archives, "Procès-verbaux," 13 Jun. 1844, 2: 28-29.

[71] T[anneguy] Duchâtel, "Circulaire [with marginal heading: "Instructions concernant la suppression et la vente des papiers inutiles"]," Paris, 24 Jun. 1844, AN, box AB Vf 1, folder "Archives départementales (1820-1857)...."

But the Commission was not just reshaping departmental archives to fit the new system of classification; it was also reshaping the role of the departmental archivist. Interior Minister Duchâtel's circular of 1839 had not only required departmental administrations to appoint a permanent archivist (as François Morand had suggested in 1838) but had also reserved the right to review all such appointments. In 1841, the Archives Commission took on the responsibility of reviewing departmental appointees on the Minister's behalf.[72] Far from simply rubber-stamping these appointments, the Commission undertook painstaking evaluations of each nominee. What were the Commission's criteria? The most formal discussion of the Commission's conception of a "good archivist" can be found in the "General Regulations for Departmental Archives" it prepared in March 1843:

> The functions of the Archivist include the preservation and organization [*mise en ordre*] of papers and documents of all kinds, the making of inventories, [and] the communication and copy of documents. He directs the work of the Employees assigned to assist him. He looks after the security of the premises, the cleanliness and management of the depository, and the maintenance of the fixtures. He is responsible for events that might be attributed to a lack of care and supervision on his part.[73]

Although this passage seems to emphasize the archivist's role as preserver, in its monthly discussions of archival nominees (as in its discussions of archival depositories), the Commission consistently subordinated preservation to classification. The Commission only occasionally cited candidates' attention to safety and cleanliness, but it never neglected to comment on their ability to adhere to classification by *fonds*. In fact, the Commission seems to have used the inventories submitted by these candidates (who had often assumed their functions pending ministerial

---

[72] Duchâtel, "Circulaire," 8 Aug. 1839, col. 878. Duchâtel presented these demands as clarifications of the law of 10 May 1838, which among many other provisions unrelated to archives, had required departmental administrations to include in their budgets the cost of the "protection and preservation" of their archives (see "Loi sur les attributions des conseils-généraux et des conseils d'arrondissement," *Le Moniteur universel*, 13 May 1838, p. 1221). The Archives Commission began reviewing archival appointees in November 1841 (see its "Procès-verbaux," 1: 24).

[73] T[anneguy] Duchâtel, "Circulaire [with marginal heading, "Archives départementales. Envoi d'un règlement général de ces archives"]," Paris, 7 Mar. 1843, AN, box AB Vf 1, folder "Archives départementales (1820-1857)...," p. 3.

approval) to determine their fitness as official archivists. Hence the unhappy experience of the archivists nominated to head the depository of the Ille-et-Vilaine, who had to submit inventories at least three times over as many years before finally obtaining the Commission's approval.[74]

Chartistes were by no means exempt from this stringent review; in 1844, the Commission called Louis Redet (class of 1834) "skillful and hardworking" but deplored the many gaps in his inventory of the former Abbey of Montierneuf.[75] Nevertheless, the Commission clearly hoped that the newest generation of Ecole des Chartes graduates would provide the classification experts necessary for the complete and consistent application of Circular No. 14. Much of its first meeting was spent debating how best to use the school's students to "establish order" in departmental collections. One suggestion, offered by the head of the Royal Archives, amounted to an elaboration of the existing program of missions; armed with Duchâtel's various instructions, young *chartistes* would set out for the most neglected of provincial depositories, relaying their findings to the Paris Commission. Later that year, the Commission did send a freshly-minted Archivist-Paleographer, Louis de Mas Latrie, on mission to the furthest reaches of the Ariège to classify the region's archives.[76] Over the course of the 1840s, however, the Commission became increasingly committed to a second approach: assigning *chartistes* as permanent archivists. During an 1842 meeting, for example, they agreed that more *chartistes* were needed in departmental depositories and formally requested that the Minister remind the school's graduates about existing vacancies.[77] Ecole des Chartes students were "born candidates" for departmental archivist positions, as one member explained, and the Commission had to help them fulfill their professional destinies.

How did it happen, then, that only four graduates of the Ecole des Chartes became departmental archivists in the period 1841-48?[78] Some members of the Commission worried that the prospect of spending an entire career in an isolated provincial depository was unappealing to *chartistes* used to the pleasures of Paris, especially given the salaries offered by most

---

[74] See especially Commission des archives, "Procès-verbaux," 18 Apr. 1844, 2: 4-5.

[75] Ibid., 11 Jul. 1844, 2: 32-33.

[76] Ibid., 25 May 1841 and 10 Dec. 1841, 1: 7, 32.

[77] Ibid., 17 Mar. 1842, 1: 69.

[78] Léon Aubineau, in the Aube (1841) and later in the Indre-et-Loire (1842); Paul Marchegay, in the Maine-et-Loire (1841); Gabriel Eysenbach, in the Nièvre (1842); and Philippe Guignard, in the Aube (1843).

departmental administrations.[79] It is certainly not hard to believe that some new Archivist-Paleographers (many of them less than twenty-five years old) would have balked at the idea of abandoning the social and intellectual attractions of the capital; yet there was likely another reason for the lack of *chartistes* in departmental archivist positions, one never explicitly acknowledged by the Archives Commission. By the 1840s, the graduates of the Ecole des Chartes were no longer simply the pawns of the Academy of Inscriptions (as they had been in the 1820s) or the Historical Works Committee (as they were in the 1830s) but had come into their own as members of the Société de l'Ecole des Chartes, the alumni organization formed in 1839. Although the new society was in many respects dependent upon the French state, it nevertheless exercised its independence as a private association to challenge official policy, both directly and indirectly. While the state (in this case represented by the Archives Commission, an official agency of the Minister of the Interior) hoped to mold *chartistes* into expert classifiers who would carry Circular 14 into the farthest corners of France, the Société de l'Ecole des Chartes offered its own conception of the Archivist-Paleographer, one not yet explicitly tied to archival classification.

The available records of the early Society include the minutes of its monthly meetings as well as the contents of its journal, the *Bibliothèque de l'Ecole des Chartes*, first published in 1840. As Nancy Bartlett has recently pointed out, these texts do not offer any substantive commentary either on the classification scheme of 1841 or on archival classification more generally.[80] The notion of *respect des fonds*, so central to the work of the Archives Commission, is completely absent. In fact, these sources show that the Society actually avoided the topic of classification. During its December 1839 meeting, the group voted not to publish any "instructions to archivists regarding their classification work," noting that Duchâtel's instructions would soon be appearing.[81] Two years later, Vallet de Viriville presented an "article on the organization of departmental archives" (probably based on

---

[79] See for example Commission des archives, "Procès-verbaux," 25 May 1841, 2: 12.

[80] Nancy Bartlett, "La naissance de la Société de l'Ecole des chartes: les chartistes entre l'histoire et l'administration," in *L'Ecole nationale des chartes: histoire de l'école depuis 1821*, ed. Yves-Marie Bercé, Olivier Guyotjeannin, and Marc Smith (Thionville, France: Gérard Klopp, 1997), pp. 237-239.

[81] "Société de l'Ecole des chartes. Registre No 1. Fondation de la Société. Procès-Verbaux des Séances. Procès-Verbal de la Séance du 5 décembre 1839," AN, box 11 AS 2, volume for 1839-41, pp. 63-65.

his August 1841 *Archives historiques du département de l'Aube*, which includes a vigorous attack on the slow pace of archival classification along with the classificatory "concordance" discussed above), but then quickly retracted it in response to grumblings from his colleagues.[82] Classification, it seems, had no place on the Society's agenda.

While one might assume that the Society eschewed debate about archival classification in order to demonstrate its support for ministerial policies, the Society's records suggest otherwise. Vallet did not retract his article on departmental archives out of loyalty to the Minister of the Interior but in the name of the "good harmony and unity of opinions that until the present has not ceased to reign among the members of the Society." Moments later, the rest of the organization endorsed his appeal to unity, agreeing that "in the future no member of the Society [would] publicly manifest his personal opinion on the organization or the future of the Ecole des Chartes without consulting the Society first."[83] Though Society members evidently had serious disagreements about archival classification and their role in it (fueled, no doubt, by the flurry of competing classification schemes recently developed by Vallet and other missionary *chartistes*), they determined that resolving these disputes was less important than ensuring solidarity. And indeed throughout the 1840s, the Society worked hard to both build internal consensus and rebuff external challenges, in the process often directly attacking ministerial policies.

From its first meeting in April 1839, it was clear that the Society would not be just another forum for scholarly exchange but also a vigorous advocate for the professional advancement of its members. The main topic of conversation was not medieval diplomatics but rather the "means of bringing about an amelioration in the position [and] future of the students of the Ecole des Chartes."[84] In the eyes of the Society, the government had been appallingly negligent in its enforcement of the 1829 Ecole des Chartes ordinance, which had promised graduates of the school positions in state-owned archives and libraries.[85] The Society therefore committed itself to publicizing and condemning the hiring of non-*chartistes*, both in letters of protest to the Minister of the Interior and in the pages of its official journal,

---

[82] "Société de l'Ecole royale des chartes. Procès-verbaux des séances de la société et du conseil. 1841-1842. -- 1842-1843," 2 Dec. 1841, AN box 11 AS 2, fol. 7r.

[83] Ibid.

[84] "Réunion du Conseil [de la Société de l'Ecole des Chartes]," 12 Apr. 1839, AN, box 11 AS 2, folder "Statuts, 1839-1843," p. [1].

[85] See chap. 2.

the *Bibliothèque de l'Ecole des Chartes*. For the journal's inaugural issue, member Martial Delpit prepared a lengthy "Historical Note" in which he argued that while the Ecole des Chartes had rendered countless services to the French state over the years, the central government had repeatedly violated *chartistes'* "rights" to official posts. If the government wished to reap the benefits of the school's expertise, it would put an end to the many "infractions" of the 1829 ordinance.[86] Subsequent issues reiterated this claim, including a note in the anonymous "Chronicle" section whenever a non-*chartiste* obtained a position in a public depository.

The Society occasionally complained about the appointment of outsiders as departmental archivists. In the early 1840s, for instance, it wrote the Minister of the Interior to protest the hiring of a "M. de Courson" at the "archives of Bretagne."[87] Society member Hercule Géraud made a more sweeping complaint in the 1841 *Bibliothèque de l'Ecole des Chartes*, arguing that while the Minister had once claimed that departmental archives "*needed* Archivist-Paleographers," prefects hired archivists from everywhere *but* the Ecole des Chartes.[88] Nevertheless, the Society was not only or even particularly concerned about departmental archivist positions. Some of its most strident criticism highlighted unfair hiring practices at the Royal Archives in Paris. For example, in July 1840, the Society's governing council told the Minister of the Interior:

> We recently had the honor of reminding your Excellence that a royal ordinance of 11 November 1829 reserves for the students of the Ecole des Chartes half of the librarian and archivist positions that you have at your disposal. Since then, two people absolutely foreign to our Institution have been called to important functions at the Royal Archives…. We are far from believing we can supervise the actions of your administration; but [the 1829 ordinance]…has not ceased to be misunderstood for ten years, and to let it [lapse] would be to annul from now on the resolution we have made to take every opportunity to affirm it by legal means.[89]

---

[86] Martial Delpit, "Notice historique sur l'Ecole royale des Chartes," *BEC* 1 (1840): 17.

[87] Société de l'Ecole des Chartes to Monsieur le Ministre, [between 1839 and 1843], AN, box 11 AS 2, folder "Statuts, 1839-1843," p. [1].

[88] H[ercule] Géraud, "De l'organisation projétée des archives départementales," *BEC* 2 (1841): 505-505. Géraud's emphasis.

[89] Conseil de la société de l'Ecole Royale des Chartes [H. Bordier, L. Lacabane, Adre. le Noble, E. de Fréville, J. Quicherat, H. Géraud, Le Roux de Lincy, and L. Douët D'arcq] to Monsieur le Ministre de l'Intérieur, Paris, 8 Jul. 1840, AN, box

The group raised similar objections to the exclusion of *chartistes* from posts in public libraries. When both the Arsenal and the Royal Library passed over qualified Archivist-Paleographers in 1843, the *Bibliothèque*'s editors said they were hardly surprised; the 1829 ordinance was a "deceptive act" [*acte menteur*] that had provided only empty promises to unsuspecting *chartistes*.[90] Thus while the Archives Commission worked to identify *chartistes* with departmental archives, the Society's members identified themselves less with a particular kind of collection than with a certain set of skills, in their view obtainable only at the Ecole des Chartes.

What were these skills? How did the graduates of the school conceive of their own expertise? The most telling source on this point is the *Bibliothèque de l'Ecole des Chartes*, whose editors and (with rare exceptions) contributors were all Ecole des Chartes alumni.[91] From the pages of the *Bibliothèque*, it is clear that the graduates of the Ecole des Chartes thought of themselves first and foremost as readers and interpreters of medieval texts. The preface to the first volume announced that the journal would be "devoted to the study of history and literature according to original documents," and would therefore feature work in both "paleography" and "criticism." Articles would include discussions of "fragments of ancient authors, pieces of medieval literature, poems of the troubadours and trouvères, chronicles and histories, charters, diplomas, inscriptions, etc." as well as "essays on little-known or distorted facts, verification of inexact assertions advanced by historians, biography of important and forgotten personages, restitutions of corrupted texts, [and] research on ancient French dialects."[92] By the sixth volume (1844-45), the editors made their mission even more explicit, adding

---

AB Va 6, folder "1830-1848. Droit du Garde général dans la nomination des chefs de section et employés...," pp. [1-2]. See also *BEC* 1 (1840): 582-583.

[90] *BEC* 5 (1844): 102-103. Hercule Géraud (class of 1839 and member of the Society's governing council) was apparently so angered by an 1843 decision to hire a non-*chartiste* at the Bibliothèque Mazarine that he drafted a scathing article on the subject for the *BEC*. The article, never published, is in his notebook, "Résumé du Cours de Diplomatique de Mr. Guérard. Notes diverses," AEC-SC, series B, item 2, fols. 72r-74v.

[91] The journal included occasional contributions from non-*chartistes*, though these were usually scholars closely associated with the school (e.g., Jean-Marie Pardessus, head of the school's advisory board). See Charles Samaran, "Le centenaire de notre revue, la 'Bibliothèque de l'Ecole des chartes' depuis un siècle," *BEC* 100 (1939): 257-280.

[92] *BEC* 1 (1840): i-ii.

after "Bibliothèque de l'Ecole des Chartes" the subtitle, "Scholarly journal devoted principally to the study of the Middle Ages."

By publishing their own scholarly review, the members of the Society were not only demonstrating their mastery of medieval paleography and criticism but also staking a proprietary claim to these fields. While the journal had some four hundred subscribers by the late 1840s (ranging from King Louis-Philippe to the future Napoleon III and from Guizot to Chateaubriand), the editors increasingly excluded non-*chartistes* from publishing in its pages, implying that only graduates of the school had the training necessary for the proper evaluation of medieval sources.[93] The editors also made this claim rather more pointedly in a series of notes in the "Chronicle" section of the journal. In 1843, for example, they described a case recently brought before the Parisian court, in which the French state had attempted to demonstrate its rights to forests belonging to the town of Soucy by pointing to a set of thirteenth-century charters. Since the charters were in medieval Latin (a language whose "barbarism," the journal's editors added smugly, they understood "better than anyone"), the state's lawyers "did not understand at all the meaning of the text[s]," and therefore "the court referred the examination of the difficult titles to M. Lacabane [a *chartiste*], who easily clarified their interpretation."[94] The moral of the story was clear: *chartistes* alone were capable of contending with the difficulties posed by medieval texts.

Chartistes' expertise in medieval paleography was by no means lost on the Interior Minister's Archives Commission. As early as 1839, Duchâtel had argued that graduates of the Ecole des Chartes, "versed in the study of charters and ancient monuments," would be especially useful in classifying "historical" (i.e., pre-1790) archives, and the Commission seems to have taken care in assigning *chartistes* to departmental archives known to possess rich collections of older documents.[95] Nevertheless, it also chastised *chartistes* for their "repugnance for dealing with the administrative [post-1790] part of

---

[93] On the journal's subscribers, see Marie-Clothilde Hubert, "Réseaux, appuis, rayonnement: les premiers souscripteurs de la *Bibliothèque de l'Ecole des chartes* (1839-1851)," in *L'Ecole nationale des chartes: histoire de l'école depuis 1821*, pp. 232-236. On the increasing exclusion of non-*chartistes*, see Samaran, "Le centenaire," p. 264-268 and Jean Le Pottier, "Histoire et érudition. Recherches et documents sur l'histoire et le rôle de l'érudition médiévale dans l'historiographie du XIXe siècle" (Thesis, Ecole nationale des Chartes, 1979), p. 107.

[94] *BEC* 5 (1844): 517-518.

[95] Duchâtel, "Circulaire," 8 Aug. 1839, col. 878.

the archives."[96] From the Commission's perspective, it seems, the proper classification of entire collections was ultimately more important than the painstaking evaluation of individual historical sources, while for the Société de l'Ecole des Chartes, this evaluation lay at the heart of the *chartistes'* endeavor.

Though historical expertise was clearly the linchpin of the Society's sense of collective identity, an intriguing entry in the *Bibliothèque*'s "Chronicle" for 1842 suggests this identity contained two other components as well. The entry begins with the provocative declaration: "Nothing demonstrates in a more peremptory fashion the necessity of a close and rigorous supervision of the nomination of departmental archivists than the scandalous affair that has just been debated before the Assizes Court of the Indre-et-Loire." The focus of the trial, the entry explains, was Jean-Claude-Marius Seytre (who, as we saw earlier, took courses at the Ecole des Chartes before leaving Paris to become the archivist of the Indre-et-Loire in Tours). In 1842, "having involved himself in the Indre-et-Loire elections with far too much zeal," Seytre "sensed that remaining in the Touraine was henceforth forbidden [to him]," and arranged to be transferred to the archives of the Aube instead. But no sooner had Seytre arrived in the Aube than "infinitely more serious accusations were raised against him." Lawyers in the Indre-et-Loire charged Seytre with stealing "printed books, manuscripts, parchments, autographs, [and] art objects" from a half-dozen public libraries and archives in and around Tours. Found guilty of most of these charges, Seytre was condemned to two years in prison.[97]

The *Bibliothèque*'s account of this "scandalous affair" studiously avoids mentioning Seytre's early connection to the Ecole des Chartes. To the editors of the journal, it seems, Seytre was not only not a real *chartiste* but a kind of anti-*chartiste*, engaged in behavior antithetical to the *chartistes'* mission. The scandalous elements of Seytre's behavior were apparently two-fold: first, and most important, he stole some of the very treasures he was charged to protect. A full-fledged *chartiste*, the *Bibliothèque* implies, would never have plundered public collections in this way. Yet the entry also mentions another failing: Seytre's overzealous involvement in local elections. Though the *Bibliothèque* hardly gives this point much attention, it is worth noting because it offers the first inkling of what would soon become an important component of the *chartiste*'s self-conception: political neutrality. Until the 1840s, descriptions of *chartistes* in particular and French archivists

[96] Commission des Archives, "Procès-verbaux," 1: 27.
[97] *BEC* 4 (1843): 308-309.

in general made no mention of their personal attachment to (or detachment from) political debates; but by the latter half of the century, as we will see, graduates of the school had come to pride themselves on their "objective" stance in relation to French politics. This emerging commitment to political neutrality may also help explain why the Society was so reluctant to discuss archival classification. If, as this chapter has tried to demonstrate, the 1841 scheme represented a political argument in archival form, the Society's decision not to discuss the scheme may indicate an unwillingness to engage with this argument.

Considering that in the final decade of the July Monarchy, the graduates of the Ecole des Chartes assembled themselves into an organized Society, began publishing their own scholarly journal, and started articulating their "rights" as public-minded conservators and neutral historical experts, can one argue that they had at last become "professionalized"? As Jan Goldstein explains in her now-classic *Console and Classify: The French Psychiatric Profession in the Nineteenth Century*, deciding what counts as a "profession" can be quite tricky, not least because the twentieth-century English term "profession" has no nineteenth-century French equivalent. Goldstein nonetheless draws on recent work in sociology to isolate four basic attributes of a "profession":

> (1) a body of esoteric knowledge, mastery of which is indispensable qualification for practice; (2) monopoly—that is, recognition of the exclusive competence of the profession in the general domain to which its body of knowledge refers; (3) autonomy, or control by the profession over its work, including who can legitimately do that work and how the work should be done; and (4) a service ideal—a commitment or ethical imperative to place the welfare of the public or of the individual client above the self-interest of the practitioner, even though the practitioner is earning a living through exercise of the profession.[98]

Given these criteria, it may be more fitting to describe the *chartistes* of the 1840s as "proto-professional" rather than "professional." While the members of the Société de l'Ecole des Chartes clearly had begun to think of themselves as a self-monitoring group with a legal claim on certain kinds of work, they did not yet wield the monopoly on departmental archivist positions that would come with the Second Republic. Nor had they fully elaborated the body of knowledge (including classification and preservation as well as paleography and history) that would distinguish their late nineteenth-century successors. Finally, though they constantly vaunted their

---

[98] Jan Goldstein, *Console and Classify: The French Psychiatric Profession in the Nineteenth Century* (Cambridge: Cambridge University Press, 1987), pp. 10-15.

"services" to state and scholarship, they had not yet articulated their duties
to the "public" to the extent that they would in the 1850s and 1860s. Like
Goldstein's "alienists" in this same period, the *chartistes* of the 1840s were a
profession in formation.[99]

One of the key steps in the transformation of the corps of *chartistes* into a
full-fledged profession was the December 1846 reorganization of the Ecole
des Chartes. Since its establishment in February 1821, the school had
already undergone one major reorganization, in November 1829. In both
1821 and 1829, the elaboration of the school's mission and curriculum had
fallen to just a few men: the Minister of the Interior and two or three
prominent scholars. Yet the 1846 reorganization involved a much broader
array of politicians and intellectuals, including, for the first time, both
individual *chartistes* and the Société de l'Ecole des Chartes. As we have seen,
the Society and the state's Archives Commission promoted two rather
different conceptions of the ideal *chartiste*. To the Society, the *chartiste* was an
expert decipherer and consummate medieval scholar, while to the Archives
Commission he (never she) was above all a classifier, defining and stabilizing
archival order in accordance with the 1841 circular. In the waning years of
the July regime, these two conceptions came together—if somewhat
uneasily—in the Ecole des Chartes curriculum that would shape state
approaches to libraries and archives for the next twenty years.

Although Guizot had talked of revamping the Ecole des Chartes as early
as 1830, serious plans for the school's reorganization did not get underway
until 1840, perhaps in part due to urgings from the Société de l'Ecole des
Chartes, formed the previous year.[100] A packet of anonymous scribbled
notes, labeled "Plans for the reform of the School" dates to around 1840.[101]
Yet the first substantive proposal came from Jean-Marie Pardessus, head of

---

[99] In future work, I hope to offer a more extended comparison between the
professionalization of Archivist-Paleographers and the professionalization of other
groups in mid-nineteenth-century France.
[100] The only substantive proposal for a reform of the 1829 curriculum from before
1840 is "De l'Ecole des Chartes, de son Etat actuel, & des Réformes qui lui sont
nécessaires (Septembre 1830)," presented to Guizot by student Auguste Savagner
(AN, box F17-4024; nearly identical text in AN, box M257B). It is not clear
whether Guizot responded to Savagner's suggestions (which, like those of his late
July Monarchy successors, emphasized historical training).
[101] AEC, folder "Ecole des Chartes. établie...."

the school's governing commission, in 1841.[102] Pardessus argued for maintaining the two existing courses (the elementary course on "decipherment" taught by Guérard and the advanced course on diplomatics and paleography taught by Champollion-Figeac) but suggested adding a third, which he described as

> a history course on the political, ecclesiastical, civil, and judicial institutions and the geography of France in the Middle Ages, in which the professor, instead of losing himself in theories, hypotheses, [and] systems, would only draw his demonstrations and explanations from contemporary and authentic documents.[103]

Pardessus' proposal is intriguing on two counts. On the one hand, it advocates a rather dramatic expansion of the school's mission; instead of teaching only the internal analysis of individual documents (decipherment, translation, dating, and authentication), the school would now offer instruction on broader shifts in medieval institutions and territories. For the first time, "history," not just diplomatics and paleography, would enter the curriculum. On the other hand, Pardessus recommends a particular kind of historical training, one based on "contemporary and authentic documents" rather than "theories, hypotheses, [and] systems." Though Pardessus does not accuse anyone in particular of "losing himself" in flights of historical fancy, his comment might be taken as an indirect critique of the kind of history then being professed by Jules Michelet at the Collège de France. While Michelet, also head of the Historical Section at the Royal Archives, was certainly no stranger to "authentic" medieval documents, his immensely popular public lectures quickly moved away from his particular sources to ponder the identity and future of France.[104] Pardessus was proposing a different sort of history, one more narrowly rooted in contemporary sources and, perhaps, less given to political musings.

We find a similar proposal in an 1846 letter from Ernest de Fréville (Ecole des Chartes class of 1839) to the Minister of Public Instruction. Fréville asked that the Minister augment the school's curriculum with a

---

[102] Unfortunately, this governing board, the *Commission de l'Ecole des Chartes*, has left few traces.

[103] AN box F17-4024 contains a "Note de M. Pardessus, sur l'Ecole des Chartes" (Paris, 2 Mar. 1841) as well as an unsigned and undated "Note sur l'école des chartes" that can be clearly attributed to Pardessus and dated to before 1846. The contents of both notes are quite similar, including some passages that are repeated verbatim. The passage quoted here is from the undated manuscript, p. [7].

[104] See Fauquet, *Michelet*.

course on the great "chroniclers" [*annalistes*] of the French past. Yet what Fréville had in mind was no impassioned review of France's struggles and successes. He argued instead for a careful dissection of existing chronicles in order to determine "what parts...merit confidence, [and] what others must be suspected of partiality, ignorance, or plagiarism." For in Fréville's view, "as soon as one studies the history of France with care, one notices not only that much highly necessary information is completely lacking, but also that numerous points are not well established."[105] The only way to avoid having to rewrite the chronicles from scratch, he explained, was to test their claims against the "solid guarantees" of original documents. For Fréville, then, as for Pardessus, studying history was not about developing overarching narratives or elaborate theories but about establishing historical truths through the painstaking analysis of primary sources. Hence adding a course in French history to the offerings of the Ecole des Chartes did not mean replicating courses already offered at other institutions but instead building on the methods already taught at the school to create a particularly *chartiste* approach to the study of history.

Yet not everyone agreed that adding courses in French history—even courses based on authentic documents—was what the school needed most. In early 1843, Augustin Thierry wrote his good friend, Public Instruction Minister Villemain, to recommend a major reevaluation of the Ecole des Chartes' curriculum. He claimed that while the two existing courses had "merit," they did not provide "sufficient instruction." By "sufficient instruction," Thierry explained, "I do not at all mean to express the complete understanding of the sources of our history, but the simple notions that ought to suit the title of <u>Archivist Paleographer</u>." In Thierry's view, although the school had been awarding this title for nearly fourteen years, it had yet to properly train either archivists or paleographers. His letter to Villemain takes each of these terms in turn:

> The title of <u>archivist</u> presupposes theoretical and practical knowledge about which the two successive courses, the one that teaches the reading of charters and the one that aims to teach their comprehension, cannot give the faintest smattering; for nothing in the program of these two courses is related to the classification of archives, the production of catalogues, [and]

---

[105] Ernest de Fréville to Monsieur le Ministre Secrétaire d'Etat de l'Instruction publique, Paris, 10 Apr. 1846, AN, box F17-4024, pp. [1-3].

the preparation of inventories [and] notes on diplomas and manuscripts.[106]

Without training in cataloguing and classification, Thierry argued, the degree granted by the Ecole des Chartes was nothing more than an "illusory title that is far from offering the administration the guarantees of the protection and organization [*mise en ordre*] of our archives that it seems to promise." The label of "paleographer" was equally misleading:

> If the word <u>paleographer</u> is not taken in its most limited sense, [as one with] the ability to read ancient acts, if one applies it, as one must, to the conditions of special study and of various genres required for cooperation in the great historical publications undertaken by the government, it is certain that in this regard as well there is a gap in the lessons at the Ecole des Chartes.

According to Thierry, while the young Benedictines of the eighteenth century had undergone a "long noviciate" before beginning work on their great compendia, their nineteenth-century successors were put to work after just two introductory courses, thus forcing the academicians and historians in charge of the government's publication projects to waste valuable time completing their training.[107] As long as the Ecole des Chartes failed to provide training both in archival classification and in manuscript publication, its "Archivist-Paleographers" would have little to offer the July Regime.

Thierry's solution to the inadequacies of the school's curriculum was a new course, which would treat both the "[t]heory of archival classification and the theory of the publication of diplomas and other historical documents." As he explained in a second letter to Villemain, the first part of this course would emphasize the "rules" of archival classification, the critical evaluation of existing inventories and catalogues, and finally "practical exercises" in the preparation of inventories of medieval sources.[108] The second half of the course would turn to the details of historical publication, including "the order and arrangement of documents, the collation of manuscripts, prolegomena and commentaries, annotation and cross-references, tables of contents, [etc.]." In Thierry's view, the combination of all these lessons in classification and publication would do more than just fill

---

[106] Augustin Thierry to Mon cher ami [Villemain], Paris, 18 Jan. 1843, AN, box F17-4024, p. [2].

[107] Ibid., pp. [2-3].

[108] Augustin Thierry to Mon cher ami [Villemain], Paris, 7 Feb. 1843, AN, box F17-4024, p. [4].

out the curriculum of the Ecole des Chartes; it would constitute the first formal instruction in an ancient and revered science: "the science of historical sources and proofs." This science was not the same as history but instead a "science exterior to history," characterized by "its own rules and methods." It was the task of the Ecole des Chartes to reinvigorate this neglected science.

Was Thierry's proposal perhaps a much-delayed response to François Morand, the provincial archivist who in 1838 had pleaded for his help in developing a corps of permanent archivists and a program for archival classification? We cannot tell. Yet regardless of Thierry's immediate motivations, his letters to Villemain offer an intriguing counterpoint to the proposals submitted by Pardessus and Fréville. Both of these proposals had implied that by extending its reach beyond diplomatics and paleography to "history," the Ecole des Chartes would offer a corrective to the grandiose and error-ridden accounts of historians both past and present. *Chartistes*, in other words, would not only become historians, but better and more truthful historians than all the rest. In contrast, Thierry's proposal envisioned *chartistes* not as historians, but as archivists (classifiers of historical collections) and paleographers (editors of original sources). Furthermore, while Pardessus and Fréville had spoken only in terms of the benefits their courses might provide to scholarship (e.g., the "solid guarantees" vaunted by Fréville), Thierry emphasized the benefits his new course would bring to the French state. Properly trained archivists would respond to the current administration's need for the "protection and organization" of France's archives, while appropriately skilled paleographers would help complete the government's compendia of historical sources. Thus if Pardessus and Fréville might be seen as articulating some of the arguments expressed by the Société de l'Ecole des Chartes, Thierry might be seen as articulating the wishes of the Orleanist state, both from the perspective of the Historical Works Committee (which wanted paleographers for its historical publications) and the Archives Commission (which wanted archivists to carry out its classification program).

It therefore took someone involved in all of these organizations to begin to bring these different conceptions of the Ecole des Chartes together. That person was Benjamin Guérard, Ecole des Chartes class of 1823, professor of the elementary course on "decipherment" since 1831, and active member of both the Historical Works Committee and the Archives Commission.[109] Guérard had long argued that *érudits*, or experts in the study of original documents, were the only true historians of his era. For example, in an 1829 review of Guizot's lecture course in modern history at the Paris Faculty of Letters, Guérard roundly condemned the "rational and purely speculative method" adopted by "history professors at the Collège de France and the Faculty of Letters." In Guérard's view, only historical instruction based on the methods of the Benedictines, that is, based on the careful analysis of "contemporary monuments," was capable of promoting the "progress of history."[110] Consequently, in 1837, he lobbied vigorously, though unsuccessfully, for the vacant chair in history at the Collège de France (eventually awarded to Michelet).[111] Yet even as he promoted the *chartistes'* methods as the only truly "historical" methods, Guérard also helped construct an image of the *chartiste* as expert classifier and state servant. At the first meeting of Duchâtel's Archives Commission, in May 1841, Guérard argued for teaching the students of the Ecole des Chartes how to classify departmental archives:

> Without a doubt, the studies [undertaken at] this school suitably prepare students for the exploration of ancient documents, but not for the work of classification. They are capable of undertaking paleographic studies, but not at first of organizing archives. It is very important for the success of their work that they be given a good method.[112]

Both of these visions of the Ecole des Chartes are present in Guérard's proposal for the reorganization of the school, submitted sometime in the early 1840s.[113] Much like Pardessus, Guérard suggested adding a third-year course in French history, which he hoped would cover "geography, history,

---

[109] On Guérard see Natalis de Wailly, *Notice sur M. Daunou...suivie d'une notice sur M. Guérard* (Paris: Dumoulin, 1855), partially reproduced in *BEC* 16 (1855): 385-411. On Guérard's participation in the Historical Works Committee, see chap. 2.

[110] Benjamin Guérard, review of *Cours d'histoire moderne...*, by [François] Guizot, *L'Universel*, 15 Oct. 1829. For a thoughtful analysis and full transcription of this review, see Le Pottier, "Histoire et érudition," 86-96 and 511-515. Guérard made a similar argument on the opening day of his elementary course in 1831; see "Ecole des Chartes, Discours d'ouverture du cours de première année," *France littéraire* 1 (1832): 268-280.

[111] See Fauquet, *Michelet*, chap. 7.

[112] Commission des Archives, "Procès-verbaux," 25 May 1841, 1: 14.

[113] The note "sur la division des cours de l'école" attributed to Guérard, describes courses to be taught in 1844 (AN, box F17-4024).

origins, customs, institutions, both national and feudal; people and land conditions; coins and measures in use in France during the Middle Ages." Yet he also sided with Thierry in calling for instruction in archival classification. His plan for the second-year course included not only the "principles of chronology and forms of dates," already covered under the 1829 curriculum, but also the "classification of texts and distinction of different kinds of documents," and, more specifically, the "arrangement of archives according to the plan adopted and published by Monsieur the Minister of the Interior for departmental and communal archives."[114] Guérard's *chartistes*, then, would be both erudite historians and official classifiers.

After years of proposals and counter-proposals, Narcisse de Salvandy (the successor to Thierry's friend Villemain as Minister of Public Instruction) officially reorganized the Ecole des Chartes in December 1846.[115] Responding to demands voiced both by state agencies and by the growing corps of *chartistes*, Salvandy's ordinance greatly increased the size and status of the school by enlarging its budget, granting it new classroom space, increasing the number of professors and students, guaranteeing a salary to its graduates, and, most important, dramatically expanding and revising its curriculum.[116] Though one might expect that the new curriculum would have placed more emphasis on classification (apparently the state's leading concern) than on historical analysis, it in fact featured both subjects, suggesting that both the Archives Commission and the Société de l'Ecole des Chartes had managed to make their voices heard. As in Guérard's proposal, the new curriculum included a second-year course in archival classification as well as third-year courses in "political, ecclesiastical, and civil geography" and "history of the political institutions of France in the Middle Ages."[117]

---

[114] Ibid., p. [1].

[115] For the budgetary debates in the Chamber of Deputies that helped prepare the way for the December 1846 ordinance, see *Le Moniteur Universel*, 27 May 1846, pp. 1541-1543.

[116] For the text of the ordinance, signed by Salvandy and King Louis-Philippe, see *BEC* 8 (1847): 170-173; and *Le Moniteur universel*, 6 Jan. 1847.

[117] Interestingly, the classification course does not appear in the ordinance itself, only in the full list of courses elaborated by the school's governing council and published in 1847. See Ecole des Chartes, Conseil de Perfectionnement, "Procès-verbaux," 8 Feb. 1847, AEC (bound volume covering 1 Feb. 1847 to 11 Jan. 1864), pp. [14]-15.

Yet the new program did more than simply reproduce Guérard's outline; undoubtedly under the influence of Jean-Antoine Letronne (head of the Royal Archives, member of the Archives Commission, and now "Director" of the Ecole des Chartes), the curriculum extended both aspects of Guérard's proposal, recasting both the work of the *chartiste*-historian and the work of the *chartiste*-classifier.[118] In addition to the new courses in geography and medieval institutions, the third-year program also included lessons in the "archeology and arts of the Middle Ages," and "elements of civil law, canon law, and feudal law," thus stretching the limits of "erudite history" even further than Guérard had envisioned.[119] Perhaps more significant, the 1846 ordinance made an "*acte public*," or what quickly became known as a "thesis," one of the primary requirements for the degree of Archivist-Paleographer. While *chartistes* had long been publishing articles on medieval sources in their *Bibliothèque de l'Ecole des Chartes*, now this historical writing was formally incorporated into their training.[120] Students were expected not only to have mastered diplomatics, paleography, geography, medieval institutions, law, archeology, and art, but to have learned how to conduct their own analyses of "original monuments" and present their findings in coherent narrative form. The curriculum had become, in Letronne's words, "a sort of *encyclopedia* of the history of France, which nonetheless contains nothing superfluous or useless to its subject."[121]

---

[118] The 1847 program is nearly identical to a note "on the nature and gradation of instruction" at the Ecole des Chartes, attributed to Letronne and probably produced before September 1846 (the date of an anonymous "Note pour Monsieur le Ministre" that mentions a proposal "that is believed to be by Monsieur Letronne"). See AN, box F17-4024.

[119] On the new course in archeology, see Jacques Thirion, "L'archéologie à l'Ecole des chartes"; and on the course in law, see Gérard Giordanengo, "La chaire d'histoire des droits civil et canonique," both in *L'Ecole nationale des chartes: histoire de l'école depuis 1821*, pp. 86-91 and 72-81, respectively. According to Thirion, it was a *chartiste*, Jules Quicherat, who came up with the idea for a course in archeology; unfortunately, Quicherat's proposal has not survived.

[120] Though, as Olivier Guyotjeannin points out in "Naissance de la thèse (1849-1914)" (*L'Ecole nationale des chartes: histoire de l'école depuis 1821*, pp. 92-105), it was many years before the school's professors and administrators developed a regular system for evaluating student theses.

[121] [Jean-Antoine] Letronne in *Ecole Royale des Chartes. Séance d'inauguration (5 mai 1847)* (Paris: Impr. Paul Dupont, 1847), reproduced in *BEC* 8 (1847): 450-455. Passage quoted is from *BEC* p. 452. Italics in original.

Not everyone liked the idea of the *chartiste* as encyclopedic historian. In a forty-three page brief written just months before the passage of the 1846 ordinance, Pardessus argued that plans for the school had gotten out of hand. Though his earlier proposals had called for the expansion of the school's curriculum, now Pardessus feared that it was expanding too much:

> Diplomatics is the science of reading, understanding, and evaluating documents generically known as Diplomas and Charters. This science can undoubtedly also include the reading and appreciation of manuscripts that contain historical narratives, [and] literary and scholarly compositions.

> But if one wanted to extend the instruction at the Ecole des Chartes [in this way], the career would become too vast; one would be obliged to talk about the various branches of human knowledge that would be treated in the manuscripts [being studied]: it would be necessary to review in succession poetry, theology, philosophy, all the way through music…One would come to find no more limits, because all [fields of] human knowledge hold together and follow on one another.

Lest the Ecole des Chartes become an "encyclopedic school of the Middle Ages," Pardessus warned, professors would have to limit their lessons to diplomatics and paleography, eliminating all "accessories."[122] Yet in the final years of the history-obsessed July Monarchy, Pardessus' argument found no supporters; the new *chartistes*, though schooled in the methods of diplomatics and paleography, were, in theory, to extend their scholarly reach to every aspect of French history.

Just as the 1846 ordinance expanded early conceptions of the *chartiste*'s role as historian, it also significantly extended previous ideas about the *chartiste*'s role as classifier. While both Thierry and Guérard had argued for a course on the classification of state archives, the course inaugurated in early 1847 under the professorship of former "missionary" Vallet de Viriville was entitled "Classification of archives *and public libraries*" [my emphasis].[123] Where did this idea come from? As we know, while the July regime employed a few *chartistes* at the Royal Library and occasionally sent others to explore the bibliographic treasures of public libraries, it had hardly encouraged them to become public librarians.[124] And even though the

---

[122] [Jean-Marie] Pardessus, "Note confidentielle sur les matières qui paraissent devoir constituer l'enseignement de l'Ecole des Chartes," Pimpeneau près Blois, 18 Jun. 1846, AN, box F17-4024, pp. 1-5.

[123] The lecture notes Vallet de Viriville prepared for this course, which he taught between 1847 and his death in 1868, are in AEC-SC.

[124] See chap. 2.

Société de l'Ecole des Chartes had sometimes protested against the hiring of non-*chartistes* in public libraries, it had never associated library work with classification. Part of the inspiration for the inclusion of library classification in the new curriculum may have come from Guérard's proposal, which does not mention library classification but does include lessons on ancient and medieval books and on the preparation of manuscripts catalogues. Nevertheless, the draft of a letter buried in the unprocessed archives of the Ecole des Chartes suggests that the more immediate catalyst was Vallet himself. In June 1846, it seems, Vallet wrote to the Minister of Public Instruction to argue for replacing the current "elementary" course (which emphasized the "decipherment" of medieval texts) with a new course in three parts, one for each of the specialists the Ecole des Chartes was supposed to train: *érudits*, librarians, and archivists. The second part of this course, "Ideas for the use of librarians," would cover the following:

> Abridged history of libraries.—Summarily introduce the current organization of our great national [sic] library…Explain the origin, formation, and current composition of our public libraries.—Duties and functions of a librarian.—On the construction, the furnishing, [and] physical maintenance of libraries.—Creation of catalogues.—Instructions and practical knowledge related to the classification, distribution, binding, and preservation of printed books as well as manuscripts.[125]

Though Vallet's description hardly seems revolutionary today, in the context of the late July Monarchy it held out the possibility of a dramatic reinvention of the state's approach to its Old Regime collections. Since the 1790s, the central government had rarely shown much interest in public libraries. While the July Monarchy hoped to mine libraries for their "historical monuments" (usually manuscripts), it left library management almost entirely to local officials. As we saw in the previous chapter, this disdain for public libraries was likely connected to the regime's anxiety about the disorderly and even revolutionary potential of the library-going "public." But under Vallet's plan, the Ecole des Chartes would train state experts to organize, catalogue, and maintain public libraries (including both unique "monuments" and printed books), implying perhaps a new confidence in the reading public. Yet if we compare his proposal with the curriculum actually instituted in 1846, we can see that out of all the

---

[125] [Vallet de Viriville], draft of letter to Monsr. le Ministre de l'Instruction publique (with marginal heading, "Projet d'un nouveau cours de notions élémentaires à l'Ecole des chartes et demande de la chaire par l'auteur de ce projet"), Paris, 6 Jun. 1846, AEC-SC, Vallet de Viriville Papers, pp. 1-3.

components of his course on libraries, the Minister chose to adopt only the lessons on library classification. Though Vallet's proposal hinted at a reemerging interest in the public and public instruction, the late July Monarchy could see public libraries only through the lens of classification.

Both components of the new Ecole des Chartes curriculum—the classification of libraries and archives and the study of national history—can be seen as conservative efforts to buttress the monarchy of King Louis-Philippe. By training expert classifiers, the school would help separate the potentially volatile archives of the 1790s from the properly "historical" documents of the Old Regime. Meanwhile, by training erudite historians, it would help present the July Monarchy as the logical outcome of the nation's long evolution. If the framers of the new curriculum did not describe their aims in quite these terms, they nevertheless readily acknowledged the school's conservative leanings. At the school's reopening ceremonies in May 1847, Director Jean-Antoine Letronne remarked:

> Do you not also admire [the fact] that these young people, having become entirely free after having passed [their] examinations, abandoned thus to themselves, resist, with the force of the healthy impulse that they have received, the preoccupations, the tastes of the moment, and do not fall into any of these literary, political, or religious aberrations that so many of the most distinguished young intellects let themselves get caught up in these days? No, Messieurs, none of our young paleographers has entered into these conspiracies against common sense that we witness every day. No matter how hard I look, I cannot see that any of them has even dreamed of inventing a philosophical system or the smallest of new religions!"[126]

However, as we will see in Chapter 4, neither the students of the Ecole des Chartes nor the state collections in their charge were immune to the "preoccupations of the moment." As the July Monarchy fell to the Second Republic in early 1848, *chartistes*, archives, and libraries would be reenvisioned once again.

---

[126] Letronne in Ministère de l'Instruction Publique, *Ecole Royale des Chartes. Séance d'inauguration (5 mai 1847)* (Paris: Impr. Paul Dupont, 1847), p. 11. Also in *BEC* 8 (1847): 454.

Chapter Four

Revolutionary Libraries and Reactionary Archives? *Chartistes* in the Service of the Second Republic and Early Empire

If in the early months of 1847 the Ecole des Chartes seemed poised to help buttress the July Monarchy against political instability, it soon became clear that no amount of archival reclassification or historiographical reconstruction could protect the regime against a new revolution. Within months of the school's reorganization, four major histories of the 1789 revolution appeared in booksellers' shops.[1] At the same time, Louis-Philippe's republican opponents began holding large public meetings—thinly disguised as "banquets"—in major French cities. When in early 1848 the government attempted to shut down one of these meetings, France once again went into revolt. Parisian workers hurt by the recent economic crisis and frustrated by the government's inflexibility led the fighting that toppled the constitutional monarchy and brought in the Second Republic. And by the first week of March, the students of the formerly Orleanist Ecole des Chartes had assembled a delegation to proclaim their dedication to the revolutionary government. After considering a proclamation likening themselves to the "Parisian bourgeois of the Middle Ages," the students opted instead for a more republican formulation, saluting the new government as the culmination of "the progressive development of French liberty."[2]

---

[1] Alphonse de Lamartine, *Histoire des Girondins*; Louis Blanc, *L'histoire de la Révolution française*; Alphonse Esquiros, *L'histoire des Montagnards*; and Jules Michelet, *L'histoire de la Révolution française* all appeared in 1847.

[2] Reported by H[enri] d'Arbois de Jubainville, Ecole des Chartes class of 1851, in his *Deux manières d'écrire l'histoire: critique de Bossuet, d'Augustin Thierry et de Fustel de Coulanges* (Paris: Librairie Emile Bouillon, 1896), pp. 109-111. On the disintegration of the July Monarchy in 1847-1848, see especially André Jardin and André-Jean Tudesq, *Restoration and Reaction, 1815-1848*, trans. Elborg Forster (Cambridge: Cambridge University Press, 1983), originally published as *La France des notables* (Paris: Seuil, 1973); and Maurice Agulhon, *The Republican Experiment, 1848-1852*,

Though the Ecole des Chartes was quick to shed its Orleanist allegiances in the early days of the Second Republic, the school could hardly have been described as a hotbed of revolutionary agitation. After all, the school's students waited until *after* the defeat of Louis-Philippe to declare their republican devotions. The corps of *chartistes* did not so much rebel against the July Monarchy, then, as follow the French state as it shifted from monarchy to republic. Indeed, the school's students went out of their way to emphasize the continuity of the state and its cultural institutions. According to the March 1848 issue of the *Bibliothèque de l'Ecole des Chartes*:

> The political events of the end of the month of February, the fall of the monarchy of 1830 and the return of the French Republic, must not change anything about the country's literary institutions...The new order of things changes only the names of literary establishments. The first among our libraries, which was called either the King's Library or the Royal Library, has again taken on the title of National Library...; [and] the Ecole Royale des Chartes becomes the Ecole Nationale des Chartes.[3]

Four years later, the school underwent a similar transformation, changing its name to the "Ecole Impériale des Chartes" just as Emperor Napoléon III began his reign. When the French state became a republic, the Ecole des Chartes became republican; when the state became an empire, the Ecole des Chartes became imperial. In one sense, then, the 1846 reorganization of the school had been remarkably successful. Before the reorganization, *chartistes* and the French state had not always seen eye to eye. The school's alumni organization, the Société de l'Ecole des Chartes, had often challenged state archival policies as well as state conceptions of the archivist. Yet with the 1846 curriculum—essentially a compromise between the Société and the Minister of Public Instruction—came a new alliance between *chartistes* and the French government that in 1848 and again in 1852 would prove resistant even to the most drastic changes in political regime.

Because the Ecole des Chartes so closely shadowed the movements of the French state after 1846, the activities of the newly-reorganized school and its students offer particularly telling indications of how the government conceived of archives and libraries in the tumultuous years around 1848. The records of these activities show that in this period, the state's approach to its book and manuscript collections moved in a kind of cycle. In 1846, as

---

trans. Janet Lloyd (Cambridge: Cambridge University Press, 1983), originally published as *1848 ou l'apprentissage de la République, 1848-1852* (Paris: Seuil, 1973).
[3] *BEC* 9 (1847-48): 277-278.

the July Monarchy was beginning to wane, the government's attentions were focused on provincial archives, and, in particular, on classifying these archives in a way that would both promote political order and suppress revolutionary ideas. Then in the heady days of 1848, as we will see, the new republican government instituted a set of radically different policies, working to revive public libraries and redeem revolutionary history. Yet no sooner had the new republic started to articulate these policies than it began to question their merit, and by the time Louis-Napoléon-Bonaparte had been elected president in December 1848 (paving the way for his coup d'état in 1851 and his ascension as Emperor Napoléon III in 1852), the state had begun to return to organizing provincial archives and trying to avoid the revolutionary past. While tracing the circular path of the state's policies in this period, this chapter also shows that the circle was not perfect: though in certain respects the archival policies of the Bonapartist 1850s reprised those of the Orleanist 1840s, they were not identical. In the wake of France's third revolution, the Bonapartist regime developed a political and archival order that was all its own.

    The deposed king Louis-Philippe was still making his way to exile in England when the new republican government began its campaign to develop public libraries. While the First Empire, Bourbon Restoration, and July Monarchy had repeatedly passed over state libraries in favor of state archives, thus subordinating published books to "original" manuscripts and the disturbingly indefinable reading "public" to a narrow audience of *érudits*, the Second Republic not only shifted its attention from archives to libraries but moved to extend the limits of the library-going "public" to include new categories of readers. On February 25, 1848, the first full day of republican rule, the new Minister of Public Instruction asked a prominent Paris publisher to help him create a national network of communal libraries.[4] Three weeks later, the same Minister appointed a special commission— including archival classification theorist Natalis de Wailly as well as longtime Ecole des Chartes supporter Ferdinand de Lasteyrie—to undertake a critical

---

[4] The plan, by publisher Alexandre Paulin, has not survived. See A[lexandre-Pierre] Freslon, "Circulaire relative à l'établissement de bibliothèques communales populaires," 1 Dec. 1848, in *Recueil de lois, décrets, ordonnances, arrêtés, circulaires, etc. concernant les bibliothèques publiques, communales, universitaires, scolaires et populaires*, ed. Ulysse Robert (Paris: H. Champion, 1883), p. 208.

review of public libraries in the city of Paris.[5] The Minister and his new
commission seem to have envisioned a two-fold strategy. On the one hand,
they would force existing libraries (those created or enlarged during the first
French Revolution) to become more "public." In April, for example, the
commission required all Paris public libraries to remain open in the
evenings, and called upon the recent graduates of the Ecole des Chartes to
staff these added shifts.[6] On the other hand, the government planned to
construct a host of new libraries for the "instruction" of French workers and
peasants. As the Minister of Public Instruction explained to departmental
prefects in early December:

> the republican government ranks among its primary duties the task of
> procuring the well-being and happiness of the people through the spread
> of enlightenment [*lumières*]. The development of primary instruction is
> undoubtedly one of the best ways of attaining this result; but school
> lessons, once considered a luxury, today a need, must from now on be
> envisioned only as an excellent preparation. Indeed, why should
> instruction be a privilege, since intelligence is not?[7]

In order to cultivate the intelligence of the laboring classes—now eligible
to vote under the republic's policy of universal suffrage—public libraries
would pick up where elementary schools left off. Libraries scattered
throughout Paris and the provinces would provide reading both "practical
and professional," ranging from "works on religion and morality" to "good
writings on the new institutions that France has just given herself." While
previous governments had provided libraries only for "the man of state, the
scholar, the man of letters, [and] the artist," now state libraries would be
available to all.[8]

Proponents of the Second Republic's public library campaign were well
aware that such programs amounted to a major revival of the public library

---

[5] [Hippolyte] Carnot (Le Ministre Provisoire au département de l'Instruction
publique et des Cultes) and P. Colli[n?], [Arrêté], 15 Mar. 1848, AN box F17-3476,
folder "Commission d'Organisation des Bibliothèques Publiques. 1848."

[6] *BEC* 9 (1848): 359. See also Ecole des Chartes student Edouard Garnier's letter
requesting an evening shift assignment, 1 May 1848, AN, box AB IVc 1, folder
"Garnier."

[7] Freslon, "Circulaire," p. 207.

[8] Ibid., pp. 207-208. See also the reference to a proposal for workers' libraries in
A[lphonse-Honoré] Taillandier (Président de la commission) and F[élix] Ravaisson
(secrétaire) to Monsieur le Ministre, 5 Jul. 1848, AN Box 3476, folder
"Commission...," p. [1].

projects of the 1790s. Indeed, they took every opportunity to vaunt the policies of the First Republic as justification for the policies of the Second. Perhaps the best example of this eagerness to invoke a "revolutionary" tradition of public library development is the "Critical and historical note on the Ecole des Chartes" submitted by Auguste Vallet de Viriville to the Minister of Public Instruction in April 1848.[9] Vallet, a *chartiste* who had recently been appointed to teach library and archival classification at the Ecole, praised the "immortal founders" of the First Republic for recognizing that

> [p]ublic libraries are in a way a universal school, the progressive and unlimited complement to all schools. They thus offer one of the most powerful vehicles of instruction, one of the most precious tools that have been placed in the hands of the public authority to be used for the good of all.[10]

Hence the great architects of the revolutionary system of public instruction—Talleyrand, Condorcet, and Grégoire—had all included public libraries in their educational proposals. Yet after the Revolution, Vallet claimed, public libraries "were delivered...to an abandonment, a sterility, an anarchy that one would have to experience to understand."[11] As evidence of this pattern of neglect, Vallet pointed to the uneven development of the Ecole des Chartes. Though the school "now

---

[9] The "Note historique et critique sur l'Ecole des Chartes -- Projet d'annexion de cette Ecole au Collège de France," Paris, 14 Apr. 1848, in AN box F17-4024 is unsigned, and the name "M. Genin" is written in a different hand at the top. Jean Le Pottier has therefore quite understandably surmised that the manuscript is the work of François Genin, prominent philologist and official at the Ministry of Public Instruction, or that of one of Genin's associates (see Le Pottier's "Histoire et érudition: recherches et documents sur l'histoire et le rôle de l'érudition médiévale dans l'historiographie française du XIXè siècle" (Thesis, Ecole nationale des Chartes, 1979)). However, across the top of Vallet de Viriville's personal copy of his 1848 *BEC* article on the history of the Ecole des Chartes is the following note: "An off-print copy of this article was sent by the author on 14 April 1848 to the Minister of Public Instruction and Religions [*Cultes*], along with a report proposing the annexation of the Special School for History [Vallet's proposed name for the Ecole des Chartes] to the Collège de France" (AEC-SC, Vallet de Viriville Papers). The addition of Genin's name may indicate that the Minister forwarded Vallet's report to Genin (who also served on the Paris public libraries commission named in mid-March).

[10] [Vallet de Viriville], "Note historique," p. [3].

[11] Ibid., p. [5].

function[ed] in a more or less normal and satisfactory manner" as a training ground for archivists, it had repeatedly failed to get its graduates hired as public librarians, despite the promises of the 1829 and 1846 ordinances. In the future, Vallet predicted, the school's role as trainer of public librarians would undoubtedly become the most important of its three missions (to train *érudits*, archivists, and librarians), but only if the new government would return public libraries to "their place in the edifice of public instruction."[12] If the Second Republic wished to continue the great revolutionary tradition of public instruction, it would revitalize public libraries and reform the Ecole des Chartes.

Given this enthusiasm for the educational programs of the 1790s, it is perhaps not surprising that the *chartistes* of the Second Republic also became involved in a government effort to bring the history of the Revolution back into the official history of France. In July 1848, the Minister of Public Instruction named historians Jules Michelet and Henri Martin as well as Ecole des Chartes director Jean-Antoine Letronne and *archiviste-paléographe* Jules Quicherat (a lifelong friend of Michelet) to a commission charged with "revising the program of instruction in French history and modern history used in the Republic's secondary schools, and with preparing a new curriculum that will include the history of the French Revolution."[13] Thus while the *chartistes* of the late July Monarchy had helped to remove the Revolution from the realm of "history" (through the creation of the departmental archives series L), the *chartistes* of 1848 attempted to do just the opposite, encouraging all French citizens to study the revolutionary era.

Yet if the records of the Ecole des Chartes would so far seem to depict a stark contrast between the library and archival policies of the Second Republic (which envisioned *chartistes* as public librarians and revolutionary historians) and those of the late July Monarchy (which saw them as state archivists and medieval historians), this is not the whole story. For at the very moment that the school was becoming involved in a state campaign to revive both revolutionary library projects and revolutionary history, it was also beginning to lend its expertise to a republican effort to limit public

---

[12] Ibid., p. [7]. Of course Vallet, as the instructor for the new Ecole des Chartes course on library and archival classification, had a personal interest in strengthening the school's connections to public libraries.

[13] Le Ministre de l'Instruction publique et des cultes to [Jules] Quicherat (répétiteur général à l'Ecole nationale des chartes), 15 Jul. 1848, AEC-SC, series B, item 103. See also *BEC* 9 (1848): 531. As far as I can tell, the commission never fulfilled its charge.

library access and put a rather more negative spin on the first revolution. The focal point of this effort was none other than Guillaume Libri Carrucci dalla Sommaia: mathematician, *érudit*, and library-thief *extraordinaire*.[14]

The aptly named Libri (Italian for "books") was a Tuscan count who had been forced into exile after supporting an insurrection against the Habsburgs in 1831. Making his new home in Paris, he quickly found a niche among the Orleanist elite. By the late 1830s, he had become a professor of geometry at the Sorbonne, an editor at the *Journal des Savants*, and a close friend of such luminaries as Frédéric Chopin, Prosper Mérimée, and François Guizot. He had also begun to amass an enormous collection of books and manuscripts, ranging from a rare edition of Castiglione's *Book of the Courtier* to a ninth-century manuscript of Boethius' *De Arithmetica*. In 1841, his evident familiarity with rare materials (as well as his powerful connections) won him a post as head of the *Catalogue général des manuscrits des bibliothèques publiques* (General catalogue of manuscripts in public libraries) and allowed him to spend much of his time on official expeditions to provincial libraries, where local officials granted him unrestricted access to their historical collections. As early as 1843, however, rumors began circulating that Libri was stealing from the very libraries he was assigned to inventory.[15] Libraries in the south of France were missing priceless sixteenth-century volumes, while the Arsenal Library in Paris could no longer locate a series of letters by Henri IV. But it was not until after Libri had sold some of his most valuable manuscripts to the British Lord Ashburnham and begun making plans to sell off his printed books that the monarchy launched an investigation. On February 4, 1848, the state prosecutor at last filed a report on Libri's activities; however, Foreign Affairs Minister Guizot, undoubtedly hoping to shield his longtime friend against

---

[14] As I did not fully appreciate the importance of the Libri Affair until after I had completed my archival research in France, the present discussion relies only on materials available in the United States. In future work, I hope to incorporate some of the documentary sources available in Paris and elsewhere.

[15] According to the most recent study of Libri, P. Alessandra Maccioni-Ruju and Marco Mostert's *The Life and Times of Guglielmo Libri (1802-1869), scientist, patriot, scholar, journalist, and thief: a nineteenth-century story* (Hilversum: Verloren, 1995), the first accusation against Libri appeared in an unsigned article by Hercule Géraud, Ecole des Chartes class of 1839, in the *Univers* of 28 Jun. 1843. Géraud and his fellow *chartistes* were apparently angry at having been excluded from the commission on the *Catalogue général des manuscrits* (even though, as we saw in the previous chapter, at least two *chartistes* did cataloguing work on the commission's behalf). Unfortunately, I was not able to locate a copy of Géraud's article.

criminal prosecution, quickly buried the incriminating *dossier* among his
ministerial files.

The *dossier* did not remain buried for long, however. Less than three
weeks later, a throng of revolutionaries stormed the Ministry of Foreign
Affairs, ransacked Guizot's office, and made off with the contents of his
private files. Within the month, the state's official newspaper, the *Moniteur
universel*, had published the prosecutor's report, and the new republican
government had reopened the case against Libri. The investigating
magistrate assigned to the case faced a tremendously daunting task, for Libri
(who had immediately fled to London) had left behind an enormous
collection of books, manuscripts, and personal papers, most of them stashed
in his Latin Quarter apartment. Thus in August the Minister of Public
Instruction appointed a committee of "experts" to examine Libri's
belongings and determine whether the accusations of thievery were true.
While the Minister might have selected any number of prominent librarians
or bibliophiles to sit on this committee, he instead chose three *archivistes-
paléographes*: Ludovic Lalanne, Henri Bordier, and Félix Bourquelot.[16] The
three *chartistes* spent more than a year sifting through Libri's possessions
before filing a lengthy report to the judge in August 1849. Drawing almost
exclusively on this report, the court quickly convicted Libri of stealing state
property and in June 1850 sentenced him *in absentia* to ten years hard
labor.[17]

The French court's verdict divided the European intellectual elite,
pulling librarians, scholars, and publishers alike into an extended pamphlet
war over Libri's supposed crimes. Libri's defenders included writer Prosper
Mérimée, publisher Jacques-Charles Brunet, librarian Paulin Paris, as well
as the recently deposed François Guizot, while on the opposing side were
arrayed the students of the Ecole des Chartes, the head of the National
Library, and provincial librarians from across France. Perhaps the most
heated moment in the case came when Mérimée published a lengthy

---

[16] The Minister at first appointed five *chartistes* (Lalanne, Bordier, and Bourquelot as
well as Louis de Mas-Latrie and Jules Quicherat) in addition to one non-*chartiste*,
Chabaille, who was a friend of Libri. However, the committee quickly narrowed to
three, after Lalanne et al. apparently acted to remove Chabaille. See Maccioni-
Ruju and Mostert, *Life and Times*, p. 243.

[17] The most thorough and balanced account of the case is Maccioni-Ruju and
Mostert's *Life and Times*. See also Giuseppe Fumagalli, *Guglielmo Libri* (Firenze: L. S.
Olschki, 1963), and Barbara McCrimmon, "The Libri Case," *Journal of Library
History* 1, no. 1 (1966): 7-32.

defense of Libri—including a detailed accounting of the "errors" committed by the state's experts—in the spring 1852 *Revue des deux mondes*. The article prompted not only a caustic reply from Lalanne, Bordier, and Bourquelot but also a harsh reprimand from the Paris court, which sentenced Mérimée to two weeks in jail for maligning the state's investigation.[18] The case remained a topic of frequent scholarly debate even into the late 1880s, when another *chartiste*, Léopold Delisle, offered apparently indisputable evidence that Libri had indeed stolen thousands of literary treasures from France's public collections.[19]

Most recent accounts of the *affaire Libri* present it as a kind of morality tale, scandalous proof that librarians everywhere must be forever vigilant over their public collections. In a contribution to the anthology *Histoire des bibliothèques françaises* (1991), for example, Marcel Thomas cautions his readers that instances of such "diabolical cleverness" are not unusual, and "it would be risky indeed to declare that they have all been discovered."[20] For our purposes, however, Libri's story is less important for what it teaches us about the vulnerability of public libraries than for what it tells us about the changing preoccupations of the French Second Republic. After all, the Libri affair was not the only case of library theft under dispute in this period, nor was it the only case of library theft involving the Ecole des Chartes. In 1851, the writer Félix-Sébastien Feuillet de Conches published his *Réponse à une incroyable attaque de la Bibliothèque nationale* (Response to an incredible attack by the National Library), in which he claimed that the head of the Library had unjustly accused him of stealing a letter by Michel de Montaigne from the library's manuscripts department. According to Feuillet, the *Bibliothèque de l'Ecole des chartes* had severely biased the case against him by publishing repeated defenses of the Library in its pages.[21] In

---

[18] See V. de Mars in *Revue des deux mondes* 1852, pp. 1221-1222. On the "battle of pamphlets" more generally, see Maccioni-Ruju and Mostert, *Life and Times*, chap. 18.

[19] Léopold Delisle, *Catalogue des manuscrits des fonds Libri et Barrois* (Paris: H. Champion, 1888).

[20] Marcel Thomas, "Détournements, vols, destructions," *Histoire des bibliothèques françaises* (Paris: Promodis, 1991), 3: 269-270.

[21] F[élix Sébastien] Feuillet de Conches, *Réponse à une incroyable attaque de la Bibliothèque nationale, touchant une lettre de Michel de Montaigne* (Paris: Laverdet, 1851). Feuillet was apparently most upset by *chartiste* Ludovic Lalanne's argument in favor of the National Library in an 1850 review of Achille Jubinal's *Une lettre inédite de Montaigne* (*BEC* 11, pp. 267-271). See also Le Pottier, "Histoire et érudition," pp. 123-124.

yet another case of library theft, the suspect came from within the Ecole des Chartes itself. In March 1848, Jacques-Joseph Champollion-Figeac, longtime professor of diplomatics at the school and a manuscripts curator at the National Library, was fired from both of his posts for "illegal possession of documents belonging to the state."[22] Interestingly, although Champollion-Figeac had by then been teaching at the Ecole des Chartes for more than seventeen years, it does not appear that any *chartistes* came to his defense in 1848; the *Bibliothèque de l'Ecole des Chartes*, for instance, gave only the briefest mention of Champollion-Figeac's departure, calling him an "elderly septuagenarian whose brother [Egyptologist Jean-François Champollion] has attained glory throughout Europe," and likening his case to that of Libri.[23] What is more, according to Champollion-Figeac biographer Charles-Olivier Carbonell, it may even have been students of the Ecole des Chartes who first accused Champollion-Figeac of stealing from the state.

Given that the primary and secondary literature on French libraries records no other major cases of library theft in the period 1800-1870, we must ask: why did these cases suddenly surface during the Second Republic? And why in each case was the Ecole des Chartes cast in the role of prosecutor?[24] Perhaps the most obvious answer is that these indictments were simple acts of political revenge. Libri and Champollion-Figeac (and likely Feuillet as well) were ardent supporters of the July regime; thus the coincidence of their actions and the 1848 revolution created the perfect opportunity for republicans to humiliate the Orleanist elite in what the pro-Libri London *Daily News* called a "Reign of Terror."[25] Libri, of course, bore the added stigma of being a foreigner; as a successful Italian (and an openly nationalist one at that), he undoubtedly proved an appealing target for a new government eager to prove its "Frenchness." As for the Ecole des Chartes, it had not only immediately sided with the republican government

---

[22] Charles-Olivier Carbonell, *L'autre Champollion: Jacques-Joseph Champollion-Figeac (1778-1867)* (Toulouse: Presses de l'Institut d'études politiques de Toulouse et l'Asiathèque, 1970), p. 255.

[23] *BEC* 9 (1848): 359.

[24] The only other case of library theft I am aware of did not come until 1873, when Auguste Harmand of the Troyes municipal library, was convicted (again with the help of two *chartiste* "experts") of stealing books from his own collection. See Françoise Bibolet, "La Bibliothèque municipale de Troyes," *Revue française d'histoire du livre* (Jul.-Sept. 1976): 307.

[25] Maccioni-Ruju and Mostert, *Life and Times*, p. 243.

but also contained within its ranks a number of staunch republican supporters, among them Henri Bordier and Jules Quicherat, two of the original "experts" in the Libri case.

On one level, then, the Libri, Feuillet, and Champollion-Figeac cases can be interpreted as so many republican attempts to retaliate against the Orleanist regime; on another level, however, the cases might be read as indicators of the Second Republic's growing discomfort with its early pro-public initiatives. The new government had acted almost immediately to open public libraries to the widest possible audience; state collections both old and new planned to invite even the poorest laborers to explore their intellectual treasures. Yet the highly-publicized scandals of Libri and company pointed to one of the potential drawbacks of public library access: the loss and destruction of national property. If the head of the state's public library catalogue and a senior professor at the Ecole des Chartes could not be trusted in public collections, who could? For many of the *chartistes* and politicians of the Second Republic the implication of the scandals was clear: public collections (and their users) had to be subjected to a far greater degree of official surveillance. If the new "public" was to be larger and more powerful than in regimes past, it seems, it also had to be more carefully watched and controlled than ever before.

The Libri, Champollion-Figeac, and Feuillet de Conches cases suggest that the increasingly Bonapartist republican regime had begun to have similar misgivings about emulating the French Revolution. Early Second Republic library supporters like Vallet de Viriville presented the library policies of the 1790s as inspirational models, proof of the wisdom of the first revolution's educational vision. Yet the book-theft scandals of the late 1840s redirected public attention to the negative consequences of revolutionary programs. Claimants on both sides of the Libri and Feuillet cases blamed the scandals at least partly on the "chaos" wrought by revolutionary confiscations. The defendants argued that French libraries had been in such grave disorder since the 1790s that it could no longer be proven that library X really owned volume Y or that manuscript Z had not actually been stolen decades ago and then sold to the accused thief through a reputable dealer. Bibliophile Paul Lacroix, for example, claimed to have found more than one hundred books in Paris shops that bore the marks of the National Library.[26] In a similar vein, Feuillet de Conches complained that although the Library

---

[26] Paul Lacroix [also known as the "bibliophile Jacob"], *Les cent et une: lettres bibliographiques à M. l'administrateur général de la Bibliothèque nationale* (Paris: Paulin, 1849-50).

had accused him of stealing a letter by Montaigne, there was no record of any such letter in the library's catalogue, for the catalogue contained only a fraction of the Library's confiscated collections. Thus he had become, he claimed, a victim of the "anarchy" of the Library:

> If [the Library] associates itself with progress, let us remember that as far as catalogues are concerned, progress means completing, improving, [and] undertaking skillfully what is to be done, not vainly [redoing] what is already well done. Could not all these little cataloguing *coups d'état* be a form of that pompous and deceptive socialism that confiscates everything, even liberty, in order to level it all, and ultimately puts only anarchy and chaos atop the debris?[27]

The *chartistes,* for their part, while maintaining that the disorder of French libraries had often been exaggerated (particularly by foreigners), argued that the lack of orderly catalogues had both encouraged thefts and made prosecuting them more difficult.[28] Thus while the first revolution had generated admirable ideas about the creation and use of public collections, it had also doomed these collections to decades of loss and confusion. To resolve this problem, both sides seemed to agree, France's collections required not so much classification (as the late July Monarchy had emphasized) as cataloguing, for only an accurate record of public holdings would end the dangerous uncertainty over ownership that had been unleashed by the revolutionary upheaval.

In the library robbery scandals of the Second Republic, therefore, we can see the emergence of a much more hesitant and conservative attitude toward public libraries than that expressed in contemporary proposals for the bibliographic enlightenment of workers and peasants. The apparent lesson of the Libri, Feuillet, and Champollion-Figeac cases was that the revolutionary model of the public library could only be taken so far. If the public library of the Second Republic was to offer "universal" instruction, it

---

[27] Feuillet de Conches, *Réponse*, p. 37. Given the strongly political overtones of this passage, it would be interesting to find out whether Feuillet's essay, published sometime in 1851, was written before or after Louis-Napoléon Bonaparte's *coup d'état* of 2 December.

[28] *BEC* 10 (1849): 381-382; Lud[ovic] Lalanne, H[enri] Bordier, and F[élix] Bourquelot, *Affaire Libri. Réponse à M. Mérimée...*, 2d. ed. (Paris: Panckoucke, 1852), p. 10. For an example of how foreign coverage of the Libri case emphasized the revolutionary disorder of French libraries, see *The Case of M. Libri. Reprinted from "Bentley's Miscellany," for July 1, 1852* (London: Richard Bentley, 1852), p. 8.

also had to have comprehensive records; if it was to be freely accessible to the public, it also had to be carefully supervised by the republican state.

Beyond pointing up the ambivalences of the Second Republic's approach to public libraries, the library thievery scandals are also significant for what they reveal about the evolving identity of the Ecole des Chartes. Though graduates of the school had long functioned as state experts—in the guise of historical researchers, missionaries, and archivists—this role had never been so apparent as it was at the time of the *affaire Libri*. The Paris court not only allowed the *chartistes* full control of the Libri investigation but then accepted their findings utterly without question. While such authority undoubtedly increased the fame and prestige of the Ecole des Chartes, it also opened the school to unprecedented attacks. In the school's attempts to respond to these attacks, we can see it continuing to elaborate the nature of its expertise as well as its relationship to the French state.

According to Libri's and Feuillet's supporters, *chartistes* were singularly unqualified to serve as scholarly experts. The Libri camp delighted in pointing out that despite their many years of paleographical training, the three *chartistes* assigned to the case had made multiple errors in identification and translation. For example, they had mistakenly transcribed the Latin heading *Bibliothecae S. IO* (for the library of the San Giovanni convent) as *Bibliothecae S. 10* (or as one friend of Libri put it, the library of the "holy ten").[29] Here was the Latin of the Ecole du Droit (School of Law), said Mérimée, not the Latin of the Ecole des Chartes.[30] Even worse, Libri's backers claimed, the supposedly preservationist *chartistes* had been physically careless with Libri's books, dropping rare volumes along his apartment staircase and in the street. Indeed, Libri's friends wondered whether the school's graduates knew anything about books at all. As Mérimée wrote in 1852:

> one wondered [in 1848] whether the experts would offer the guarantees of experience necessary for an investigation, because one can be very good at spelling out Merovingian charters and understand nothing about bibliography...Personally, I maintain that it would have been better to entrust the expertise, or what the indictment calls the *technical research*, to known bibliophiles, or even to booksellers or bookbinders...[31]

Thus despite the Second Republic's efforts to involve the Ecole des Chartes in the world of public libraries, to its opponents, the school was not

---

[29] *The Case of M. Libri*, p. 10.
[30] Mérimée, "Le procès," p. 318.
[31] Ibid., p. 312.

prepared to train bibliographers, only paleographers—and rather inept ones at that. In the case of the "expert" *chartistes*, joked one British journalist, the term "expert" was less likely derived from the Latin *expertus* ("experienced") than from *expers* ("lacking").[32]

The school's responses to these accusations are intriguing. *Chartistes* and their supporters mounted a considerable effort to defend their scholarly expertise. In their 1852 *Réponse à M. Mérimée*, for example, Lalanne, Bordier, and Bourquelot tried to combat Mérimée's "reproaches of thoughtlessness and flightiness" by rebutting his list of "errors" point for point. They claimed that Mérimée himself had made numerous errors, due to his willingness to rely on Libri's own testimony rather than the collections in question, and they noted that they would "always be ready" to answer further attacks. Yet despite the *chartistes'* apparent enthusiasm for their new role as republican librarians, they never directly engaged with the Libri camp's charge that they were incompetent bibliographers. Though they defended their knowledge of specific books in Libri's collection, they made no claim to mastery of bibliography in general. Thus given the opportunity to define themselves as expert librarians (rather than as archivists or *érudits*), the corps of *chartistes* shied away, a move that would often be repeated under Emperor Napoléon III.

Beyond attacking Lalanne, Bordier, and Bourquelot as "inexpert," the Libri side also argued that *chartistes* as a group were unfit to participate in the investigation because of their long-standing religious, professional, and political biases. According to Mérimée, the graduates of the school had borne a collective grudge against Libri ever since the early 1840s, when the aggressively anti-clerical count had attacked the school as a Jesuit stronghold.[33] To make matters worse, Mérimée explained, Libri had worked to exclude *chartistes* from the 1841 *Catalogue des manuscrits*, thereby depriving them of much-needed professional posts.[34] Feuillet, for his part, paid special attention to the school's political prejudices, arguing that "at the time of the February revolution,…a coterie had taken over the [*Bibliothèque de l'Ecole des Chartes*] and had transformed it into a nest of malicious scandal-mongers," and, "like these others who, speaking for themselves alone, [yet] call themselves the People," they "claimed the right to insult at random."[35] The combined effect of all these prejudices, argued a British supporter of Libri,

---

[32] *The Case of M. Libri*, p. 4.
[33] Mérimée, "Le procès," p. 310.
[34] Ibid. See also Maccioni-Ruju and Mostert, *Life and Times*, p. 176.
[35] Feuillet de Conches, *Réponse*, pp. 39-40.

was that the report ultimately filed by the committee of "experts" in 1849 "resemble[d] a bad article written by a partisan in a strong party review."[36]

The Ecole des Chartes offered two responses to these claims. During the trial itself, the school maintained what might be described as a loud silence on the Libri Affair. In other words, rather than clamoring to refute their opponents' characterization of the school as a haven for rabid republicans and fanatical Jesuits (an odd combination, in any case), the *chartistes* repeatedly affirmed their "duty" to avoid discussing the Libri trial. For example, the spring 1849 issue of the *Bibliothèque de l'Ecole des Chartes* proclaimed:

> On Monday, April 30th, M. Libri published,…under the title *Letter to M. Falloux containing the story of an odious persecution*, a volume in which the Ecole des Chartes, and particularly those of its members whom the court has appointed to assist it in the judicial investigation against M. Libri, are the object of vulgar invective. Until the day that the court gives its verdict, it is the duty of the Ecole des Chartes to ignore such attacks.[37]

After the trial was over, the *chartistes* broke with this policy of dutiful silence, only to adopt a second, equally measured approach. Lalanne, Bordier, and Bourquelot's *Réponse à M. Mérimée*, for example, gave a self-consciously dispassionate reply to the Libri camp. Instead of responding to the "vulgar invective" of Libri and company in equally emotional terms, the authors explicitly limited themselves to a scholarly refutation of their alleged "errors." As they stated in their concluding sentence, "[w]e would have had the right to complain bitterly [about the "grave accusations" of the opposition]; but for us it was enough to be right."[38]

In course of the Libri Affair, then, the Ecole des Chartes worked at developing a brand of scholarly neutrality that would remain one of its hallmarks for the remainder of the nineteenth century. On the one hand, by reaffirming its allegiance to the Republic, the school tacitly adopted a political position. While it might have refused to become involved in a dispute pitting the republican regime against former Orleanist leaders, it chose to lend its support to the republican prosecution. And while it might have tried to counter the Libri camp's accusations of bias with claims to political and religious neutrality, it chose instead to let the accusations stand. Yet on the other hand, the school also adopted an apolitical stance. As we saw in the previous chapter, the Société de l'Ecole des Chartes had already

---

[36] *The Case of M. Libri*, p. 4.

[37] *BEC* 10 (1849): 326.

[38] Lalanne, Bordier, and Bourquelot, *Affaire Libri*, p. 25.

begun to establish this position in the early 1840s by refusing to discuss the volatile issue of archival classification and condemning the involvement of archivists in political debates. During the Libri Affair, the Society's policy seemed to become school policy, as the Ecole not only refused to advertise its republican allegiances but also carefully avoided explicitly political discussions. From the late 1840s on, the school would be both strongly pro-state and strongly anti-political.[39]

In the years following the Libri verdict, as republican President Louis-Napoléon Bonaparte gradually transformed himself into Emperor Napoléon III, the state's misgivings about the public instruction proposals of the early republic became much more evident. Around 1850, just as the Bonapartist government began working to limit universal suffrage and repress leftist organizations, it also began to abandon its plans for workers' libraries and revolutionary instruction.[40] Soon even the grand old public libraries that had figured in the Libri Affair (the National Library, the Arsenal, the municipal libraries in the departments, etc.) had fallen off the central government's agenda. The Minister of Public Instruction did help promote the Imperial Library's monumental *Catalogue de l'histoire de France*, the first volume of which was published in 1855, as well as a "Statistical Table of Public Libraries in the Departments," which appeared in 1857.[41] Yet these

---

[39] On the adoption of a similar stance by university-trained historians in the 1870s and 1880s, see William Keylor, *Academy and Community: The Foundation of the French Historical Profession* (Cambridge: Harvard University Press, 1975), esp. chap. 5.

[40] On the abandonment of the educational programs inaugurated in 1848, see the introduction to Katherine Auspitz, *The Radical Bourgeoisie: The Ligue de l'enseignement and the origins of the Third Republic, 1866-1885* (New York: Cambridge University Press, 1983). On the Bonapartist repression of revolutionary groups, see especially John M. Merriman, *The Agony of the Republic: The Repression of the Left in Revolutionary France, 1848-1851* (New Haven: Yale University Press, 1978).

[41] Bibliothèque impériale, *Catalogue de l'histoire de France* (Paris: Firmin Didot, 1855-95). As far as I know, only one *chartiste*, Charles Marty-Laveaux, contributed to the first volume of this catalogue, though others may have joined in the late 1850s. A second subject catalogue, the *Catalogue des sciences médicales*, followed in 1857. For the statistical table, see Ministère de l'Instruction publique et des cultes, *Tableau statistique des bibliothèques publiques des départements, d'après des documents officiels recueillis de 1853 à 1857 (Extrait du Journal Général de l'Instruction Publique)* (Paris: Imprimerie Paul Dupont, 1857). The 1853 circular that announced this project can be found in AN, box F2 I 378[15], folder "Bibliothèques Comles. Objets généraux." Neither Graham Keith Barnett's *Histoire des bibliothèques publiques en France de la Révolution à 1939* (Paris:

projects do not seem to have been part of a larger program to develop public libraries. Nor do they appear to have drawn upon the revolutionary discourse of universal access and popular instruction. On the contrary, as Christian Amalvi points out in an intriguing analysis of the Imperial Library, the classification scheme of the 1855 *Catalogue* serves to subordinate revolutionary themes.[42]

Rather than pursuing the early Republic's policy of public library reform, the Bonapartist state of the 1850s launched a new program of archival organization. At the center of this program was a series of measures aimed at bringing provincial archives under the exclusive control of *archivistes-paléographes*. In February 1850, largely at the urging of the Archives Commission (which had continued to meet despite the 1848 upheaval), the Minister of the Interior decreed that in the future all departmental archivists were to be selected from among the graduates of the Ecole des Chartes. If a *chartiste* was not available, the department would be permitted to hire an outside candidate, but only if he had obtained a special "certificate of ability" from the Archives Commission, and only then with the explicit approval of the Minister himself.[43] While it took some time for *archivistes-paléographes* to make their way into the smaller and more remote

---

Promodis, 1987) nor the relevant articles in vol. 3 of *Histoire des bibliothèques françaises* mentions any other significant state initiatives on public libraries in the 1850s.

[42] Christian Amalvi, "La périodisation du passé national dans le catalogue de l'Histoire de France du département des imprimés de la Bibliothèque nationale," in *Périodes. La construction du temps historique. Actes du Ve colloque d'histoire au présent* (Paris: Editions de l'Ecole des Hautes Etudes en Sciences Sociales et Histoire au Présent, 1991), pp. 15-20. Around 1858, state interest in public libraries began to revive; I will discuss this phenomenon in the following chapter.

[43] Louis-Napoléon Bonaparte (Le Président de la République) and Ferdinand Barrot (Le Ministre de l'Intérieur, "Décret," 4 Feb. 1850, in Ministère de l'Intérieur, *Archives Départementales, Communales et Hospitalières. Bibliothèques Administratives. Recueil des lois et instructions qui régissent le service* (Paris: Imprimerie administrative Paul Dupont, 1860), p. 57. The report by Barrot that prompted this decree is in AN, box AB XXXI 41. For the certification examination administered to non-*chartistes* (a sort of summary version of the examinations given at the Ecole des Chartes itself) see J[ules] Baroche (Le Ministre de l'intérieur), "Circulaire [with marginal heading: "Archives départementales. Nomination des archivistes"]," Paris, 10 Jul. 1850, AN, box AB Vf 1, folder "Archives départementales (1820-1857)...." In a circular of 15 Apr. 1852 (in AN, box AB XXXI 41, based on a more general decree of 25 Mar. 1852), the new Interior Minister, Persigny, modified this ruling somewhat, maintaining that while prefects still had to choose archivists from the Ecole des Chartes, they no longer needed to obtain ministerial permission first.

departments, the decree had an immediate and marked effect: in 1850, there were only four *chartistes* in France's eighty-odd departmental archives; by 1852, there were twelve; by 1861, twenty-seven; and by 1900, seventy-four.[44] Thus *chartistes*, who in the first half of the century had rarely ventured out of Paris except on temporary missions, began to see the provinces as their rightful administrative and intellectual territory.[45]

Starting in 1853, the Imperial regime overlaid this network of departmental archivists with a complementary system of archival inspectors, also drawn from the ranks of the Ecole des Chartes. Again the catalyst for this development was the Archives Commission, which in early 1852 determined that a "permanent inspection" of departmental archives could be highly effective "if the men charged with verifying, controlling, [and] facilitating" the work of departmental archivists were "in a position to do so with great and incontestable superiority."[46] Evidently, such men could only be found at the Ecole des Chartes, for in 1854 the Interior Minister appointed two *chartistes*, Eugène de Stadler and Francis Wey (joined by a third, Eugène de Rozières, in 1858, and a fourth, Martin Bertrandy, in 1862) as Inspectors-General of Departmental Archives.[47] The Minister also

---

[44] These statistics are based on my own compilation of records from the AEC, AN, and departmental archives, as well as on data provided in Vincent Mollet, "La conquête des archives départementales," in *L'Ecole nationale des chartes: histoire de l'école depuis 1821*, ed. Yves-Marie Bercé, Olivier Guyotjeannin, and Marc Smith (Thionville, France: Gérard Klopp, 1997), pp. 253-262.

[45] Indeed, the connection between the school and departmental archives had become so strong by the late nineteenth century that Arthur Giry (class of 1870) complained that "[t]he official goal, as it were, of the Ecole des Chartes is to provide the departments with conscientious archivists" ("L'Ecole des chartes," *République française*, 16 Apr. 1875, p. 3, cols. 2-3). It is interesting to consider that the February 1850 decree on departmental archivists came just one month before the passage of the famous Falloux Law, which gave the Catholic Church more influence over French schools. Though the archival decree makes no mention whatsoever of religion, given the Libri-era connection between *chartistes* and Jesuits, it is possible that sending *archivistes-paléographes* into the provinces fit into a larger effort to extend the Church's influence over cultural institutions in the provinces.

[46] Commission des archives départementales et communales, "Procès-verbaux," 8 Apr. 1852, AN, AB XXVI 3*, p. 93.

[47] AN, box F2 I 378[10]. See also Vincent Mollet, "Les archives départementales du Tarn de 1790 à 1946: constitution et mise en valeur d'un patrimoine écrit," (Thesis, Ecole nationale des chartes, 1992), p. 130; and Jean-Yves Mariotte, introduction to *La Haute Savoie vers 1865*, by Henry Terry (Annecy, France: Gardet, 1977), pp. 7-11. I am grateful to Jean-Yves Mariotte for sharing his work on Francis Wey with me.

began charging some departmental archivists with the inspection of communal archives (which were generally staffed by non-*chartistes*).[48] The combined effect of the new ruling on departmental archivists and the new system of archival inspections was a hierarchical network of *archivistes-paléographes* ready to extend the Paris government's vision of archival organization to even the tiniest towns in France.[49]

What was the purpose of this network? What about it was identifiably "Bonapartist"? And what impact did it have on provincial archives, many of which had remained wholly indifferent to the classification crusades of the 1840s? Here I will try to answer these questions by drawing upon ministerial rulings, inspection reports, scholarly journals (including the *Bibliothèque de l'Ecole des Chartes*), and, most important, records from seven departmental archives: those of the Allier (in Moulins), Aube (Troyes), Indre-et-Loire (Tours), Lot-et-Garonne (Agen), Maine-et-Loire (Angers), Nièvre (Nevers), and Seine-et-Oise (now the Department of the Yvelines, in Versailles). I selected these seven archives in part because unlike many other departmental collections, they still contain substantial internal records (annual reports, personnel files, administrative correspondence, archival inventories, etc.) from the period 1848-1860.[50] More important, these archives hired their first *chartistes* relatively early (in the 1840s or 1850s) and

---

[48] An 1857 Interior Ministry circular to prefects made departmental archivists responsible for overseeing the classification and inventory of communal archives in their regions (Billault, "Circulaire [with marginal heading: "Instructions pour le classement et l'inventaire sommaire des Archives communales antérieures à 1790"]," 25 Aug. 1857, AN, box AB XXXI 41), but even before that some departmental archivists had begun conducting annual tours of communal collections (see, for example, *chartiste* Henri d'Arbois de Jubainville's reports on the archives of the Aube in AN, box F2 I 367[12]).

[49] This new network of *chartistes* was undoubtedly all the more influential because in 1854 the Interior Ministry's Archives Commission underwent a reorganization that apparently greatly reduced its power. At the same time, the Minister created a new Archives Bureau, but in the 1850s, at least, this bureau seems to have limited itself primarily to administrative tasks, leaving most of the policymaking to the departmental archivists, Inspectors-General, and, of course, the Minister himself. See Le Pottier, "Histoire et érudition," p. 214.

[50] Some of these records are duplicated or completed by materials in the AN series F2 I. The following discussion also draws occasionally on AN materials from other departments that hired *chartistes* in this period (notably the Oise and the Jura) although I was not able to visit these depositories in person and therefore have only partial documentation for them.

then continued to hire more *chartistes* in subsequent decades. Their records are therefore particularly useful for assessing the impact of the first major wave of departmental archivists to come out of the Ecole des Chartes.[51]

Of course, conclusions based on so small a sampling (roughly eight percent) of departmental collections must necessarily be considered preliminary. Even a far more comprehensive study of local records would still contain important gaps; for example, a number of documents from this period suggest that some local politicians and scholars were rather resistant to *chartistes'* efforts to inventory and classify their collections, yet the records maintained by the archives themselves generally do not document these struggles.[52] Nevertheless, even this limited set of sources can help us understand how the Imperial state (if not local officials and *érudits*) thought about French archives—and about the French past. Historians have paid considerable attention to the historiographical ambitions of the July Monarchy, late Second Empire, and Third Republic, but they have largely ignored those of the early Second Empire.[53] By exploring the early Empire's treatment of archives, we can begin to investigate what made the historiographical strategies of the early Empire distinct from regimes both before and after.

---

[51] For many years, the only histories of departmental archives were to be found either in archival guidebooks or in brief articles published in provincial journals. More recently, however, several *chartistes* have begun to study the history of departmental collections. See especially the work of Vincent Mollet, including "La conquête des archives départementales," and his 1992 Ecole des Chartes thesis, both cited above; as well as his "Les chartistes dans les Archives départementales avant le décret de 1850, *BEC* 151 (1993): 123-154. Also quite useful is Ecole des Chartes professor Olivier Guyotjeannin's recent article, "Les premières années des archives départementales françaises (1796-1815)," in *Les archives en Europe vers 1800: les communications présentées dans le cadre de la journée d'études du même nom aux Archives générales du Royaume à Bruxelles le 24 octobre 1996*, Miscellanea Archivistica Studia, no. 103 (Brussels: Archives générales du royaume et archives de l'état dans les provinces, 1998), pp. 7-36.

[52] See for example the discussions of potential conflicts with local governments in Commission des Archives, "Procès-verbaux," 1849-1850, AN, AB XXVI 2*.

[53] For a discussion of recent work on the July Monarchy, see chapters 2 and 3. On the late Second Empire and Third Republic, see for example Keylor, *Academy*, and Charles-Olivier Carbonell, *Histoire et historiens: une mutation idéologique des historiens français, 1865-1885* (Toulouse: Privat, 1976). The same pattern is apparent in studies of the Second Empire more generally; historians tend to prefer the cultural, political, and economic projects of the 1860s to those of the 1850s.

The *archivistes-paléographes* that set out for departmental archives in the 1850s saw themselves—much like the Jesuit missionaries of centuries past—as bearers of order in a chaotic land. Their annual reports, addressed to the departmental prefect and usually forwarded to the Ministry of the Interior, are filled with comments such as this one, from an 1851 report on the Archives of the Indre-et-Loire by *chartiste* Augustin Deloye:

> The department's archives seem never to have been divided into two large classes, one covering everything prior to 1790, the other covering everything after that [as prescribed by the 1841 circular]. Everywhere the old archives had become invaded and penetrated by the modern ones, and presented to the eye the strangest medley [*la plus étrange bigarrure*]…I never understood better than at that moment the priceless advantages of a regular and uniform order for all departmental archives, which allows a newly-arrived archivist to become acquainted with his depository in a few hours.[54]

In 1852, Henri d'Arbois de Jubainville offered a similar account of his first year as a departmental archivist, noting that the historical archives were in a "deplorable state," their *fonds* "mixed" and "in the greatest disorder." At the end of the decade, Paul Thomeuf echoed the complaints of d'Arbois and Deloye, writing that due to the "faulty classification" of his (non-*chartiste*) predecessor, "disorder reigns in all its splendor, and…the confusion is unequaled."[55]

Into this unparalleled confusion, claimed the *chartiste* archivists of the 1850s, they brought the organizing power of the "precepts" of the Ecole des Chartes.[56] Of course, they were not the only ones who believed that the Ecole alone provided the expert knowledge necessary for the reordering of provincial collections. In the report that prompted the February 1850 decree on the hiring of departmental archivists, the Minister of Public

---

[54] [Augustin] Deloye (L'archiviste du département), "Archives départementales d'Indre et Loire. Rapport annuel de l'Archiviste. 1851," 23 Aug. 1851, AN, box F2 I 371⁵, p. 15. Interestingly, although Deloye's immediate predecessor in the Indre-et-Loire, Léon Aubineau, was also a *chartiste*, Deloye never mentions him by name, perhaps eager to distance himself from his insufficiently organized colleague.

[55] H[enri] d'Arbois de Jubainville (Archiviste du dept.), "Rapport à Monsieur le Préfet de l'Aube sur la situation des Archives départementales & communales," 18 Dec. 1852, AN, box F2 I 367¹², p. [2]; [Paul] Thomeuf, "Rapport de l'archiviste [of the Jura]," [1859], AN, box F2 I 371¹⁰, p. [2].

[56] [Célestin Port], "Rapport sur le 1e semestre 1854 [for the archives of the Maine-et-Loire]," 1854, AD Maine-et-Loire, 384 T 3, fol. 10v.

Instruction commented on the inadequacy of the non-*chartistes* then responsible for most departmental depositories:

> Do they all have the paleographical concepts indispensable for [their work]? Can they all, more particularly, decipher the writings from the various centuries of our history, writings that are so varied, so changeable, with such numerous and complicated abbreviations?..Have their linguistic studies been sufficient to understand the various idioms in use in France up until the moment of the constitution of the political unity of the country? Have they all, finally, the historical knowledge without which a mass of documents—that alone can elucidate the mores, customs, local institutions, [and] intimate details of feudal and communal organization— remain an indecipherable enigma? It is doubtful.

The solution, according to the Minister, was to "narrow the circle" of potential archivists to graduates of the Ecole des Chartes, or, as he put it, to "men [who are] still young, hard-working, zealous, full of devotion to their work, and above all who possess the specialized knowledge necessary for the accomplishment of their mission."[57]

As this passage suggests, the image of the departmental *archiviste-paléographe* constructed by government officials and by archivists themselves included a physical and moral element as well as an intellectual one. The Minister of Public Instruction decried the tendency of departmental prefects to appoint as archivists "elderly employees who can no longer serve in the [administrative] offices and to whom the guardianship of the archives is given either as a retirement pension or as a pension supplement." The young graduates of the Ecole des Chartes, he claimed, would bring a much-needed "bodily vigor" to archival work.[58] At the same time, archival officials argued, they would bring the kind of moral rectitude required of guardians of the nation's treasures. During an Archives Commission meeting in April 1850 (just two months before Guillaume Libri's conviction for theft), one commissioner proclaimed that "two conditions are necessary to create a good archivist: the specialized knowledge that his functions require, and an honorable character." Indeed, he claimed, it might create "very great drawbacks to introduce men whose morality was not certain into [departmental] depositories."[59] In a similar vein, Inspector-General of

---

[57] Ferdinand Barrot, "Rapport à M. le Président de la République," Paris, 4 Feb. 1850, AN, box AB XXXI 41, p. 3.

[58] Ibid., pp. 3-4.

[59] Commission des Archives, "Procès-verbaux," 11 Apr. 1850, AN, AB XXVI 2*, p. 161.

Departmental Archives Francis Wey noted in 1858 that he had serious doubts about a non-*chartiste* who had applied for the post of archivist of the Jura; while the man was an excellent paleographer, a recent prison stint had put his "morality" in question. "The job of archivist is a position of trust," Wey declared; "the administration must be represented before [public] opinion by pure agents."[60] The graduates of the Ecole des Chartes, those "new Benedictines," would furnish such agents.

This mid-nineteenth-century image of the archivist *chartiste*— transforming a disorderly and neglected provincial depository with his combination of scholarly expertise, youthful vigor, and unassailable honor— has been cultivated and maintained by generations of Ecole alumni. In 1904, for example, Henri Moranvillé described the changes wrought by Charles Grandmaison, class of 1850, in the archives of the Indre-et-Loire: "The depository that came under his direction had been badly mistreated by an archivist from outside the Ecole des Chartes, and one can imagine what it is like to organize archives in which thefts have been committed." Yet Grandmaison persevered, inventorying the archive and more than doubling its contents. As a result, though "order had not prevailed before him," he transformed the archives to such an extent that, according to Moranvillé, "one can say he nearly created them."[61] Similarly, in a 1938 history of the archives of the Seine-et-Oise, Henri Lemoine argued that the first *chartiste* had "revolutionized" the collection:

> So as to bring a bit of order to the [depository], Charles-Marie-Henri Saint-Marie Mévil, *archiviste-paléographe* of the class of 1854, was appointed assistant archivist on February 12, 1858. It is important to recognize—and this is the glory of the Ecole des Chartes—that from that moment on, everything changed.[62]

---

[60] Francis Wey, "Rapport à S. Exc. M. le Ministre de l'Intérieur," 25 Sept. 1858, AN, box F2 I 371[9], p. 8.

[61] H[enri] Moranvillé, "Charles de Grandmaison," in H[enri] Moranvillé and H[enry?] Faye, *Ch. de Grandmaison (1824-1903)* (Tours: Imprimerie Paul Bousrez, 1904), pp. 5-8. The guilty outsider mentioned by Moranvillé was probably Jean-Claude-Marius Seytre, convicted of stealing from archives in and around Tours during his tenure as departmental archivist. See chap. 3, footnote 97.

[62] Of course, there were exceptions to this rule: in the Nièvre, for example, the non-*chartiste* archivist Félix Leblanc-Bellevaux turned out to be much more capable and organized than his *chartiste* predecessors (see AN, box F2 I 374[5], and AD Nièvre, folder "Archives départemales [sic]. Rapports au Ministre et Correspondance ministérielle, 1851-1910"). On Mévil, see H[enri] Lemoine, *Les Archives de Seine-et-*

But what did the *chartiste* "revolution" actually entail? Based on their administrative correspondence and annual reports, it appears that the departmental *archivistes-paléographes* of the early Empire concentrated on four main tasks: classification, inventory, inspection, and centralization. In the abstract, none of these tasks seems particularly remarkable, or particularly "Imperial"; however, as we will see, together they constituted a fairly coherent Bonapartist strategy for bringing provincial archives into the service of the French state. Let us examine each of these tasks in turn before considering the political context in which they became so important.

Given the *chartistes'* conception of themselves as bearers of "order," it is not surprising that the departmental archivists of the early Empire spent the vast majority of their professional time classifying and inventorying their collections. Undoubtedly well trained in Vallet de Viriville's new course on the "Classification of Archives and Public Libraries" (which gave pride of place to departmental archives), the *archivistes-paléographes* of the 1850s immediately set about bringing their collections in line with the 1841 circular on archival classification.[63] Documents produced before 1790 became "historical archives," those produced after 1800 "administrative archives," and those in between "archives of the intermediary period" (though there were exceptions to this pattern, as we will see in a moment). Indeed, most archivists structured their annual reports entirely around the divisions of the 1841 scheme, beginning with Series A and ending with Series Z. They even adopted the organic language of *respect des fonds*, referring blithely to the "physiognomy" of ecclesiastical cartularies and the "natural order" of princely archives.[64] They became, in effect, the young

---

Oise de 1790 à 1888 (Versailles: Imprimerie Coopérative "La Gutenberg," 1938), pp. 15-16. According to the archives of the Ecole des Chartes, Mévil actually graduated from the school in 1847, not 1854.

[63] Vallet de Viriville's lecture notes are in AEC-SC. On the details of the 1841 circular, see chap. 3.

[64] See for example Ch[arles] L[oyseau] Grandmaison, "Archives départementales d'Indre-et-Loire. Rapport annuel de l'archiviste. 1858," 18 Aug. 1858, AN, box F2 I 371[5], who claimed to be doing his best to "find and preserve the actual physiognomy of the old collections of charters" using eighteenth-century inventories (p. [8]). Interestingly, the prefect then picked up on this language in making his own report to the Minister the following year, saying that Grandmaison had "endeavored to return the former physiognomy of these ten-century-old collections of charters, whose debris, until recently scattered and seemingly chaotic, are today united in a natural and methodical order...." (Préfet d'Indre-et-Loire, "Rapport,"

apostles of documentary classification that the archival reformers of the 1840s had long hoped to dispatch to provincial posts.

Yet if the archival administrators of the late July Monarchy had focused almost exclusively on developing a uniform system of classification, those of the early Empire worked increasingly to fix that system in place through the production of archival inventories. In January 1854, an Interior Ministry circular to departmental prefects announced the launch of a national collection of archival inventories known as the *Inventaires sommaires*. The Minister asked that each departmental archivist fill out pre-printed forms with the series, dates, pagination, content, and physical location of every box, bundle, and volume in his depository. While one copy of the inventory would remain in the department, another would be sent to Paris to be united with other inventories from around the country.[65] Within months of the circular's issue, archivist *chartistes* across France had made the inventory their primary concern. The Inspectors-General of Departmental Archives, meanwhile, helped ensure that the inventory was prepared according to ministerial specifications; an inspection checklist from the mid-to-late 1850s, for example, includes no less than sixty-six questions about the progress of the *Inventaires sommaires* (e.g., "On average, how many articles does Monsieur the Archivist inventory per day?…Is the paper used for the inventory and indexes 45.8 cm long and 30 cm wide, the dimensions of the model form?") but only half as many questions about other issues of archival administration.[66]

---

in *Procès-verbal des délibérations du Conseil général du département d'Indre-et-Loire précédé du Rapport du préfet. Session de 1859*, AD Indre-et-Loire, T 1395, p. 91).

[65] [Victor] F[ialin] de Persigny (Le Ministre de l'intérieur), "Instructions à transmettre aux archivistes, pour l'inventaire des archives départementales," 20 Jan. 1854, AN, box AB Va 7. Also in *Revue archéologique* 10 (1853): 747-750. The 1841 circular had also called for the preparation of inventories (based on *bulletins*, or cards, created for each box, packet, or volume), but placed far more emphasis on the classification process itself.

[66] Inspection générale des archives départementales, pre-printed questionnaire, after 1853 (header reads "Exercice 185."), AN, box F2 I 378[10]. Interestingly, *chartistes*' interest in archival inventory extended even to the Imperial Archives in Paris; in 1855, *chartiste* Henri Bordier, who after serving as an "expert" in the Libri case had worked for several years at the Archives, published his *Les archives de la France* (Paris: Dumoulin, 1855), which in lieu of an official inventory of the collections (not begun until the end of the decade) offered scholars an overview of the depository's contents.

On one level, the Empire's preoccupation with archival inventories points to a renewed interest in defining provincial archives as state property. The July Monarchy had tried to lay claim to the depositories supposedly abandoned by earlier governments, but the Second Empire's inventory project pushed this effort one step further. By laboriously recording the contents of every box in every departmental archive, the central government seemed to be preparing to defend itself not only against thieves (the Guillaume Libris of the archival world) but also against local officials and scholars eager to hoard precious documents. And indeed, throughout this period, the Archives Commission and the Inspectors-General proclaimed that departmental archives were not truly departmental, but rather national collections that had simply been entrusted to the guardianship of local officials. For example, in concluding a discussion of the status of a collection recently donated to the archives of the Nord, a Commission member declared that "[a]ccording to the firm opinion of the commission," departmental archives were "considered a dependency of the general archives of the State," and hence "their placement in the prefectures" had "no other aim but to facilitate research."[67] By hiring Paris-trained *chartistes* to prepare detailed inventories of these collections, the central government affirmed its control over all French archives.

Nevertheless, the *Inventaires sommaires* were clearly not intended solely as official records of state property. For as historians familiar with departmental collections are well aware, *Inventaires sommaires*, or "summary inventories," do not describe every document in every folder in every box in the depository. Unlike the *Inventaires analytiques* (analytical inventories) more common in the twentieth century, *Inventaires sommaires* provide more or less description depending on the supposed historical value of the document.[68] Thus in the *Inventaire sommaire* for the Maine-et-Loire, we find a folio-by-folio description of the medieval cartulary of the Abbey of Saint-Maur-sur-Loire,

---

[67] Commission des Archives, "Procès-verbaux," 19 Dec. 1850, AN, AB XXVI 2*, p. 206.

[68] In 1909, departmental archives stopped producing *Inventaires sommaires* and began working on *Inventaires analytiques*, which list all documents regardless of their historical value and do not include excerpts. See Le Directeur du Secrétariat et de la Comptabilité, "Rapport à Monsieur le Ministre de l'Intérieur, sur la situation des Archives départementales en 1875," 29 Jun. 1876, AN, box AB XXXI 15, and, more generally, *La pratique archivistique française*, ed. Jean Favier (Paris: Archives nationales, 1993), pp. 158-159 for discussions of the various research tools produced by departmental archives.

including dozens of synopses and Latin transcriptions, while we find only one line for an eighteenth-century register of the abbey's properties and revenues.[69] The decision to vary the level of description in this way was undoubtedly in part practical; if the departmental archivists of the 1850s (who rarely had assistants) had attempted truly comprehensive analytical inventories, their work might have been reduced to an impossibly slow pace. Yet the summary inventory also allowed the administration to promote certain sources as historically valuable while suppressing others completely. At the same time, because the state does not seem to have provided any explicit guidelines for making these sorts of judgements, the *Inventaire sommaire* project undoubtedly further bolstered the "expert" authority of departmental archivists, and, more specifically, of departmental *archivistes-paléographes*. The new generation of *chartistes* would not only put departmental archives in order but also draw upon their historical training to determine what facets of their now-orderly collections would be seen by archival researchers.[70]

Surprisingly, the departmental archivists of the 1850s do not seem to have made these determinations with any clear notion of the archival "public" in mind. Their official correspondences and annual reports rarely use the word "public"; in fact, some reports never mention archival researchers at all. Especially toward the end of the decade, some archivists begin to note the number of "communications" (i.e., documents retrieved from the depository) but generally without any discussion of the readers for whom these documents were retrieved.[71] As the next chapter will

---

[69] Célestin Port, *Inventaire sommaire des archives départementales antérieures à 1790…Maine-et-Loire. Archives ecclésiastiques. Série H. Clergé régulier* (Angers: Lachèse et Cie., 1898). On the campaign to publish the *Inventaires sommaires*, see chap. 5.

[70] In later work, I hope to compare the *Inventaires sommaires* of the late 1800s and the *Inventaires analytiques* of the 1900s in order to identify patterns in the kinds of documents included in (and excluded from) the earlier guides. I also plan to investigate whether these patterns have any relationship to the curriculum of the Ecole des Chartes. Did graduates of the school impose a particularly *chartiste* conception of history on their departmental archives, or did they follow their own interests?

[71] The annual number of "communications" in the departments included in this study seems to have varied considerably, from roughly 200 to roughly 1,400 items. A line in the inspection questionnaire cited in footnote 66 above suggests that an 18 Feb. 1854 circular required departmental archivists to keep a record of documents retrieved for readers (a *registre des communications*). Unfortunately, I have been unable so far to locate the text of this circular.

demonstrate, this situation changed rather dramatically around 1860, as archivists at all levels of the state archival administration began to direct their attention outward toward the reading "public"; through the late 1850s, however, archivists usually focused inward, concentrating on the work of classification and description rather than on public access.

In the few instances in which departmental *archivistes-paléographes* did talk about the archival public in the 1850s, it was usually in the context of the task that (after classification and inventory) consumed most of their professional energies: inspection. In his February 1850 report to Louis-Napoléon, the Minister of Public Instruction had called for the "active surveillance" of provincial archives, and the *archivistes-paléographes* of the 1850s seemed eager to respond to this charge. While the Inspectors-General conducted regular reviews of departmental (and sometimes communal) collections, many departmental archivists undertook inspections of communal depositories in their own departments. For instance, in the department of the Aube, Henri d'Arbois de Jubainville began inspecting communal archives in 1852 and by 1854 was inspecting more than one hundred a year.[72] For the most part, these inspections focused on the physical conditions of documents and collections, pointing out misnumbered shelves, disintegrating cartons, and leaky rooftops. Yet on occasion, they also attended to the people interested in using these collections. In 1859, Lot-et-Garonne archivist Ernest Croset (who often signed his reports "Archivist-Inspector") noted that while the departmental archives in Agen were accessible only to "*érudits* of established morality," and only then "under the surveillance of the Archivist in charge," communal archives had no such restrictions, leading to appalling "abuses" such as loss and theft.[73] For the archivist *chartistes* of the early Empire, as for the court "experts" of the Libri Affair, both state collections and their users had to be kept under careful watch.

---

[72] See AN, box F2 I 367[12], as well as Henri d'Arbois de Jubainville, *Voyage paléographique dans le département de l'Aube. Rapport à M. le préfet sur une inspection faite en 1854 dans les archives communales et hospitalières du département...*(Paris: A. Durand, 1855). D'Arbois was apparently one of the first departmental archivists to take such an active interest in communal archives, for the *BEC* of late 1853 made special note of his efforts, citing them as evidence that all departmental archivists should be charged with the inspection of communal depositories (*BEC* 15, p. 207).

[73] E[rnest] Croset, "Rapport présenté à Monsieur le Préfet sur la situation des Archives du département," 8 Aug. 1859, AD Lot-et-Garonne, box 3 T 3, pp. 7-8.

Yet the Empire's network of *archivistes-paléographes* did more than extend the eye of the state outward to the distant communes of the French provinces; it also produced an opposite motion, bringing information and documents from the provincial collections back to the center. The last of the four major tasks of the new departmental archivist, then, was to promote centralization. He did so in part by relaying inspection reports, archival inventories, and other records back up the administrative chain to the Ministry of the Interior. Under this new bureaucratic system, the central government began to produce and concentrate more information about provincial archival holdings than ever before. By amassing what would soon become a kind of archive on archives, the Imperial regime both illustrated its growing control over departmental collections and ensured that it could maintain that control into the future.

Beyond working to centralize information about provincial archives, the archivists of the 1850s also helped to centralize the archives themselves. In a campaign that became increasingly aggressive over the course of the decade, the Imperial government tried to concentrate all "historical" (pre-1790) documents in a given department in that department's central archives.[74] Though in some cases this meant tracking down isolated documents that had wound their way into the hands of private collectors or local organizations, more often it meant combing the smaller public archives in the region for old and rare materials that could be transferred to departmental headquarters. While the departmental archivist was out inspecting a communal depository for orderliness and cleanliness, he would also be quietly scanning the shelves for medieval charters and feudal registers.

In the 1850s, departmental archivists generally offered two justifications for incorporating the yellowing contents of local depositories into the main departmental collection. The first was that the precious vestiges of the Old Regime would be far better used and preserved at the departmental archives. As archivist Ernest Croset explained to the prefect of the Lot-et-Garonne:

> the ancient titles dispersed among the communes...lost their local utility
> the day that the administrative units that produced them ceased to exist.

---

[74] In the mid-1850s, archival officials in Paris even discussed bringing these departmental collections under the control of the Imperial (i.e., central) Archives, but the Minister of State ultimately rejected this idea (see AN, box AB I 1; box AB II 14, folder "1855," and box F17-13540, folder "Archives. Décret d'organisation. 22 Décembre 1855").

The records of the local registry offices [*Etat civil*], which may become—if brought together—a useful source of information on the movement of the population before the Revolution, uselessly clutter up the city hall in communes created in modern times, or whose former [church] parishes have disappeared.

What was more, Croset argued,

since the secret of ancient writings has been lost among populations ignorant of the past, the communal constitutions, the sovereign privileges, [and] the donation charters slowly amassed in [pre-revolutionary] abbeys...become lost, get sold, or pass into the hands of an amateur lacking the instruction necessary to understand them and the sense of justice to return them.[75]

The solution, then, was to bring all communal archives produced before 1790 under the "expert" supervision of the departmental archivist. Perhaps realizing that such a move was not likely to sit well with communal administrators, Croset and his prefect (Alphonse Paillard, also a graduate of the Ecole des Chartes) claimed that the communes would not be permanently surrendering their historical collections to the departmental archives but instead merely sending them out on loan. As Paillard assured the region's mayors:

It would not enter my mind to deprive the communes of a sacred property. The commune will thus remain the owner [*propriétaire*] of its titles: the prefectoral [i.e., departmental] archives will only be their trustee [*dépositaire*]. But there, placed under the vigilant eye of a skillful and responsible guardian, carefully analyzed, methodically classified, they will form a series of documents available for all [kinds of] research and from which erudition will draw great benefits.[76]

Useless and neglected at the communal level, the historical remnants of Old Regime institutions would get the care and attention they deserved from the "skillful and responsible" departmental archivist.

The second—and far more common—justification for centralizing historical archives in departmental depositories was rooted in the late July Monarchy's notion of *respect des fonds*.[77] According to this argument, while under the Old Regime, France's archives had constituted an orderly array

---

[75] E[rnest] Croset, "Minute. Rapport sur les archives Départementales et Communales," 5 Aug. 1858, AD Lot-et-Garonne, box 3 T 3, p. [5].

[76] Alph[onse] Paillard, circular to the mayors in the Lot-et-Garonne, in *BEC* 20 (1859): 461.

[77] See chap. 3.

of documentary *fonds*, the French Revolution destroyed this order, first by confiscating these *fonds* in the name of the nation, and then by redistributing them among a new set of archival depositories. Since the administrative boundaries of the new regime did not map neatly onto those of the old, the argument went, this process of documentary redistribution was often messy and inaccurate; the records of a single pre-revolutionary province would wind up in several different departments, while the archives of a feudal territory would be divided among a number of departmental and communal collections. The job of the departmental archivist, then, was to "reintegrate" the Old Regime *fonds* scattered around the department and around the country, thus reestablishing the organic wholeness of the pre-revolutionary collections. And since in this case the "reintegrated" documents belonged "naturally" to the departmental archive, they would be considered not temporary loans or deposits but permanent additions to the department's collection.[78]

Not surprisingly, the first formal appeal for archival "reintegration" came in the 1841 circular on *respect des fonds*.[79] Yet it was not until the first major wave of *archivistes-paléographes* hit the departments in the 1850s that reintegrations began in earnest. Departmental archivists trawled communal and judicial depositories for documents to fill the "gaps" in their own collections, while Inspectors-General urged them on, reporting each new transfer in detailed reports to the Ministry. Due to this program of reintegrations, as well as to the contemporaneous effort to get communal archives to deposit their historical collections with the department, the provincial archival landscape of the 1860s looked quite different from that of the 1840s. The archives of the Old Regime—now defined as "historical archives"—became concentrated in departmental depositories, where they could be organized, inventoried, and, most important, supervised by the expert archivists of the Ecole des Chartes.

---

[78] The most passionate statement of this position can be found in the "Rapport d'ensemble sur les diverses branches du service des Archives," submitted to the Interior Minister by the Inspectors-General of Departmental Archives in April 1866 (AN, box AB XXXI 15; also in BN mss., n.a.f. 22385).

[79] On p. 13 of T[anneguy] Duchâtel (Ministre Secrétaire d'Etat au département de l'Intérieur), "Circulaire [with marginal heading, "Instructions pour la mise en ordre et le classement des archives départementales et communales"]," Paris, 24 Apr. 1841, AN, box AB Vf 1, folder "Archives départementales (1820-1857)," we find: "We must also anticipate that within the limits of the department we may discover documents that, according to their nature and their origin, belong to the central prefectoral depository and that should be reintegrated into it."

In certain respects, the early Empire's effort to classify, inventory, inspect, and centralize provincial archives by stationing eager young *archivistes-paléographes* in departmental depositories around the country can be seen as an extension of the archival campaigns of the late July Monarchy. Like the Orleanist regime of the 1840s, the Bonapartist one of the 1850s spent most of its administrative energies on provincial archives rather than Parisian archives or public libraries. Both governments approached these provincial collections with a kind of crusading fervor, showing themselves eager to transform supposedly filthy and chaotic depositories into clean, orderly state collections. And for the most part, the Empire seems to have accepted the July Monarchy's vision of archival order, from its policies of "reintegration" and *respect des fonds* to its classification of documents into those before 1790, those after 1790, and those of the "intermediary period." Bonapartist officials even openly praised the work of their Orleanist predecessors, touting the 1841 circular as a work of great wisdom and foresight.[80]

This willingness to emulate the archival policies of the July Monarchy is somewhat surprising; after all, the First Napoleonic Empire had so often promoted itself as the crowning achievement of the French Revolution, so one might have expected the Second Empire to follow suit, celebrating its revolutionary roots and—perhaps—embarking on a new investigation of revolutionary archives.[81] Yet Louis-Napoléon's archival administrators at times seem to have been even more intent upon isolating and suppressing the archives of the 1790s than were their Orleanist predecessors. With the violence of France's most recent revolution undoubtedly fresh in their minds, they worked to keep Series L a series apart. For example, while the Interior Minister of the early 1840s had been willing to let Seine-et-Oise archivist Breval do away with Series L, in the late 1850s, *chartiste* Inspector-General Eugène de Stadler had no tolerance for what he called Breval's "incredible obstinacy" in dividing the series up among Series M through Z:

> Mr. Breval most often proceeded unmethodically, following his whims, and according to a peculiar style that led him to undo what had already been done [and] to classify documents in an order that conflicts with that

---

[80] See for example Barrot, "Rapport," p. [2].

[81] On Napoléon III's efforts to imitate Napoléon I (and on his belief that Napoléon I's Empire represented the fulfillment of the revolutionary destiny), see Stuart L. Campbell, *The Second Empire Revisited: A Study in French Historiography* (New Brunswick, NJ: Rutgers University Press, 1978), esp. chap. 1.

so judiciously prescribed for all archivists by ministerial instructions: classification by *fonds* of origin.[82]

The new generation of departmental *archivistes-paléographes*, for their part, studiously avoided the "intermediary period," often mentioning every other series in their annual reports except Series L. If their reports did mention the 1789 revolution, it was usually only to bemoan the thefts and burnings of archival documents, or what *chartiste* Charles Grandmaison called "these senseless holocausts."[83]

There were some indications that attitudes toward the "intermediary period" were about to change. In 1852, Indre-et-Loire archivist Augustin Deloye appealed—though unsuccessfully—for a general inventory of departmental archives from what he termed the "revolutionary era."[84] Then in the mid-1850s, several *archivistes-paléographes* stationed in departmental archives began to produce inventories of Series L, despite the lack of ministerial instructions on the subject.[85] Nevertheless, even the archivists bold enough to begin exploring this series seemed convinced that its contents were still too volatile for widespread scholarly use. They explained that they were merely preparing the way for a future generation of historians for whom the French Revolution would be an appropriate subject of scholarly study. Grandmaison, for example, noted in his annual report for 1853 that he had begun reviewing the documents in Series L because they would "one day be useful and precious materials for the writers who will [then] take a serious interest in the role the Revolution played in our regions."[86] Grandmaison's colleague in the Maine-et-Loire, Célestin Port, made this argument even more forcefully in his report for 1856:

---

[82] E[ugène] de Stadler, "Rapport à S. Exc. M. le Ministre de l'Intérieur et de la Sûreté générale [sur les archives départementales de Seine-et-Oise]," 15 Feb. 1859, AN, box F2 I 376[12], p. [3]. On the Minister of the Interior's earlier reaction to Breval, see chap. 3.

[83] Charles L. Grandmaison, *Notice historique sur les archives du département d'Indre-et-Loire* (Tours: Imprimerie Ladevèze, 1855), p. 7.

[84] [Augustin] Deloye, "Archives départementales d'Indre-et-Loire. Rapport annuel de l'archiviste à Monsieur le Préfet. 1852," 20 Aug. 1852, AN, box F2 I 371[5], p. 9.

[85] See for example [Henri] d'Arbois de Jubainville, "Rapport à M. le Préfet de l'Aube sur la situation des archives du département au 1er Août 1857," 1 Aug. 1857, AN, box F2 I 367[12], p. [4]; and E[rnest] Croset, "Rapport présenté à Monsieur le Préfet sur la situation des Archives du département," 1 Aug. 1859, AD Lot-et-Garonne, box 3 T 3, p. 1.

[86] Ch[arles] L[oyseau] Grandmaison, "Archives d'Indre et Loire. 1853. Rapport de l'archiviste," Aug. 1853, AN, box F2 I 371[5], p. [3].

[W]hen the public passions and angers die along with the last survivors of those dismal struggles, and it will be possible to look directly at the impassive face of history, [now] still veiled by the smoke of combat, this whole shapeless chaos [of documents] will radiate with a bright light and with unexpected lessons.[87]

Although nearly seventy years had passed since the fall of the Bastille, the archives of the Revolution were still hot to the touch. And despite the preliminary forays of the mid-1850s, it would be twenty years more before the central government would begin encouraging its departmental archivists to organize and publicize their revolutionary collections.[88]

Just as surprising as the Empire's lack of enthusiasm for the departmental archives of the 1790s is its apparent lack of interest in those of the early 1800s. Although an Imperial commission spent much of the 1850s preparing Napoleon I's correspondence (located primarily at the central Archives in Paris) for publication, this fascination with the First Empire does not seem to have extended to provincial collections.[89] While the post-revolutionary *archives administratives* (Series K and M through Z) presumably contained extensive records of the First Empire's dealings in the provinces, the *archivistes-paléographes* of the Second Empire—like those of the July Monarchy—generally ignored these collections in favor of the archives of the Old Regime. At the Ecole des Chartes, for example, Professor Vallet de Viriville "dictated at length the first part of the [1841 classification] framework, applicable to archives prior to 1790" and "commented upon and developed each of the articles in this part of the table," yet gave only a "rapid analysis" of the second part of the framework, applicable to archives after 1790.[90] Once posted in departmental archives, Vallet's students had

---

[87] Célestin Port, "Rapport sur les Archives Départementales de Maine et Loire (1855-1856)," 7 Aug. 1856, AN, box F2 I 373¹, p. [5]. See also Eugène Lelong, *Célestin Port, 1828-1901* (Angers: Germain et G. Grassin, 1902), pp. 22-23. Interestingly, Grandmaison and Port stood at opposite ends of the political spectrum; while Grandmaison was a Catholic conservative, Port was an anti-clerical republican.

[88] On the 1874 circular calling for the classification of Series L, see the epilogue.

[89] See *Correspondance de Napoléon Ier, publiée par ordre de l'Empereur Napoléon III* (Paris: Plon, J. Dumaine, 1858-70). Several *chartistes*, including Athanase Cucheval-Clarigny, Félix Rocquain de Courtemblay, and Auguste Baillet contributed to this publication in the late 1850s and 1860s, but none of the departmental archivists included in this study make any mention of the project.

[90] [Auguste Vallet de Viriville], packet of lecture notes, labelled "Archives," AEC-SC, fol. 47v. Vallet's emphasis.

little choice but to follow his lead, for the nationwide *Inventaire sommaire* project of 1854 covered only the archives of the Old Regime (Series A through I). While archivists could (and sometimes did) create inventories for the later series, their departmental prefects and Inspectors-General pressed them to finish their "historical" inventories first.[91] Hence these archivists' annual reports often pause over every box and folder in their Old Regime series but rarely devote more than a few lines to the archives of the later period.

The early Empire's eagerness to follow the late July Monarchy in rejecting the departmental archives of the French Revolution and promoting those of the Old Regime suggests that from the perspective of archives, the conservatism of the 1850s was not so different from that of the 1840s. Both the late July Monarchy and the early Second Empire emphasized centralization, standardization, and surveillance.[92] Both rejected revolutionary collections, even though popular revolutions had helped bring them to power. And both, it seems, preferred to view the Old Regime, not the New, as their "history."[93] Despite (or more likely because of) the political upheaval of 1848, the new Bonapartist regime returned to the policies of its Orleanist precursor.

So what made the archival and historical policies of the 1850s unique? The question is difficult to answer, for unlike the July Monarchy, the early Empire never set forth a clear and coherent historical program. In the 1830s and 1840s, Orleanist historians like François Guizot, Augustin Thierry, and

---

[91] A checklist of questions designed for the Inspectors-General asked, "Does the work required by the modern [post-1790] papers allow the archivist enough time to attend to the archives prior to 1790 on a regular basis?" (see footnote 66 above).

[92] Indeed, it was in part the sense of continuity between the centralizing impulses of the July Monarchy and those of the Second Empire that helped push Alexis de Tocqueville to begin work on *The Old Regime and the French Revolution* (1856). See François Furet, "Tocqueville," in *A Critical Dictionary of the French Revolution*, ed. François Furet and Mona Ozouf, trans. Arthur Goldhammer (Cambridge, MA: Harvard/Belknap, 1989), pp. 1021-1032; originally published as *Dictionnaire critique de la révolution française* (Paris: Flammarion, 1988).

[93] It is possible that the Imperial government chose to emphasize the archives of the Old Regime over those of the New as a way of trying to link Napoléon III to the long line of pre-revolutionary kings. After all, as Michael Paul Driskel points out in *As Befits a Legend: Building a Tomb for Napoleon, 1840-1861* (Kent, OH: Kent State University Press, 1993), for much of the 1850s, Persigny and Napoléon III planned to bury Napoléon I at the Basilica of Saint-Denis, the traditional resting place of French kings.

Ludovic Vitet had led an energetic campaign to unite the French behind a common historical vision. In project after project, they tried to convince the French populace that the bourgeoisie of 1830 was the same bourgeoisie that had led the French nation through centuries of struggles, from the urban revolts of the Middle Ages to the massive upheaval of 1789.[94] But the revolution of 1848 sent this generation of historian-politicians scattering and put in its place a cadre of career administrators generally less prone to sweeping statements of historiographical vision. Nevertheless, if we look more closely at these officials' discussions of provincial archives, we can see the makings of an identifiably "Imperial" historiographical strategy.

Perhaps the most common underlying theme in the work of archival administrators from this period is the importance of local history. Of course, the historians of the 1830s and 1840s had also encouraged the study of local history (particularly the history of medieval municipalities) but only insofar as it helped corroborate the larger story of the nation's advance. Cities and regions were studied for their similarities, not their differences. By contrast, the ministers, archivists, and inspectors of the 1850s promoted local history without implying that local studies would—or should—buttress a certain conception of national history. For example, in his 1854 circular on the *Inventaires sommaires*, clearly intended as a nationwide compilation of archival inventories, Interior Minister Persigny never once mentioned "France" or the "nation," noting only that

> [t]his is an enterprise worthy of all the government's solicitude, for the old archives, which have preserved for us the official traditions of the past [by] providing a summary of their annals, still contain the history particular to each of the provinces, localities, and families; the history of landed and movable property; finally, the history of science, art, public law, customs, and mores.[95]

Interestingly, for Persigny, the value of these various histories was not just intellectual or political but eminently practical. As he told the Archives Commission in early 1854: "it is due to industrial development that public opinion and the government have become concerned with the organization [*mise en ordre*] and inventory of archives." Properly inventoried, local historical collections would offer residents valuable "lessons" about "the projects and experiments attempted in the sciences, arts, industry,

---

[94] See chap. 3.
[95] Persigny, "Instructions," in *Revue archéologique*, p. 747.

commerce, agriculture, etc."[96] Departmental archives would become a valuable point of reference not only for scholars but also for local participants in the slow industrialization of the French countryside.[97]

Although neither the Archives Commission nor the archivists and inspectors they helped supervise seems to have shown much interest in the industrial or commercial uses of regional archives, they did follow Persigny in emphasizing the uniqueness of local historical collections. While the reports filed by departmental archivists (both *chartistes* and non-*chartistes*) during the July Monarchy often pointed to their affiliations with national historical projects like the *Documents inédits* series, those of the early Empire were far more likely to mention their own work on local sources.[98] Throughout the 1850s, graduates of the Ecole des Chartes posted in departmental depositories turned out dozens of publications in local history, from specialized inventories to collections of texts to narrative accounts. They published so much, in fact, that according to Charles-Olivier Carbonell, archivists were by the mid-1860s the most prolific of all French historians.[99] For example, *chartiste* Charles Beaurepaire, appointed archivist of the Seine-Inférieure (now the Seine-Maritime) in 1851, published multiple histories of Rouen and its environs, from *La Normandie illustrée* [Illustrated Normandy] (1852) to *Notes sur la prise du château de Rouen par Ricarville en 1432* [Notes on the capture of Rouen castle by Ricarville in 1432] (1856). Meanwhile in the Allier, Beaurepaire's colleague Alphonse Chazaud devoted himself to the study of the Bourbonnais, producing articles on medieval Bourbon rulers for the *Bibliothèque de l'Ecole des Chartes* and local scholarly journals. At the same time, *chartistes* like Beaurepaire and Chazaud encouraged other scholars to study their regions by founding and supporting local historical societies.[100]

---

[96] Commission des Archives, "Procès-verbaux," [18?] Jan. 1854, AN, AB XXVI 3*, p. 159. Persigny made a similar argument in an 1862 speech to the Historical and Archeological Society of Forez (see *BEC* 24 (1863): 237-244).

[97] On industrialization in France, see Rondo Cameron, *France and the Economic Development of Europe, 1800-1914* (Princeton, NJ: Princeton University Press, 1961), and François Caron, *An Economic History of Modern France*, trans. Barbara Bray (New York: Columbia University Press, 1979).

[98] Interestingly, according to Jean Le Pottier, at about the same time, the government agency responsible for the *Documents inédits*, the Historical Works Committee, shifted its focus to local history and began taking a greater interest in provincial scholarly societies ("Histoire et érudition," pp. 194-195).

[99] Carbonell, *Histoire et historiens*, p. 251.

[100] See Le Pottier, "Histoire et érudition," p. 213.

The *archivistes-paléographes* of this period do not seem to have been concerned that their work as local historians might distract them from their work as classifiers, cataloguers, and inspectors of archival documents. On the contrary, they argued that the study of local history was one of their most important professional duties. In an 1852 report on the archives of the Maine-et-Loire, for example, *chartiste* Paul Marchegay defended his work on behalf of the historical *Revue de l'Anjou*:

> choosing the old documents to be printed [in the journal], offering the tribute of [my] experience to collaborators frightened by the breadth of the research and the difficulty of the scripts, and encouraging through constant efforts the auspicious impetus that literary as well as erudite works have received in the Anjou, all this is also to fulfill [my] functions as an archivist.[101]

The Inspectors-General of Departmental Archives appear to have encouraged this conception of the archivist's role, congratulating archivists on their recent publications and applauding their "erudition" in reports to the Minister of the Interior.[102] In this sense, the archivist *chartistes* of the 1850s were the logical product of the Ecole des Chartes curriculum of 1846; trained in both archival classification and historical analysis, they were prepared both to apply the 1841 circular and to produce scholarly works.[103] Yet if the 1846 curriculum had envisioned *chartistes* (even those stationed in the provinces) as national historians, carefully constructing a documentary lineage for the then-Orleanist state, the archivists of the 1850s were more likely to serve as local historians, revealing the forgotten glories of the Anjou, the Savoie, or the Bourbonnais.

Another way in which these archivists broke with Orleanist strategy was by extending their gaze beyond the medieval period to encompass the entire Old Regime. Even though the "historical" period defined by the 1841 circular did not end until 1790, the archival and historical projects sponsored by the July regime had concentrated almost exclusively on the

---

[101] P[aul] Marchegay, "Archives de Maine et Loire. Rapport sur les travaux du 1er semestre de 1852," 24 Aug. 1852, AN, box F2 I 373¹, p. [13].

[102] See for example Inspector Francis Wey's review of Charles Grandmaison in "Rapport à M. le Ministre de l'Intérieur sur les archives de la Préfecture de Tours," 3 Jul. 1858, AN, box F2 I 371⁵. See also Wey's fictional travelogue, *Dick Moon en France, journal d'un Anglais de Paris* (Paris: Librairie de L. Hachette, 1862), in which he praises the Imperial government's use of *chartistes* to help "revive the provinces" and create a healthy sense of regional history and "local patriotism" (pp. 343-345).

[103] On the debate over the 1846 curriculum (still in place in the 1850s), see chap. 3.

Middle Ages. With the rise of Napoléon III, this pattern began to shift. While the courses taught at the Ecole des Chartes (as well as the articles published in the school's *Bibliothèque*) continued to emphasize medieval history, the *chartistes* assigned to departmental archives began to explore later periods.[104] In 1855, for instance, d'Arbois de Jubainville reported that the most fascinating of the historical treasures he had discovered during his inventory of the archives of the Aube were from the sixteenth and seventeenth centuries, documents like the 1559 itinerary of Jean de Luxembourg and the 1697 minutes of the local *Arrière-Ban* (assembly of nobles).[105] Meanwhile, Inspector-General Francis Wey reminded the Minister of the Interior that the archives of the Seine-et-Oise contained a mine of valuable information on life at Versailles on the eve of the Revolution.[106] Yet the most memorable example of this trend is Indre-et-Loire archivist Charles Grandmaison's work on behalf of historian Alexis de Tocqueville. In the summer of 1853, Tocqueville came to the departmental archives in Tours to begin work on *The Old Regime and the French Revolution*. In his efforts to assist his illustrious visitor, the young Grandmaison devoted himself to organizing the eighteenth-century records of the local provincial government, or intendancy. Though trained as a medievalist, Grandmaison quickly warmed to the pre-revolutionary sources and indeed continued to vaunt their historical value long after Tocqueville's departure.[107] The archives of Louis XVI were becoming just as historically compelling as those of his medieval ancestors.

---

[104] For the examination questions given to the school's students in this period, see the minutes of the Ecole's *Conseil de perfectionnement*, or governing board, in the AEC, as well as scattered references in AN, box F17-4049 and F17-4050 (in one box) and box F17-4051.

[105] [Henri] d'Arbois de Jubainville, "Rapport à Monsieur le Préfet de l'Aube sur la situation des Archives du Département," 31 Dec. 1855, AN, box F2 I 367[12].

[106] Francis Wey, "Rapport à M. le Ministre de l'Intérieur sur les archives départementales de Versailles," 22 Oct. 1856, AN, box F2 I 376[12], p. 8.

[107] See Charles de Grandmaison, "Sejour d'Alexis de Tocqueville en Touraine, préparation du livre sur l'ancien régime, juin 1853-avril 1854," *Le Corréspondant* 114 (1879): 926-949, also published separately in 1893 by the Librairie Nouvelle. See also Richard Herr, "The Archives of Touraine," in *Tocqueville and the Old Regime* (Princeton, NJ: Princeton University Press, 1962), pp. 3-8. For Tocqueville's nod to Grandmaison, see *L'ancien régime et la Révolution*, 2nd ed. (Paris: Michel Lévy, 1856), p. 9. For the correspondence between Tocqueville and Grandmaison, see AD Indre-et-Loire, box 8 F 9/2, Fonds Grandmaison.

That the archival administrators of the 1850s were willing to encourage a broader range of historical projects—from detailed studies of local monuments to scholarly investigations of pre-revolutionary assemblies— suggests that the early Empire may have been open to a wider spectrum of cultural and political allegiances than was the late July Monarchy. The Orleanists had tried to rally the entire country around a particular conception of French history. They seemed to believe that if they could enlist enough scholars and muster enough documents, they might be able to instill the (literate) public with a sense of connection to the bourgeois regime. From the perspective of archives, at least, the early Empire seems to have taken the opposite tack, helping its subjects to investigate both medieval communes and absolutist kings, both regional customs and Parisian decrees. While this approach to national history may at first seem like no approach at all, it may have been one particularly well-suited to the political predicament of the early Empire. Following the bitter conflicts of 1848, an overwhelming majority of Frenchmen had voted in support of Louis-Napoléon, later Napoléon III. As a number of historians have argued, much of Napoléon's appeal lay in his ambiguity: at once a prince and a populist, a technocrat and a utopian thinker, a dictator and a Liberal, he offered something for everyone.[108] The Empire's approach to archives can thus be seen as an effort to sustain this broad support by helping a range of scholars (and particularly scholars in the countryside, the traditional mainstay of Bonapartist support) find their histories in the nation's archives. Its very lack of a historical program, then, was a program in itself.

We cannot forget, however, that along with this apparent openness and eclecticism came a good measure of regulation and repression. If the Imperial administration opened the broad sweep of the Old Regime to scholarly exploration, it nevertheless continued to mark the revolutionary period as forbidden territory. And while it encouraged provincial scholars to study their local treasures, it brought most of those treasures under the watchful eye of Paris-trained *archivistes-paléographes*. We might say, then, that the Empire's historiographical strategy was to promote a range of historical identifications, but within clear limits. Historical research under Napoléon III could look beyond the medieval bourgeoisie, but only within the

---

[108] See for example Theodore Zeldin, *The Political System of Napoleon III* (New York: W.W. Norton, 1958); Matthew Truesdell, *Spectacular Politics: Louis-Napoléon Bonaparte and the Fête Impériale, 1849-1870* (New York: Oxford University Press, 1997), and James F. McMillan, *Napoléon III* (New York: Longman, 1991).

boundaries of the now far more centralized and standardized system of state archives and state archivists.

The contrast between the Bonapartist regime's emphasis on archival organization and the early Second Republic's focus on library experimentation points to a pattern that had begun to emerge in the early 1800s but was not fully visible until mid-century. While the more conservative post-revolutionary regimes (the Bourbon Restoration, the late July Monarchy, the late Second Republic, and the early Second Empire) concentrated their efforts on state archives, the more left-leaning governments (the early Second Republic, and, to a lesser extent, the early July Monarchy) looked to public libraries. Even though the 1789 revolution had taken considerable interest in archival organization and indeed had pioneered the idea of "national" archives, under later regimes archives seemed to become linked with opposition to the revolution, libraries with support for it. State-owned libraries seemed to be associated with expanded public education, increased political participation, and thus with the possibility of new political upheavals. Archives, meanwhile, were linked with the controlled production of national history, which was seen as essential to political unity and stability. This pattern was to continue under the late Second Empire, as the increasingly "liberal" Bonapartist state again turned to the question of public libraries. Yet the late Empire was no revolutionary republic; even as it worked to enact liberal reforms, it also tried to maintain its strict control of public politics. As it struggled to balance experimentation and conservatism, it began to explore the relationship between public libraries and state archives, and the proper relationship of each to the modern French state.

Chapter Five

The Challenge of the Public: Defining Libraries and Archives in the Late Second Empire

Unlike the Bourbon Restoration, the July Monarchy, and the Second Republic, all of which became increasingly conservative over time, the Second Empire was far more liberal at the time of its collapse in 1870 than at its inception in 1852. The early Empire, eager to suppress the revolutionary passions of 1848, had allowed few opportunities for political debate, yet the Empire of the 1860s gradually opened the way for opposition groups—and especially those on the left—to express their views publicly. The first indicator of the Empire's new approach was the general amnesty of 1859, which unlike earlier amnesties, allowed political exiles to return to France without asking them to make any declaration of submission to the Imperial regime. The following year, in 1860, the Emperor inaugurated a series of reforms that while stopping short of creating a parliamentary government, significantly increased the power and visibility of the popularly elected *Corps législatif* (Legislative body). When combined with a set of measures designed to reduce restrictions on the press, these reforms promoted what one historian has called the "revival of political life" in France. Indeed, this revival was so vigorous that it pushed Napoléon III to enact even more reforms, culminating in the quasi-parliamentary "Liberal Empire" of 1869. How long this new compromise between authoritarianism and republicanism might have lasted, we cannot know, for in September 1870, the Second Empire fell to Prussian troops, thus preparing the way for the Third Republic.[1]

---

[1] Historians have offered various reasons for the relaxation of restrictions in the 1860s, some pointing to Napoléon III's personal commitment to political reform, others to increasing pressure from opposition groups (especially republicans and Liberals) unsatisfied by the Empire's early efforts at political reconciliation. See Theodore Zeldin, *The Political System of Napoleon III* (New York: W.W. Norton, 1958), and *Emile Ollivier and the Liberal Empire of Napoleon III* (Oxford: Clarendon Press, 1963); chap. 1 of Stuart L. Campbell, *The Second Empire Revisited: A Study in French Historiography* (New Brunswick, NJ: Rutgers University Press, 1978); and Philip Nord, *The Republican Moment: Struggles for Democracy in Nineteenth-Century France*

The new openness in the world of politics in the 1860s coincided in the world of archives and libraries with a rather dramatic reorientation toward the reading public. In the wake of the Second Republic's experiments in public library reform, the *chartistes* of the 1850s had hardly ever noted the existence of readers, let alone reflected on the nature of the "public." However, just around the time of Napoléon III's legislative reforms, *chartistes* at all levels of archival and library administration began invoking the public with greater and greater frequency. In the provinces, departmental archivists spoke more often of the public's "needs" and of new policies designed to meet them. In the capital, archivists and librarians alike began touting their "public services" and applauding the Empire's new "liberality" toward users of state collections. And in 1869, the Minister of Public Instruction once again reorganized the Ecole des Chartes, this time splitting the existing course on the classification of archives and libraries into two new courses, one on archival classification and one on "Bibliography and the Classification of Public Libraries." Arguing that *chartistes* needed more "practical" training than that provided by the 1846 curriculum, the framers of the new program hoped to prepare students more effectively for work as public librarians.[2]

It is rather tempting to read these developments as a return to the public library policies of 1848. Perhaps after a decade spent inventorying, centralizing, and inspecting provincial archives, the French state was once again ready to open its historical collections to the *grand public* and ready to ask its corps of *chartistes* to shift their attention from state archives to public libraries. Perhaps on the eve of the Third Republic, in other words, the French state was prepared to revive the policies of the Second Republic. However, if we look more closely at discussions of libraries and archives in the 1860s, we find that the situation was rather more complicated, both for the state and for the Ecole des Chartes. In the final decade of Napoléon III's reign, librarians and archivists became enmeshed in two major debates about the role of public libraries in France. The first of these emerged along

---

(Cambridge: Harvard University Press, 1995). The quotation is from William E. Echard, "Reform," in *Historical Dictionary of the French Second Empire, 1852-1870* (Westport, CT: Greenwood Press, 1985), p. 544.

[2] For the 1869 decree as well as the ministerial report that preceded it, see *BEC* 30 (1869): 122-125. On the development of the new curriculum, see Ecole des Chartes, Conseil de Perfectionnement, "Procès-verbaux," 29 Dec. 1868 and 12 Apr. 1869, AEC (bound volume covering 1864-1876), pp. 90-99; as well as correspondence between the Conseil and the Minister in AN, box F17-4024.

with the "popular library" movement of the early 1860s. Convinced that France's supposedly "public" libraries were inadequate to the needs of the literate population, leaders of this movement pressed the Ministry of Public Instruction to re-evaluate its long-standing policies. Meanwhile, a second and much more bitter debate pitted France's two largest collections—the Imperial Library and the Archives of the Empire—against each other in a five-year battle that began in a dispute over a set of historical manuscripts and ended in a struggle over the proper distinction between "public libraries" and "state archives." As we will see, in both of these debates, the French state proved either unwilling or unable to articulate a clear role for its public libraries. Moreover, rather than pushing the Ecole des Chartes into a position of new prominence in public libraries, these debates actually linked the school more strongly with the world of state archives.

Although the idea of a "popular library," aimed at the instruction, edification, and (most often) moralization of the masses, has its roots in the eighteenth century, efforts to create popular libraries in France remained relatively sporadic until the latter half of the Second Empire, when booksellers, industrialists, workers, and artisans began setting up popular collections in neighborhoods and towns around the country.[3] The movement to create these collections seems to have begun in 1858, when several Parisian journalists began calling for the development of popular libraries.[4] Three years later, typographer Jean-Baptiste Girard responded to this call by founding the *Société des Amis de l'instruction* (Society for the Friends of Instruction), aimed at organizing libraries by and for the working classes. For a monthly fee, workers of both sexes who wanted access to "professional" as well as "literary" works could not only borrow books but also participate in the administration and development of the collections. The first of these libraries opened in the third *arrondissement* of Paris in 1861, and several others followed by the end of the decade.[5] Other popular library

---

[3] On the history of the popular library movement, see the work of Noë Richter, notably *Les bibliothèques populaires* (Paris: Cercle de la Librairie, 1978) and "Les bibliothèques populaires et la lecture ouvrière," in *Histoire des bibliothèques françaises* (Paris: Promodis, 1991), 3: 513-535.

[4] Graham Keith Barnett, *Histoire des bibliothèques publiques en France de la Révolution à 1939* (Paris: Promodis, 1987), p. 140; and Jean Hébrard, "Les bibliothèques scolaires," in *Histoire des bibliothèques françaises*, 3: 548.

[5] Bibliothèque des Amis de l'Instruction (IIIe arrondissement), *Exercice 1861-1862. Historique. Compte rendu financier. Statuts. Liste des donateurs* (Paris: Imprimerie de J.

associations did not create libraries themselves but rather tried to encourage
the spread of popular libraries by compiling lists of "good books," providing
book binding and distribution services, and by drumming up donors. The
most famous of these was the *Société Franklin*, founded in 1862, which by the
end of the Second Empire had recruited 700 businessmen, industrialists,
and bureaucrats to discuss reading lists and prepare documents such as the
Society's "Instructions on the formation of a popular library."[6] Another
influential group was the *Société des bibliothèques communales du Haut-Rhin*
(Communal Library Society of the Haut-Rhin), founded by Jean Macé and
a group of Mulhouse industrialists in 1863.[7] Yet there were smaller popular
library "propaganda" societies all over France, from major cities like Lyon
and Bordeaux to small towns like Bacouel (population 214).[8]

Historians have identified a number of reasons for this explosion of
activity. On the one hand, the expansion of both elementary and adult
education meant that the reading public was far larger—and more socio-
economically diverse—in the late nineteenth century than ever before.[9] On

---

Claye, 1862), pp. 6-8. See also Marie-Josèphe Beaud, Jean Grigorieff, and Georges-
Guillaume Kerourédan, eds., *Lectures et lecteurs au XIXe siècle: la Bibliothèque des Amis de
l'Instruction* (Paris: Bibliothèque des Amis de l'Instruction du 3e arrondissement,
1985); Pascale Marie, "La Bibliothèque des Amis de l'instruction du IIIe
arrondissement: un temple, quartier du Temple," in *Les lieux de mémoire*, ed. Pierre
Nora ([Paris]: Gallimard, 1984), vol. 1, pp. 323-351; and Jacqueline Guilbaud,
"Bibliothèque des Amis de l'instruction du IIIe arrondissement," in *Patrimoine des
bibliothèques de France*, ed. Anne-Marie Reder (Paris: Payot, 1995), 1: 158-159.

[6] See Société Franklin pour la propagation des bibliothèques populaires. *I. Notice sur
la Société Franklin, II. Instruction pour la fondation d'une bibliothèque, III. Catalogue populaire
de la Société Franklin..., IV. Nouveaux statuts de la Société Franklin...*([Paris]: Siège de la
Société, Sept. 1864). See also Barnett, *Histoire des bibliothèques*, pp. 143-144; and Jean
Hassenforder, "Histoire d'une tentative pour la promotion des bibliothèques
populaires: la Société Franklin," *Education et bibliothèques* 6 (Mar. 1963): 21-36.

[7] See especially Katherine Auspitz, *The Radical Bourgeoisie: The Ligue de l'enseignement
and the Origins of the Third Republic, 1866-1885* (Cambridge: Cambridge University
Press, 1983), pp. 74-76.

[8] For a summary of regional activities, see Barnett, *Histoire des bibliothèques*, pp. 145-
152.

[9] For this argument, see Barnett, *Histoire des bibliothèques*, pp. 140-141. On literacy
and education more generally, see François Furet and Jacques Ozouf, *Reading and
Writing: Literacy in France from Calvin to Jules Ferry* (Cambridge: Cambridge University
Press, 1982), originally published as *Lire et écrire: l'alphabétisation des français de Calvin à
Jules Ferry* (Paris: Editions de minuit, 1977); and James Smith Allen, *In the Public Eye:*

the other hand, France's "public libraries" (that is, the municipal libraries of the provinces as well as the Imperial Library, Arsenal, Mazarine, and Sainte-Geneviève libraries in Paris) seemed less accessible and less relevant than ever before. Even at the time of the French Revolution, when most of these libraries were formed, their collections had been dominated by theological and historical works of little interest to most French readers; by the Second Empire, despite efforts to expand their holdings through legal deposit and other means, these libraries only appeared more stuffy and outdated. Members of the *Société Franklin* and other popular library groups of the 1860s never tired of describing public collections as too old, too scholarly, and too dilapidated for widespread use.[10] And in fact most public libraries served only a narrow audience of local *érudits*; according to an 1857 government survey, the vast majority of municipal libraries (303 out of 341) had fewer than twenty-one readers per day, and 105 of these 303 had no readers at all.[11] While there were important exceptions to this pattern, notably the ever-crowded Imperial and Sainte-Geneviève libraries in Paris, as a system, the Second Empire's public libraries could not meet the demands of the Second Empire's readers.[12]

If the surge of interest in popular libraries was in part related to this longtime disjuncture between public library supply and demand, it was undoubtedly also connected in the more immediate term to the revival of the left in the early 1860s. Certainly, not all supporters of popular libraries were members of the political opposition; most of the *Société Franklin*'s members, for example, were Imperial loyalists.[13] Yet among the popular library movement's most vocal backers were both socialist activists and republican politicians. Jean-Baptiste Girard, creator of the *Société des Amis de l'instruction* and co-founder of the *Société Franklin*, was a veteran of the socialist-led "associationist" movement of 1848. Imprisoned along with

A History of Reading in Modern France, 1800-1940 (Princeton, NJ: Princeton University Press, 1991), esp. chap. 2.

[10] See Barnett, *Histoire des bibliothèques*, p. 140; and Richter, *Bibliothèques populaires*, chap. 1, "L'inadaptation des bibliothèques traditionnelles."

[11] Ministère de l'Instruction Publique et des Cultes, *Tableau statistique des bibliothèques publiques des départements, d'après des documents officiels recueillis de 1853 à 1857* (Paris: Imprimerie Paul Dupont, 1857), summarized in Agnès Marcetteau-Paul, "Les bibliothèques municipales," in *Histoire des bibliothèques françaises*, 3: 444.

[12] On public libraries in this period, see footnote 4 as well as the articles in *Histoire des bibliothèques françaises*, vol. 3, and *Patrimoine des bibliothèques*, both of which include extensive bibliographies of local studies.

[13] Nord, *Republican Moment*, p. 210. See also Auspitz, *Radical Bourgeoisie*, p. 70.

other associationists in the early 1850s, he resurfaced in the early 1860s to advocate popular libraries as a means of working-class liberation.[14] Another outspoken member of the *Société Franklin* was Jules Simon, republican deputy from the Department of the Seine and future leader of the Third Republic. Like many republicans in the 1860s, he was looking for ways to appeal to the working classes. Popular libraries seemed an ideal way to both gain workers' support and inculcate them with republican values.[15] Thus in an 1863 article in the *Revue des Deux-Mondes*, Simon presented popular libraries as agents of political progress. He argued that while the great revolutions of 1789 and 1848 had promised liberty and equality for all, these promises had only been fulfilled for the literate population. Despite the opportunities provided by universal suffrage, only the educated could read campaign posters and follow legislative changes. Simon's solution to this problem was two-fold: first, he explained, sounding a key republican theme, France had to improve its elementary education system. Second, and "perhaps better," France had to establish popular libraries, which would "spread the taste for reading" among the working classes and thus create the "desire" for more and better schools.[16] Thus, as he explained in an 1865 speech, the book would become "the symbol of the last and most fecund of revolutions," completing the work of 1789 and extending political freedom to all.[17]

Perhaps because the popular library movement's leadership included members of the political opposition, the movement often appeared wary of government involvement. Simon, for example, argued that however much

---

[14] For the intriguing story of Girard's political career, see Ian Frazer, "Jean-Baptiste Girard (1821-1900): Fondateur des Bibliothèques des Amis de l'Instruction (1861)," in Beaud, Grigorieff, and Kerourédan, *Lectures et lecteurs*, pp. 53-72.

[15] Nord, *Republican Moment*, pp. 208-211. Of course, the group of politicians and activists describing themselves as "republicans" in this period was extremely diverse. For a useful overview of these sub-groups, see Joel S. Cleland, "Republicanism," in *Historical Dictionary of the Second Empire*, pp. 550-555.

[16] Jules Simon, "L'instruction primaire et les bibliothèques populaires," *Revue des Deux-Mondes* (15 Sept. 1863): 349-375.

[17] Jules Simon, "Société d'enseignement professionel du Rhône. Conférence de M. Jules Simon (député de la Seine). Les bibliothèques populaires," *Revue bleue* (11 Feb. 1865): 174-179. It would be worth investigating further the relationships among socialist, republican, and Bonapartist supporters of popular libraries. While some suggest that the socialists were quickly silenced and excluded by the more centrist groups, others argue that some popular library associations remained socialist throughout the 1860s. See the contributions by Ian Frazer and Odile Vacher in *Lectures et lecteurs*.

the state might claim to "put itself above partisanship," it would inevitably transform popular libraries into instruments of official propaganda.[18] Yet Simon's fellow *Société Franklin* member, Ecole des Chartes professor Auguste Vallet de Viriville, offered a different view.[19] Like Simon, Vallet saw libraries as the natural complement to public schools. As he told his library classification students in the mid-1860s, "[l]ibraries are establishments that are directly connected to public instruction. They are schools of the first rank, the highest schools, since it is there that [great] minds have deposited their riches." He also agreed that libraries had to be open to all, reminding his classes that "[o]ne of the conditions of [libraries'] utility is that they be accessible to everyone.... The most important thing for a library is accessibility."[20] And like other popular library proponents, Vallet believed that the existing system of public libraries was in a pitiful state. In an 1867 article in *Le Temps*, he recounted the tale of an unnamed public library in the center of France whose librarian was a retired dance instructor who "hardly knew how to read or write." When said librarian became too old even to move his legs, the city hired a replacement, a "sordid" man who served in his position for twenty-seven years, only for it to be discovered, upon his death, that he had kept some fifteen hundred of the library's volumes locked away in a filthy, debris-filled cavern.[21]

However, while many popular library advocates believed that the organization of more useful and accessible collections was best left to private initiative, Vallet urged the French government to draw on the enthusiasm for popular libraries to help revive and expand the public library system. Indeed, in Vallet's view, the effervescence of the popular library movement demonstrated that library reform was in the "general interest" and thus worthy of the "intervention of the State." As Vallet explained in 1867:

> On all sides, in fact, in the light of good sense and in the sunshine of patriotism, new buds are growing on the old withered trunk of so-called *public* libraries. Private associations, with their zeal and their money, are

---

[18] Simon, "L'instruction," pp. 366-369. See also Frazer, "Jean-Baptiste Girard," and Richter, *Bibliothèques populaires*.

[19] On Vallet's earlier discussions of public libraries, see chap. 3.

[20] Auguste Vallet de Viriville, quoted in F[rançois] Molard, "Cours de Mr. Vallet de Viriville. Classement des Archives et des Bibliothèques. 1864-65," Bibliothèque municipale d'Auxerre, ms. 382, pp. 3 and 34.

[21] A[uguste] Vallet de Viriville, *L'Ecole des chartes: son passé, son état présent, son avenir* (Paris: Ch. Schiller, 1867), pp. 22-24 (first published in *Le Temps*, 8 and 11 Sept. 1867).

organizing collections of books that will be in touch with the intellectual and current needs of the population. The great issue of libraries will thus inevitably come back within the legislative purview.[22]

The challenge for the state, then, was to revitalize public libraries in a way that brought them, too, more in touch with the needs of the population. Even though the public libraries in the provinces had been virtually abandoned to local governments since 1803, it was time for the central government to reassert its control:

> While leaving to the communes the liberty and right that belongs to them, in my opinion, good order will not come into being in this branch of the administration until the day when the legislator pursues measures for libraries analogous to those that have been so successful for departmental archives.[23]

If, Vallet suggested, the central government would pay as much attention to public libraries as it did to state archives, the private organization of popular libraries would no longer be necessary.

Given Vallet's long-standing efforts to strengthen the ties between public libraries and the Ecole des Chartes, it is not surprising that his lectures and essays from the mid-1860s foresaw a prominent role for *chartistes* in what he hoped would be a massive campaign to make public libraries more "popular." His 1864-1865 classification course began, like many of his articles and essays, with the reminder that *chartistes* were more than just archivists. "Three kinds of people come out of the Ecole des Chartes," he said, "1. archivists, 2. librarians, 3. *érudits*." He then launched a series of lessons about the history and organization of public libraries, telling his students:

> We begin with libraries…given the general movement of minds toward that part of our studies. Several of our departments have already instituted communal [i.e., popular] libraries, and among them the Bas-Rhin has particularly distinguished itself. It is important that we understand libraries thoroughly because they form a part of the sphere in which we are called to act. We can also thus contribute to the movement we spoke of; [we can] guide it and in doing so prove to the innovators that we have already preceded them on this path.[24]

---

[22] Ibid., p. 25. Vallet's emphasis.

[23] Ibid.

[24] Vallet quoted in Molard, "Cours," pp. 1 and 3 [p. 2 is blank]. For more on Vallet's lectures on public libraries, see the packet of lecture notes labelled

According to Vallet, though the government had repeatedly promised the school's graduates positions in public libraries, these promises had gone unfulfilled.[25] Now was the time to let *chartistes*, as the rightful heads of public libraries, extend the popular library movement's ideals of utility and accessibility to all state-owned collections.

Vallet's repeated disquisitions on the possible convergence of popular and public libraries do not seem to have won any converts at the Ecole des Chartes in the 1860s. There is no evidence that any of Vallet's students or colleagues shared his interest in leading a major reorganization of the public library system.[26] Nor does Vallet seem to have attracted any followers among Napoléon III's chief ministers. This is not to say, however, that the French government was oblivious to the burgeoning popular library movement. In fact, many local officials, including a number of town mayors, actively supported the establishment of popular libraries, whether by helping to purchase books and supplies, offering municipal buildings for popular library use, or simply by granting the projects their official approval.[27] In certain cases, local officials actually spearheaded the effort to create popular collections; for example, in 1865, the mayor of the eleventh *arrondissement* of Paris founded a "municipal popular library" in his district. Impressed by the library's success, the Prefect of the Seine (the famous Baron Haussmann) appointed city librarian Alexandre de Saint-Albin

---

"Bibliothèques" in AEC-SC, Vallet de Viriville Papers; and Léopold Pannier, "Cours de M. Vallet de Viriville, 9 Juillet [18]67" [in notebook also containing "Ecole des Chartes. Cours de Mr. J. Quicherat. 21 nov 1866"], AEC-SC, series B, item 6. For examples of Vallet's earlier discussions of *chartistes* as librarians, see especially [Vallet de Viriville], draft of letter to Monsr. le Ministre de l'Instruction publique (with marginal heading, "Projet d'un nouveau cours de notions élémentaires à l'Ecole des chartes et demande de la chaire par l'auteur de ce projet"), Paris, 6 Jun. 1846, AEC-SC, Vallet de Viriville Papers; and his "Note historique et critique sur l'Ecole des Chartes -- Projet d'annexion de cette Ecole au Collège de France," Paris, 14 Apr. 1848, AN, box F17-4024.

[25] See especially Vallet de Viriville, *L'Ecole des Chartes*, p. 25.

[26] To my knowledge, Vallet was the only *chartiste* who participated in the popular library associations of the 1860s. An 1856 letter from the Prefect of the Somme to the Minister of the Interior (AN, box F2 I 378[15], folder "Bibliothèques Comles. Objets généraux") notes that Louis Boca, Ecole des Chartes class of 1837 and the department's head archivist, had been appointed to a local commission to oversee the creation of "popular libraries in the rural communes," but I do not know what became of this project.

[27] Barnett, *Histoire des bibliothèques*, pp. 146-148.

"Inspector of Libraries in the *Arrondissements*" and charged him with instituting a similar collection in every district in Paris. Though Haussmann's initiative produced only one other *arrondissement* library in the 1860s, it indicates that even the most powerful of local officials took an interest in the extension of "popular" collections.[28]

If some local administrators were eager to subsidize and even organize popular libraries, the central government was rather more wary. In an April 1860 report to Napoléon III, Minister of Public Instruction Gustave Rouland recommended using the duplicate copies of books owned by the Imperial Library to establish "free and public reading rooms" throughout Paris and thus promote "popular instruction."[29] By the end of May, however, Rouland's idea had metamorphosed into an initiative that was at once more and less ambitious than his earlier plan. In a set of instructions to departmental prefects, Rouland called for the establishment of a "small library-cabinet," in every elementary school classroom in France.[30] On the one hand, these *bibliothèques scolaires* ("school libraries"), which numbered some 14,000 by the end of the Empire, had much in common with the popular libraries created by private associations and local governments. Though their collections were located in elementary classrooms, they were intended to be available to the students' families as well. By the late 1860s, their holdings were also meant to support the curricula of evening courses for adults. As Rouland put it, the goal was to provide not just young Frenchmen but the whole "laboring population" with "a collection of interesting and useful works."[31] On the other hand, the school library

---

[28] Ibid., p. 142; Richter, *Bibliothèques populaires*, pp. 53-54. See also Maurice Caillet, "L'inspection générale des bibliothèques, *Bulletin des bibliothèques de France* 16, no. 3 (Mar. 1971): 152-157; and Denis Guérin, "La lecture publique à Paris au XIXe siècle," *Bulletin des bibliotheques de France* 28, no. 2 (1983): 145.

[29] [Gustave] Rouland, *Ministère de l'Instruction Publique et des Cultes. Bibliothèque Impériale. Rapport à l'Empereur* (Paris: Imprimerie Paul Dupont, April 1860), p. 19.

[30] See [Gustave] Rouland, "Circulaire relative à l'établissement de bibliothèques scolaires dans les écoles primaires publiques," 31 May 1860, and related laws (1862-1867) in Ulysse Robert, *Recueil de lois, décrets, ordonnances, arrêtés, circulaires, etc. concernant les bibliothèques publiques, communales, universitaires, scolaires et populaires...*(Paris: H. Champion, 1883), pp. 209-228.

[31] Rouland in Robert, *Recueil*, p. 209. The number of school libraries comes from Hébrard, "Bibliothèques scolaires," p. 551. Interestingly, one of the earliest proponents of school libraries was Joseph-Marie Degérando, the Ideologue and philanthropist behind the creation of the Ecole des Chartes (see Barnett, *Histoire des*

network amounted to something less than a national system of popular libraries. The collections formed in the late Empire remained quite modest; according to figures provided by Graham Keith Barnett, the average school library contained only eighty-six volumes as of 1870.[32] Even Rouland himself recognized that these libraries were less substantial than existing popular collections, noting in his 1860 circular that while a "vast organization of communal libraries" would best fulfill the goal of providing worthwhile reading for the working classes, "this organization presents difficulties that only a multiple combination of wills and sacrifices would be capable of resolving."[33] The central government was not prepared to create popular collections on the scale established by private and local groups.

Historians have often disagreed about the significance of the late Imperial network of school libraries, some seeing it as a poor substitute for a national system of popular or communal libraries, others applauding it as a necessary first step toward such a system.[34] Yet regardless of how one views the school library campaigns of the 1860s, it is clear that they did not occasion the kind of reconceptualization of the "public library" suggested by Vallet de Viriville. For Vallet, popular libraries were simply the latest and most advanced stage in the development of public libraries (the "buds" growing on the aging "trunk"), but for the late Imperial state, popular libraries and public libraries were separate entities. While government officials were clearly interested in establishing new library collections for the working classes (whether in the form of "popular" municipal libraries or in the form of school libraries), they seemed not at all interested in developing existing public libraries into collections that might serve all classes of the French population. Indeed, they hardly seemed interested in developing public libraries at all; contrary to what one might expect in an era in which the term "public" was constantly invoked by politicians and administrators alike, there seem to have been few official interventions in the world of public libraries in this period. With the important exception of the Imperial

---

bibliothèques, p. 152; and Richter, "Les bibliothèques populaires et la lecture ouvrière," p. 517-518).

[32] Barnett, *Histoire des bibliothèques*, p. 156 notes that ca. 1870 there were 14,395 school libraries with a total of 1,239,165 volumes. See also Eugen Weber, *Peasants into Frenchmen: The Modernization of Rural France* (Stanford: Stanford University Press, 1976), p. 454.

[33] Rouland in Robert, *Recueil*, p. 210. See also Richter, *Bibliothèques populaires*, p. 51.

[34] For an excellent overview of the historiography on school libraries, see Hébrard, "Bibliothèques scolaires."

Library (which I will discuss shortly), public libraries were largely absent from the legislative agenda of the 1860s, and if public librarians wished the situation otherwise, their complaints were not heard by the central government.[35]

Some historians of public libraries have described the Napoleonic regime's unwillingness to fuse popular and public libraries as a "failure," a glaring example of French "backwardness" (*retard*) in relation to the Americans and the British in this period.[36] Here, however, I am less concerned with comparing French public libraries to their Anglo-American counterparts than with understanding why the Bonapartist regime of the 1860s dealt with public libraries as it did.[37] One element of the explanation is practical: since the bulk of most public library collections consisted of historical books and manuscripts of more interest to scholars than to workers or schoolchildren, it was undoubtedly easier to establish "small library-cabinets" in local schools than to reorganize public libraries. However, practical considerations are only part of the answer. It also appears that the late Empire had strong political misgivings about the extension of libraries to the "popular" classes. In April 1864, Interior Minister Paul Boudet dispatched a circular marked "confidential" to departmental prefects. The circular recalled that in the last two years, private associations like the *Société Franklin* had "instituted in various places

---

[35] This conclusion is based on the ministerial records at the AN. It would be useful to see if the records kept by individual municipal libraries paint a similar picture.

[36] See especially Jean Hassenforder, *Développement comparé des bibliothèques publiques en France, en Grande-Bretagne, et aux Etats-Unis dans la seconde moitié du XIXe siècle (1850-1914)* (Paris: Cercle de la librairie, 1967); Henri-Jean Martin, "Bibliothèques publiques et bibliothèques populaires," in *Histoire de l'édition française* (Paris: Promodis, 1985), 3: 261-267; and to a lesser extent Barnett, *Histoire des bibliothèques*.

[37] In this respect I am following the lead of several recent historians who have tried to study French libraries on their own terms. See Jean Hébrard, "Bibliothèques scolaires"; Olivier Tacheau, "Bibliothèques municipales et genèse des politiques culturelles au XIXe siècle: Dijon et Besançon entre 1816 et 1914," *Bullétin des bibliothécaires français* 40, no. 4 (1994): 44-51; and especially Laure Léveillé, "Les petites bibliothèques de la République: aux origines de la lecture publique parisienne, des années 1870 aux années 1930," (Doctoral thesis, Université de Paris X-Nanterre, Jan. 1998). As Léveillé explains in her contribution to vol. 4 of *Histoire des bibliothèques françaises* (Paris: Promodis, 1992), "Fascinations étrangères et naissance de la lecture publique," the "backwardness" argument has its origins in the early twentieth century, when library reformers like Eugène Morel began urging France to conform to the Anglo-American model of the public library.

in the Empire popular libraries, whose object is to promote the reading of books particularly destined for the working class." Boudet then added:

> The government's intention is not to thwart the development of an undertaking that seems to have an honorable goal, but its duty is to see to it that as they multiply, popular libraries do not encourage abuses which would change the primary purpose of these establishments and transform them into hotbeds of propaganda or political intrigue.

In order to prevent popular libraries from becoming "revolutionary schools" or "so many centers of propaganda," prefects were to maintain careful surveillance of these new collections, particularly by monitoring their catalogues for books containing "dangerous or subversive theories."[38] Such language suggests that while Napoléon III's ministers were willing to take the limited step of establishing school libraries, they worried about the political consequences of developing large-scale collections for "popular" audiences. If opened to the *grand public*, public libraries might promote "revolutionary" thinking, and while the late Empire was ready to make certain overtures to the political opposition, it was not willing to risk another French revolution.

However, before we dismiss the late Empire's decision to separate popular from public libraries as a purely conservative maneuver, we should consider that the popular library movement was not the only force working to define public libraries in the 1860s. At the same time that public library administrators were trying to respond to groups like the *Société Franklin* and the *Société des Amis de l'Instruction*, they were also trying to respond to another set of challenges, this time from the world of state archives. In order to understand these challenges, we turn to the second major public library debate of the late Empire: the struggle between the Imperial Library and the Archives of the Empire.

The conflict between the two institutions began in 1858, when a government commission appointed to evaluate the collections and services of the Imperial Library submitted its findings to the Minister of Public Instruction. The commission's report—often referred to as the "Mérimée Report" after its author, writer and former Libri defender Prosper Mérimée—recommended that the Library cede some of its collections to

---

[38] [Paul Boudet] (Le Ministre de l'Intérieur), "Circulaire. Au sujet des Bibliothèques populaires," 8 Apr. 1864, AN, box F1a 632, folder "Société Franklin. Bibliothèques municipales," pp. [1-2]. See also Auspitz, *Radical Bourgeoisie*, pp. 70-71.

other institutions in order to unify objects "of the same nature, serving the same [kinds of] studies." In particular, the commission recommended that the Library give the Imperial Archives "a large number of loose charters and charters bearing seals, and especially the collection called the Genealogical Cabinet [*Cabinet généalogique*]." In return, the Archives would give the Library some 20,000 of its historical maps.[39] The Minister of Public Instruction, while agreeing with many of the Mérimée Commission's recommendations, nevertheless decided against transferring the Genealogical Cabinet to the Archives on the grounds that it would have been too disruptive for the Library, and—for a time—the matter appeared to have been settled.[40]

Two years later, in November 1860, the Emperor shifted control of the Imperial Library from the Ministry of Public Instruction to the Ministry of State, which was already responsible for the Imperial Archives. Seeing in this shift the opportunity to submit the Library-Archives issue to a new authority, Archives Director Léon de Laborde asked the Minister of State to

---

[39] P[rosper] Mérimée ("au nom de la Commission chargée d'examiner les modifications à introduire dans l'organisation de la Bibliothèque Impériale"), "Rapport présenté à S. Exc. le Ministre de l'Instruction publique et des cultes," (Paris: Imprimerie impériale, 27 Mar. 1858) (also in *Le Moniteur Universel*, 20 Jul. 1858, pp. 905-906). See also Barbara McCrimmon, "Mérimée as Library Reformer," *Journal of Library History* 4, no. 4 (1969): 297-320; and Jean-François Foucaud, "Le rapport Mérimée," in *Histoire des bibliothèques françaises*, 3: 306. Mérimée's report was not the first to suggest the transfer of these manuscripts and charters to the Imperial Archives; see for example [François-André] Isambert, "Prolégomènes," in *Recueil général des anciennes lois françaises, depuis l'an 420 jusqu'à la révolution de 1789...*, ed. [Athanase Jean Leger] Jourdan, Decrusy, and [François-André] Isambert (Paris: Berlin le Prieur, [1822-33]), p. l; the discussion of a report by Georges Cuvier in [Pierre-Paul] Royer-Collard, "Rapport à Monsieur le Ministre Secrétaire d'Etat au département de l'Instruction publique," 31 Oct. 1832, AN, box F17-13504, pp. 39-41; and the 1853 proposal discussed in Jean Le Pottier, "Histoire et érudition. Recherches et documents sur l'histoire et le rôle de l'érudition médiévale dans l'historiographie du XIXe siècle" (Thesis, Ecole nationale des Chartes, 1979), p. 238.

[40] See Rouland, "Rapport à l'Empereur," *Le Moniteur Universel*, 20 Jul. 1858, p. 905. An Imperial decree dated 14 Jul. 1858 (published in the same issue of *Le Moniteur Universel*, p. 905) reflected Rouland's recommendations, ordering a number of changes in the administration of the Imperial Library but making no mention of an exchange with the Archives.

consider an exchange between the two institutions.[41] Evidently intrigued, the Minister appointed a new commission, this time under the leadership of Marshal Vaillant, to investigate the issue.[42] The Vaillant Commission spent months reviewing the two collections and interviewing their personnel before voting by a narrow majority to recommend a substantial transfer of documents from the Library to the Archives. The Library would give up not only the Genealogical Cabinet (a wide-ranging collection documenting the evolution and status of the French nobility) but also all "charters and diplomas" that could be removed from the Library's Manuscripts Department without "mutilating or lacerating" any volumes.[43] To justify these recommendations to the Minister, the Commission appointed member Félix Ravaisson to prepare a report, finally submitted in early 1862.[44] However, the head of the Library, Jules Taschereau, backed by the minority members of the Commission (including Vaillant himself) lobbied vigorously against the Ravaisson report, arguing that it went far beyond even the views expressed by the members of the majority.[45] The Minister of State therefore rejected Ravaisson's recommendations, ordering a limited exchange of documents but keeping the Library's manuscripts collection largely intact. Though it took another year of wrangling over the details,

---

[41] For the text of the decree transferring the Library to the Ministry of State, see *BEC* 22 (1861): 207. For Laborde's proposal, see his letter to Monsieur le Ministre, Paris, 23 Jan. 1861, AN, box F17-13541.

[42] A[lexandre] Walewski (Le Ministre d'Etat) and Eug. Marchand (Le Conseiller d'Etat Secrétaire Général), "Arrêté," 22 Apr. 1861, AN, box F17-13541, folder "Constitution de la Commission. 1861." In addition to Vaillant, the Commission included Parieu, Amédée Thierry, De Saulcy, Latour du Moulin, the Comte Napoléon de Champagny, Boulatignier, Taillandier, and the Baron de Guilhermy, all high government officials, as well as Empis, the Inspector General of Libraries; Félix Ravaisson, philosopher and Institut member; and Dard, the commission's secretary.

[43] See Commission de la Bibliothèque Impériale et des Archives de l'Empire, "Procès-verbaux, 1861-1862," AN, box F17-13541, especially fols. 16v-17v.

[44] Félix Ravaisson, *Rapport adressé à S. Exc. le Ministre d'Etat au nom de la Commission instituée le 22 avril 1861* (Paris: Typographie E. Panckoucke, 1862).

[45] See especially [Jules] Taschereau to Son Excellence Monsieur le Président de la Commission de la Bibliothèque Impériale et des Archives de l'Empire [Vaillant], Paris, 27 Jan. 1862; and Le Ma[récha]l Vaillant to Son Excellence le Ministre d'Etat, Paris, 12 Mar. 1862, both in AN, box F17-13541.

both the exchange and the fighting finally came to an end in mid-1863, five years after the appearance of the Mérimée report.[46]

In certain respects, the arguments generated by this debate were specific to the Imperial Library and Archives. Much of the voluminous correspondence produced during the conflict consists of detailed discussions about the various decrees governing the two institutions (some dating to before the Revolution) and how these rulings ought be interpreted in the context of the Second Empire.[47] One might therefore argue that this debate tells us little about conceptions of French libraries and archives in general. However, the conflict's participants—and, as we will see, especially those on the side of the Imperial Archives—constantly pushed the debate from the realm of specifics into that of abstract definitions. Throughout the controversy, Archives Director Laborde pressed the Vaillant Commission for a "definitive solution" to the dispute, one that would determine "if there were in the past, [and] if there ought to be in the future, archives and libraries, archivists and librarians."[48] In a similar vein, Ravaisson's report argued that the commission's job had been not only to decide whether a Library-Archives exchange was appropriate but also to determine "as far as possible" what counted as "archival documents [*pièces d'archives*]" and what counted as "library documents [*pièces de bibliothèques*]."[49] What might have remained a petty struggle over a collection of genealogical manuscripts consequently became a major debate about the differences between a public library and a state archive. Was a library properly an agglomeration of many different historical materials or simply a collection of books? Was an archive the holding tank for administrative documents or a center for historical research? While post-revolutionary French governments had long treated archives and libraries as companion institutions, now state officials were forced to think about what made them distinct.[50]

---

[46] For the 19 Apr. 1862 ministerial order demanding a limited exchange of documents as well as the early 1863 correspondence about the final details of the exchange, see AN, box F17-13541.

[47] See especially AN, box 13541.

[48] Cte. [Léon] de Laborde to Son Excellence le Maréchal Vaillant, Paris, 14 May 1861, AN, box F17-13541, p. [12].

[49] Ravaisson, *Rapport*, p. 5.

[50] In recent years, several historians have begun to explore the Library-Archives debate. See Françoise Hildesheimer, "Les Archives nationales au XIXe siècle: établissement scientifique ou administratif?" *Histoire et archives* 1 (1997): 106-135; *Les Archives de France: Mémoire de l'Histoire* (Paris: Honoré Champion, 1997), esp. p. 54; and her "Echec aux Archives: la difficile affirmation d'une administration," *BEC*

If late Imperial archivists, librarians, and government officials were well aware that Library-Archives dispute was about how to define public libraries and state archives, it may be only in retrospect that we can see that it was also about how to define the Ecole des Chartes. From the beginning, in fact, one of the school's best-known graduates found himself at the very center of the dispute. Léon Lacabane—a member of the school's first graduating class, former president of the Société de l'Ecole des Chartes, and recently appointed as the school's Director—was in 1858 also the head of the Imperial Library's Genealogical Cabinet. Since Lacabane knew the Cabinet's contents better than anyone, the Imperial Archives asked to acquire both Lacabane and the collection in his charge. Spokesmen for the Library (including Lacabane himself) countered by arguing that Lacabane could only conduct his work within the context of the Library's collections.[51] Meanwhile, as we will see, the Archives also declared (though without any explicit reference to Lacabane), that *chartistes* in general were better suited to archival work than to library administration. Remarkably, though a number of *chartistes* participated in the dispute on both sides, none seems to have construed the conflict as a challenge to the school's identity. Nevertheless, from the vantage point of the late twentieth century, I will argue, the controversy can be seen as an important turning point in the school's development.

Throughout the controversy, and whether the topic of discussion was archives or libraries, charters or *chartistes*, the Imperial Archives managed to set the terms of the debate. Led by the seemingly indefatigable Laborde, the Archives camp constantly challenged the Library to define its collections and its mission. The discussion that follows therefore tries to isolate the key elements of the Archives' complex and sometimes contradictory arguments before turning to the Library's efforts to counterpunch. We will see that

---

156 (1998), esp. p. 102. See also Nancy Bartlett, "Respect des fonds: The Origins of the Modern Archival Principle of Provenance," in *Bibliographical Foundations of French Historical Studies*, ed. Lawrence McCrank (New York: Haworth Press, 1991), pp. 107-115; and Le Pottier, "Histoire et érudition," pp. 226-246. However, while these studies have emphasized the debate's implications for the Archives, here I give equal attention to its implications for the Imperial Library and for public libraries more generally.

[51] See the copy of Lacabane's "Observations sur le projet de réunir le Cabinet des Titres et Généalogies aux Archives de l'Empire," [Apr. 1858], submitted to Vaillant by Library head Jules Taschereau on 21 May 1861, in AN, box F17-13541, folder "Pièces annexées…." See also the anonymous "Note sur le Cabinet des Titres de la Bibliothèque Impériale," [Apr. 1861], in the same AN box.

while Laborde's supporters spent most of their energy trying to identify the differences between libraries and archives, they also claimed certain "library" attributes (especially publicity) for the "modern" Imperial Archives, thus depriving the Library's rebuttals of much of their force.

The Archives camp argued that the basic distinction between libraries and archives lay in what Laborde called "the nature of their collections."[52] Laborde and his supporters described this "nature" differently in different contexts (and sometimes even in the space of a single Commission meeting), but they most often maintained that archival materials were "official" or "authoritative" while library materials were not. What did it mean to be "authoritative"? According to Laborde, authoritative sources were the product of a "constituted authority" and thus carried "authority" themselves.[53] While Laborde himself never offered a definition of a "constituted authority," the members of the Commission seem to have interpreted this phrase to mean the French government, both past and present. As Parieu explained in a May 1861 meeting, a document would be considered archival "if it emanate[d] from the French public authority, or from one of the various powers that the state has absorbed."[54] Thus the Imperial Archives, not the Imperial Library, was the appropriate depository for the charters, diplomas, ordinances, and other "official" documents produced by the Old Regime.[55] While the Library might properly contain manuscripts or books about the "public authority" (such as chronicles), it was not to contain sources produced by the authority itself.

---

[52] Laborde to Monsieur le Ministre, 23 Jan. 1861, AN, box F17-13541, p. [1].

[53] Laborde in "Archives de l'Empire. Procès-verbaux des Conférences du Directeur général avec les Chefs de Section," 9 Apr. 1861, AN, box AB VII 1, p. 58. For other descriptions of archives as "official" and "authoritative," see Commission de la Bibliothèque Impériale et des Archives de l'Empire, "Procès-verbaux," esp. fols. 8r-8v.

[54] Parieu in Commission de la Bibliothèque Impériale et des Archives de l'Empire, "Procès-verbaux," 16 May 1861, fol. 15v. Parieu's definition also contained other components to which I will return in a moment.

[55] These examples are from Laborde, "Archives de l'Empire. Procès-verbaux des Conférences," 9 Apr. 1861, p. 58. Of course, the Archives did not contain all "official" Old Regime materials; some were located in departmental and communal archives. The Commission began to address the touchy question of how to distinguish between the provincial archives and the central or "Imperial" archives, but as this issue was not a key component of the Library-Archives dispute, I will not discuss it here.

However, in the course of the Commission's deliberations, the Archives side came to find their definition of archival documents as products of the public authority too restrictive. The central collection up for dispute, the Library's Genealogical Cabinet, contained both documents produced by the royal government and documents produced by individual nobles and families. Representatives from the Library therefore argued that the Cabinet ought to remain where it was. For example, Natalis de Wailly, who had left the Imperial Archives for the Library's Manuscripts Department in 1854, claimed that while there were certain "series of official [genealogical] documents" that rightfully belonged at the Archives, "[o]ur Genealogical Cabinet contains private documents [*documents privés*] that are not the necessary annex or accessory to the titles deposited at the archives."[56] The Archives countered by offering an even broader definition of archival sources. Archives, they said, contained not only materials produced by the public authority but also all sources in the "public interest."[57] To support this claim, they pointed especially to the 1855 decree regulating the Imperial Archives, which had described the collection as containing "all documents in the public interest whose preservation is judged useful."[58] Under this definition, even seemingly "private" documents like the familial correspondence and titles in the Genealogical Cabinet, could be considered archival sources.

Thus far, the Archives camp's argument would seem to rest on a conception of archival sources as primarily administrative: archives would include all documents produced by the government as well as all documents considered in the "public interest." Yet Laborde and his supporters were also eager to present archives as historical collections. While Commission member Parieu's first criterion for describing a given manuscript as an "archival document" was that it "emanate from the French public authority," he also included all manuscripts of interest to "the history of France or [the] various provinces and communes."[59] Indeed, as several historians have pointed out, Laborde often seemed to be using the Library-Archives dispute as a means of establishing the Archives as the premiere site

---

[56] De Wailly in Commission de la Bibliothèque Impériale et des Archives de l'Empire, "Procès-verbaux," 10 May 1861, fol. 11r.

[57] Ibid., fols. 16v-17r.

[58] Napoléon [III] and Achille Fould (Ministre d'Etat), "Décret," 22 Dec. 1855, in Direction des Archives, *Lois, décrets, arrêtés, règlements relatifs 1. aux Archives nationales, 2. aux Archives départementales* (Paris: 1905), p. 17. Also in *BEC* 17 (1856): 188-190.

[59] See footnote 54. Interestingly, Parieu later voted against the Archives.

for historical research in France. Even as he affirmed the Archives role as an administrative resource, he also touted its potential as a historical trove, declaring for example in a February 1863 letter to Vaillant that with the proper inventories, the Archives would become "the active center of ongoing studies destined to shine a new light on our national history."[60]

The Archives camp never went so far as to argue that library collections were irrelevant to historical research; indeed, Laborde willingly acknowledged that libraries and archives had in common "the same goal of historical utility."[61] Nevertheless, the Archives side repeatedly suggested that while libraries might contain works *about* the past, archives contained the "true" and "original" remnants of the past itself. As Laborde explained to his section heads as they prepared for a visit from the Vaillant Commission in April 1861:

> It is important above all to make the Commission understand the distinction between the two great establishments in question...At the archives, all the acts emanating from a constituted authority: charters, diplomas, ordinances, letters patent, treaties, accords, recognitions, and all sealed documents. At the Library, all that constitutes a work [*ouvrage*], a second-hand project based on original or other documents.[62]

One of Laborde's employees, the *chartiste* Edgard Boutaric, made a similar point in his enthusiastic review of Ravaisson's report for the 1863 *Bibliothèque de l'Ecole des Chartes*. In Boutaric's view, no reader of the journal needed to be reminded of the historical "utility" of "charters, diplomas, and other authentic documents," for it was a matter of "common consent [*de l'aveu de tous*]," that archives contained "the true sources of our national history."[63]

---

[60] Cte. [Léon] de Laborde to Son Excellence le Ministre d'Etat, Paris, 7 Feb. 1863, AN, box AB VI 1, p. [3]. See also Le Pottier, "Histoire et érudition," pp. 228-243; and Hildesheimer, *Les Archives de France*, p. 54.

[61] Le Marquis [Léon] de Laborde, *Les Archives de la France: leurs vicissitudes pendant la Révolution, leur régénération sous l'Empire* (Paris: Vve. Renouard, 1867), p. 64. This book, published at the end of Laborde's reign as Archives Director, reprises many of the arguments he had begun to develop during the struggle with the Imperial Library.

[62] Laborde, "Archives de l'Empire. Procès-verbaux des Conférences," 9 Apr. 1861, p. 58.

[63] E[dgard] Boutaric, "Les Archives de l'Empire: à propos d'un rapport de M. F. Ravaisson," *BEC* 24 (1863): 252. Interestingly, while Laborde himself occasionally hinted that only archival documents were truly "authentic," (as in the 10 May 1861 Vaillant Commission meeting, in which he noted that the "ancient jurisconsults determined that an archival document [that had been] taken out of its depository lost its authentic character"), he rarely pushed this point, apparently hoping to

Of course, the claim that "original" or "authentic" documents like charters and diplomas were the only true sources of historical understanding was not new; what was new, however, was the argument that such sources ought to be reserved for archival collections alone.[64] According to the supporters of the Imperial Archives, while libraries offered historians books and manuscripts about French history, they could not—and should not—provide any materials that might be considered "original" historical sources.

At certain moments in the Library-Archives debate, the Archives side seemed poised to push this claim one step further. As early as March 1858, while the Mérimée Commission (of which Laborde was a member) was still preparing its recommendations, Laborde urged the Minister of State to centralize all Old Regime ministerial records at the Imperial Archives, asking, "Where can the spirit of history be found?...In books, no; in archives, yes. Centralize then [France's] historical documents."[65] The implication here was that archives could be distinguished from other collections not only by their origins (as the products of a "constituted authority") or their utility (for historical study or for the "public interest") but also by their format: archives were not books. We find a rather more explicit formulation of this argument in Ravaisson's 1862 report. Ravaisson explained that while in ancient times, the terms "archives" and "libraries" were "synonyms," by the late fourteenth century "one could distinguish more clearly between books and titles, and libraries became separate from archives." Thus it was, continued Ravaisson, that Camus, the first head of

---

[64] deflect the Library's argument that transferring the Genealogical Cabinet to the Archives would taint the Archives with "false documents." Laborde even went so far as to acknowledge that the Archives' greatness did not reside in "a complete purity and [in] the impossibility of arguing that any of its documents are forged," for "in this respect," he agreed, "they are fallible" (Laborde to Vaillant, 14 May 1861, AN, box F17-13541, p. [9-10]).

[64] This argument seems to anticipate the rise of the modern French historical profession in the late 1860s. As a new group of historians (many of them connected with the new Ecole pratique des hautes études, founded in 1868) tried to define their expertise, they also worked to define their sources and place of work, focusing their attentions on archives. I will discuss the professionalization of history at greater length in the epilogue.

[65] Cte. [Léon] de Laborde, "Rapport de Mr. le Directeur général à S. Ex. le Ministre d'Etat, sur le développement excessif des Archives spéciales de l'administration, et sur l'inexécution du Décret qui prescrit la rédaction des inventaires et leur réunion aux Archives de l'Empire," Mar. 1858, AN, box AB VI 1, p. [20].

the National Archives, understood that "'Libraries are composed of *books* just as libraries are composed of *titles*.'" Though Ravaisson seemed to include manuscript volumes in his conception of "books," provided they constituted literary or scientific "works," representatives of the Imperial Library worried that even under this definition the Library's Manuscripts Department stood to lose up to three-fourths of its holdings.[66] If Ravaisson had his way, Library Director Taschereau feared, the term "library" [*bibliothèque*] would be reduced to its ancient Greek definition: a collection of books.[67]

A key element of the Archives side's strategy, then, was to argue for differences in the "nature" of library and archival collections, to the increasing disadvantage of the Imperial Library. However, Laborde and his supporters also tried to strengthen their case by claiming that archivists and librarians treated their collections differently. While archives organized their materials by *fonds*, libraries organized both their books and their documents by subject. As a result, Laborde argued, the various "archival" manuscripts owned by the Imperial Library had been removed from their natural *fonds* and placed in topical categories, creating innumerable frustrations for scholars. As Laborde explained to the Vaillant Commission:

> The Library's *fonds* of charters and diplomas includes a large number of loose documents from archival *fonds* that are currently housed at the [Imperial Archives], notably the Cluny and St. Denis *fonds*. A distinguished writer, having consulted the Cluny *fonds* on deposit at the Archives, did not think that there would be loose documents from this *fonds* at the Imperial Library, and this error, which it should not have been possible for him to make, led him to publish an incomplete work.[68]

The solution, of course, was to transfer these materials to the Imperial Archives, where they could be reunited with their original *fonds*. In May 1861, Laborde and his Archives section heads planned for this merging of *fonds*, agreeing that the Library's "archival" sources could not simply be

---

[66] Ravaisson, *Rapport*, pp. 6-9. His emphasis.

[67] Taschereau to Son Excellence Monsieur le Président de la Commission de la Bibliothèque Impériale et des Archives de l'Empire [Vaillant], 27 Jan. 1862, AN, box F17-13541, p. 30. For another example of the Library camp's reaction to Ravaisson's claim, see Natalis de Wailly, *La Bibliothèque Impériale et les Archives de l'Empire. Réponse au rapport de M. Ravaisson* (Paris: Imprimerie de Ad. R. Lainé et J. Havard, 1863), p. 10.

[68] Laborde in Commission de la Bibliothèque Impériale et des Archives de l'Empire, "Procès-verbaux," 6 May 1861, fols. 5r-5v.

absorbed as they were, for it was "important to distinguish between real *fonds* [*fonds réels*] and artificial *fonds* [*fonds factices*], that is, *fonds* created by the randomness of sales offers and by the caprices of collectors." The archivists "proclaim[ed] *respect for the real fonds,* and the advisability of distributing the documents from the artificial *fonds* among the series containing their analogues."[69] Though forced into "artificial" categories at the Imperial Library, France's charters, diplomas, and other "archival" sources would join their "real" *fonds* at the Imperial Archives.

The Archives camp's declaration of *respect des fonds* is intriguing. As we saw in Chapter Three, this principle was first articulated in 1841 in the context of a classification program for departmental archives, not the central (then Royal) Archives. Indeed, the organicist notion of *respect des fonds* seems to have emerged partly in reaction to the more methodical classification system in use at the Archives since the time of Napoléon I.[70] And despite urgings to the contrary, the Archives had largely maintained Daunou's classification scheme even as departmental collections all over France were converting to organization by *fonds*.[71] It was thus not until the conflict with the Library in the early 1860s that the Archives began not only to subscribe to the idea but to tout it as a defining characteristic of all

---

[69] "Archives de l'Empire. Procès-verbaux des Conférences," 4 May 1861, p. 69. My emphasis.

[70] See chap. 3.

[71] For example, in an 1850 report to Laborde's predecessor, Chabrier, Jules Michelet (then head of the Archives' Historical Section) had called for a new inventory that would avoid "systematic" classifications and instead "ask the documents themselves for advice" in order to create a "natural" classification scheme. While he did not use the phrase *respect des fonds*, he recommended "leaving the old collections in their entirety" and "preserving the famous *fonds*" rather than dividing them into sections as Daunou had done ("Rapport sur l'inventaire général du dépôt de la section historique," 3 Jul. 1850, AN, box AB IX 2). Five years later, *chartiste* and former Archives employee Henri Bordier made an even more forceful argument in his *Les archives de la France* (Paris; Genève: Dumoulin, 1855). In his discussion of the Imperial Archives, Bordier declared: "the only good and true method, as regards archival classification, is classification by *fonds*.... Classification by *fonds* is the essential basis of all archival organization; hence it is recommended as the first and principal prescription to the archivists in the departments" (p. 51). See Christine Nougaret, "De Natalis de Wailly à MIRA: 150 ans de normalisation des instruments de recherche aux Archives nationales," in *Histoires d'archives: recueil d'articles offert à Lucie Favier par ses collègues et amis* (Paris: Société des amis des Archives de France, 1997), p. 87. I would therefore disagree with Bartlett, "Respect," who suggests that Bordier opposed the adoption of *respect des fonds*.

archives. By the late 1860s, Laborde was even more outspoken on this point, proclaiming in *Les Archives de la France*:

> For those who henceforth would not understand [the differences between libraries and archives]…, I will summarize my opinion in very few words and tell them: a library is something, archives are someone. This *something* can be distributed, cut up, parceled out according to all bibliographical systems…It is quite otherwise with that *someone* that lives and breathes; do not dismember him; it would be far too cruel to rob him of his head in order to put it in this room, to tear off his arms and legs to scatter them elsewhere, because the heart only beats on the condition that one respects the entire body [*qu'on respectera le corps entier*].[72]

Interestingly, despite Laborde's evident enthusiasm for the idea of organic—and therefore indivisible—archival *fonds*, neither he nor his successors managed to completely reclassify the Archives according to *respect des fonds*. The sheer size of the collections made a thoroughgoing reorganization seem hopelessly daunting. Nevertheless, from the 1860s on, *respect des fonds* became the classificatory ideal, guiding the production of inventories and the organization of new acquisitions.[73]

The final component of the Archives camp's argument about the differences between archives and libraries—and between the Imperial Archives and the Imperial Library—focused on personnel. The Archives tried to convince the Vaillant Commission that the Library's charters and diplomas would be better preserved, organized, and communicated at the Imperial Archives in part because archivists, unlike librarians, had acquired the relevant scholarly tools in their studies at the Ecole des Chartes. As Laborde wrote to Vaillant in May 1861:

---

[72] Laborde, *Les Archives de la France* (1867), p. 64. In a manuscript that appears to be a partial draft of this publication, Laborde actually uses the phrase *respect des fonds*. Here he argues that the central government's regulation of departmental archives has perhaps been too heavy-handed, and that the only principles that ought to apply to all departmental collections are: "*respect des fonds*, within the *fonds* respect for the folders [*dossiers*], and within the folders respect for the chronological order in which the documents were added" (See Laborde, "Projet d'un nouveau classement des Archives," 1866 [name, title, and date all from folder cover], AN, box AB XVI 1, p. 12).

[73] See Nougaret, "De Natalis," pp. 87-89; and her "Classement et description: des principes à la pratique," in *La pratique archivistique française*, ed. Jean Favier (Paris: Archives nationales, 1993), pp. 135-186.

Let us keep in mind the composition of the Archives' personnel, recruited entirely from the top of the Ecole des Chartes graduating class, and remember that in the last twenty years, forty-two students were placed in archives, twelve of them at the Archives of the Empire, while in the same period of time, only four or five students were able to get themselves placed in libraries. Is not the consequence of this that paleographical criticism is more trustworthy in our establishment than in any other?[74]

Laborde sounded a similar note in a January 1863 planning session with his section heads, reminding them that the Archives was far better equipped to prepare inventories of French historical documents because the Archives, unlike the Imperial Library, had a core group of "new Benedictines" from the Ecole des Chartes:

The resources and components of these [inventory] projects exist at the Archives alone. The Ecole des Chartes prepares new Benedictines, the only kind possible in modern times: brought together to work, dispersed to live, enjoying the comforts of family life, drawing from their continuous contact with the world an understanding of which intellectual needs are most important to satisfy, and who, sure of their means of survival, will work with devotion for the administration as well as for their personal renown.[75]

For Laborde, then, even though the Ecole des Chartes had produced a number of librarians (among them Léopold Delisle, the future director of the Imperial Library), the school's most important ties were to the world of state archives.

As Laborde summed up his views on the differences between archives and libraries in 1867, he again emphasized the distinction between archivists and librarians, making it clear that he considered the terms "archivist" and "Archivist-Paleographer" synonymous:

I have neither the desire nor the right to institute proceedings against librarians, [that] phalanx of celebrities that occupies the first rank in the world of letters...I would like merely to establish the nuance that

---

[74] Laborde to Vaillant, 14 May 1861, AN, box F17-13541, p. [12]. Indeed, all sixteen archivist positions that became available during Laborde's tenure as Archives Director were filled by *chartistes* (see Le Pottier, "Histoire et érudition," p. 235).

[75] Laborde, 13 Jan. 1863, quoted in Françoise Hildesheimer, "Les premiers chartistes aux Archives nationales," in *L'Ecole nationale des chartes: histoire de l'école depuis 1821*, ed. Yves-Marie Bercé, Olivier Guyotjeannin, and Marc Smith (Thionville, France: Gérard Klopp, 1997), p. 244.

distinguishes them from archivists. To be an Archivist-Paleographer one must have done brilliantly on difficult examinations [and] to have obtained one's diploma.[76]

After having graduated from the Ecole des Chartes (which, as Laborde was careful to remind his readers, was then housed at the Imperial Archives), archivists engaged in work very different from that of librarians. In Laborde's view, librarians—despite their "celebrity" status—did little more than fetch books:

> Everything conspires in a library to fatigue the employees...To sit at a desk for six hours at a time in order to give a banal crowd copies of Dulaure and Monteil, volumes of Voltaire, Rousseau, and the *Encyclopédie*; to leave this task only to reshelve the issued volumes and start again the next morning, such is the cycle in which the librarian moves....[77]

In an archive, however, "everything cooperates to fortify the intelligence, to extend the views, to hone the judgment of the archivist." While library catalogues increasingly were making it possible for readers to do their library research by themselves, archives were so massive and complex that researchers always required an archivist's help. Confronted with a request for materials on a certain subject, the archivist would often embark on an extended hunt for relevant sources:

> The archivist gets an exact explanation of what he [the researcher] wants, immediately brings him documents of which he was not aware, [documents] which extend the horizons of his subject, put him on the path of historical truth (so often distorted in his mind by books), and reveal insights that change his whole plan.[78]

Since in Laborde's view archives were the source of historical truth, the Ecole des Chartes's Archivist-Paleographers were the gatekeepers of that truth, or what Laborde called, invoking a Restoration-era phrase, the "historian's auxiliaries."[79] Librarians, by contrast, would soon come to offer

---

[76] Laborde, *Les Archives de la France* (1867), p. 65.

[77] Ibid., p. 66.

[78] Ibid., pp. 66-67.

[79] Ibid., p. 65. On Restoration conceptions of the *chartiste*, see chap. 1. Of course, to describe *chartistes* as historians' "auxiliaries" implied that they were not historians in their own right, even though many *chartistes* clearly saw themselves as full-fledged historians. I will discuss the increasing marginalization of *chartistes* in the rapidly professionalizing world of historical research in the epilogue.

little more to historical researchers than their ability to find and reshelve those secondary sources of historical knowledge, books.

As one might expect, the staff and supporters of the Imperial Library reacted angrily to the Archives camp's repeated challenges. Library Director Taschereau sent dozens of long, impassioned letters to the Vaillant Commission and the Minister of State, pleading for protection against Laborde's demands. Meanwhile, Taschereau's right-hand man, manuscripts curator and former archivist Natalis de Wailly, tried to drum up support for the Library among his fellow *érudits*, eventually publishing a lengthy "Response to the Report by Monsieur Ravaisson," in 1863.[80] Key members of the Vaillant Commission also came to the Library's defense by painting Ravaisson as an extremist who was out of touch with the real opinions of commission members. All of these efforts undoubtedly helped convince the Minister of State to keep the Genealogical Cabinet and other manuscripts at the Imperial Library. However, if the Library won the battle against the Archives in 1863, it might be said that it lost the war. While the Archives managed to present a series of general arguments about the differences between archives and libraries (and between Archivist-Paleographers and librarians), the Library never forwarded a set of equally abstract claims. Though the Library defended itself against the Archives' specific requests (i.e., for the transfer of loose charters and diplomas and the Genealogical Cabinet), as we will see, it did not mount any serious challenge to the Archives' more general demands (for—depending on the context—all "official" documents, all documents in the public interest, all "original" historical documents, or all documents, period). The result was that archivists, not librarians, got to have the final word on the appropriate division of labor between state archives and public libraries.[81]

---

[80] See for example De Wailly's April 1861 letter to librarian (and future Imperial Archives Director) Alfred Maury (Bibliothèque de l'Institut de France, ms. 2656, dossier XXVI, item 7) asking for his help in curbing the Archives "appetite" for Imperial Library manuscripts. De Wailly's critique of Ravaisson was published as *La Bibliothèque Impériale et les Archives de l'Empire.*

[81] In 1867, Henri Bordier's *Les inventaires des Archives de l'Empire. Réponse à M. le marquis de Laborde…contenant un errata pour ses préfaces et ses inventaires* (Paris: Librairie Bachelin-Deflorenne) did attempt to refute some of Laborde's more general arguments against the Library, but only in the context of a much broader attack on Laborde's administration and without any apparent aim to rally the Library's supporters for a new offensive against the Imperial Archives.

The basic difference between the argumentative strategies of the Archives and the Library is perhaps most clearly revealed in the way each side deployed a key contemporary trope: the Haussmannization of Paris.[82] In April 1861, Laborde urged the Minister to provide a definitive statement about the differences between archives and libraries, adding in his conclusion:

> When it came to putting in the Boulevard Sebastopol, all of Paris criticized the idea; on opening day, all of Paris admired it. The Library administration will do the same thing, and when the decree has been handed down, it will wonder how it could ever have so vigorously opposed such a salutary, logical, and simple measure.[83]

For Laborde, the world of archives and libraries, like the city of Paris, needed logical divisions and clear boundaries. Not so for Library Director Taschereau, who in February 1862 argued (though with no apparent reference to Laborde's earlier comment) that to divide up the Library's manuscript collections would be akin to "opening a street through the middle of the chancel of Notre Dame in order to maintain a straight line."[84] While Laborde pushed for clean Haussmannian lines, Taschereau stressed the importance—even sanctity—of historical tradition. Throughout the debate, Taschereau and his supporters consistently maintained that general distinctions between "archives" and "libraries" were irrelevant; all that mattered was the validity of the Imperial Library's legal and historical claims to its collections. For example, in his 1863 response to Ravaisson, De Wailly argued that Ravaisson's definition of an archival document could stand "as a general and abstract rule, without being in the least way applicable to an establishment that is governed not by theoretical principles

---

[82] "Haussmannization" refers to the process by which Emperor Napoléon III and chief administrator Baron Haussmann drastically remodeled Paris in the 1850s and 1860s. Applauded by some for creating grand boulevards and impressive vistas, the renovation was condemned by others for destroying historic neighborhoods. See David Pinkney, *Napoléon III and the Rebuilding of Paris* (Princeton, NJ: Princeton University Press, 1958); and David Jordan, *Transforming Paris: The Life and Labors of Baron Haussmann* (New York: Free Press, 1995).

[83] [Laborde] to [Ministre d'Etat], 5 Apr. 1861, AN, box F17-13541. One can also find what appears to be a draft of this letter in AN, box AB Va 7, folder "1861-1866. Echange entre les Archives et la Bibliothèque Impériale."

[84] J[ules] Taschereau to Sa Majesté l'Empereur, 12 Feb. 1862, AN, box F17-3436, folder "Echanges entre la Bibliothèque Impériale et les Archives de l'Empire. 1863," p. [1].

but by actual texts."[85] Unless the Archives could prove its legal right to the collections of the much older and more established Imperial Library, no substantial exchange could take place.

Despite the Library's emphasis on legal and historical arguments, it occasionally moved to engage with the more general claims put forth by the Imperial Archives. For instance, the Library sometimes seemed to appropriate the archival principle of *respect des fonds* for its own purposes, describing its manuscripts collection as an indivisible set of *fonds*. While Library supporters never used the exact phrase *respect des fonds*, they frequently came close. In 1858, for example, Public Instruction Minister Rouland refused to uphold the Mérimée Commission's recommendation for a transfer because "to transport the [genealogical] collection to the archives would be to render some *fonds* absolutely incomplete [*décompleter absolument*] and thus deprive them of nearly all of their value."[86] In 1862, Vaillant wrote of the Library's manuscripts that one could not "respect these collections too much [*trop respecter ces Collections*]."[87] Many of their colleagues used language that was much more organic, often rivaling the vivid imagery of their archivist opponents. During a Vaillant Commission meeting, for example, minority member Taillandier asked Laborde if it would really be necessary to "dismember the *fonds*" maintained by the Library.[88] Library Director Taschereau used similar language, describing the proposed transfer as a "barbaric" act that would "mutilate" and "dismember" the Library's collections.[89]

While such language would suggest that the Library side believed that the principle of *respect des fonds* applied to libraries as well as archives, the Library's defenders never made this argument explicit. Though they often maintained that the various components of the Department of Manuscripts (including the Genealogical Cabinet) were interrelated and complementary, they never claimed that these collections were organized by provenance. In

---

[85] De Wailly, *Bibliothèque Impériale*, p. 11. For more on the substance of the Library's legal arguments, see Hildesheimer, "Les Archives nationales," pp. 120-134.

[86] Rouland, "Rapport à l'Empereur," 20 Jul. 1858, p. 905.

[87] Vaillant to Ministre d'Etat, Paris, 12 Mar. 1862, AN, box F17-13541.

[88] Taillandier in Commission de la Bibliothèque Impériale et des Archives de l'Empire, "Procès-verbaux," 10 May 1861, fol. 10v.

[89] Taschereau to Sa Majesté, 12 Feb. 1862, AN, box F17-3436, pp. [1-2] ; and Taschereau to Son Excellence Monsieur le Maréchal, Président de la Commission des Archives de l'Empire & de la Bibliothèque Impériale, Paris, 6 Mar. 1862, AN, box F17-13541.

fact, when given the opportunity to argue for how the archival concept of *respect des fonds* might apply to libraries, the Library camp appeared hesitant. In a particularly heated Vaillant Commission meeting attended by representatives from both the Library and the Archives, Vaillant asked De Wailly: "What should be understood by the word *fonds*? Is it a unity, a complete body?" Since it was De Wailly, in his earlier incarnation as an Imperial Archives employee, who had been the chief architect of the 1841 circular that first articulated the principle of *respect des fonds*, we might expect that his response would have provided a clear summary of this principle and how it applied to the Library-Archives debate. Instead, he gave the rather cryptic reply: "No, at the Library our *fonds* are encyclopedic compilations [*des recueils encyclopédiques*]."[90] This statement was perhaps meant to imply that libraries had their own kind of *fonds, fonds* generated by the cumulative acquisitions of generations of librarians rather than by the "natural" activities of institutions and individuals, yet still worthy of the same "respect." However, De Wailly made no attempt to elaborate on this claim, either before the Commission or in his published refutation of Ravaisson. What is more, by allowing this statement to remain unexplained, he may even have undermined the Library's case, since by suggesting that the Library's collections were not a "unity" or a "complete body," he also implied that they could be easily divided, and thus transferred to the Archives.[91]

The Library came somewhat closer to directly confronting the Archives' definitions of archives and libraries in a set of claims about the "publicity" of its collections. The Library argued that while it was perfectly acceptable for the Archives to collect "administrative" documents, once these documents became old enough to be considered "historical," they ought to fall to the Library, because historical documents needed to be publicly accessible, and the Library, unlike the Archives, was firmly oriented toward the public. For example, De Wailly claimed that the Library had as many manuscripts as it did in part because the archival administrators of the revolutionary period had recognized that

> there are necessary points of contact between archives and libraries. The former, it is true, are established for the needs of the administration and the latter for the needs of scholarship; but, as archival papers age and are

[90] Vaillant and De Wailly in Commission de la Bibliothèque Impériale et des Archives de l'Empire, "Procès-verbaux," 10 May 1861, fol. 10v.
[91] My interpretation of De Wailly's role in the debate thus differs somewhat from those of Hildesheimer ("Les Archives nationales") and Bartlett ("Respect").

for this reason less frequently consulted for [administrative] affairs, they tend more and more to take on a historical character, until finally the administration allows or orders that they pass from the half light of archives to the full light of libraries.[92]

We find a similar argument in Vaillant's March 1862 letter to the Minister of State:

[O]ne has only to visit the Library to recognize that there everything is organized with research in mind, that the communication [of holdings] is prompt and, as everyone says, liberal. At the Imperial Archives, a communication must be requested by letter; [the request] gives rise to an investigation and is not approved until several days later. The nature of the documents found there requires that it be this way. The attributions of each establishment must be clearly indicated and well understood by the public: at the Imperial Library, historical and literary documents,—at the Archives, administrative documents.[93]

De Wailly and Vaillant's supporters seemed eager to reinforce this claim at every turn. Commission minority member Taillandier noted that "the principal mission of the employees of the Imperial Library is to be of service to the public," while "at the Archives, communications to researchers [*travailleurs*] are just an accessory to the work of the employees and research is difficult."[94] Similarly, Taschereau testified before the Commission that a nobleman had decided to donate his family's "archives" to the Imperial Library because he wanted them to be communicated "as are all our other historical documents, with an extreme liberality."[95]

The Archives made no attempt to challenge the claim that the Library offered "extreme liberality" and public accessibility. Nor did it try to dispute the idea that historical sources ought to be easily accessible while administrative documents ought to be more carefully guarded. Indeed, Laborde and his supporters often reminded the Vaillant Commission that the Archives exercised all the "prudence" and "discretion" necessary to protect both the French state and individual French subjects and their

---

[92] De Wailly, *Bibliothèque Impériale*, p. 18.

[93] Vaillant to Ministre d'Etat, Paris, 12 Mar. 1862, AN, box F17-13541, p. 9.

[94] Taillandier in Commission de la Bibliothèque Impériale et des Archives de l'Empire, "Procès-verbaux," 6 May 1861, fol. 6r.

[95] Taschereau in Commission de la Bibliothèque Impériale et des Archives de l'Empire, "Procès-verbaux," 3 May 1861, fol. 4v.

families from the inappropriate exposure of archival sources.[96] However, the Archives' camp moved to undercut the Library's case by arguing that when it came to "historical" sources, the Archives were just as "public" as the Library. Laborde acknowledged that this had not always been the case; some of his predecessors had placed heavy restrictions on archival research.[97] Yet, he maintained, the Archives had changed. Since his arrival in 1857, they had become truly "liberal." As he explained to the Minister of State in February 1863:

> For the last six years, all my efforts have tended to make the Archives of the Empire just as accessible to researchers as public libraries and to leave no difference between the communication of printed books and the communication of archival papers except that which is required by the security of the State, by the nature of administrative acts, and by the interest of families.[98]

For Laborde, then, there was no need to place outdated administrative documents in public libraries, for archives could manage both historical and administrative documents, both restricted and public collections.

Laborde lent weight to this claim by pointing to the two major projects he had instituted as Archives Director. The first of these was an ambitious plan to create and then publish a set of inventories of Imperial Archives collections. While the Archives had participated in a number of publication projects over the years, including the Historical Works Committee's *Documents inédits* series, at the time of Laborde's arrival, it had no substantial published inventories, leaving researchers to rely on the unofficial guide published by *chartiste* Henri Bordier in 1855.[99] Laborde therefore proposed that the Archives publish a series entitled "Inventories and Documents" that would offer a comprehensive survey of the depository's collections as well as excerpts from its most important sources, thereby facilitating archival

---

[96] See Commission de la Bibliothèque Impériale et des Archives de l'Empire, "Procès-verbaux," esp. 6 May 1861, fol. 5v, and 16 May 1861, fols. 17r-17v.

[97] Ibid., 6 May 1861, fol. 5r.

[98] Laborde to Ministre d'Etat, 7 Feb. 1863, AN, box AB VI 1, p. [1].

[99] Bordier, *Les archives*. According to Laborde, Bordier's inventory was based not on the archives themselves but on existing internal inventories. See Marquis [Léon] de Laborde to Son Excellence le Maréchal Vaillant, Ministre de la Maison [de l'Empereur], Paris, 29 Mar. 1867, AN, box F17-13545, folder "Inventaire sommaire. 1867," p. [2].

research for what he described as the "erudite public."[100] In order to accomplish this task, Laborde directed his section heads to put aside their usual investigations and begin work on both a general inventory and a set of specialized inventories. By December 1862, three of these inventories, all by graduates of the Ecole des Chartes, were moving to press, and by the end of the decade, several others, including a general "Summary Inventory," had been completed.[101]

In the preface to one of these inventories, Laborde hinted at what would become his second major effort to open the Archives' historical collections to the public: the Museum of the Archives of the Empire, now known as the Museum of the History of France. Laborde's preface called publicity the "soul of the collections and the core of scholarship," and noted that there were "two kinds of publicity," one that "a good inventory" brought to the "studious public" at home, and the other that archives offered this same public in a "museum or reading room."[102] Laborde had actually been

---

[100] See [Léon de] Laborde, "Rapport sur les inventaires de documents historiques qui pourraient être immédiatement publiés par les Archives de l'Empire. Adressé à S. E. Monsieur le Ministre d'Etat et de la Maison de l'Empereur par le directeur général des Archives," 11 Aug. 1857, AN, box AB VI 1. On the decision to use the title "Inventaires et documents," see "Archives de l'Empire. Procès-verbaux des Conférences du Directeur général avec les Chefs de Section," 12 Jul. 1860, AN, box AB VII 1, pp. 42-46.

[101] The first three inventories were: the *Layettes du Trésor des chartes*, by Alexandre Teulet; the *Collection de sceaux*, by Louis Douët d'Arcq; and the *Actes du Parlement de Paris*, by Edgard Boutaric. See "Archives de l'Empire. Procès-verbaux des Conférences du Directeur général avec les Chefs de Section," 23 Dec. 1862, AN, box AB VII 1, pp. 92-93. For a fuller discussion of Laborde's publication program, see Françoise Hildesheimer, "Les premières publications des Archives," in *Histoire de France, historiens de la France: actes du colloque international, Reims, 14 et 15 mai 1993*, ed. Yves-Marie Bercé and Philippe Contamine (Paris: Société de l'histoire de France, 1994), pp. 281-299. I will discuss the disagreements about whether or not to include the revolutionary period in these inventories in the epilogue.

[102] Laborde quoted in Anatole de Barthélemy, "Archives de l'Empire, Inventaires et documents, premier article (Collection des sceaux, par M. Douët Darcq, première partie, t. Ier, Impr. imp.)," *Revue archéologique* 7 (1863): 241. Laborde offered a similar formulation, though without the key term "museum," in his 7 Feb. 1863 letter to the Ministre d'Etat, AN, box AB VI 1, p. [1]. According to his successor, Alfred Maury, Laborde also remodeled the Archives' reading room, open since 1846, but I have not found any other discussions of this project. See AN, box AB VII 1, folder "Notes de travail demandées aux Archivistes par Mr. Alfred Maury, Directeur général au moment de la rédaction du Rapport remis au Ministre de la

planning for an archives museum since 1858, when, newly arrived from his
earlier position as a curator at the Louvre, he proposed expanding the
existing display of archival seals to include a wide range of treasures from
the Archives' collections.[103] By the time of the Library-Archives conflict, he
had assembled a "Museum Commission" (composed largely of *chartistes*),
charged with organizing exhibits that would, in Laborde's words, "facilitate
the work of the public's eyes so that it [the public] will reap the greatest
possible profit."[104] After nearly a decade of planning, the Museum finally
opened its doors in the summer of 1867, and thus, claimed opening speaker
(and *chartiste*) Léon Gautier, the "sources of our history" became "a public
thing [*une chose publique*]."[105]

Interestingly, at the very moment that Laborde was working to
demonstrate the "publicity" of the Imperial Archives, officials responsible
for provincial archives were also taking measures to attract the scholarly
public. As we saw in the previous chapter, departmental archivists had spent
most of the 1850s developing *Inventaires sommaires* for their "historical" (pre-
1790) collections. In 1861, Interior Minister Persigny announced that it was
time that these manuscript inventories "pass into publicity," and ordered the
departments to begin publishing their completed guides.[106] The first
inventories appeared in 1862, and by 1867, forty-one volumes had been
printed under the Interior Minister's stamp.[107] The *chartistes* responsible for

---

Maison de l'Empereur et des Beaux-Arts le 1er Juillet 1868, sur l'administration des
Archives depuis 1852."

[103] The existing *Musée sigillographique* (Sigillographical Museum) had been established
by Laborde's predecessor Jean-Antoine Letronne in 1847. See Jean-Pierre Babelon,
ed., *Centenaire du Musée de l'Histoire de France: l'oeuvre du Marquis de Laborde aux Archives
nationales* (Paris: Archives nationales, 1968), pp. 28-29.

[104] Laborde in "Procès-verbaux des séances de la Commission du Musée," 7 Oct.
1861, AN, box AB XII 4, p. 4.

[105] Léon Gautier, "Le musée des Archives de l'Empire. Discours d'ouverture," *BEC*
29 (1868): 514.

[106] [Victor] F[ialin] de Persigny, "Circulaire," 12 Aug. 1861, in Ministère de
l'instruction publique et des beaux-arts, *Lois, instructions et règlements relatifs aux Archives
départementales, communales et hospitalières* (Paris: H. Champion, 1884), pp. 64-65. See
also Vincent Mollet, "Les archives départementales du Tarn de 1790 à 1946:
constitution et mise en valeur d'un patrimoine écrit," (Thesis, Ecole nationale des
Chartes, 1992), pp. 293-294.

[107] For the ministerial correspondence associated with the publication of the
Inventaires sommaires, see AN, box F2 I 378[14]. For a tally of volumes published, see Le
Pottier, "Histoire et érudition," p. 216.

departmental archives seemed enthusiastic about the Minister's publication project, calling it a "great monument to national history," and "one of the vastest literary enterprises ever undertaken by a government."[108] They also recognized that the publication of the *Inventaires* marked a new phase in their work as archivists. Auguste Bosvieux, archivist of the Lot-et-Garonne, explained in 1864 that while "the importance of [the] precious remains of the past is no longer in doubt, and their preservation has been assured by the organization of the archives administration," archivists had just come to realize that "it was not enough to collect and to preserve; the treasures that had been gathered also had to be made known and appreciated: they had to be used."[109] In Bosvieux's view, the publication of the *Inventaires sommaires* would finally allow his collections to be used by historical researchers.

Some departmental *archivistes-paléographes* gave more subtle indications that their attention was shifting from organizing and preserving their collections to publicizing them. Nearly all of the departmental archivists included in this study began devoting more space to "communications" and "expeditions" (i.e., the delivery of official copies of archival documents) in their reports during the late 1850s and early 1860s. This shift is particularly noticeable in the case of the Department of the Aube, where in 1857 archivist Henri d'Arbois de Jubainville stopped organizing his annual reports by internal task (classification, stamping of documents, etc.) and began organizing them into two main sections: "interior," which he defined as "classification of the documents in the depository," and later as "order work," and "exterior," in which he included "communication to prefectoral offices, to the administrations, [and] to the public," as well as "the delivery of expeditions."[110] By 1864, he had dropped the "prefectoral offices" and "administrations," leaving in his second section only "relations with the public."[111] While d'Arbois never discussed the social composition of this

---

[108] Sainte Marie Mévil, "Rapport annuel sur le service des archives départementales [Seine-et-Oise]," 1 Aug. 1862, AD Yvelines, Box 3T/AD 3, p. [8]; C[élestin] Port, "Rapport sur les Archives Départementales [Maine-et-Loire] (Août 1861-1862)," 2 Aug. 1862, AN, box F2 I 373¹, p. [12].

[109] A[uguste] Bosvieux, "Rapport de l'Archiviste [Lot-et-Garonne]," 1 Aug. 1864, AN, box F2 I 372¹², p. 9.

[110] [Henri] d'Arbois de Jubainville, "Rapport à M. le Préfet de l'Aube sur la situation des archives du département au 1er Aout 1857," 1 Aug. 1857, AN, box F2 I 367¹², p. [1]. For more on the seven departmental archives covered in this study, see chap. 4.

[111] [Henri] d'Arbois de Jubainville, "Rapport à Monsieur le Préfet de l'Aube sur la situation des archives départementales," 30 Jul. 1864, AN, box F2 I 367¹², p. [1].

"public," it is clear that he and his fellow Archivist-Paleographers were now going about their "order work" with an audience of readers in mind.

Of course, opening the historical collections of the departmental and Imperial archives to the public created its own problems. How were archivists to determine when an administrative document became "historical" and therefore appropriate for public consumption? How could they be sure not to release "private" or "secret" records too early? As Félix Ravaisson explained in his 1862 Vaillant Commission report, such determinations were not so difficult to make in departmental depositories, which since 1841 had been separated into "historical" (pre-1790) and "administrative" (post-1790) sections. The Imperial Archives, however, were not divided so neatly; instead of two sections, the central archives had four: historical, administrative, legislative/judicial, and the secretariat (for internal records).[112] Ravaisson therefore advised reorganizing the Imperial Archives to look more like the departmental archives, dividing them at the year 1789, 1800, or even possibly 1804, into "historical" and "administrative" collections. The former, Ravaisson explained, could be communicated "to the public without reservation," while the latter would be subject to special restrictions.[113] But Laborde disagreed; in 1867, he declared his opposition to the idea of "two great divisions," preferring to maintain a more fluid boundary between historical and administrative, public and secret.[114] Interestingly, it was probably his unwillingness to establish firm boundaries that cost him his job later that same year. When a noted scholar, the Comte d'Haussonville, published some unflattering selections from Napoléon I's correspondence, then housed at the Imperial Archives and supposedly off-limits to scholars, the Emperor placed the blame on Laborde, eventually replacing him as Archives Director in late 1867.[115]

---

[112] See above, footnote 58.

[113] Ravaisson, *Rapport*, pp. 201-204.

[114] Laborde, *Les Archives de la France* (1867), p. 166. For what Laborde's discussion of these two divisions suggests about changing conceptions of the revolutionary period, see the epilogue. On the 1897 decision to finally reorganize the Archives into a *section ancienne* (pre-revolutionary materials) and a *section moderne* (for post-revolutionary materials), see Hildesheimer, *Les Archives de France*, p. 59.

[115] For an overview of the *affaire d'Haussonville*, see Le Pottier, "Histoire et érudition," pp. 252-263. We can look forward to a fuller discussion of the affair in the forthcoming dissertation by Jennifer Milligan of Rutgers University.

Yet if there were (and still are) varying perceptions of the boundary between "administrative" and "historical" archives, no one outside of the Imperial Library in the 1860s seems to have questioned the Archives' right to own historical documents, nor its ability to give the "studious" public sufficient access to these documents. If anything, French scholars were eager to applaud Laborde for his efforts to increase the "publicity" of the Archives' historical materials.[116] In this sense, he and his supporters appear to have successfully rebutted the Imperial Library's claim that historical sources were better placed in the "full light" of a public library than in the "half light" of a state archive. While the Archives camp never challenged the Library's capacity to serve the general public, they argued persuasively that scholars in search of the "true" sources of French history would be well served at the Imperial Archives.

When we put the Library-Archives dispute together with the debate over popular libraries, we can see that French public libraries were in a difficult spot in the 1860s. Popular library advocates painted them as dusty collections of antiquated materials, well-suited to scholarly research but hopelessly ill-suited to the educational needs of the working classes. The Imperial Archives, meanwhile, described public libraries as mere purveyors of books, useful for the "banal crowd" of library visitors but of only secondary interest to the "studious public" seeking the real vestiges of the French past. From one perspective, public libraries were not prepared to serve the general public; from the other, they were not prepared to serve the scholarly one. This is not to say, of course, that the challenges presented by the popular library movement and the Imperial Archives left no possibility for public libraries to carve out a new role for themselves. Nevertheless, the fact remains that neither public librarians nor the ministerial officials to whom they reported made any concerted effort in the 1860s to redefine and reinvigorate the public library. As a result, French public libraries in this period found themselves in an awkwardly immobile position, caught between the pull of the "popular" and the pull of the "erudite." No example may illustrate this point more effectively than the new Imperial Library reading rooms that opened—to great fanfare—in the summer of 1868.

---

[116] The only exception I know of is Bordier's *Les inventaires*, which includes among its many criticisms of Laborde the charge that creating the exhibits for the Archives Museum meant "dismembering" archival *fonds* and thus hindering scholarly research (see esp. pp. 27-28). However, even Bordier made no attempt to challenge Laborde's general program of archival "publicity."

Since 1833, all visitors to the Library's main book collection had shared a single reading room. University students and Academy members rubbed elbows with local workers and retirees, causing some critics to complain that the reading room was becoming little more than a place for "idle" souls to keep warm in the winter. Thus in 1868, largely in response to the recommendations of the Mérimée Commission, the Library opened two reading rooms: one, housed in the spectacular new Salle Labrouste, was restricted to approved card-holders and intended for "serious studies," the other, housed in the old main reading room, was described as "absolutely public" and contained a smaller collection of books and periodicals deemed appropriate for everyone from the man of leisure to the artisan or worker.[117] Unable to reconcile the scholarly and the popular, the Library simply split its public services in two.

The state's inability to fashion a clear role for public libraries in the era of the popular library movement and the Library-Archives debate is significant in two respects. First, the peculiar predicament of public libraries in the 1860s points to some of the challenges associated with the "liberalization" of the authoritarian Empire. Though eager to present itself as attentive to the wishes of the "public," the late Imperial regime seemed unsure about how to define this group. It was clearly unprepared to incorporate the working-class "people" targeted by popular libraries into the general "public"; yet as its inattention to existing public libraries suggests, it was not sure how to engage with the elite (or non-"popular") public, either. Similarly, while the relaxation of press laws and the reactivation of certain parliamentary procedures revealed the Bonapartist regime's interest in extending the boundaries of "public" knowledge, the library debates of the 1860s point to the difficulty of managing such knowledge. Were all sources (in this case, books and documents) equally public? What were the appropriate public uses of such sources (general instruction? the production of national histories?)? And when did a source pass from the realm of state

---

[117] The second room, known as "Room B," remained open until 1935, only to reemerge, in rather altered form, as the public portion of the new National Library at Tolbiac. For a fascinating discussion of Room B, see Eve Netchine and Edmée Strauch, "La 'salle B' ou 70 ans de lecture publique à la Bibliothèque nationale," in *Mélanges autour de l'histoire des livres imprimés et périodiques*, ed. Bruno Blasselle and Laurent Portes (Paris: Bibliothèque nationale de France, 1998), pp. 242-266. I am grateful to Eve Netchine for helping me to clarify details of the room's development.

secrecy to the realm of publicity? The late Empire was the first post-revolutionary regime to begin addressing these questions in a serious way.

Beyond indicating the difficulty of crafting a "public" politics in the 1860s, the library debates of the late Empire are also significant as a major turning point in the development of the three institutions at the center of this study: libraries, archives, and the Ecole des Chartes. Until the late 1850s, the various French governments had rarely made strong distinctions between archival and library collections. Though (with the important exception of the Second Republic) they devoted much more attention to archives than to libraries, they never explicitly articulated their reasons for this preference. Moreover, particularly in the 1820s and 1830s, they often mined public libraries for the same sorts of historical documents found in state archives, without making any attempt to confine these materials to one institution or another. Yet after the Library-Archives conflict of the early 1860s, public libraries and state archives took on increasingly distinct identities. As a new generation of French historians worked to style itself as a coherent "scientific" profession in the late 1860s and 1870s, it elaborated upon Laborde's claims about archives as containers of historical "truth," and began to regard a long stint in the archives—not the library—as an indispensable rite of passage.[118] Public libraries, meanwhile, became more firmly associated with the "secondary" (rather than "original") sources appropriate to the instructional needs of the general public. Though the popular-public split remained in place for most of the nineteenth century, the turn of the twentieth century saw the increasing centralization of both popular and public libraries as well as the more widespread adoption of the Anglo-American model of the public library as an instructional center open to all members of the literate population.[119]

For the Ecole des Chartes, too, the 1860s proved a crucial turning point. Both the movement to create popular libraries and the struggle between the Imperial Library and Archives opened up the possibility of recasting the Ecole as a school for public librarians. Yet despite Vallet de Viriville's repeated attempts to present *chartistes* as the natural leaders of a new and more accessible system of public libraries, neither his colleagues within the

---

[118] On the rise of the historical profession, see the epilogue.

[119] See Léveillé, "Les petites bibliothèques"; Anne-Marie Chartier and Jean Hébrard, *Discours sur la lecture (1880-1980)* (Paris: Bibliothèque publique d'information, Centre Georges-Pompidou, 1989); and especially Martine Poulain, ed., *Histoire des bibliothèques françaises*, vol. 4, *Les bibliothèques au XXe siècle, 1914-1990* (Paris: Promodis, 1992).

school nor his friends in the popular library movement seemed eager to follow his lead. At the same time, both historians and archival administrators consistently reinforced the school's connection to state archives, extending the school's monopoly over archival positions and, like Laborde, touting the "expertise" chartistes brought to archival collections.[120] The early Third Republic did see the rise of several highly influential *chartiste* librarians, notably Léopold Delisle, Ernest Coyecque, and Charles Sustrac; nevertheless, the school never came to play the same role in the making of republican library policy that it played in the creation of state archival policy. A 1904 attempt to reorganize the Ecole as the "National Professional School for Archivist-Librarians," met with no success. Meanwhile, a new generation of French librarians committed to the Anglo-American vision of the public library began developing their own professional examinations and certificates, culminating in the creation of the Ecole Nationale Supérieure des Bibliothèques (the National Library School, now the Ecole Nationale Supérieure des Sciences de l'Information et des Bibliothèques, or the National Library and Information Science School, near Lyon).[121] Now the state would look to new librarians and new educational institutions in its attempts to reorganize and reform the nation's libraries.

---

[120] In 1887, graduates of the school obtained a monopoly on archivist posts at the National Archives. See Jules Grévy (le Président de la République) and Berthelot (Le ministre de l'instruction publique), "Décret," *Journal officiel*, 17 May 1887, p. [2].
[121] See Daniel Renoult, "Les formations et les métiers," in *Histoire des bibliothèques françaises*, 4: 421-445; Denis Pallier, "Histoire et évolution du métier de bibliothécaire," *Bulletin d'informations de l'Association des bibliothécaires français* no. 164 (1994): 47-54; and Jean-Pierre Seguin, *Eugène Morel et la lecture publique: un prophète en son pays* (Paris: Centre Georges Pompidou, 1994). On the reorganization proposals of 1904, see the "Chronique" section of the *BEC* for 1904-1906; Bruno Delmas, "Les débuts de la formation des bibliothécaires," *Histoire des bibliothèques françaises*, 3: 138-139; as well as AN, box F17-3348.

Epilogue

By the early years of the Third Republic (1870-1940), an important phase in the history of archives, libraries, and the Ecole des Chartes had come to a close. Since its founding in 1821, the school had been the focal point of multiple state efforts to contend with the masses of books and documents declared "national" and "public" during the French Revolution. Shifts in conceptions of the school and its students had reflected key changes in the state's approach to its library and archival collections. However, by the 1870s, the school was no longer such a telling indicator of government policies. As we have seen, the public library debates of the 1860s tended to weaken the connection between the Ecole des Chartes and public librarianship. Despite the ongoing presence of *chartistes* in major public library collections, it would be librarians from outside the school who would do the most to shape policies under a republican regime increasingly committed to an Anglo-American conception of the public library. Meanwhile, two other developments—both of which began to surface in the late 1860s and had become fully apparent by the 1870s—also worked to alter the relationship between the Ecole des Chartes and the French state. Once envisioned as the premier training ground for both archivists and historians, the school saw its role become increasingly circumscribed as new historical institutions rose around it. At the same time, the French government, long convinced that the archives and libraries of the Old Regime alone constituted French national history, began looking to books and documents produced after 1789—and especially to those produced between 1790 and 1800—for historical source material. While individual *chartistes* made substantial contributions to this effort, as an institution the Ecole tended to cede the initiative to new groups of scholars.

The last third of the nineteenth century saw major changes in the teaching and practice of history in France. Until the late 1860s, the Ecole des Chartes had been the only French institution training students in the practices of historical research and criticism. If a young Frenchman wanted to teach history in secondary schools, he could take history lecture courses at the prestigious Ecole Normale. If he wanted to understand the broad currents of historical change, he could attend public lectures by the great orators of the Collège de France and University Faculties. But if he wanted to learn how to locate, translate, and evaluate "original" documents, he could do so only at the Ecole des Chartes or on his own. Given the small size of the Ecole (generally fewer than thirty students), this meant that most of the scholars publishing historical works in this period had no formal methodological training.[1] However, by the end of the century, such training was not only considered crucial to historical practice but was also available at a variety of French educational institutions.[2]

Part of the stimulus for this change came from a new generation of reformist historians (among them a number of *chartistes*); the other part came from the French state. In the late 1860s, a number of young historians began to push for the more widespread application of "scientific" historical methods, that is, the careful authentication, decipherment, and critique of "original" (and generally archival) documents. The year 1866 saw the establishment of two new, aggressively "scientific" historical journals: the *Revue des questions historiques* and the *Revue critique d'histoire et de littérature*. Though politically opposed—the first was vigorously Catholic and legitimist, the second more centrist-republican—both journals proclaimed the supremacy of historical erudition and lambasted scholars who had been careless in their research. Perhaps not surprisingly, the editorial boards of both publications were dominated by graduates of the Ecole des Chartes: Marius Sepet and Léon Gautier at the *Revue des questions historiques*, and Paul Meyer and Gaston Paris at the *Revue critique*. While the *Bibliothèque de l'Ecole des chartes* had long published and reviewed works of historical erudition, now a new group of *chartistes* was taking a more active approach to promoting the school's view of history.[3]

The methodological concerns articulated by the *Revue critique* and the *Revue des questions historiques* in the late 1860s found their fullest expression in what is often regarded as the first "professional" historical journal in France, the *Revue historique* of 1876. Like its late Imperial precursors, the *Revue*

---

[1] I use the term "he" intentionally here; on how historical institutions and practices worked to exclude both female historians and "femininity" more generally, see Bonnie G. Smith, *The Gender of History: Men, Women, and Historical Practice* (Cambridge: Harvard University Press, 1998). For a social analysis of historical practitioners in the 1860s, see Charles-Olivier Carbonell, *Histoire et historiens: une mutation idéologique des historiens français, 1865-1885* (Toulouse, Privat, 1976).

[2] William R. Keylor, *Academy and Community: The Foundation of the French Historical Profession* (Cambridge: Harvard University Press, 1975); Gérard Noiriel, "Naissance du métier d'historien," *Genèses* 1 (1990): 61; Louis Halphen, *L'histoire en France depuis cent ans* (Paris: Librairie Armand Colin, 1914), pp. 143-152.

[3] On the development of these journals, see Carbonell, *Histoire et historiens*, especially part 4, chapters II and IV.

historique had strong ties to the Ecole des Chartes. Gabriel Monod, the journal's founder and intellectual leader, had audited courses at the school in the 1860s, while co-founder Gustave Fagniez had graduated from the school in 1867 and begun working as a professional archivist shortly thereafter.[4] In addition, more than a third of the journal's early collaborators were *chartistes*.[5] Yet if the *Revue* drew heavily on *chartistes'* expertise, it also claimed to offer a more expansive vision of history than that provided either by the Ecole des Chartes or by its venerable *Bibliothèque*. As Monod explained in his introduction to the inaugural issue, the *Revue historique* was intended to combine the "erudite" history of the Ecole des Chartes and the "literary" history of the Faculties and the Ecole Normale to create a new history that would be both analytic and synthetic, both rooted in documentary "fact" and supportive of general conclusions. He hoped this new "scientific" history would not only help unite the various political factions of the new republic but also help French scholars compete with their supposedly more advanced counterparts across the Rhine.[6]

In the closing decades of the nineteenth century, the "scientific" approach espoused by the *Revue historique* drew legions of adherents. The journal became the center of a scholarly movement aimed at reinvigorating a nation humiliated by the Franco-Prussian War and divided by the Paris Commune with a more "virile" and "truthful" history.[7] Partly in response to pressure from this movement, the republican state began a massive reorganization of higher education, including a major reform and extension of historical training. Here again the developments of the 1870s and 1880s had their roots in the late 1860s. In July 1868, Public Instruction Minister Victor Duruy (himself a historical scholar) worked with the leaders of the *Revue critique* (including, by then, Gabriel Monod) to establish the Ecole Pratique des Hautes Etudes. Modeled on the intensive seminars that Monod, Gaston Paris, and others had experienced on visits to German universities, the courses in the school's fourth section, "historical and

---

[4] Ibid., as well as Carbonell's "La naissance de la *Revue historique,* une revue de combat (1876-1885)," *Revue historique* 255, no. 2 (1976): 341-348. On Fagniez, see *Titres et travaux de M. Fagniez (Gustave-Charles)* (Paris: Imp. F. Pichon, [1895]). According to Carbonell, Fagniez left the journal in 1881, probably due to deepening political and religious disputes with Monod.

[5] See G[abriel] Monod and G[ustave] Fagniez, "Avant-propos," *Revue historique* 1 (1876): 2-5.

[6] See Carbonell, "La naissance," p. 344.

[7] Keylor, *Academy*, chap. 2; Smith, *Gender*, chap. 4.

philological sciences," were meant to provide a bridge between the general history lectures of the Ecole Normale and the more technical courses of the Ecole des Chartes. Young *chartistes* (who comprised nearly all of the historical section's students in its early years) would come to the new school to learn broader applications of their paleographic and diplomatic skills, while *normaliens* would come to learn how to test their historical understanding on "original" sources.[8]

After the fall of the Second Empire, the combined forces of the scientific history movement and the republican state moved to extend the seminar-based training first offered at the Ecole Pratique to the various University Faculties. Instead of giving large public lectures, history professors would now offer small seminars to which only their most promising students were invited. As Bonnie Smith explains, these seminars created a kind of "brotherhood" of historians that extended not only across France but throughout Western Europe and the United States. While in previous decades historians had not been a particularly cohesive group, united only by scholarly societies or large historical projects (like the *Document inédits* series), now they were more likely to have a certain educational background, one based on seminar courses and the careful study of primary documents. This "brotherhood" acquired even greater strength and influence as the state not only revamped the University's historical curriculum but expanded it, adding new professorial chairs and more student scholarships. History was beginning to take on the trappings of a modern profession.[9]

On the one hand, the rise of professional, "scientific" history brought great rewards to the Ecole des Chartes. Indeed, several historians have called the final decades of the nineteenth century the school's "golden age."[10] Scientific historians throughout Europe and North America

---

[8] For the Imperial decree establishing the Ecole pratique, see *BEC* 29 (1868): 538-543. On the presence of *chartistes*, see G[abriel] Monod to Monsieur le Directeur [Alfred Maury], Paris, 20 Mar. 1869, AN, box F17-13617, transcribed in Jean Le Pottier, "Histoire et érudition: recherches et documents sur l'histoire et le rôle de l'érudition médiévale dans l'historiographie française du XIXè siècle" (Thesis, Ecole nationale des chartes, 1979), pp. 501-505. See also Keylor, *Academy*, pp. 25-26; and Carbonell, "La naissance," pp. 341-342. On the role of historical scholars like Monod, Hippolyte Taine, and Ernest Renan in organizing university reforms, see George Weisz, *The Emergence of Modern Universities in France, 1863-1914* (Princeton: Princeton University Press, 1983), esp. chap. 2.

[9] Keylor, *Academy*, chap. 3.

[10] See for example Odile Krakovitch, "Les chartistes et l'histoire de la Révolution," in *L'Ecole nationale des chartes: histoire de l'école depuis 1821*, ed. Yves-Marie Bercé,

applauded the school as a model of rigorous, impartial scholarship. At the same time, *chartistes* found themselves in high demand as historians obsessed with unearthing "virgin" documents engaged in massive searches of French archives.[11] Perhaps the greatest validation of the Ecole's teachings came in 1897, when it was officially incorporated into the University system and moved from its cramped quarters at the National Archives to its current location at the Sorbonne.[12] The following year, *chartiste* Charles-Victor Langlois and *normalien* Charles Seignobos, then co-teaching the Sorbonne's first course in historiography, published some of their lessons as *Introduction aux études historiques*, which quickly became the basic manual for all aspiring historians.[13] As one historian wrote begrudgingly in 1910, the Ecole des Chartes seemed to have "seized control of the Sorbonne."[14]

On the other hand, the widespread adoption of the school's erudite methods meant that the school's own curriculum was no longer quite so unique. Young men who wanted to be trained as historians could now attend the Ecole Pratique, the Sorbonne, or one of the other French Faculties of Letters. As a result, the Ecole des Chartes became ever more strongly associated with the training of archival administrators, or "historians' auxiliaries." In a 1906 *Revue historique* article, for example, Monod argued that the school's essential function was as "a preparatory school for archivists."[15] Interestingly, many twentieth-century historians have assumed, based on such characterizations, that the school had always been responsible primarily for training archivists. This study has shown, however, that although the Ecole had always had strong connections to French archives (and had early on been described as a school for historical "auxiliaries"), it had also been envisioned as a training ground for librarians and historians. Thus the Ecole des Chartes of the period 1821-1870 not

---

Olivier Guyotjeannin, and Marc Smith (Thionville, France: Gérard Klopp, 1997), p. 136; and Le Pottier, "Histoire et érudition," p. 275.

[11] On the "fetishization" of archival documents (often described in highly gendered terms), see Smith, *Gender*, chap. 4.

[12] Keylor, *Academy*, p. 64. See also Christian Hottin, "19, rue de la Sorbonne. L'Ecole, ses bâtiments, sa décoration," in *L'Ecole nationale des chartes: histoire de l'école depuis 1821*, pp. 142-148.

[13] Ch[arles]-V[ictor] Langlois and Ch[arles] Seignobos, *Introduction aux études historiques* (Paris: Hachette, 1898). On their course, see Keylor, *Academy*, chap. 3.

[14] Lucien [pseud.], "L'Ecole des chartes et la Sorbonne," *Revue politique et parlementaire* 65, no. 195 (1910): 528.

[15] Gabriel Monod, "La situation de l'enseignement supérieur," *Revue historique* 91 (May-Aug. 1906): 312.

only helped shape the historical profession of the Third Republic but was in turn reshaped by it. As the "scientific" history movement (with its many *chartistes*) helped remake the Sorbonne as the center of professional historical education, it also worked to recast the Ecole des Chartes as the center of professional archival studies.

The second major development working to alter the school's role after 1870 was the state's decision to turn its attention away from the books and documents of the Old Regime to those of the Revolution and nineteenth century. As we saw in the previous chapter, the new republican government showed much greater interest in popular and university libraries, both of which tended to emphasize recently-published books and periodicals, than had earlier regimes. Yet the shift to "modern" materials is even more striking in the case of French archives. After decades of focusing its "order work" on pre-revolutionary documents, the government began pushing for the preservation and organization of "modern," and particularly revolutionary, archival sources.

Historians most often associate the turn to revolutionary sources with the centennial celebrations of 1889, and, indeed, it was not until the late 1880s and 1890s that published inventories and collections of revolutionary-era archival documents started to appear.[16] Nevertheless, we can see the beginnings of this shift in the 1870s, and even as early as the late 1860s. In his 1867 treatise, *Les Archives de la France*, Imperial Archives Director Léon de Laborde challenged the idea of a strict division between pre-revolutionary, "historical" archives and modern, "administrative" ones:

> It has been proposed that we split the entire archive along chronological lines into two large sections, creating old archives and modern archives. The years 1750, 1789, 1800, [and] 1804 have [all] been put forward as dividing lines. They are arbitrary, will be debatable for every scholar, and with the passing of years will all become meaningless. *There was a transformation between the two periods, but not a rupture.* All the administrative processes continued under other names; the new officials charged with directing these processes protected the same interests.[17]

---

[16] See especially Krakovitch, "Les chartistes," and her "La découverte des sources révolutionnaires, il y a cent ans: les inventaires et collections de documents sur la Révolution publiés à l'occasion du Centenaire," *Gazette des archives* 148 (1990): 157-177.

[17] Le Marquis [Léon] de Laborde, *Les Archives de la France: leurs vicissitudes pendant la Révolution, leur régénération sous l'Empire* (Paris: Vve. Renouard, 1867), p. 167. My emphasis. For one of these proposals, see the unsigned "Archives de l'Empire.

Laborde therefore refused to follow the departmental archives in erecting what he described as a "wall of China" between pre-revolutionary and revolutionary or "modern" archives.[18]

Remarkably, just as his book was going to press, departmental archivists were also questioning the wisdom of a strict revolutionary "rupture," apparently without any prodding from Laborde. An 1867 ministerial circular written by the four Inspectors-General of provincial archives (all *chartistes*) advised prefects that although previous instructions had divided departmental collections at 1790, since the "old institutions were not destroyed all at once on a fixed date, and since several of them persisted for a certain time," it would be wise to continue the inventories of Old Regime institutions until they were officially replaced by "new powers," whether that was before or after 1790. The circular also asked that departmental archivists give "particular care" to the "documents of the revolutionary period, as well as to the so-called <u>Intermediary</u> administrations." "Like the other historical papers," these "precious sources" were to be "fully classified," according to divisions "analogous to those of the earlier archives."[19] When one official complained that the new circular would lead to "completely arbitrary" classifications, the Inspectors-General replied that it was the date 1790 that was arbitrary, for it forced archivists to cut Old Regime *fonds* that ended in 1787 or 1808 in two unwieldy pieces. "In sum," they explained, the 1790 division "represents only in imperfect fashion the

---

Section Législative et Judiciaire. Cadre qu'il semblerait bon d'étudier pour arriver à une meilleure repartition et juxtaposition des papiers," 3 Jun. 1867, AN, box AB XVI 1, folder "1866. Projet d'un nouveau classement...."

[18] Laborde, *Les Archives de la France*, p. 174. In a document that looks to be a partial draft of this book (also in AN, box AB XVI 1, folder "1866. Projet d'un nouveau classement..."), Laborde explicitly condemns the 1841 circular for "imposing" this split on departmental archives. However, the claims about the revolutionary "rupture" and "wall of China" that appear in these two sources do not appear in his *Les Archives de la France pendant la Révolution* (Paris: Imprimerie de J. Claye, 1866), which was first published as the introduction to the Archives' inventory of historical monuments and is in many respects identical to his 1867 book.

[19] La Vallette (Le Ministre de l'Intérieur), "Circulaire [with heading: "Archives départementales, communales et hospitalières. Instructions complémentaires sur la rédaction des Inventaires Sommaires"]," 28 May 1867, AD Aube, box 3 T 131. La Vallette's emphasis. Reproduced in Ministère de l'instruction publique et des beaux-arts, *Lois, instructions et règlements relatifs aux Archives départementales, communales et hospitalières* (Paris: H. Champion, 1884), pp. 70-74.

distinction between the old order and the new order."[20] Like Laborde, then, they recommended blurring the boundary between the Old and New Regimes, and expanding the category of "historical" documents to include those of the revolutionary period.

Nevertheless, in the 1860s, key Imperial officials remained wary of drawing too much attention to revolutionary documents, as is clear from a set of exchanges between Laborde and the Minister of State. When in early 1863, Laborde announced his plans to publish inventories of the records of the revolutionary tribunals and the decrees of the Committee of Public Safety, the Minister's advisor recommended strongly against it:

> Must a scholarly establishment that has more than enough documents to choose from allocate its resources to a quite recent period, about which the newspapers and official papers of the time give a sufficient understanding, and which only recall crimes and misfortunes? When all of the government's efforts tend toward the appeasement of revolutionary and retrograde passions, it would be difficult to understand a publication produced by a public administration with this sad epoch as its subject and bearing in large print the adopted phrase: *Inventory published by order of the Emperor.*[21]

The Minister readily accepted this recommendation, instructing Laborde to postpone the two inventories.[22] Yet by the late 1860s, Laborde was again declaring his intention to publish revolutionary-era inventories, and had assigned at least two of his *chartistes* to work on these projects. Clearly

---

[20] For the criticism of the circular, see the unsigned "Note pour Monsieur le Conseiller d'Etat, Secrétaire général" (with table, "Dates jusqu'auxquelles existèrent les anciennes Institutions judiciaires, administratives et écclesiastiques"), 28. Mar. 1868. For the reply, see Comité de l'Inspection générale des Archives Départementales, Communales et Hospitalières [E. de Stadler, Francis Wey, M. Bertandy, and Eugène de Rozière], "Exposé de l'Affaire communiquée: Examiner s'il n'y aurait pas lieu de rédiger une note complémentaire de la Circulaire du 28 Mai 1867," 31. Mar. 1868, both in AN, box AB XXXI 50, folder "Circulaire du 28 mai 1867."

[21] Cte. [Léon] de Laborde to Son Excellence le Ministre d'Etat, 7 Feb. 1863, AN, box AB VI 1; [Marchand?] (Ministère d'Etat. Secrétaire général. Bureau du personnel), "Note au Ministre," 9 Feb. 1863, AN, box F17-13544 and 13545, folder "Archives Nationales. Inventaires," p. [4]. Italics in original.

[22] Cte. Walewski to M. le Cte. de Laborde, 23 Feb. 1863, AN, box F17-13544 and 13545, folder "Archives Nationales. Inventaires."

displeased, the new Minister quickly reminded him that the revolutionary era was to be avoided. Just months later, Laborde was relieved of his post.[23]

After the fall of the Second Empire, government leaders proved much more willing to tackle the archives of the 1790s. While for the Imperial state, these documents recalled only "crimes and misfortunes," for the new republic, they recalled the great innovations of their political predecessors. Now that republicanism, long associated with violence and chaos, had begun to emerge as a stabilizing force, the revolutionary legacy became a treasure to be explored, not a danger to be suppressed. As early as 1873, work had begun on a new ministerial decree aimed at encouraging departmental archivists to classify and describe their revolutionary sources. That spring, Inspector-General Eugène de Rozière, one of the four inspectors responsible for the 1867 circular discussed above, began drafting a document that followed up on the earlier circular's more general claims about the "historical" quality of revolutionary archives with specific instructions about how to organize these documents.[24] In 1874, the Interior Ministry's Archives Commission, newly reconstituted under Natalis de Wailly, took on Rozière's project, working with nearly a dozen departmental archivists (all of them *chartistes*) to complete the instructions.[25] The final circular, dated November 1874, explained that while earlier governments had been "preoccupied" with the pre-1790 series, now was the time to move to "all the registers and dossiers of the revolutionary period,

---

[23] On *chartistes* Emile Campardon and Jules Guiffrey's work on revolutionary sources, see J. J. Guiffrey to Monsieur Maury, [after Aug. 1871], AN, box AB IVc 3, folder "Guiffrey," and AN, box AB VI 1, folder "Notes de travail demandées aux Archivistes par Mr. Alfred Maury...." In June 1863, the Archives were moved from the Ministry of State to that of the "Maison de l'Empereur et des Beaux-Arts," headed by the Maréchal Vaillant. In a 4 Mar. 1867 letter to Laborde (AN, box F17-13545, folder "Archives Nationales. Inventaires."), Vaillant emphasized his support for Walewski's earlier decision. On Laborde's dismissal, see chap. 5. See also the useful discussion in Le Pottier, "Histoire et érudition," pp. 250-264.

[24] See the May 1873 correspondence between Rozière and archivists Henri d'Arbois de Jubainville and Charles Beaurepaire in AN, box AB XXXI 50, folder "Circulaire du 11 novembre 1874."

[25] For the Commission's deliberations, see "Commission supérieure des Archives départementales, communales et hospitalières. Procès-verbaux des séances," 1874-1879, AN, box AB XXVI 4* (the next two volumes, 5* and 6*, appear to be missing); and "Commission supérieure des Archives...Séances de la Commission," 1874-1923, AN, box AB XXVI 1. For the departmental archivists' comments on the proposed circular, see AN, box AB XXXI 50.

which contain the liquidation of the Old Regime and the first attempts at a new regime," and which had "suffered" from their "prolonged abandonment." Nevertheless, at the urging of at least one departmental archivist, the circular also instructed departments to "bring a great deal of prudence and moderation to the preparation of notes intended for the inventory" and to avoid including "indications that might serve to revive local hatreds, today extinguished, or to undermine respect for [local] families."[26]

In the 1880s and 1890s, such concerns seemed to evaporate as the republican government—newly confident after weathering a series of political crises—devoted ever more attention to revolutionary sources. In 1885, the Historical Works Committee formed a special commission on the "publication of original historical documents related to the French Revolution," while in 1886 the Paris municipal government created a similar commission for the publication of materials on the role of the capital in the revolutionary upheaval. Then in early 1886, the Sorbonne established its first chair in the history of the revolution. Soon French publishers were turning out dozens of inventories and compilations of revolutionary documents, from the minutes of the revolutionary Committee of Public Instruction to the records of the 1789 Estates-General.[27] Now the documents of both the Revolution and the Old Regime were "public" information.

Although *chartistes* played a crucial role in designing the 1874 circular and although a number of them (including the indefatigable Alexandre Tuetey) devoted countless hours to the organization and publication of revolutionary documents, the Third Republic's push to recover the archival vestiges of the French Revolution was led for the most part not by *chartistes* but by professional historians.[28] Of course, this had been the case with earlier state archival campaigns, such as the Orleanist investigations of the archives of the medieval bourgeoisie. What was different in the 1880s was that the historians leading the campaign increasingly worked to cast the

---

[26] Gal. de Chabaud de la Tour (Le Ministre de l'Intérieur). "Circulaire [with marginal heading: "Archives départementales. Instruction pour le classement des séries L et Q"]," Paris, 11 Nov. 1874, AN, box F17-4024.

[27] See footnote 16 above, as well as Keylor, *Academy*.

[28] Krakovitch, "Les chartistes." The key exception here is Etienne Charavay (class of 1869), member of the Historical Works Committee's commission and co-founder of the Société d'histoire de la Révolution. See Maurice Tourneux, "Etienne Charavay: sa vie et ses travaux," *La Révolution française* 38 (Mar. 1900).

graduates of the Ecole des Chartes as professionally unprepared for and personally unsuited to the task at hand. The most biting criticism of the school came from none other than the holder of the new Sorbonne chair in the history of the revolution, Alphonse Aulard. In an 1887 article on the archives of the southwest, Aulard reported that despite the 1874 circular, hardly any of the archives he had visited had inventories for Series L, and those inventories that did exist were full of mistakes. "How are such errors possible?" he asked, replying: "the archivists, as I was aware, and as I saw, are all educated and zealous. But, with few exceptions, they are educated about the Middle Ages, zealous about the Middle Ages." The young graduates of the Ecole des Chartes, trained on cartularies, diplomas, and charters, had neither the preparation nor the inclination to evaluate the archives of the 1790s. Unless the Ecole's curriculum was drastically revamped, departmental archivists would continue to "fail seriously in their duties" to historical study.[29]

A number of *chartistes* worked to defend themselves against such attacks, especially when, during the Dreyfus Affair, the anti-Dreyfusard camp claimed that the *chartistes* testifying for the defense did not know enough about contemporary documents to evaluate the famous *bordereau*; and when, in 1906, Aulard stepped up his accusations by describing *chartistes* themselves—not just their studies—as "not very modern."[30] Graduates of the school and their supporters pointed out that both the Ecole's curriculum and a number of recently submitted student theses dealt with the post-medieval period, up to and including the years of the French Revolution.[31] The Professional Association of French Archivists, founded in 1905,

---

[29] F[rançois]-A[lphonse] Aulard, *Les archives révolutionnaires du sud-ouest: Landes, Basses et Hautes-Pyrénées, Gers, Haute-Garonne, Tarn, Lot, Tarn-et-Garonne, Lot-et-Garonne, Gironde* (Paris: Charavay Frères, 1888), pp. 8-9 and 45-46; first published in *La Révolution française* 13 (14 Dec. 1887).

[30] For a fascinating discussion of the participation of *chartistes* in the Dreyfus Affair (*chartistes* were called to serve as experts on both sides), see Bertrand Joly, "L'Ecole des Chartes et l'Affaire Dreyfus," *BEC* 147 (1989): 611-671. A[lphonse] Aulard, "Chartistes et archivistes," *Revue internationale de l'enseignement* 51 (15 May 1906): 414; first published in *L'Aurore* (16 Apr. 1906). For a similar attack on the school, this time by one of Aulard's most famous students, see Albert Mathiez, "Le classement et l'inventaire des archives départementales," *Revue d'histoire moderne* 9 (1907-1908): 72-83.

[31] On the changes in the school's curriculum to include the revolutionary period, see for example Eugène Lelong, *Célestin Port, 1828-1901* (Angers: Germain et G. Grassin, 1902), pp. 84-85.

prepared a "list of works on the revolutionary and contemporary period, published by Archivist-Paleographers."[32]Nevertheless, however caricatural, the image of the *chartiste* as a medieval specialist with little interest in modern documents seemed to stick. Thus as the Third Republic began to put aside the Old Regime collections seized during the French Revolution—long the obsession of the national government—and to confront the collections produced by the Revolution itself, it was less likely to channel these efforts through the Ecole des Chartes.

In the twentieth century, the development of French archives and libraries remained closely connected to changes in national politics, as the prolonged debates about the new National Library at Tolbiac and the bitter conflicts over the archives of the Vichy regime can attest. Yet the idea that the books and documents nationalized in the 1790s offered the key to national unity and political stability had come and gone. And the state school charged with locating, classifying, and publicizing those materials, the Ecole des Chartes, had taken its place among the many other institutions now devoted to archival and library research. As the French state confronted a new set of political dilemmas, it would find new ways of putting its library and archival collections in order.

---

[32] Association Amicale Professionnelle des Archivistes Français, *Etat des travaux sur l'époque révolutionnaire et contemporaine, publiés par des archivistes-paléographes étant ou ayant été en fonctions dans les divers services d'archives* (n.p., May 1906). For other defenses of the school, see for example Ferdinand Lot, "Chartistes et archivistes," *Revue internationale de l'enseignement* 51 (15 May 1906): 415-420; and, interestingly, Monod, "La situation."

Manuscript Sources

Ecole nationale des chartes, Paris
Archives de l'Ecole des chartes [unprocessed]:

Folder "Ecole des Chartes. établie près les Archives du Royaume...."
Three folders of notes taken by Pierre Marot in preparation for a
history of the school [apparently never completed]:
    1. "L'Ecole des Chartes."
    2. "Ecole: Histoire."
    3. "Maugard."
Volumes:
    1. "Ecole royale des Chartes. Section de la Bibliothèque du Roi.
Registre contenant les ordonnances et reglemens [sic] relatifs à
l'Ecole; et servant à l'Inscription des Elèves, 1830-1847."
    2. "Ecole des Chartes. Conseil de Perfectionnement. 1847-1867."
    3. "Ecole des Chartes. Conseil de Perfectionnement. Procès
Verbaux. 1847-1864."
    4. "Ecole des Chartes. Conseil de Perfectionnement. Procès
Verbaux. 1864-1876."
    5. "Correspondance; Arrêtés ministériels; papiers divers relatifs à
l'Ecole Nationale des Chartes. 1847, etc."
    6. "Bourses d'élèves. 1847-1866."
    7. "Traitement des professeurs. 1847-1867."
    8. "Conseil de Perfectionnement [de l'Ecole des Chartes]. Registre
d'inscriptions des candidats, 1845-?."

Archives nationales, Paris
On the Ecole des Chartes:

AF IV 1289, d. 74, 75, 77. Secrétairerie d'état Impériale. Ministère de
l'Intérieur. Mesures proposées pour encourager les lettres. Rapport
et pièces relatifs aux encouragemens [sic] accordés aux lettres, 2
avril 1807.
D XXXVIII 2, d. 20. Comité d'instruction publique. [Mémoire sur
l'enseignement relatif aux Chartes], n.d.

F17-1144, d. 2, pièces 224-225. Présidence du Conseil des Ministres, 1821.

F17-2933s through 3014. Missions, [including those by *chartistes* Roziere, Mas Latrie, Guessard, Bastard, Montaiglon, Certain, Delisle, Delpit, Vallet de Viriville, Boutaric, and Marchegay].

F17-3250 through 3297. Travaux historiques et scientifiques. Publications [folders on *chartistes* ca. 1834-1875].

F17-4024 and 4025. Ecole des Chartes. Organisation et enseignement. Budget.

F17-4026 through 4035. Ecole des Chartes. Dépenses, 1821-1872.

F17-4044 and 4045. Ecole des Chartes. Traitements d'expectative des archivistes-paléographes, 1847-1873; Indemnités diverses, 1835-1898.

F17-4046 through 4048. Ecole des chartes. Personnel, 1821-1894 [actually through 1900].

F17-4049 and 4050. Ecole des chartes. Promotions, 1847-1900.

F17-4051. Ecole des Chartes. Thèses, 1848-1898.

F17-4052 and 4053. Ecole des Chartes. Archivistes départementaux, 1829-1900.

F17-13554. Demandes de création de chaires, Collège de France, an XII-1900, folder "Projet de décret pour ajouter au Collège de france une Ecole Spéciale de Géographie et d'histoire, 1807."

F17-13606. Ecole des chartes. Organisation, règlements, décrets, et arrêtés, 1846-1932.

M257B, Folders 1 and 2. Travaux de la Commission de l'Ecole des Chartes, 1823-1839.

On the Société de l'Ecole des Chartes:

11 AS 1. Statuts de la Société, 1839-1921.

11 AS 2. Vie de la Société. Registres de déliberations, procès-verbaux des séances, 1839-1940.

11 AS 3. Réunions de la Société, 1839- .

11 AS 11. Correspondance, 1839- .

11 AS 17, d. 1. Legs de Vallet de Viriville, 1908.

11 AS 22. Elèves.

On state archives:

AB I 1. Lois, décrets et arrêtés relatifs à l'organisation et à l'administration des Archives, 1789-1860.

AB II 9 through 16. Correspondance administrative des Archives du Royaume, 1816-1870.

AB III 1. Ordres, instructions et notes de service des gardes et directeurs généraux des Archives, 1791-1940.

AB IV^A 1. Archives nationales. Personnel, 1789-1914 [selected folders].

AB IV^B 1 and 2. Archives nationales. Personnel, demandes d'emploi, 1790-1852 [selected folders].

AB IV^C 1 through 9. Archives nationales. Personnel [selected folders].

AB V^A 1^a. Pièces relatives aux travaux executés au Palais des Archives à l'Ile des Cygnes et à l'hôtel de Soubise...; rapport présenté à l'empereur en l'an XIII; rapports adressés au garde général des Archives en 1893. An XIII-1815, 1893.

AB V^A 5 through 10. Archives nationales, Pièces et dossiers divers, an XIII-1900.

AB V^A 4*. Code des Archives, 1789-1830.

AB V^C 2*. Bureau du Triage des Titres, an VIII. Tableaux Systématiques des Archives, 1811, 1827, 1831.

AB V^F 1. Notes et rapports relatifs aux archives départementales, communales et hospitalières en général et à quelques dépôts d'archives départementales et communales en particulier, 1792-1860.

AB V^F 1*. Tableau de situation des Dépôts d'archives des départements de l'ancienne France, au 1er novembre 1812, contenant les réponses aux 16 questions adressées aux préfets par la circulaire ministérielle du 22 septembre.

AB VI 1. Etats des archives et rapports sur les archives présentés par les gardes généraux, 1791-1854. Rapports des directeurs généraux, 1857-1888.

AB VII 1*. Archives de l'Empire. Procès-verbaux des Conférences du Directeur général avec les Chefs de Section, 1857-1864.

AB VIII 1. Comptes rendus et états de travail, an IV-an XII, 1816-1833.

AB IX 1 through 3. Archives nationales, section historique, rapports mensuels, an VII - 1872.

AB XII 1. Inventaires et notes concernant la série AB, 1835-1940.

AB XII 4. Musée des Archives, 1861-1891.

AB XVI 1. Pièces relatives au classement général des Archives, an XIII-1869.

AB XVII 1 and 2. Archives nationales, publications, an VI-1855 [actually thru 1913].

AB XIX 540. Papers of Eugène de Rozière.

AB XX 1. Reglementation et Police de la Salle du Public [des Archives nationales], 1856-1957.

AB XXV 1 through 4. Organisation, Règlement des Archives, 1856-1897.

AB XXVI 1. Commission supérieure des Archives, 1860-1923 [actually 1874-1923]

AB XXVI 1* through 3* Commission des Archives départementales et communales. Procès-verbaux, 1841-1854.

AB XXVI 4*. Commission supérieure des Archives départementales, communales et hospitalières. Procès verbaux des séances, 1874-1879 [registers 5 and 6 appear to be missing].

AB XXVI 3. Commission des archives, 1854-1935.

AB XXXI 15. Archives de France. Relations avec les services administratifs. Rapports généraux sur les archives, 1866-1923.

AB XXXI 41. Circulaires de la direction des Archives de France: collection chronologique, 1792-1869.

AB XXXI 50. Circulaires de la direction des Archives de France: préparation et exécution (classement chronologique), 1854-1876.

AB XXXI 207. Organisation et fonctionnement de la D.A.F. et des services d'archives territoriaux. Bureau des archives départementales, communales et hospitalières..., 1854-191?.

AB XXXI 230. Archives départementales. Archivistes départementaux, nominations et traitements: correspondance, circulaires, divers, 1852-1923.

BB 17a 75, folder 19bis, Ch. Choisnard to Monsieur, Paris, 13 Aug. 1830.

F1a 590-592[1]. Archives du Ministère de l'Intérieur, Archives nationales, Archives diverses, 1790-1824.

F1a 593. Archives du Ministère de l'Intérieur, Archives nationales, Archives diverses, 1792-1798.

F1a 596. Archives du ministère de l'Intérieur, Archives nationales, Archives diverses, 1819-1839.

F2 I 166-353. Archival inventories [by department], ca. 1840-1900 [selected volumes only].

F2 I 367[1] through 377[12]. Archives départementales, communales et hospitalières, 1788-1889:

    367[4]. Allier, 1795-1877.

    367[12]. Aube, 1791-1872.

    367[13]. Aube, 1863-1884 [actually 1839-1884].

    371[5]. Indre-et-Loire, 1794-1882.

    371[9]. Jura, 1857-1877.

    371[10]. Jura, 1854-1873 [actually 1840-1873].

    372[12]. Lot-et-Garonne, 1796-1873.

    373[1]. Maine-et-Loire, 1791-1877.

    374[4]. Nièvre, 1793-1871.

    374[5]. Nièvre, 1839-1877.

    374[10]. Oise, 1792-1873.

    376[10]. Seine-et-Oise, 1796-1871.

    376[11]. Seine-et-Oise, 1840-1877 [actually [1839-1877].

    376[12]. Seine-et-Oise, 1842-1884.

F2 I 378[2]: Archives départementales. Personnel et divers, 1853-1879.

F2 I 378[3]. Archives départementales. Affaires diverses. Inventaires, 1856-1881.

F2 I 378[4]. Archives départementales. Recherches, correspondance, 1849-1877.

F2 I 378[5]. Archives départementales. Recherches, 1854-1882.

F2 I 378[9]. Inspection générale, 1854-1886.

F2 I 378[10]. Archives départementales. Inspection des archives. 1854-1873.

F2 I 378[15]. Archives départementales. Ensemble du service, 1845-1879 [actually 1820-1879].

F2 I 1579 through 1692. Archives départementales, communales et hospitalières, 1840-1900:

    1581. Allier, 1861-1900.

    1591. Aube, 1843-1900.

    1592. Aube, 1853-1900.

    1638. Maine-et-Loire, 1840-1900 [actually 1839-1900].

[for the remaining departments in my study, this sub-series contained only documents from after ca. 1870 or documents duplicated in other depositories]

F17-13540. Archives nationales. Organisation: lois, décrets, arrêtés, règlements, 1790-1870.

F17-13541. Archives nationales, 1790-1892 [primarily 1851-1869].

F17-13544 and 13545. Archives nationales. Recherches, communications. Inventaires des archives des ministères, 1853-1881.

On public libraries:

F1a 632. Bibliothèques municipales, scolaires, populaires, militaires, 1850-1877.

F17-1206. Dépôts littéraires et bibliothèques, 1790-1830.

F17*-2219. Commission de publication des documents historiques inedits relatifs à la Révolution de 1789, 1886-1891.

F17*-3243. Notes sur les Bibliothèques publiques de France. Tome 2. 1853- 1854.

F17-3340. Service général des bibliothèques. Textes législatifs, Circulaires, Arretés concernant l'organisation des bibliothèques, 1828-1900.

F17-3341. Service Général des bibliothèques. Copies des pièces concernant la formation des bibliothèques, 1789-1794.

F17-3342. Service Général des bibliothèques. Copies des pièces concernant la formation des bibliothèques, 1795-1815.

F17-3343 and 3344. Service Général des bibliothèques. Administration, ca. 1832-1910.

F17-3427. Catalogue général des manuscrits des bibliothèques de France, 1841-1888.

F17-3436. Service Général des bibliothèques. Echanges, 1861-1887.

F17-3346. Service des bibliothèques, 1859-1870 [actually 1853-1870].

F17-3348. Commission des archives et des bibliothèques, 1904-1906.

F17-3350. Inspection générale des bibliothèques, 1870-1913.

F17-3456. Organisation et règlements de la Bibliothèque nationale, 1832-1891.

F17-3458. Bibliothèque nationale. Organisation. Administration générale, 1790-1895.

F17-3459 and 3460. Bibliothèque nationale. Personnel. Rapports, 1830-1905.

F17-3461. Procès-verbaux du Conservatoire [de la Bibliothèque nationale], 1838-1845.

F17-3473. Bibliothèque nationale. Catalogues, 1798-1898.

F17-3476 and 3477. Bibliothèques publiques de Paris. Organisation, 1828-1900.

F17-13504. Bibliothèque nationale. Organisation, 1832-1914.

F17-13514. Bibliothèque de l'Arsenal, 1815-1930, folder "Classement des Archives de la Bastille."

On the Académie des Inscriptions:

F17-3601. Organisation, Affaires diverses, 1816-1892.

F17-3602. Publications.

F17-3603. Instructions pour des missions; Prix, legs, 1821-1872.

Archives nationales, Paris—Section contemporaine
Archives de l'Ecole des chartes, materials in-process:
Note: the "supplément" to Série B described in the typescript summary of this collection appears to be missing.

Série B:
1. Teulet, Alexandre. "Cours de l'Ecole des Chartes. Années 1831-1832. Alexandre Teulet. 1er élève pensionnaire."
2. Géraud, H[ercule]. "Résumé du cours du Diplomatique de M. Guérard.   Notes diverses." [1836-41?].
6. Pannier, Léopold. "Ecole des Chartes. Cours de Mr. J. Quicherat. 21 nov 1866 [and from other end of notebook:] Cours de M. Vallet de Viriville. 9 Juillet 67."
28. Correspondance de Léon Lacabane.
29. Notes ayant servi au cours professé par Léon Lacabane en troisième année   de l'Ecole des chartes.
103. Correspondance officielle adressée à Jules Quicherat.
106. Papiers provenant d'Anatole de Montaiglon. Notes pour son cours de Bibliographie.
174. Lettre de J. A. Letronne, Garde général des Archives et Directeur de l'Ecole des chartes, à Victor Hugo (Paris, 10 novembre 1848).

Unnumbered boxes:
Gautier, Léon. "Cours de diplomatique pontificale professé à l'Ecole des chartes, 1862."

Gautier, Léon. "Cours de diplomatique nationale professé à l'Ecole des
Chartes, 1869-1871." 2 vols.

Papers of Auguste Vallet de Viriville.

Archives départementales de l'Allier, Moulins

T 1015 (2). Lettres d'A. Chazaud au préfet, 1860-1874.

T 1020. Correspondance, circulaires, 1819-1891.

T 1021. Divers, 1809-1880.

3 J. Fonds Alphonse Chazaud.

Archives départementales de l'Aube, Troyes

3 T 19. Série B. Rapport adressé par M. de Stadler au garde général
des archives au sujet des papiers déposés dans les greniers des
prisons de Troyes (sans date).

3 T 32. Correspondance [des archives départementales], 1808-1840
[actually through 1929].

3 T 33. Correspondance [des archives départementales], 1841-1852.

3 T 34. Correspondance [des archives départementales], 1853-1880.

3 T 97. Inventaire du fonds de Montier-la-Celle par Philippe Guignard.

3 T 131 and 231 [in same box]. Circulaires et instructions, 1790-1919.

Archives départementales de l'Indre-et-Loire, Tours

T 1393. Rapports annuels, comptes rendus, et correspondance [des
archives départementales] avec la Direction des Archives de
France, 1856-1952.

T 1395. Rapports annuels…, 1843-1888 [actually through 1867].

T 1396. Rapports annuels…, 1868-1888.

T 1399. Sous-archivistes, archivistes, dossiers individuels, 1894-1922.

T 1620. Rapports annuels…, 1819-1939.

T 1623. Dossier Seytre. Vols de documents, procès, 1841-1943.

T 1624. Rapports annuels…, 1863-1937.

T 1627. Rapports annuels de l'archiviste à M. le Préfet, 1816-1888.

T 1628. Inspections générales. Rapports des inspecteurs, 1854-1923.

T 1629. Généralités (an V-1939). Correspondance (1861-1865).
Personnel…Nominations d'archivistes (1842-1943).

T 1631. Demandes de recherches et correspondance, 1840-1900
[actually 1806-1938].

8 F 9/2. Fonds Grandmaison. Famille Loizeau de Grandmaison.
Correspondance de Charles de Grandmaison vers 1850-1900.
Correspondance avec A. de Tocqueville [1854-1856].

Archives départementales de l'Isère, Grenoble
Fonds Champollion:
  30. Administration de l'Ecole royale des chartes, 1821-1837.
  31. Administration de l'Ecole royale des chartes, 1838-1867.
  57. Travaux historiques, 1831-1839.

Archives départementales du Lot-et-Garonne, Agen
3 T 1. Archives départementales. Instructions ministérielles, 1795, 1806-1940.
3 T 2 and 3. Archives départementales. Rapports annuels de l'archiviste, 1839-1940; Rapports d'inspection, 1841-1904.
3 T 9. Inventaires et repertoires des archives de la préfecture, 1814-1857.
15 J 2. Fonds Tholin. Lettres reçues d'érudits parisiens, 1867-1919.

Archives départementales de la Maine-et-Loire, Angers
Note: Box 384 T 1 (Personnel. Etats de situation. Rapports des inspecteurs généraux, 1790-1924) has been missing since ca. 1994.

384 T 3. Archives départementales. Rapport annuel de l'archiviste, 1841-1876 [actually through 1901].
384 T 12. Archives départementales. Correspondance. Expéditions, 1833-1931 [actually 1819-1931].

Archives départementales de la Nièvre, Nevers
Archives départementales. Rapports annuels au Préfet, 1834-1923.
Archives départementales. Rapports au Ministre et Correspondance ministérielle, 1851-1910.

Archives départementales du Rhône, Lyon
TA 37. Archives départementales. Correspondance ministérielle, 1819-1910.

Archives départementales de la Seine-et-Oise (now the Yvelines), Versailles
1 M 15. Personnel administratif [du département de Seine-et-Oise]. Archivistes et employés des archives, 1816-1929 [actually 1790-1929].
3 T/AD 1. Rapport annuel de l'archiviste départemental, 1807-1845.
3 T/AD 2. Rapport annuel de l'archiviste departemental, 1846-1859.

3 T/AD 3. Rapport annuel de l'archiviste départemental, 1870-1873 [actually 1860-1873].

3 T/AD 4. Rapport annuel de l'archiviste départemental, 1874-1890.

Archives de l'Institut de France, Paris
Archives de l'Académie des Inscriptions:
    E 6. Législation sur l'Ecole des Chartes, 1821-1829.
    E 78. Procès-verbaux, 1818-1823 [and "pièces annexes"].
    E 79. Procès-verbaux, 1824-1829.

Bibliothèque nationale de France, Département des manuscrits, Paris
Papiers et correspondance de Louis-Léon Gadebled (1812-1873):
n.a.f. 21576. Lettres de L. Gadebled à son père, de son père, de son frère et de differents membres de sa famille; à la suite, lettres de divers archivistesdépartementaux, classées par ordre alphabétique de départements.
n.a.f. 21577. Lettres diverses, classées par ordre alphabétique, parmi lesquelles on remarque des lettres de L. Bellaguet, Th. Bonnin, R. Bordeaux, H. Carnot, A. de Caumont, J. Desnoyers, H. Lefebvre Duruflé, A. Le Prevost, Letronne, Pardessus, A. Passy, Raoul Rochette, A. de Sainte- Beuve, N. de Wailly, etc.
n.a.f. 21578. Procès-verbaux de la Commission des Archives (1841-1847); minutes de L. Gadebled, secrétaire, suivies de projets d'instruction pour le classement et de règlement des archives départementales, etc.

Correspondance et papiers de Pierre-Claude-François Daunou (1761-1840):
n.a.f. 21910. Copies de chartes et pièces historiques.—Notes sur les Bibliothèques nationale, du Panthéon, des Archives nationales et sur la bibliothèque particulière de Daunou.

n.a.f. 22385. [Wey, Francis]. "Rapports sur les Archives," 1866.

Archives modernes:
    108. Administration. Organisation intérieure de la Bibliothèque nationale, 1818-1868.
    115-119. Personnel, Dossiers classés par ordre alphabétique des noms [selected folders].

122. L. Delisle, Dossiers administratifs. XIXe s. Histoire depuis la Révolution. Catalogues, prets, acquisitions. Personnel, etc.
662 and 663. Département des Manuscrits. Registres de présence du personnel des travaux historiques, 1836-1838.

Bibliothèque de l'Institut de France, Paris
Ms. 2656, d. 26, no. 7. N[atalis] De Wailly to Monsieur et cher confrère [Alfred Maury], Passy, 28 Apr. 1861.
Ms. 2061. Lettres à[Charles-Joseph] Marty-Laveaux.
Ms. 5685, d. 3. J.-M. Heredia, Cours de Lacabane, Bourquelot, Tardif, Quicherat, [n.d.].

Archives anciennes [de la Bibliothèque de l'Institut], antérieurs à 1944:
A 21. Correspondance administrative, 1839-1898.

Bibliothèque de l'Arsenal, Paris
Correspondence of Anatole de Montaiglon, boxes 7890-7893.

Bibliothèque Mazarine, Paris
Adminstrative correspondence, ca. 1851 [the year *chartiste* Hippolyte Cocheris was hired by the library].

Bibliothèque Sainte-Geneviève, Paris
Archives de la Bibliothèque, Personnel:
        XVIII. Dossier Lacour.
        XXI. Dossier Montaiglon.

Bibliothèque municipale d'Auxerre
Ms. 382. Molard, François. "Cours de Mr. Vallet de Viriville. Classement des archives et des bibliothèques. 1864-1865."

Select Bibliography

The Ecole des Chartes

"L'Académie des Inscriptions et les archivistes paléographes." *BEC* 71 (1910): 709-710.

"Actualité de l'histoire à l'Ecole des Chartes. Etudes réunies à l'occasion du cent cinquantième anniversaire de la *Bibliothèque de l'Ecole des chartes, 1839-1989*." *BEC* 147 (1989).

Alglave, Emile. "L'Ecole des Chartes et son enseignement." *Revue bleue* (18 Nov. 1865): 826-829, 842-848.

Arbois de Jubainville, H[enri] d'. *Deux manières d'écrire l'histoire: critique de Bossuet, d'Augustin Thierry et de Fustel de Coulanges*. Paris: Librairie Emile Bouillon, 1896.

"Les archivistes-paléographes dans les bibliothèques." *BEC* 66 (1905): 607-610.

Association Amicale Professionnelle des Archivistes Français. *Etat des travaux sur l'époque révolutionnaire et contemporaine, publiés par des archivistes-paléographes étant ou ayant été en fonctions dans les divers services d'archives*. N.p., May 1906.

Aulard, [Alphonse], and Ferdinand Lot. "Chartistes et archivistes." *Revue internationale de l'enseignement* 51 (15 May 1906): 412-420.

Bercé, Yves-Marie, Olivier Guyotjeannin, and Marc Smith, eds. *L'Ecole nationale des chartes: histoire de l'école depuis 1821*. Thionville, France: Gérard Klopp, 1997.

[Bordier, Henri]. *Programme de l'Ecole Nationale des Chartes. Historique de l'Ecole des Chartes. De la société de l'Ecole des Chartes. Renseignements nécessaires aux candidats. Recueil de pièces officielles. Personnel de l'Ecole et de la Société*. Paris: Chez Dumoulin et Chez Auguste Durand, 1848.

Bourgeois, Emile. "La question de l'Ecole des Chartes." *Revue bleue* 3d ser. (7 Apr. 1888): 469-471.

B., F. [Bourquelot, Félix?]. "Bibliothèque Royale. Ecoles [sic] des Chartes (Cours de M. B. Guérard)." *Gazette Spéciale de l'Instruction Publique* no. 29 (6 Dec. 1838): [1].

Carbonell, Charles-Olivier. *L'autre Champollion: Jacques-Joseph Champollion-Figéac (1778-1867)*. Toulouse: Presses de l'Institut d'études politiques de Toulouse et l'Asiathèque, 1970.

"La célébration à Poitiers du Centenaire de la Réorganisation de l'Ecole des Chartes [24 Janvier 1948]." *Annales de l'Université de Poitiers* 2d ser., no. 1 (1948): 5-18.

Célébration du Centenaire de Léopold Delisle, 24 octobre 1826-22 juillet 1910. Valognes, 7 novembre 1926. N.p., [1927?].

Cère, Emile. "L'Ecole des Chartes." *Nouvelle revue* 5 (1 Feb. 1883): 535-554.

C[hampollion]-F[igeac], A[imé]. "Ecole royale des Chartes." In *Dictionnaire de la conversation et de la lecture*, ed. W. Duckett, 331-332. Paris: Belin-Mandar, 1834.

Delpit, Martial. "Notice historique sur l'Ecole royale des chartes." *BEC* 1 (1840): 1-42.

Demante, Gabriel. "L'Ecole des chartes en 1840." *BEC* 59 (1898): 812-819.

Des Cilleuls, P. "Les origines de l'Ecole des Chartes et du Comité des travaux historiques au XVIIIe siècle." *Revue internationale de l'enseignement* 8 (1884): 394-402.

Dibdin, Thomas Fragnall. *A bibliographical, antiquarian and picturesque tour in France and Germany.* London: Printed for the author, by W. Bulmer and W. Nicol, Shakspeare Press, and sold by Payne and Foss [etc.], 1821.

"L'Ecole des Chartes de Dijon." *BEC* 83 (1922): 271.

"L'Ecole des chartes en 1831." *BEC* 92 (1931): 250-251.

Ecole Imperiale des Chartes. Liste des élèves pensionnaires et des archivistes-paléographes depuis la fondation de l'Ecole en 1821 jusqu'au 1er mai 1870. Nogent-le-Rotrou: Impr. de A. Gouverneur, [1870?].

Ecole nationale des chartes. *Centenaire de la réorganisation de l'Ecole des chartes: compte rendu de la cérémonie du 17 mai 1947.* Paris: Ecole nationale des chartes, 1947.

------. *Centenaire de l'Ecole des chartes, 1821-1921. Compte-rendu de la journée du 22 février 1921.* Paris: A l'Ecole nationale des chartes, 1921.

------. *L'Ecole des Chartes: notice et documents.* Paris: A. Picard et fils, 1913.

------. *Livret de l'Ecole des chartes, 1821-1966.* Paris: Ecole nationale des chartes, 1967.

Frédéricq, Paul. "L'enseignement supérieur de l'histoire à Paris, notes et impressions de voyage." *Revue internationale de l'enseignement* (1883): 745-752.

Gardner, Richard Kent. "Education for Librarianship in France: An Historical Survey." Ph.D. diss., Case Western Reserve University, 1968.

G[arnier], J[oseph]. "Souvenirs Bourguignons: la mésaventure d'un Conseiller au Parlement." *Le Bien Public* (30 Apr. 1893): 1.

Gautier, Léon. *Société de l'Ecole des Chartes. Cinquantième Anniversaire de notre fondation. Banquet du 13 juin 1889.* Paris: D. Dumoulin, 1889.

Giry, Arthur. "L'Ecole des Chartes." *République française*, 16 Apr. 1875, 1-3.

------. "Histoire de la Diplomatique." *Revue historique* 48, no. 1 (1892): 235-256.

Guérard, B[enjamin]. "Ecole des Chartes. Discours d'ouverture du cours de première année." *La France littéraire* 1 (1832): 268-280.

------. "Institutions et géographie de la France. Leçon d'ouverture de l'un des cours de troisième année professés à l'Ecole des chartes. Novembre 1847." *BEC* 9 (1848): 361-384.

------. "Discours prononcé par M. Guérard pour l'ouverture du cours de première année à l'Ecole des Chartes, en 1831 ou 1832." *BEC* 17 (1856): 1-9.

Guyotjeannin, Olivier. "Aperçus sur l'Ecole des Chartes au XIXe siècle." In *Erudicion y discurso historico, las instituciones europeas, s. XVIII-XIX*, ed. Gimeno Blay, 285-303. Valencia: Universitat de Valencia, 1993.

Hanotaux, Gabriel. "Au temps de l'Ecole des Chartes." In *Sur les chemins de l'histoire*. Paris: Librairie Ancienne Edouard Champion, 1924.

Isambert, [François-André]. Preface to *Recueil général des anciennes lois françaises, depuis l'an 420 jusqu'a la révolution de 1789...*, ed. [Athanase-Jean Leger] Jourdan, Decrusy, and [François-André] Isambert. Paris: Librairie de Plon Frères, 1822.

Jean-Bernard. *La vie de Paris, 1906*. Paris: Alphonse Lemerre, 1907.

Joly, Bertrand. "L'Ecole des Chartes et l'Affaire Dreyfus." *BEC* 147 (1989): 611-671.

Jubinal, Achille. "Ecole des Chartes." In *Paris pittoresque*, ed. G. Sarrut and B. Saint-Edme, 54-68. Paris: D'Urtubie, Worms et Cie., 1837.

Jullian, Camille. "L'Ecole des Chartes et notre histoire nationale." *Revue de Paris* 34 (Aug. 1927): 481-497.

L[edos], E[ugène]-G[abriel]. "Une visite à l'Ecole des Chartes (1834)." *BEC* 76 (1915): 606-612.

------. "Le cours de Benjamin Guérard à l'Ecole des Chartes en 1838." *BEC* 88 (1927): 171-174.

Leniaud, J.-M. "L'Ecole des chartes et la formation des élites (XIXe siècle)." *La Revue administrative* 46 (1993): 618-624.

Le Pottier, Jean. "Histoire et érudition: recherches et documents sur l'histoire et le rôle de l'érudition médiévale dans l'historiographie française du XIXè siècle." Thesis, Ecole nationale des chartes, 1979.

Lucien [pseud.]. "L'Ecole des chartes et la Sorbonne." *Revue politique et parlementaire* 65, no. 195 (1910): 522-529.

Mariotte, Jean-Yves. Introduction to *La Haute Savoie vers 1865*, by Henry Terry. Annecy, France: Gardet, 1977.

Marot, Pierre. *Institut de France. Académie des inscriptions et belles-lettres. A propos du IIIe centenaire de l'Académie. L'essor de l'étude des antiquités nationales à l'Institut, du Directoire à la monarchie de juillet...Lecture faite dans la séance publique annuelle du 22 novembre 1963.* Paris: n.p., 1963.

Martin, Henri-Jean "Les chartistes et les bibliothèques." *Bulletin des bibliothèques de France* 17 (1972): 529-537.

Mathiez, Albert. "Le centenaire de l'Ecole des chartes." *Annales révolutionnaires* 13 (1921): 174-175.

Ministère de l'Instruction Publique. *Ecole Royale des Chartes. Séance d'inauguration (5 mai 1847).* Paris: Impr. Paul Dupont, 1847.

Mirot, [Albert]. "L'Ecole des Chartes: des origines à nos jours." *La Montagne Ste. Geneviève et ses abords* no. 86 (Jun. 1964): 2-7.

Mollet, Vincent. "Les chartistes dans les Archives départementales avant le décret de 1850." *BEC* 151 (1993): 123-154.

Monod, Gabriel. "La situation de l'enseignement supérieur." *Revue historique* 91 (May-Aug. 1906): 307-313.

Mortet, Charles. "Le cours de bibliographie et de service des bibliothèques à l'Ecole des Chartes (1847-1920)." *BEC* 81 (1920): 76-92.

O[mont], H[enri]. "L'Ecole royale des chartes en 1832." *BEC* 88 (1927): 169-171.

[Omont, Henri]. "L'Ecole des Chartes de 1821 à 1832." *BEC* 89 (1928): 153-157.

Porée, Charles. *L'Ecole des Chartes, 1821-1921: coup d'oeil sur l'oeuvre des chartistes. Communication faite à la Société des Sciences historiques de l'Yonne, le 7 avril 1921.* Auxerre: Imprimerie coopérative "l'Universelle", 1922.

"Projet d'un enseignement historique et diplomatique à la Bibliothèque nationale sous la Convention." *BEC* 52 (1891): 353-355.

Prou, Maurice. *Allocution prononcée au banquet de la Société de l'Ecole des Chartes, le 23 mai 1907.* [Paris?]: par les soins des amis de M. Maurice Prou en souvenir de sa présidence de la Société de l'Ecole des Chartes, [1908].

------. "L'Ecole des chartes et l'histoire." *Revue internationale de l'enseignement* (1910): [1-11?].

------. "Nos grandes écoles, l'Ecole des chartes." *Revue des deux-mondes* 37 (Jan. 1927): 372-396.

[Quantin, Maximilien]. "L'Ecole des chartes de Dijon." *Bulletin historique et philologique du Comité des travaux historiques* nos. 1-2 (1887): 305-311.

Quynn, Dorothy Mackay. "The Ecole des Chartes." *American Archivist* 13, no. 3 (1950): 271-283.

Samaran, Ch[arles]. "A propos du premier numéro de la 'Bibliothèque de l'Ecole des chartes' (1839)." *BEC* 102 (1941): 318-328.

------. "Le centenaire de notre revue, la 'Bibliothèque de l'Ecole des chartes' depuis un siècle," *BEC* 100 (1939): 257-280.

------. "L'école des Chartes et les Chartistes." *La Revue de la Semaine illustrée* no. 8 (25 Feb. 1921): 443-457.

Société de l'Ecole des chartes. *L'Ecole des chartes et la Guerre (1914-1918): Livre d'Or, orné de 51 portraits.* Paris: n.p., 1921.

Vallet de Viriville, A[uguste]. *L'Ecole des Chartes. Son passé, son état présent,—son avenir.* Paris: Ch. Schiller, 1867.

------. "Notes et documents pour servir à l'histoire de l'Ecole royale des chartes." *BEC* 9 (1848): 153-176.

Archives

Arbois de Jubainville, Henri d'. *Voyage paléographique dans le département de l'Aube. Rapport à M. le préfet sur une inspection faite en 1854 dans les archives communales et hospitalières du département.* Paris: A. Durand, 1855.

Archives de l'Empire. *Inventaires et Documents publiés par ordre de l'Empereur sous la direction de M. le Marquis de Laborde, Directeur Général des Archives de l'Empire, Membre de l'Institut: Inventaire Général Sommaire des Archives de l'Empire.* Paris: Imprimerie Impériale, 1867.

Aulard, F[rançois]-A[lphonse]. *Les archives révolutionnaires du sud-ouest: Landes, Basses et Hautes-Pyrénées, Gers, Haute-Garonne, Tarn, Lot, Tarn-et-Garonne, Lot-et-Garonne, Gironde.* Paris: Charavay Frères, 1888. First published in *La Révolution française* 13 (14 Dec. 1887).

Babelon, Jean-Pierre, ed. *Centenaire du Musée de l'Histoire de France: l'oeuvre du Marquis de Laborde aux Archives nationales.* Paris: Archives nationales, 1968.

Barthélemy, Anatole de. "Archives de l'Empire, Inventaires et documents, premier article (Collection des sceaux, par M. Douët Darcq, première partie, t. Ier, Impr. imp.)." *Revue archéologique* 7 (1863): 241.

Bartlett, Nancy. "*Respect des Fonds*: The Origins of the Modern Archival Principle of Provenance." In *Bibliographical Foundations of French Historical Studies*, ed. Lawrence McCrank, 107-115. New York: Haworth Press, 1991.

Baudot, Marcel. "Les archives municipales dans la France de l'ancien régime." *Archivum* 13 (1963): 23-30.

Bautier, R[obert]-H[enri]. "La phase cruciale de l'histoire des archives, la constitution des dépôts d'archives et la naissance de l'archivistique, XVIe-début XIXe siècles." *Archivum* 18 (1968): 139-150.

Beaucourt, G. de. "Musée et l'inventaire sommaire des archives." *Revue des questions historiques* 13 (1873): 272-273.

Bernard, Gildas. *Guide des Archives départementales de l'Aube*. Troyes: Impr. de la Renaissance, 1967.

Bloch, Camille. *Le Classement de la Série Q (Domaines) des Archives départementales*. Paris: Au Siège de la Société [de l'histoire de la révolution française], 1916.

Bordier, Henri. *Les archives de la France, ou l'histoire des Archives de l'Empire, des Archives des Ministères, des départements, des communes, des hôpitaux, des greffes, des notaires, etc., contenant l'inventaire d'une partie de ces dépôts*. Paris: Dumoulin, 1855.

------. *Les inventaires des Archives de l'Empire. Réponse à M. le marquis de Laborde, Directeur général, contenant un errata pour ses préfaces et ses inventaires*. Paris: Librairie Bachelin-Deflorenne, 1867.

Bourgin, Georges. "Alphonse Aulard et les archives." *Cahiers d'histoire de la Révolution française* (1955): 78-80.

------. "Quelques textes sur Daunou, garde des archives." *BEC* 102 (1941): 318-328.

Boutaric, E[dgard]. "Les Archives de l'Empire: A propos d'un rapport de M. F. Ravaisson." *BEC* 24 (1863): 252-264.

Burias, J. *Guide des Archives de Lot-et-Garonne*. Agen: n.p., 1972.

Champollion-Figeac, Aimé. *Annuaire de l'Archiviste des préfectures, des mairies et des hospices…pour faire suite au Manuel de l'Archiviste….* Paris: 1862-1866.

------. *Manuel de l'archiviste des préfectures, des mairies et des hospices; contenant les lois, décrets, ordonnances, règlements, circulaires et instructions relatifs au service des archives; des renseignements pratiques pour leur éxecution et pour la rédaction des inventaires; et précédé d'une introduction historique sur les archives publiques anciennes et modernes*. Paris: Imprimerie et librairie administratives de Paul Dupont, 1860.

------. "Notice sur les archives départementales de France." *Bulletin de l'Académie Delphinale* 21 (1886): 179-209.

Charpy, Jacques. "Les archives en révolution: les premières années des Archives départementales d'Ille-et-Vilaine, 1789-1802." *Bulletin et mémoires de la Société archéologique du département d'Ille-et-Vilaine* 93 (1991): 33-60.

------. "Les premiers archivistes du Finistère et la formation des archives départementales (1790-1851)." *Bulletin de la Société archéologique du Finistère* 93 (1967): 215-272.

Combe, Sonia. *Archives interdites: les peurs françaises face à l'histoire contemporaine*. Paris: Albin Michel, 1994.

Commission des archives départementales et communales. *Tableau général numérique par fonds des archives départementales antérieures à 1790.* Paris: Imprimerie Nationale, 1848.

Courteault, H[enri]. Appendix to *Les Archives nationales de 1902 à 1936.* Paris: Didier, 1939.

Cuer, Georges. "Les archives départementales ont 200 ans." *Mémoires de la Société d'Emulation du Jura* (1996).

Daniels, Maygene F., and Timothy Walch, eds. *A Modern Archives Reader: Basic Readings on Archival Theory and Practice.* Washington, D.C.: National Archives and Records Service and the U.S. General Services Administration, 1984.

D., L. [Delisle, Léopold?]. Review of *La Bibliothèque Impériale et les Archives de l'Empire. Réponse au rapport de M. Ravaisson,* by Natalis de Wailly *BEC* 24 (1863): 350-352.

Delsalle, Paul. "L'archivistique sous l'ancien régime, le trésor, l'arsenal, et l'histoire." *Histoire, Economie, et Société* 12, no. 4 (1993): 447-472.

Derrida, Jacques. *Archive Fever: A Freudian Impression.* Trans. Eric Prenowitz. Chicago: University of Chicago Press, 1995. Originally published as *Mal d'archive: une impression freudienne.* [Paris]: Editions Galilée, 1994.

Dessalles, [Léon]. "Archives du Royaume." *Paris pittoresque,* ed. G. Sarrut and B. Saint-Edme, 278-298. Paris: D'Uturbie, Worms et Cie., 1837.

------. *Le Trésor des chartes, sa création, ses gardes et leur travaux, depuis l'origine jusqu'en 1582....* Paris: Imprimerie royale, 1844.

De Wailly, Natalis. *La Bibliothèque Impériale et les Archives de l'Empire. Réponse au rapport de M. Ravaisson.* Paris: Imprimerie de Ad. R. Lainé et J. Havard, 1863.

Direction des Archives. *Lois, décrets, arrêtés, règlements relatifs 1. aux Archives nationales, 2. aux Archives départementales.* Paris: Imprimerie Nationale, 1905.

[Duchâtel, Tanneguy]. *Rapport au Roi sur les archives départementales et communales.* Paris: Imprimerie Royale, May 1841.

Duchein, Michel. "L'accès aux archives en France de messidor an II à janvier 1979: libéralisme et frilosités." In *Histoires d'archives: recueil d'articles offert à Lucie Favier par ses collègues et amis,* 59-69. Paris: Société des amis des Archives de France, 1997.

------. "Archives, archivistes, archivistique: définitions et problématique." In *La pratique archivistique française,* ed. Jean Favier, 19-39. Paris: Archives nationales, 1993.

------. "Les bâtiments d'archives départementales en France." *Archivum* 6 (1956): 108-176.

------. "La clef du trésor. L'évolution des instruments de recherche d'archives du Moyen Age à nos jours d'après des exemples français." *Archives et bibliothèques de Belgique (Miscellanea Carlos Wyffels)* 57, nos. 1-2 (1986): 109-126.

------. "The history of European archives and the development of the archival profession in Europe." *American Archivist* 55, no. 1 (1992): 14-25.

------. "Le respect des fonds en archivistique: principes théoriques et problèmes pratiques." *Gazette des Archives* 97 (1977): 71-96.

------. "La Révolution française et les archives: la mémoire et l'oubli dans l'imaginaire républicain." *Mémoires de la commission départementale des monuments historiques du Pas-de-Calais* 25 (1987) [also published as *Liber amicorum: études historiques offertes à Pierre Bougard*. Arras: [Conseil général du Pas-de-Calais], 1987], pp. 261-265.

Duclert, V. "Archives politiques et politiques d'archives sous la IIIe République." *Jean Jaurès: Cahiers trimestriels* no. 135 (Jan. 1995): 11-19.

Farge, Arlette. *Le goût de l'archive*. Paris: Editions du Seuil, 1989.

Favier, Jean, and Lucie Favier. *Archives nationales: quinze siècles d'histoire*. Paris: Editions Nathan, 1988.

Funck-Brentano, Frantz. *Catalogue des manuscrits de la Bibliothèque de l'Arsenal, Tome Neuvième: Archives de la Bastille*. Paris: Librairie Plon, 1892.

[Gadebled, Louis-Léon]. "Notes sur les archives départementales et communales." *Bulletin de la Société de l'histoire de France* (Mar.-Oct. 1848).

Gautier, Léon. "Le musée des Archives de l'Empire. Discours d'ouverture." *BEC* 29 (1868): 513-527.

G[éraud], H[ercule]. "De l'organisation projétée des archives départementales." *BEC* 2 (1841): 499-505.

Grandmaison, Charles de. *Alexis de Tocqueville en Touraine: Préparation du livre sur l'ancien régime, Juin 1853-Avril 1854, Notes et souvenirs intimes*. Paris: Librairie Nouvelle, 1893.

------. *Notice historique sur les archives du département d'Indre-et-Loire*. Tours: Imprimerie Ladevèze, 1855.

Guyotjeannin, Olivier. "Les premières années des archives départementales françaises (1796-1815)." In *Les archives en Europe vers 1800: les communications présentées dans le cadre de la journée d'études du même nom aux Archives générales du Royaume à Bruxelles le 24 octobre 1996*. Miscellanea Archivistica Studia, no. 103. Brussels: Archives générales du royaume et archives de l'état dans les provinces, 1998.

Herr, Richard. "The Archives of Touraine." In *Tocqueville and the Old Regime*. Princeton: Princeton University Press, 1962.

Hildesheimer, Françoise. *Les Archives de France: Mémoire de l'Histoire*. Paris: Honoré Champion, 1997.

------. "Les Archives nationales au XIXe siècle: établissement scientifique ou administratif?" *Histoire et Archives* 1 (1997): 106-135.

------. *Les archives...Pourquoi? Comment? La recherche aujourd'hui dans les archives en France*. Paris: Editions de l'érudit, 1984.

------. "Echec aux Archives: la difficile affirmation d'une administration." *BEC* 156 (1998): 91-106.

------. "Périodisation et archives." In *Périodes. La construction du temps historique. Actes du Ve colloque d'histoire au présent*, 39-46. Paris: Editions de l'Ecole des Hautes Etudes en Sciences Sociales et Histoire au Présent, 1991.

------. "Les premières publications des Archives." In *Histoire de France, historiens de la France: actes du colloque international, Reims, 14 et 15 mai 1993*, ed. Yves Bercé and Philippe Contamine, 281-299. Paris: Société de l'histoire de France, 1994.

------. "Des triages au respect des fonds: les archives en France sous la monarchie de Juillet." *Revue historique* 286, no. 2 (1991): 295-312.

Krakovitch, Odile. "La découverte des sources révolutionnaires il y a cent ans: les inventaires et collections de documents sur la Révolution publiés à l'occasion du Centenaire." *Gazette des archives* 148 (1990): 157-177.

L., J. A. "Les archives départementales." *Revue archéologique* 10 (1854): 747-752.

Laborde, H[enri]-François de. *Etude sur la constitution du Trésor des chartes et sur les origines de la série des sacs dite aujourd'hui Supplément du Trésor des chartes*. Paris: Plon-Nourrit, 1909.

Laborde, [Léon] le Marquis de. *Les Archives de la France: leurs vicissitudes pendant la Révolution, leur régénération sous l'Empire*. Paris: Vve. Renouard, 1867.

------. *Les Archives de la France pendant la Révolution. Introduction à l'inventaire du fonds d'archives dit les monuments historiques*. Paris: Imprimerie de J. Claye, 1866.

Lelong, E[ugène]. *Célestin Port, 1828-1901*. Angers: Germain et G. Grassin, 1902.

Lemoine, H[enri]. *Les Archives de Seine-et-Oise de 1790 à 1888*. Versailles: Imprimerie Coopérative "La Gutenberg," 1938.

Levron, Jacques. "Les archives de Seine-et-Oise de 1790 à 1967." *Bulletin de la Commission des antiquités et des arts* 59 (1967): 101-122.

Luce, Siméon. "De l'utilité matérielle et pratique, de l'importance historique et scientifique, de la portée morale et sociale des travaux d'archives: à propos d'un discours de Son Exc. M. le comte de Persigny." *BEC* 24 (1863): 237-251.

Mahieu, Bernard. "Les inventaires d'archives selon Michelet." *Gazette des archives* 16 (1954): 16-22.

------. "Michelet aux Archives nationales." *Annuaire-Bulletin de la Société de l'histoire de France* (1946-1947): 71-86.

Maras, Raymond J. "Napoleon's Quest for a Super-Archival Center in Paris." *Consortium on Revolutionary Europe, 1750-1850: Selected Papers* (1994): 567-578.

Marchegay, Paul. *Archives d'Anjou, recueil de documents et mémoires inédits sur cette province*. Angers: Charles Labussière, 1843.

------. *Rapport sur les archives de la préfecture de Maine et Loire*. Angers: n.p., 14 Aug. 1841.

Maréchal, Michel. *Guide des Archives de l'Allier*. Yzeure: Département de l'Allier, Direction des services d'archives, 1991.

Mathiez, Albert. "Le classement et l'inventaire des archives départementales." *Revue d'histoire moderne* 9 (1908): 72-83.

Ministère de l'instruction publique et des beaux-arts. *Lois, instructions et règlements relatifs aux Archives départementales, communales et hospitalières*. Paris: H. Champion, 1884.

Ministère de l'Intérieur. *Archives Départementales, Communales et Hospitalières. Bibliothèques Administratives. Recueil des lois et instructions qui régissent le service*. Paris: Imprimerie Administrative de Paul Dupont, 1860.

Mollet, Vincent. "Les archives départementales du Tarn de 1790 à 1946: constitution et mise en valeur d'un patrimoine écrit." Thesis, Ecole nationale des chartes, 1992.

Montgomery, Frances E. "Tribunes, Napoleon, and the Archives Nationales." *Consortium on Revolutionary Europe, 1750-1850, Selected Papers* 19, no. 1 (1989): 437-459.

Morand, François. *Lettres à Augustin Thierry et autres documents relatifs à un projet de Constitution des Archives communales, proposée en 1838 et années suivantes*. Paris: J.-B. Dumoulin, 1877.

Moranvillé, H[enri], and H[enry?] Faye. *Ch. de Grandmaison (1824-1903)*. Tours: Imprimerie Paul Bousrez, 1904.

Musée des Archives nationales, documents originaux de l'histoire de France exposés dans l'Hotel Soubise, ouvrage enrichi de 1,200 fac-simile des autographes les plus importants depuis l'époque mérovingienne jusqu'à la révolution française. Paris: Henri Plon, 1872.

Nora, Pierre. "Archives et construction d'une histoire nationale: le cas français." In *Les Arabes par leurs archives (XVIe-XXe siècles)*, ed. Jacques Berque and Dominique Chevallier, 323-332. Paris: Editions du Centre national de la recherche scientifique, 1976.

Nougaret, Christine. "Classement et description: des principes à la pratique." In *La pratique archivistique française*, ed. Jean Favier, 135-186. Paris: Archives nationales, 1993.

------. "De Nathalis de Wailly à MIRA: 150 ans de normalisation des instruments de recherche aux Archives nationales." In *Histoires d'archives: recueil d'articles offert à Lucie Favier par ses collègues et amis*, 85-104. Paris: Société des amis des Archives de France, 1997.

Ollivier, Jules. "De l'importance des recherches à faire sur l'histoire générale de la France et en particulier sur l'histoire du Dauphiné." *Revue du Dauphiné* 4 (1838): 65-87.

Outrey, A[médée]. "La notion traditionnelle de titre et les origines de la législation révolutionnaire sur les archives, la loi du 7 septembre 1790." *Revue historique de droit français et étranger* 33, no. 3 (1955): 438-463.

------. "Sur la notion d'archives en France à la fin du XVIIIe siècle." *Revue historique de droit français et étranger* 31 (1953): 277-286.

Panitch, Judith M. "Liberty, Equality, Posterity? Some Archival Lessons from the Case of the French Revolution." *American Archivist* 59 (Dec. 1996): 30-47.

Périn, Jules. *Les archives départementales, leur avenir.* Paris: Librairie de l'Académie des Bibliophiles, 1866.

Piétresson de Saint-Aubin, P. "Les archives de l'Aube, 1790-1928." In *Inventaire sommaire des archives départementales antérieures à 1790. Aube. Archives écclesiastiques. Série G (Clergé seculier).* Troyes, France: Imprimerie A. Albert, 1930.

------. "Auguste Vallet de Viriville: Archiviste de l'Aube (1838-1841)." *Nouvelle revue de Champagne et de Brie* 6 (1928): 109-117.

------. "Du feudiste à l'archiviste: Jean-Baptiste et Jean-François Delion, commissaires à Terrier dans la région Troyenne (1742-1818)." In *Actes du 80e Congrès des Sociétés Savantes, Lille 1955*, 351-384. Paris: Imprimerie Nationale, 1955.

------. "Un projet de réforme des archives départementales en 1829." *Gazette des archives* (1970): 46-48.

Plaisir d'archives: recueil de travaux offerts à Danièle Neirinck. Mayenne: Imprimerie de la Manutention, 1997.

Pomian, Krzysztof. "Les archives, du Trésor des chartes au CARAN." In *Les lieux de mémoire*, ed. Pierre Nora, vol. 3, pt. 3, 162-233. Paris: Gallimard, 1992.

Posner, Ernest. "Some Aspects of Archival Development Since the French Revolution." *The American Archivist* 3 (Jul. 1940): 159-172.

Ravaisson, Félix. *Rapport adressé à S. Exc. le Ministre d'Etat au nom de la Commission instituée le 22 avril 1861.* Paris: Typographie E. Panckoucke, 1862.

Ravaisson, François, and Louis Ravaisson-Mollien. *Archives de la Bastille, d'après des documents inédits.* Paris: A. Durand et Pedonne-Lauriel, 1866-1904.

Richou, Gabriel. *Traité théorique et pratique des archives publiques.* Paris: Paul Dupont, 1883.

Rocquain, Félix. "Les travaux de Michelet aux Archives nationales." *Notes et fragments d'histoire,* 61-92. Paris: Plon, 1906.

Saint-Joanny, Gustave. *Les archives départementales et communales, à propos du projet de loi sur les conseils généraux et municipaux.* Paris: Imprimerie administrative de Paul Dupont, 1865.

Samaran, Ch[arles]. "Un cousin de Sainte-Beuve: Edmond Dupont des Archives de l'Empire. Lettres inédites." *Gazette des Archives* (1958): 52-55.

Soboul, Albert. "De la pratique des terriers à la veille de la Révolution." *Annales, Economies, Sociétés, Civilisations* 19, no. 16 (1964): 1049-1065.

Steedman, Carolyn. "The space of memory: in an archive." *History of the Human Sciences* 11, no. 4 (1998): 65-83.

Thuillier, Guy. "Les historiens locaux en Nivernais de 1815 à 1840." In *Actes du 101e Congrès national des sociétés savantes, Lille, 1976, Section d'histoire moderne et contemporaine,* 2: 349-364. Paris: Bibliothèque nationale, 1978.

------. "Les historiens locaux en Nivernais de 1840 à 1860." In *Actes du 102e Congrès national des sociétés savantes, Limoges 1977, Section d'histoire moderne et contemporaine,* 2: 319-333. Paris: Bibliothèque nationale, 1978.

------. "Les historiens locaux en Nivernais de 1860 à 1900." In *Actes du 103e Congrès national des sociétés savantes, Nancy-Metz 1978, Section d'histoire moderne et contemporaine,* 2: 403-417. Paris: Bibliothèque nationale, 1979.

Vallet de Viriville, Auguste. *Les archives historiques du département de l'Aube et de l'ancien diocèse de Troyes, Capitale de la Champagne; depuis le VIIe siècle jusqu'a 1790.* Troyes: Bouquot, 1841.

------. *Essai sur les archives historiques du chapitre de l'eglise cathédrale de Notre-Dame à St.-Omer (Pas-de-Calais).* Saint-Omer: Imprimerie de Chanvin fils, 1844.

------. "Le nouveau Musée des Archives." *Revue Nationale et Etrangère politique, litteraire et scientifique* (11 Jan. 1868): 256-258.

------. "Variétés. L'Hôtel Soubise." *Le Journal pour Tous* 2 (26 Apr. 1856): 63-64.

Villepelet, R. "Notes sur le classement et l'inventaire des papiers de l'époque révolutionnaire conservés dans les archives départementales." *Le Bibliographe moderne* 7 (1903): 377-400.

Warne, Chris. "Amateurs and Collectors: Amans-Alexis Monteil and the Emergence of a Professional Archive Culture in Nineteenth-Century France." *Australian Journal of French Studies* 33, no. 1 (1996): 45-72.

Wey, Francis. *Dick Moon en France, journal d'un Anglais de Paris.* Paris: Librairie de L. Hachette, 1862.

Libraries

Albert, J. F. M. *Recherches sur les principes fondamentaux de la classification bibliographique précédées de quelques mots sur la Bibliographie, d'un exposé des principaux systèmes bibliographiques, et suivies d'une application de ces principes au classement des livres de la Bibliothèque Royale.* Paris: Chez l'auteur, 1847.

Allen, James Smith. *In the Public Eye: A History of Reading in Modern France, 1800-1940.* Princeton: Princeton University Press, 1991.

Amalvi, Christian. "Catalogues historiques et conceptions de l'histoire." *Storia della storiografia* 2, no. 82 (1982): 77-101.

------. "La périodisation du passé national dans le catalogue de l'Histoire de France du département des Imprimés de la Bibliothèque Nationale." In *Périodes. La construction du temps historique. Actes du Ve colloque d'histoire au présent,* 15-20. Paris: Editions de l'Ecole des Hautes Etudes en Sciences Sociales et Histoire au Présent, 1991.

Arnoult, Jean-Marie. "La conservation." In *Histoire des bibliothèques françaises,* vol. 3, ed. Dominique Varry, 273-279. Paris: Promodis, 1991.

Auspitz, Katherine. *The Radical Bourgeoisie: The Ligue de l'enseignement and the Origins of the Third Republic, 1866-1885.* Cambridge: Cambridge University Press, 1983.

Balayé, Simone. *La Bibliothèque nationale: des origines à 1800.* Geneva: Droz, 1988.

------. "La Bibliothèque nationale pendant la Révolution." In *Histoire des bibliothèques françaises,* vol. 3, ed. Dominique Varry, 329-333. Paris: Promodis, 1991.

------. "Les publics de la Bibliothèque nationale." In *Histoire des bibliothèques françaises,* vol. 3, ed. Dominique Varry, 71-83. Paris: Promodis, 1991.

Balsamo, Luigi. "The Bibliography of Librarians and Historians in the Nineteenth Century." In *Bibliography: The History of a Tradition,* trans. William A. Pettas. Berkeley, CA: Bernard M. Rosenthal, 1990.

Barnett, Graham Keith. *Histoire des bibliothèques publiques en France de la Révolution à 1939.* Trans. Thierry Lefèvre and Yves Sardat. Paris: Promodis; Editions du Cercle de la librairie, 1987. Originally presented as "The History of Public Libraries in France from the Revolution to 1939." Thesis, Library Association [Great Britain], 1973.

Baudrillart, Henri. *Rapport sur les pertes éprouvées par les bibliothèques publiques de Paris en 1870-1871, adressé à M. le Ministre de l'Instruction Publique*. Paris: Impr. Paul Dupont, 1871.

Baune, Aimé. *Notice sur la bibliothèque publique de Chalon-sur-Saône*. Chalon-sur-Saône: J. Ducresne, Jun. 1834.

Beaud, Marie-Josèphe, Jean Grigorieff, and Georges-Guillaume Kerourédan, eds. *Lectures et lecteurs au XIXe siècle: la Bibliothèque des Amis de l'Instruction (Actes du Colloque tenu le 10 novembre 1984)*. Paris: Bibliothèque des Amis de l'Instruction du 3e arrondissement, 1985.

Bellet, Roger. "Une bataille culturelle, provinciale, et nationale, à propos des bons auteurs pour bibliothèques populaires (janvier-juin 1867)." *Revue des sciences humaines* 34, no. 135 (1969): 453-473.

Bernard-Griffiths, Simone, Marie-Claude Chemin, and Jean Ehrard, eds. *Révolution française et 'vandalisme révolutionnaire': Actes du colloque international de Clermont-Ferrand, 15-17 décembre 1988*. Paris: Universitas, 1992.

Bibliothèque des Amis de l'Instruction (IIIe arrondissement). *Exercice 1861-1862. Historique. Compte rendu financier. Statuts. Liste des donateurs*. Paris: Imprimerie de J. Claye, 1862.

Bibliothèque nationale. *1789: Le patrimoine libéré: 200 trésors entrés à la Bibliothèque nationale de 1789 à 1799*. Paris: Bibliothèque nationale, 1989.

Bibolet, Françoise. "La Bibliothèque municipale de Troyes" *Revue française d'histoire du livre* (Jul.-Sept. 1976): 275-324.

Blasselle, Bruno. "La bibliothéconomie, théorie et pratique." In *Histoire des bibliothèques françaises*, vol. 3, ed. Dominique Varry, 143-163. Paris: Promodis, 1991.

Blasselle, Bruno, and Jacqueline Melet-Sanson. *La Bibliothèque Nationale: mémoire de l'avenir*. Paris: Gallimard-Découvertes, 1990.

Blasselle, Bruno, and Laurent Portes, eds. *Mélanges autour de l'histoire des livres imprimés et périodiques*. Paris: Bibliothèque nationale de France, 1998.

Bondois, Paul 1885-. *Le prêt des livres et manuscrits à la Bibliothèque Impériale en 1813*. Lille: S.I.L.I.C., [1932].

Breton-Gravereau, Simone, and François Dupuigrenet Desroussilles. "'Lever la carte': la politique des catalogues de livres imprimés à la fin du XIXe siècle." *Revue de la Bibliothèque nationale* 49 (1993): 4-7.

Buchon, J[ean] A[lexandre]. "Rapport à son Exc. le Vicomte de Martignac, sur la situation des bibliothèques publiques en France." In *Rapport sur les institutions municipales de littérature, sciences et arts*. Paris: Everat, [1828?].

------. "Rapport général sur l'organisation des bibliothèques." *Revue de Paris* 5 (1829): 24-38; 6 (1829): 30-45 and 262-278.

Bulletin de la Société pour l'amélioration et l'encouragement des publications populaires. Première année. Paris: Adrien Le Clere et Ce., 1862.

Caillet, Maurice. "Les inspecteurs généraux des bibliothèques." In *Histoire des bibliothèques françaises*, vol. 3, ed. Dominique Varry, 131. Paris: Promodis, 1991.

------. "L'inspection générale des bibliothèques." *Bulletin des bibliothèques de France* 15, no. 12 (1970): 597-608; 16, no. 3 (1971): 145-159.

The Case of M. Libri. Reprinted from "Bentley's Miscellany," for July 1, 1852. London: Richard Bentley, 1852.

Casselle, Pierre. "Les pouvoirs publics et les bibliothèques." In *Histoire des bibliothèques françaises*, vol. 3, ed. Dominique Varry, 109-117. Paris: Promodis, 1991.

Champollion-Figeac, [Jacques-Joseph]. *Etat actuel des catalogues des manuscrits de la Bibliothèque royale (1er mars 1847).* Paris: Firmin Didot, [1847].

------. *Notice sur le cabinet des chartes et diplômes de l'histoire de France.* Paris: Firmin Didot, 1827.

Charmasson, Thérèse, and Catherine Gaziello. "Les grandes bibliothèques parisiennes." In *Histoire des bibliothèques françaises*, vol. 3, ed. Dominique Varry, 61-69. Paris: Promodis, 1991.

------. "Les grandes bibliothèques d'étude à Paris." In *Histoire des bibliothèques françaises*, vol. 3, ed. Dominique Varry, 359-393. Paris: Promodis, 1991.

Chartier, Anne-Marie, and Jean Hébrard. *Discours sur la lecture (1880-1980).* Paris: Bibliothèque publique d'information, Centre Georges-Pompidou, 1989.

Chartier, Roger. *The Order of Books: Readers, Authors, and Libraries in Europe between the Fourteenth and Eighteenth Centuries.* Trans. Lydia G. Cochrane. Stanford: Stanford University Press, 1994. Originally published as *L'ordre des livres: lecteurs, auteurs, bibliothèques en Europe entre le XIVe et le XVIIIe siècle.* Aix-en-Provence: Alinea, 1992.

Clarke, Jack A. "French Libraries in Transition, 1789-95." *Library Quarterly* 37, no. 4 (1967): 366-372.

Comte, Henri. *Les bibliothèques publiques en France.* Lyon: Imprimerie BOSC Frères, 1977.

Constantin, L[éopold]-A[uguste] [Léopold-Auguste Hesse]. *Bibliothéconomie. Instructions sur l'arrangement, la conservation et l'administration des bibliothèques.* Paris: J. Techener, 1839.

Curmer, Léon. *De l'établissement des bibliothèques communales en France.* Paris: Guillaumin et Cie., 1846.

[Danjou, Félix]. *Exposé succinct d'un nouveau système d'organisation des bibliothèques publiques; par un bibliothécaire.* Montpellier: Boehm, 1845.

Delessert, B[enjamin]. *Mémoire sur la Bibliothèque royale, ou l'on indique les mesures à prendre pour la transférer dans un bâtiment circulaire d'une forme nouvelle, qui serait construit au centre de la place du Carrousel.* Paris: Imprimerie de Henri Dupuy, 1835.

Delmas, Bruno. "Les débuts de la formation des bibliothécaires." In *Histoire des bibliothèques françaises*, vol. 3, ed. Dominique Varry, 119-139. Paris: Promodis, 1991.

Delon, Michel. "La bibliothèque est en feu: rêveries révolutionnaires autour du livre." *Bulletin des bibliothèques de France* 34, nos. 2-3 (1989): 117-123.

Description de la Bibliothèque de Metz. Metz: Verronnais, 1833.

Desgraves, Louis. "Le catalogage des fonds." In *Histoire des bibliothèques françaises*, vol. 3, ed. Dominique Varry, 165-181. Paris: Promodis, 1991.

------. "Les bibliothécaires." In *Histoire des bibliothèques françaises*, vol. 3, ed. Dominique Varry, 281-293. Paris: Promodis, 1991.

De Vleeschauwer, Herman J. *Library History of the XIXth century, 1750-1914.* Pretoria: Univ. of South Africa, 1965.

Dobi, Antonia. "Napoleon's Great Librarians." *Wilson Library Bulletin* 49, no. 3 (1974): 229-233.

Dufresne, Hélène. *Le Bibliothécaire Hubert-Pascal Ameilhon (1730-1811): érudition et esprit public au XVIIIe siècle.* Paris: Nizet, 1962.

Feuillet de Conches, F[élix Sébastien]. *Réponse à une incroyable attaque de la Bibliothèque nationale, touchant une lettre de Michel de Montaigne.* Paris: Laverdet, 1851.

Fierro, Alfred, ed. *Patrimoine parisien, 1789-1799: destructions, créations, mutations.* Paris: Délégation à l'action artistique de la ville de Paris; Bibliothèque historique de la ville de Paris, 1989.

Foisy, F[rançois]- M[arie]. *Sommaire d'un opuscule intitulé: Essai théorique et pratique sur la conservation des bibliothèques publiques.* Paris: Typographie de Lachevardière, [1833].

Foucaud, Jean-François. *La Bibliothèque Royale sous la monarchie de juillet (1830-1848).* Paris: Bibliothèque Nationale, 1978.

------. "Le rapport Mérimée." In *Histoire des bibliothèques françaises*, vol. 3, ed. Dominique Varry, 306. Paris: Promodis, 1991.

Franklin, Alfred. *Les anciennes bibliothèques de Paris.* Paris: Imprimerie Impériale, 1867-1870; Imprimerie nationale, 1873.

Funck-Brentano, Frantz, and Paul Deslandres. *La Bibliothèque de l'Arsenal.* Paris: Henri Laurens, 1930.

Gonod, B. *Note sur le classement des imprimés, la rédaction et la publication du Catalogue général de la Bibliothèque royale.* 2d ed. Paris: Chez Porquet, May 1847.

Grün, A[lphonse]. *Bibliothèques publiques*. Strasbourg: Imprimerie de Veuve Berger-Levrault, 1855.

Guérin, Denis. "La lecture publique à Paris au XIXe siècle." *Bulletin des bibliothèques de France* 28, no. 2 (1983): 143-153.

Harris, Michael H. *History of Libraries in the Western World*. Metuchen, NJ: The Scarecrow Press, 1984.

Hassenforder, Jean. *Développement comparé des bibliothèques publiques en France, en Grande-Bretagne, et aux Etats-Unis dans la seconde moitié du XIXe siècle (1850-1914)*. Paris: Cercle de la Librairie, 1967.

------. "Histoire d'une tentative pour la promotion des bibliothèques populaires: la Société Franklin." *Education et bibliothèques* 6 (Mar. 1963): 21-36.

Hébrard, Jean. "Les bibliothèques scolaires." In *Histoire des bibliothèques françaises*, vol. 3, ed. Dominique Varry, 547-577. Paris: Promodis, 1991.

Hessel, Alfred. *A History of Libraries*. Trans. Reuben Peiss. New Brunswick, NJ: The Scarecrow Press, 1955. Originally published as *Geschichte der Bibliotheken*. Göttingen: H. Th. Pellens & Co., a.-g., 1925.

Hoch, Philippe. "Félix Ravaisson et les débuts de l'inspection générale des bibliothèques." *Bulletin d'information de A.B.F.* no. 141, 1st trimester (1989): 44-46.

Hopkins, Judith. "The 1791 French Cataloging Code and the Origins of the Card Catalog." *Libraries and Culture* 27 (fall 1992): 378-404.

Jackson, S. L. "Tax-supported library service to the people: why is 1876-7 the nodal point?" *International Library Review* 4 (1972): 417-421.

Jacob, Paul Lacroix. "Les Bibliothèques publiques à Paris an 1831." In *Mon Grand Fauteuil*. Paris: E. Renduel, 1836.

------. *Les cent et une: lettres bibliographiques à M. l'administrateur général de la Bibliothèque nationale*. Paris: Paulin, 1849-50.

Jolly, Claude, ed. *Histoire des bibliothèques françaises*. Vol. 2, *Les bibliothèques sous l'Ancien Régime, 1530-1789*. Paris: Promodis, 1988.

Kupiec, Anne. "Le livre sauveur." *Bulletin des bibliothèques de France* 34, nos. 2-3 (1989): 124-130.

Labiche, J[ean]-B[aptiste]. *Notice sur les dépôts littéraires et la révolution bibliographique de la fin du dernier siècle, d'après les manuscrits de la Bibliothèque de l'Arsenal*. Paris: Typographie de A. Parent, 1880.

Laborde, Léon. *De l'organisation des bibliothèques dans Paris*. Paris: A. Franck, Feb. 1845.

Lalanne, L[udovic], H[enri] Bordier, and F[élix] Bourquelot. *Affaire Libri. Réponse à M. Mérimée*. 2d ed. Paris: Pancoucke, 1852.

Le Glay, [A. J. G.]. *Mémoire sur les bibliothèques publiques et les principales bibliothèques particulières du département du Nord.* Lille: Chez le concierge des Archives départementales, 1841.

Ledos, E[ugène]-G[abriel]. *Histoire des catalogues des livres imprimés de la Bibliothèque nationale.* Paris: Editions des bibliothèques nationales, 1936.

Léveillé, Laure. "Les petites bibliothèques de la République: aux origines de la lecture publique parisienne, des années 1870 aux années 1930." Doctoral thesis, Université de Paris X-Nanterre, Jan. 1998.

Longnon, Jean. Introduction to *Voyage dans l'Eubée, les Iles ioniennes et les Cyclades en 1841*, by Alexandre Buchon. Paris: Emile-Paul, 1911.

Louandre, Charles. "La Bibliothèque Royale et les bibliothèques publiques." *Revue des deux-mondes* 13 (1846): 1045-1067.

Lyons, Martyn. *Le Triomphe du livre: une histoire sociologique de la lecture dans la France du XIXe siècle.* Paris: Promodis, 1987.

Maccioni Ruju, P. Alessandra, and Marco Mostert. *The Life and Times of Guglielmo Libri (1802-1869), scientist, patriot, scholar, journalist and thief: a nineteenth-century story.* Hilversum: Verloren Publishers, 1995.

Malclès, Louise-Noëlle. "La bibliographie en France, depuis 1762 jusqu'à la fondation de l'école nationale supérieure de bibliothécaires." In *Humanisme actif: mélanges d'art et de littérature offerts à Julien Cain*, vol. 2, 117-131. Paris: Hermann, 1968.

Marcetteau-Paul, Agnès. "Les bibliothèques municipales." In *Histoire des bibliothèques françaises*, vol. 3, ed. Dominique Varry, 437-453. Paris: Promodis, 1991.

Marie, Pascale. "La bibliothèque des amis de l'instruction du IIIe arrondissement: un temple, quartier du Temple." In *Les lieux de mémoire*, ed. Pierre Nora, vol. 1, 323-351. Paris: Gallimard, 1984.

Martin, Henri-Jean. "Bibliothèques publiques et bibliothèques populaires." In *Histoire de l'édition française*, ed. Henri-Jean Martin and Roger Chartier, 3: 261-267. Paris: Promodis, 1985.

------. "The French Revolution and Books: Cultural Break, Cultural Continuity." In *Publishing and Readership in Revolutionary France and America*, ed. Carol Armbruster, 177-190. Westport, CT: Greenwood Press, 1993.

Martin, Henry. *Catalogue des Manuscrits de la Bibliothèque de l'Arsenal. Tome Huitième: Histoire de la Bibliothèque de l'Arsenal.* Paris: Plon, 1899.

McCrimmon, Barbara. "The Libri Case." *Journal of Library History* 1, no. 1 (1966): 7-32.

------. "Mérimée as Library Reformer." *Journal of Library History* 4, no. 4 (1969): 297-320.

Mérimée, Prosper. *Note d'un voyage dans le Midi de la France*. Paris: Libraire de Fournier, 1835.

------. "La Nouvelle salle de lecture au British Museum." *Le Moniteur Universel* 238 (26 Aug. 1857): 933-934.

------. "Rapport présenté à S. Exc. le Ministre de l'instruction publique et des cultes..., au nom de la commission chargée d'examiner les modifications à introduire dans l'organisation de la Bibliothèque Impériale." *Le Moniteur Universel* 201 (20 Jul. 1858): 905-907.

Michelet, [Jules]. *Rapport au Ministre de l'Instruction Publique sur les bibliothèques et archives des départements du sud-ouest de la France (août-septembre 1835)*. Paris: Imprimerie de Ducessois, 1836.

Ministère de l'Instruction Publique et des Cultes. *Tableau statistique des bibliothèques publiques des départements, d'après des documents officiels recueillis de 1853 à 1857 (Extrait du Journal Général de l'Instruction Publique)*. Paris: Imprimerie Paul Dupont, 1857.

Mortet, Ch[arles]. *Les bibliothèques publiques en France, leur formation historique et leur organisation actuelle*. Paris: Honoré Champion, 1928.

Netchine, Eve, and Edmée Strauch. "La 'salle B' ou 70 ans de lecture publique à la Bibliothèque nationale." In *Mélanges autour de l'histoire des livres imprimés et periodiques*, ed. Bruno Blasselle, and Laurent Portes, 242-266. Paris: Bibliothèque nationale de France, 1998.

Omont, Henri. "Rapport sur la Bibliothèque Nationale fait à la Commission d'Instruction Publique de la Convention Nationale." *Revue des bibliothèques* (1905): 67-98.

Pallier, Denis. "Histoire et évolution du métier de bibliothécaire." *Bulletin d'informations de l'Association des bibliothécaires français* no. 164 (1994): 47-54.

Paris, Paulin. *De la Bibliothèque Royale et de la necessité de commencer, achever et publier le catalogue général des livres imprimés*. Paris: Techener, 1847.

Pautet du Rozier, Jules. *Bibliothèque Nationale. A M. Louis-Napoléon Bonaparte, Président de la République. Rapport sur l'organisation du personnel, la reconstruction du monument, ou l'emploi de la nouvelle galerie du Louvre, et la Rédaction du Catalogue de la Bibliothèque nationale*. 2d ed. Paris: Ledoyen, 1849.

Piers, H[ector Beaurepaire]. *Notice historique sur la bibliothèque publique de la ville de St-Omer*. Lille: Imp. Ve. Libert-Petitot, 1840.

Ravaisson, Félix. *Rapports au Ministre de l'Instruction Publique sur les bibliothèques des départements de l'ouest, suivis de pièces inédites*. Paris: Joubert, 1841.

Reder, Anne-Marie, ed. *Patrimoine des bibliothèques de France: un guide des régions*. Paris: Payot, 1995.

Riberette, Pierre. *Les Bibliothèques Françaises pendant la Révolution (1789-1795): Recherches sur un essai de catalogue collectif.* Paris: Bibliothèque Nationale, 1970.

------. *Le conseil de conservation et la formation des bibliothèques françaises.* Paris: Bibliothèque Nationale, 1966.

Richard, Hélène. "Catalogue collectif et échange de documents: un utopie révolutionnaire." *Bulletin des bibliothèques de France* 34, nos. 2-3 (1989): 166-173.

Richter, Noë. *Les bibliothèques populaires.* Paris: Cercle de la librairie, 1978.

------. "Les bibliothèques populaires et la lecture ouvrière." In *Histoire des bibliothèques françaises*, vol. 3, ed. Dominique Varry, 513-535. Paris: Promodis, 1991.

------. "Lecture populaire et lecture ouvrière: deux composantes du système de lecture français." *Bulletin des bibliothèques de France* 28, no. 2 (1983): 123-134.

Robert, Ulysse. Preface to *Catalogue général des manuscrits des bibliothèques publiques de France: Départements—Tome Premier, Rouen*, by Henri Omont. Paris: Librairie Plon, 1886.

------, ed. *Recueil de lois, décrets, ordonnances, arrêtés, circulaires, etc. concernant les bibliothèques publiques, communales, universitaires, scolaires et populaires.* Paris: H. Champion, 1883.

Rouland, [Gustave]. *Ministère de l'Instruction Publique et des Cultes. Bibliothèque Impériale. Rapport à l'Empereur.* Paris: Imprimerie Paul Dupont, April 1860.

------. "Rapport à l'Empereur par S. Exc. le Ministre de l'instruction publique et des cultes concernant la reorganisation de la Bibliothèque Impériale; decret y annexé." *Le Moniteur Universel* 201 (20 Jul. 1858): 905.

Sax, Joseph L. "Heritage Preservation as a Public Duty: The Abbé Grégoire and the Origins of an Idea." *Michigan Law Review* 88, no. 5 (1990): 1142-1169.

Seckel, Raymond Josué. "Bibliométrie, bibliographies, classifications." In *Mesure(s) du livre: colloque organisé par la Bibliothèque nationale et la Société des études romantiques, 1989*, ed. Alain Vaillant, 41-56. Paris: Bibliothèque nationale, 1992.

Seguin, Jean-Pierre. *Eugène Morel et la lecture publique: un prophète en son pays.* Paris: Centre Georges Pompidou, 1994.

Simon, Jules. "L'instruction primaire et les bibliotheques populaires." *Revue des deux-mondes* (15 Sept. 1863): 349-375.

------. "Société d'enseignement professionnel du Rhône...Les bibliothèques populaires." *Revue bleue* (11 Feb. 1865): 174-179.

"Société Franklin, pour la propagation des Bibliothèques municipales, autorisée par arrêté de S. Exc. le ministre de l'intérieur, en date du 19 septembre 1862." *Journal de la librairie* (31 Jan. 1863).

Société Franklin pour la propagation des bibliothèques populaires. *I. Notice sur la Société Franklin, II. Instruction pour la fondation d'une bibliothèque, III. Catalogue populaire de la Société Franklin..., IV. Nouveaux statuts de la Société Franklin.* [Paris]: Siège de la Société, Sept. 1864.

Tacheau, Olivier. "Bibliothèques municipales et genèse des politiques culturelles au XIXe siècle: Dijon et Besançon entre 1816 et 1914." *Bulletin des bibliothèques de France* 40, no. 4 (1994): 44-51.

Taschereau, Jules. "A Son Excellence Monsieur le ministre de l'Instruction publique et des cultes." In *Catalogue de l'histoire de France*. Vol. 1. Paris: Firmin Didot, 1855.

Techener, J[acques]. *Considérations sérieuses à propos de diverses publications récentes sur la Bibliothèque Royale, suivies du seul plan possible Pour en faire le Catalogue en trois ans.* Paris: Au Bureau du *Bulletin du Bibliophile*, 1847.

------. *De l'amélioration des anciennes bibliothèques en France et de la création de nouvelles bibliothèques appropriées au perfectionnement moral du peuple.* Paris: Guiraudet et Jouaust, n.d.

------. *Sur les améliorations à apporter aux bibliothèques des villes de province.* Paris: Imprimerie de Madame Veuve Huzard; Imprimerie de L. Bouchard-Huzard, [1839].

Ternaux-Compans, H[enri]. *Lettre à M. le Ministre d'Instruction Publique sur l'état actuel des bibliothèques publiques de Paris.* Paris: Delaunay, 1837.

Thomas, Marcel. "Détournements, vols, destructions." In *Histoire des bibliothèques françaises*, vol. 3, ed. Dominique Varry, 263-271. Paris: Promodis, 1991.

------. "Les manuscrits." In *Histoire des bibliothèques françaises*, vol. 3, ed. Dominique Varry, 172-175. Paris: Promodis, 1991.

Tourneur-Aumont, J. "Idées bibliographiques en l'an II: Les rapports d'Urbain Domergue et Henri Grégoire." *Revue des Bibliothèques* 37 (1927): 362-391.

Varry, Dominique. "D'un siècle à l'autre." In *Histoire des bibliothèques françaises*, vol. 3, ed. Dominique Varry, 625-631. Paris: Promodis, 1991.

------. "Il faut que les Lumières arrivent par torrents: la Révolution française et la création des bibliothèques publiques: projets et réalités." *Bulletin des bibliothèques de France* 34, nos. 2-3 (1989): 160-165.

------. "Aux origines de la bibliothèque publique de Belfort." *Bulletin de la société belfortaine d'émulation* (1989): 49-58.

------. "La profession de bibliothécaire en France à l'époque de la révolution française." *Revue de synthèse* 4th ser. (Jan. 1992): 29-39.

------. "Les saisies révolutionnaires: une source inexploitée." In *Transactions of the Eighth International Congress on the Enlightenment*. Studies on Voltaire and the Eighteenth Century, nos. 303-305 (Oxford: The Voltaire Foundation, 1992).

------. "Vicissitudes et aléas des livres placés sous la main de la Nation." In *Révolution française et vandalisme révolutionnaire: actes du colloque international de Clermont-Ferrand, 15-17 décembre 1988*, ed. Simone Bernard-Griffiths, Marie-Claude Chemin, and Jean Ehrard, 277-284. Paris: Universitas, 1992.

------, ed. *Histoire des bibliothèques françaises*. Vol. 3, *Les bibliothèques de la Révolution et du XIXe siècle, 1789-1914*. Paris: Promodis, 1991.

Vitet, L[udovic]. *Rapport à M. le ministre de l'interieur sur les monumens [sic], les bibliothèques, les archives, et les musées des départemens [sic] de l'Oise, de l'Aisne, de la Marne, du Nord et du Pas-de-Calais*. Paris: Imprimerie Royale, 1831.

Wintzweiller, Marguerite. *La Bibliothèque Sainte-Geneviève de jadis à aujourd'hui: Exposition organisée à l'occasion du Centenaire de son installation dans les bâtiments actuels, 1851-1951*. Paris: n.p., 1951.

Historians and Historical Projects

Augustin-Thierry, A. *Augustin Thierry (1795-1856) d'après sa correspondance et ses papiers de famille*. Paris: Librairie Plon, 1922.

Baker, Keith Michael. *Inventing the French Revolution: Essays on French Political Culture in the Eighteenth Century*. New York: Cambridge University Press, 1990.

Bann, Stephen. *The Clothing of Clio: A Study of the Representation of History in Nineteenth-Century Britain and France*. Cambridge: Cambridge University Press, 1984.

Barret-Kriegel, Blandine. *Les historiens et la monarchie*. Paris: Presses universitaires de France, 1988.

Bautier, R[obert]-H[enri]. "Le Comité des travaux historiques et scientifiques." In *Histoire de l'édition française*, ed. Henri-Jean Martin and Roger Chartier, 3: 224-225. Paris: Promodis, 1985.

------. "Le Comité des travaux historiques et scientifiques, bilan d'activité, 1945-1965." In *Humanisme actif: mélanges d'art et de littérature offerts à Julien Cain*, vol. 1, 29-46. Paris: Hermann, 1968.

------. "Le recueil des monuments de l'histoire du tiers état et l'utilisation des matériaux réunis par Augustin Thierry." *Annuaire-Bulletin de la Société de l'histoire de France* (1944): 89-118.

Bercé, Françoise. "Arcisse de Caumont et les sociétés savantes." In *Les lieux de mémoire*, ed. Pierre Nora, vol. 2, pt. 2, 534-565. Paris: Gallimard, 1986.

------, ed. *Les premiers travaux de la commission des monuments historiques, 1830-1840*. Paris: Picard, 1979.

Beugnot, [Arthur Auguste]. *Les Olim, ou Registres des arrêts rendus par la cour du Roi sous les règnes de Saint Louis, de Philippe le Hardi, de Philippe le Bel, de Louis le Hutin et de Philippe le Long (1254-1318)*. Paris: Imprimerie royale, 1848.

Blanchet, Adrien et al. *Les Travaux de l'Academie des Inscriptions et Belles-Lettres: Histoire et Inventaire des Publications*. Paris: C. Klincksieck, 1947.

Boer, Pim den. *History as a Profession: The Study of History in France (1818-1914)*. Trans. Arnold J. Pomerans. Princeton: Princeton University Press, 1998.

Bréquigny, [Louis Georges Oudart Feudrix de] and [Jacques-Joseph] Champollion-Figeac. *Lettres de rois, reines et autres personnages des cours de France et d'Angleterre depuis Louis VII jusqu'à Henri IV, tirées des Archives de Londres par Bréquigny, et publiées par M. Champollion-Figeac*, Paris: Imp. Royale, 1839-47.

Burton, June K. *Napoleon and Clio: Historical Writing, Teaching, and Thinking During the First Empire*. Durham, NC: Carolina Academic Press, 1979.

Carbonell, Charles-Olivier. "Guizot, homme d'Etat, et le mouvement historiographique français du XIXe siècle." In *Actes du Colloque François Guizot (Paris, 22-25 octobre 1974)*, 219-237. Paris: Au siège de la société [de l'histoire du Protestantisme français], 1976.

------. *Histoire et historiens: une mutation idéologique des historiens français, 1865-1885*. Toulouse: Privat, 1976.

------. "La naissance de la *Revue historique*, une revue de combat (1876-1885)," *Revue historique* 255 (Apr.-Jun. 1976): 331-351.

Carroll, Kieran Joseph. "Some aspects of the historical thought of Augustin Thierry (1795-1856)." Ph.D. diss., Catholic University of America, 1951.

Champollion-Figeac, [Jacques-Joseph], ed. *Documents historiques inédits tirés des collections manuscrites de la Bibliothèque Royale et des archives ou des bibliothèques des départements*. Paris: Firmin Didot, 1841.

Charmes, Xavier. *Le Comité des travaux historiques et scientifiques (histoire et documents)*. Paris: Imprimerie Nationale, 1886.

Chastel, André. "La Notion de Patrimoine." In *Les lieux de mémoire*, ed. Pierre Nora, vol. 2, pt. 2, 405-450. Paris: Gallimard, 1986.

Crossley, Ceri. *French Historians and Romanticism: Thierry, Guizot, the Saint-Simonians, Quinet, Michelet.* London: Routledge, 1993.

Dacier, Bon-Joseph. *Rapport historique sur les progrès de l'histoire et de la littérature ancienne depuis 1789, et sur leur état actuel, presenté à sa majesté l'Empereur et Roi, en son conseil d'état, le 20 février 1808, par la Classe d'Histoire et de Littérature ancienne de l'Institut.* Paris: Imprimerie Imperiale, 1810.

Denieul Cormier, Anne. *Augustin Thierry: l'histoire autrement.* [Paris]: Publisud, 1996.

De Wailly, Natalis. *Eléments de Paléographie. Pour servir à l'étude des documents inédits sur l'histoire de France publiés par ordre du Roi et par les soins du Ministre de l'Instruction Publique.* Paris: Impr. Royale, 1838.

Dussaud, Réné. *La Nouvelle Académie des inscriptions et belles-lettres (1795-1914).* Paris: Paul Geuthner, 1947.

Fauquet, Eric. *Michelet, ou, la gloire du professeur de l'histoire.* Paris: Editions du Cerf, 1990.

Fermigier, André. "Mérimée et l'inspection des monuments historiques." In *Les lieux de mémoire*, ed. Pierre Nora, vol. 2, pt. 2, 593-609. Paris: Gallimard, 1986.

Furet, François. "Michelet." *Proceedings of the British Academy* 76 (1990): 63-72.

Gasnault, Pierre. "Motivations, conditions de travail et héritage des Bénédictins de Saint-Maur." *Revue d'histoire de l'église de France* 71 (Jan. 1985): 13-23.

Gauchet, Marcel. "Les Lettres sur l'histoire de France d'Augustin Thierry." In *Les lieux de mémoire*, ed. Pierre Nora, vol. 2, pt. 1, 247-316. Paris: Gallimard, 1986.

------, ed. *Philosophie des sciences historiques: Textes de P. Barante, V. Cousin, F. Guizot, J. Michelet, F. Mignet, E. Quinet, A. Thierry.* Lille: Presses Universitaires de Lille, 1988.

Gautier, Léon. "De l'avenir des études historiques." *Revue des questions historiques* (1866): [3]-9.

Georgel, Chantal. "The Museum as Metaphor in Nineteenth-Century France." In *Museum Culture: Histories, Discourses, Spectacles*, ed. Daniel J. Sherman and Irit Rogoff, 113-119. Minneapolis: University of Minnesota, 1994.

Gerson, Stephane. "Pays and nation: the uneasy formation of an historical patrimony in France, 1830-1870." Ph.D. diss., University of Chicago, 1997.

Gossman, Lionel. "Augustin Thierry and Liberal Historiography." *History and Theory* Beiheft 15, no. 4 (1976): 1-83.

------. "History as Decipherment: Romantic Historiography and the Discovery of the Other." *New Literary History* 18, no. 1 (1986): 23-57.

Greene, Christopher M. "Romanticism, Cultural Nationalism, and Politics in the July Monarchy: The Contribution of Ludovic Vitet." *French History* 4 (Dec. 1990): 487-509.

Grell, Chantal. *L'histoire entre érudition et philosophie: étude sur la connaissance historique à l'age des lumières.* Paris: Presses universitaires de France, 1993.

Gruner, Shirley M. "Political Historiography in Restoration France." *History and Theory* 8 (1969): 346-365.

Guérard, Benjamin, ed. *Cartulaire de l'abbaye de Saint-Père de Chartres.* Paris: Imprimerie de Crapelet, 1840.

Guizot, [François]. "Allocution de M. Guizot [2 Aug. 1837]." *Mémoires de la Société des Antiquaires de Normandie* 11 (1840): xli-xlv.

------. *Mémoires pour servir à l'histoire de mon temps.* Paris: Michel Lévy, 1860.

Halphen, Louis. *L'histoire en France depuis cent ans.* Paris: Librairie Armand Colin, 1914.

Institut de France. *L'Académie des Inscriptions et Belles-Lettres.* Paris: Auguste Picard, 1924.

Johnson, Douglas. *Guizot: Aspects of French History, 1787-1874.* London: Routledge and Kegan Paul, 1963.

Kelley, Donald R. *Historians and the Law in Post-Revolutionary France.* Princeton: Princeton University Press, 1984.

Keylor, William R. *Academy and Community: The Foundation of the French Historical Profession.* Cambridge, MA: Harvard University Press, 1975.

Knibiehler, Yvonne. *Naissance des sciences humaines: Mignet et l'histoire philosophique au XIXe siècle.* Paris: Flammarion, 1973.

Knowles, David. *Great Historical Enterprises.* London: Thomas Nelson and Sons, 1963.

Langlois, Ch[arles]-V[ictor], and Ch[arles] Seignobos. *Introduction aux études historiques.* Paris: Hachette, 1898.

Mabillon, Jean. Excerpt from "On Diplomatics." In *Historians at Work*, ed. Peter Gay and Victor G. Wexler, 2: 161-198. New York: Harper and Row, 1972.

Marrinan, Michael. *Painting Politics for Louis-Philippe: Art and Ideology in Orléanist France, 1830-1848.* New Haven: Yale University Press, 1988.

Maury, L[ouis]-F[erdinand]. *L'ancienne Académie des Inscriptions et Belles-Lettres.* Paris: Didier et cie., 1864.

Mellon, Stanley. *The Political Uses of History: A Study of Historians in the French Restoration*. Stanford: Stanford University Press, 1958.

Mérimée, Prosper, and Ludovic Vitet. *La naissance des monuments historiques: la correspondance de Prosper Mérimée avec Ludovic Vitet (1840-1848)*. Paris: Comité des travaux historiques et scientifiques, 1998.

Ministère de l'Instruction publique et des beaux-arts. *Comité des travaux historiques et scientifiques, missions [scientifiques et littéraires], bibliothèques, archives: bibliographie de leurs publications au 31 decembre 1897*. Paris: Impr. Nationale, 1898.

Monod, G[abriel]. "Introduction. Du progrès des études historiques en France depuis le XVIe siècle." *Revue historique* 1 (Jan.-Jun. 1876): 5-38.

Neveu, Bruno. "L'histoire littéraire de la France et l'érudition bénédictine au siècle des Lumières." *Journal des savants* (1979): 73-113.

Noiriel, Gérard. "Naissance du métier d'historien." *Genèses* 1 (Sept. 1990): 58-85.

Pardessus, Jean-Marie. *Institut royal de France. Rapport fait à l'Académie royale des inscriptions et belles-lettres, au nom de la commission des travaux littéraires, sur la continuation des tables des chartes imprimées, et la publication des textes des chartes concernant l'histoire de la France…dans la séance du 20 mars 1835*. Paris: Firmin-Didot, [1835].

Poulot, Dominique. "The birth of heritage: 'le moment Guizot'." *Oxford Art Journal* 11, no. 2 (1988): 40-56.

------. *Musée, nation, patrimoine, 1789-1815*. Paris: Gallimard, 1997.

------. *'Surveiller et s'instruire': la Révolution française et l'intelligence de l'héritage historique*. Oxford, England: Voltaire Foundation, 1996.

Rapports au Ministre. *Collection de documents inédits sur l'histoire de France publiés par l'ordre du Roi et par les soins du Ministre de l'instruction publique*. Paris: Imprimerie royale, 1839.

Rapports au Roi et pièces. Collection de documents inédits sur l'histoire de France. Paris: Imprimerie royale, 1835.

Rollo, Lorraine A. "François Guizot and the Making of a New History, 1787-1830." Ph.D. diss., SUNY-Buffalo, 1990.

Rosanvallon, Pierre. *Le Moment Guizot*. Paris: Gallimard, 1985.

Samaran, Charles. *L'histoire et ses méthodes*. Encyclopédie de la Pléiade, vol. 11. Paris: Gallimard, 1961.

Schmitz, Philibert. *Histoire de l'ordre de Saint-Benoît*. [Paris]: Maredsous, 1942-56.

Sherman, Daniel. *Worthy Monuments: Art Museums and the Politics of Culture in Nineteenth-Century France*. Cambridge: Harvard University Press, 1989.

Smith, Bonnie G. *The Gender of History: Men, Women, and Historical Practice.* Cambridge: Harvard University Press, 1998.

------. "Gender and the Practices of Scientific History: The Seminar and Archival Research in the Nineteenth Century." *American Historical Review* 100, no. 4 (1995): 1150-1176.

Theis, Laurent. "Guizot et les institutions de mémoire." In *Les lieux de mémoire,* ed. Pierre Nora, vol. 2, pt. 2, 569-590. Paris: Gallimard, 1986.

Thierry, Augustin. *Recueil des monuments inédits de l'histoire du Tiers Etat.* Paris: Firmin Didot Frères, 1850.

Valensise, Marina, ed. *François Guizot et la culture politique de son temps: Colloque de la Fondation Guizot-Val Richer.* Paris: Gallimard, 1991.

Ventre-Denis, Madeleine. "La première chaire d'histoire du droit à la faculté de droit de Paris (1819-1822)." *Revue historique du droit français et étranger* 45 (Oct. 1975): 596-622.

------. *Les sciences sociales et la faculté de droit de Paris sous la Restauration. Un texte précurseur: l'ordonnance du 24 mars 1819.* Paris: Aux Amateurs de Livres, 1985.

Walch, Jean. *Les Maîtres de l'histoire, 1815-1850: Augustin Thierry, Mignet, Guizot, Thiers, Michelet, Edgard Quinet.* Paris: Editions Slatkine, 1986.

Williams, Elizabeth. "Prosper Mérimée et l'archéologie médiévale du Midi de la France en 1834." *Annales du Midi* 93 (Jul. 1981): 293-312.

Index

Printed in the United Kingdom
by Lightning Source UK Ltd.
130559UK00001B/174/P